The
Final
Countdown
Vol. 1

FIRST PRINTING

Billy Crone

Dan Mank

Received
9/22/17

Cover Design:
Chris Taylor

To my wife, Brandie.

Thank you for being so patient
with a man full of dreams.
You truly are my gift from God.
It is an honor to have you as my wife
and I'm still amazed that you willingly chose
to join me in this challenging yet exhilarating
roller coaster ride called the Christian life.
God has truly done exceedingly abundantly above all
that we could have ever asked or even thought of.
Who ever said that living for the Lord was boring?!
One day our ride together will be over here on earth,
yet it will continue on in eternity forever.
I love you.

Contents

Preface..*vii*

1. *The Jewish People*...................................... 9

2. *Modern Technology*.................................... 53

3. *Worldwide Upheaval*...................................105

4. *The Rise of Falsehood*................................. 155

5. *The Rise of Wickedness*................................ 251

6. *The Rise of Apostasy*................................ Vol.2

7. *One World Religion*................................. Vol.2

8. *One World Government*.............................. Vol.2

9. *One World Economy*................................Vol.2

10. *The Mark of the Beast*............................. Vol.2

How to Receive Jesus Christ.............. 325
Notes....................................327

Preface

Unfortunately, in the Church today, the study of prophecy has been forsaken under the assumption that one can't really know for sure what it all means and therefore we should refrain from teaching it. Yet, when you think about it, this is actually a slap in the face to God; for a majority of the Holy Scriptures deal directly or indirectly with prophetic issues. Why would God put prophecy in the Bible if it wasn't meant to be understood? Do we dare say that He is playing cat and mouse with us? In addition, how can one say that they are being faithful to present the whole counsel of God when they leave a major portion of it, prophecy, out of the picture?

Bible prophecy has a wonderful way of bringing home two crucial truths that seem to be long forgotten in the American Church. One truth is that this world is not going to last forever. A flood destroyed it the first time and the next time it will be by fire. This forces you and I, the Christian, to stop living merely for the temporary things of this world, thus wasting our lives, and instead to get busy storing up treasures in heaven which last forever. Is that not needed today? Additionally, Bible prophecy drives home the second truth of God being absolutely sovereign. He is in full control of all things at all times. So much so that God has already mapped out mankind's history. Therefore, only the student of Bible prophecy can rightly discern the times in which we live. Best of all, because God is sovereign, no matter how uncomfortable things may get, we can still be at peace knowing that our Lord reigns and that He will soon return to take us to be with Him.

What you are about to read will most assuredly shock you and certainly push you out of your comfort zone. If it doesn't, then you might want to check your pulse. Lest you think I'm making this material up, I invite you to check it out for yourself. This is why everything has been meticulously documented. This is not a time to react in fear but in faith. Our hope is not to be here, but in Heaven. Remember, God is sovereign! One last piece of advice; when you are through reading this book will you please *READ YOUR BIBLE*? I mean that in the nicest possible way. Enjoy, and I'm looking forward to seeing you someday!

Billy Crone
Las Vegas, Nevada
2017

Chapter One

The Jewish People

What I'm about to share with you is a true story. I'm not making it up. This really happened. Here it goes:

"There was a man working on his motorcycle on his patio while his wife was in the kitchen. The man was racing the engine on the motorcycle when it accidentally slipped into gear. The man, still holding on to the handlebars, was dragged through the glass patio doors onto the floor inside the house.

The wife, hearing the crash, ran into the dining room and found her husband laying on the floor, cut and bleeding, the motorcycle laying next to him and the patio door shattered. So the wife ran to the phone and summoned an ambulance.

Because they lived on a fairly large hill, the wife went down the several flights of stairs to the street to escort the paramedics to her husband. After the ambulance arrived and transported the man to the hospital, the wife placed the motorcycle upright and pushed it outside.

Well, seeing that gas was spilled on the floor, the wife got some paper towels, blotted up the gasoline, and threw the towels in the toilet. The husband was treated at the hospital and released to come home.

Upon arriving at home, he looked at the shattered patio door and the damage done to his motorcycle and he became despondent. So he went to the bathroom, sat down on the toilet and smoked a cigarette.

After finishing the cigarette, he flipped it into the toilet bowl while still seated. The wife, who was in the kitchen, heard the loud explosion and her husband screaming. So she ran into the bathroom and found her husband lying on the floor.

His trousers had been blown away and he was suffering burns on his hindquarters and the back of his legs. So the wife again ran to the phone to call the ambulance.

The very same paramedic crew was dispatched and the wife met them at the street. The paramedics loaded the husband on the stretcher and began carrying him to the street.

While they were going down the stairs to the street accompanied by the wife, one of the paramedics asked the wife how the husband had burned himself. She told them and the paramedics started laughing so hard, they slipped and tipped the stretcher, dumping the husband out.

That's right, he fell down the remaining stairs and broke his arm, all in one day."[1]

Now, how many of you would say that's a pretty bad day? Believe it or not, I think I've actually discovered a day that's even worse than that one! It goes something like this. It's when you wake up one morning only to realize that your family has totally disappeared. So you run to turn on your TV to see what's happening and there you watch a special worldwide news report declaring that millions of people all over the planet are missing. Then, you see your loved one's Bible sitting on the coffee table and it suddenly dawns on you that your family was right after all when they kept telling you about the Rapture of the Church. To your horror, you realize that you've been left behind and have been catapulted into the 7-year Tribulation that's coming upon the whole world. For those of you who may not know, the time of the Tribulation is not a party. It's an outpouring of God's wrath on a wicked and rebellious planet. In fact, Jesus said in Matthew 24 it would be a "time of greater horror than anything the world has ever seen or will ever see again," and that "unless that time of calamity was shortened, the entire human race would be destroyed!"

But praise God, God is not only a God of wrath; He's a God of love as well. Because He loves us, He's given us many warning signs to wake us up so we'd know when the Tribulation was near and Christ's Second Coming was rapidly approaching. Therefore, to keep people from experiencing the ultimate bad day of being left behind, we're going to begin a journey in this book called *The Final Countdown.* What we're going to do is look at ten signs given by God to lovingly wake the Church up, and given so that the lost would commit their lives to Him before it's too late. There's no time to waste, so let's get started.

The **tenth sign** on *The Final Countdown* is none other than **The Jewish People**. One of the first and foremost important prophetic events on God's end time calendar is concerning the Jewish people. In short, if you want to know how close we are to the end, pay attention to the Jewish people. Why? Because from God's viewpoint, Jerusalem is the center of the earth! Think about it. This is where the line of the Messiah started. King David ruled from there. This is where Jesus the actual Messiah died on a cross. This is where the End Times culminate with the Battle of Armageddon outside of Jerusalem. This is where Jesus returns at His Second Coming and this is where Jesus reigns after His Second Coming.[2] It's all in Jerusalem! Therefore, if you want to know how close we are to the end, you've got to pay attention to Jerusalem and the Jewish people. That's why the Lord prophesied specific events in minute detail that would happen to the Jewish people alone, giving us a clear indication as to when we really are living in the Last Days. The following are just a few of these specific prophesies being fulfilled today concerning The Jewish People showing us just how close we really are to the Last Days.

I. First End Time Prophecy Concerning the Jewish People - Israel Would Return to the Land

Isaiah 43:1-6 "But now, this is what the LORD says – He Who created you, O Jacob, He Who formed you, O Israel: "Fear not, for I have redeemed you; I have summoned you by name; you are Mine. When you pass through the waters, I will be with you; and when you pass through the rivers, they will not sweep over you. When you walk through the fire, you will not be burned; the flames will not set you ablaze. For I am the LORD, your God, the Holy One of Israel, your Savior; I give Egypt for your ransom, Cush and Seba in your stead. Since you are precious and honored in my sight, and because I love you, I will give men in exchange for you, and people in exchange for your life. Do not be afraid, for I am with you; I will bring your children from the east and gather you from the west. I will say to the north, 'Give them up!' and to the south, 'Do not hold them back.' Bring my sons from afar and my daughters from the ends of the earth."

Ever since the destruction of the Jewish Temple in 70 AD, the Jewish people have been scattered all over the earth. However, during the past century alone, millions of Jews have returned to Israel fulfilling this very prophecy. In fact, just like the Bible said, they not only came specifically from the east, the west, the north and the south, but they came in that exact order! First from the East, in the early 1900's when many of the Jews living in the Middle East moved to Israel. Then from the West, during the mid-1900's, hundreds of thousands of Jews living in the West (Europe and the United States) began moving to Israel. Then from the North, during the 1980's, Russia finally began to allow hundreds of thousands of Jews to return to Israel. Next from the South, Israel struck a deal with Ethiopia's communist government and on the weekend of May 25, 1991, 14,500 Ethiopian Jews were airlifted to Israel. Now, more Jews are returning to Israel every single year from all over the world. First from the East, West, North, and South.[3] Just like the Bible said they would! When? In the Last Days!

II. Second End Time Prophecy Concerning the Jewish People - Israel Would Become a Nation Again

Isaiah 11:11-12 "In that day the Lord will bring back a remnant of his people for the second time, returning them to the land of Israel from Assyria, Lower Egypt, Upper Egypt, Ethiopia, Elam, Babylonia, Hamath, and all the distant coastlands. He will raise a flag among the nations for Israel to rally around. He will gather the scattered people of Judah from the ends of the earth."

Ever since 721 BC approximately fourteen different peoples have possessed the land of Israel. Yet as we saw, the Bible specifically said that the nation of Israel would one day be reborn. One day they would regain their independence. Can anyone guess what happened on May 14, 1948? That's right, after waiting centuries and centuries, the people who were scattered all over the world, not only returned to the land, but they also became a nation again! From out of nowhere and against all odds, Israel was reborn. Then in 1967 the Jewish people even recaptured the city of Jerusalem. Just like the Bible said they would! When? In the Last Days!

III. Third End Time Prophecy Concerning the Jewish People - Israel Would Be Brought Forth in One Day

Isaiah 66:8 "Who has ever seen or heard of anything as strange as this? Has a nation ever been born in a single day? Has a country ever come forth in a mere moment? But by the time Jerusalem's birth pains begin, the baby will be born; the nation will come forth."

For those of you who may not know, on May 14, 1948, at precisely 4 pm, the members of the People's Council signed the proclamation and the declaration was made that, "The State of Israel is established. This meeting is ended." Israel not only became a nation again, but it was brought forth as a nation, literally in one day.[4] In fact, it was such an obvious fulfillment of Bible prophecy that even the Jewish people themselves knew they were fulfilling a prophecy made over 2,500 years earlier as this report shows:

"The Founding of the state of Israel in 1948 followed a United Nations recommendation for the amicable deportation of British forces from Palestine. Israel's first Prime Minister David Ben Gurion proclaimed the state's independence on May 14th 1948 and opened its borders on Jewish immigration. The new state took the Star of David as its symbol.

For centuries, people have predicted the end of the world, through a depression that nearly destroyed a generation, nations were at war, rulers and dictators tried to conquer the world and wipe out an entire race. But one major prophecy was yet to be fulfilled. The rebirth of Israel in 1948 was the super sign. What we haven't seen happen in the context of all the other prophecies coming true, until 62 years ago, we haven't seen the rebirth of the state of Israel.

At the end of WWII, the British advanced the League of Nations mandate for Palestine, which included the responsibility for securing the establishment in Palestine of a national home for the Jewish people. But without American support, the plan would fail.

President Franklin Roosevelt promised Saudi King Saud the United States would not endorse any policy regarding Palestine without notifying them first. But in the spring of 1945, FDR died leaving Vice President Harry Truman with the burdens of a complex foreign policy.

Truman faced intense opposition for any plan to create a Jewish State, all the while also facing equally intense support. Eventually he would back the plan for a Jewish State and in May 1948, the President announced his support for UN Resolution 181, a partition plan to divide Palestine between Jews and Arabs.

The United Nations would never have voted Israel as a State had it not been for Harry Truman, who learned at the knee of his Sunday School teaching mother, that if you ever get a chance to help Israel, you ought to help Israel.

Ezekiel 37:25 reads: 'They will live in the land I gave to my servant Jacob, the land where your fathers lived. They and their children and their children's children will live there forever, and David my servant will be their prince forever.'

That was prophesied and you see pictures of the War of Independence in 1948 and the Six Day War, and soldiers, who were somewhat secular; who were not necessarily religious, were weeping because they felt they had translated the words of the prophet."[5]

Isn't it interesting how even the non-religious secular Jewish people recognized the prophetic importance of their becoming a nation again? To the point where they sensed it, they felt it, they even wept over it. However, most of us have no clue of the importance of that date and how it proves just how close we really are to the end. Israel not only became a nation again, but it was brought forth as a nation, literally in one day. Just like the Bible said! When? In the Last Days!

IV. Fourth End Time Prophecy concerning The Jewish People - Israel Would Be a United Nation Again

Ezekiel 37:21-22 "And give them this message from the Sovereign LORD: I will gather the people of Israel from among the nations. I will bring them home to their own land from the places where they have been scattered. I will unify them into one nation in the land. One king will rule them all; no longer will they be divided into two nations."

In about 926 BC, the Jewish people became a divided nation. The Northern ten tribes were called Israel, and the Southern two tribes were called Judah. But when the Jewish people regained independence in 1948, for the first time in 2,900 years, Israel was again united as a single nation, not two.[6] Just like the Bible said! When? In the Last Days!

V. Fifth End Time Prophecy Concerning the Jewish People - Israel's Currency Would Be the Shekel

Ezekiel 45:12,13,16 "The standard unit for weight will be the silver shekel. This is the tax you must give to the prince. All the people of Israel must join the prince in bringing their offerings."

Here we see how the Bible clearly predicted that in the future temple sacrifices, the people of Israel would not just be paying their taxes, but specifically paying them in shekels. However, the problem is that Israel's currency wasn't the shekel, it was the pound. That is, until 1980, when it just so happened it was changed to the shekel, and they use it even to this very day.[7] Just like the Bible said! When? In the Last Days!

VI. Sixth End Time Prophecy Concerning the Jewish People - Israel Would Blossom as a Rose in the Desert

Isaiah 35:1-2 "Even the wilderness will rejoice in those days. The desert will blossom with flowers. Yes, there will be an abundance of flowers and singing and joy! The deserts will become as green as the mountains of Lebanon, as lovely as Mount Carmel's pastures and the plain of Sharon. There the LORD will display his glory, the splendor of our God."

To understand the significance of this prophecy, you have to first understand the history and characteristics of the land of Israel. From the very beginning, the land that was promised to the Israelites was totally different from the land they came from. They came out of Egypt and the desert to, "The Promised Land." This "Promised Land" was a good land. In fact, in the Old Testament it was called "a good land" sixteen times and "a land flowing with milk and honey" twenty-three times. There was something special about that land.[8] Even up to the time of Josephus, a first century Jewish historian, he mentioned how the land was still very prosperous and fertile. He stated:

"For the whole area is excellent for crops and pasturage and rich in trees of every kind, so that by its fertility it invites even those least inclined to work on the land. In fact, every inch of it has been cultivated by the inhabitants and not a parcel goes to waste. It is thickly covered with towns, and thanks to the natural abundance of the soil, the many villages are so densely populated."[9]

However, all that changed after nearly 2,000 years of foreign conquerors harshly abused the land. They left Israel a complete wasteland. In fact, listen to the comments of people who visited Israel prior to 1948:

"After the scattering of the Jews beginning in 70 AD with the destruction of the Temple, the land became desolate, unable to grow much of anything. During the 2,000 years of Israel's exile from its land, numerous empires have conquered the Land, and countless wars were fought for its possession. And yet, astonishingly, no conqueror ever succeeded in permanently settling the Land. Neither have they been able to cause it to bloom.

In 1845 Alfon Lamartine said in his book, 'Recollections from the East,' that, 'Outside the walls of Jerusalem we saw no living being, heard no living voice. We encountered that desolation and that deadly silence which we would have expected to find at the ruined gates of Pompeii. A total eternal dread spell envelopes the city, the highways and the villages.'

When Mark Twain visited Israel in the 1860's, he reported that Israel was a barren wasteland with no trees. He said, 'The further we went the hotter the sun got and the more rocky and bare. Repulsive and dreary the landscape became.'

In describing the territory around the Sea of Galilee, he called it a, 'blistering, naked, treeless land.' He spoke of the villages as, 'ugly, cramped, squalid, uncomfortable and filthy.' He added that the villages are, 'a solitude to make one dreary…unpeopled deserts…rusty mounds of barrenness.'

And then he looked towards the barren Judean hills in Israel, and wrote, 'Close to us was a stream and on its banks a great heard of curious looking Syrian sheep and the sheep were gratefully eating gravel. I do not state this as a petrified fact – I only suppose they were eating gravel because there did not appear to be anything else for them to eat.'

Then in 1905, the Prime Minister of the Netherlands observed, 'The Jews have come in vain. Only God can check the blight of the inrushing desert.'"[10]

Interestingly enough, that's exactly what God did. No foreign conqueror was able to make Israel bloom again, no matter how hard they tried, but when the Jewish People began to return to the land, everything changed! They began to immediately work at getting the land back into shape. For them, and them alone, the land began to respond. One author in the 1800's counted the trees there and reported that there were less than 1,000. Now today, due to a massive tree replanting program, there are over 1.2 billion trees in Israel and half their trees are forest trees, and the other half are fruit trees, and this has not only helped to increase the rainfall by over 450%, but Israel, the former desert, is now the breadbasket of the Middle East and is exporting fruit all over the world.[11]

Speaking of their fruit, it is out of this world! It's not only huge it's incredibly sweet and delicious. That's because, it just so happens, when the Jewish people arrived, they not only replanted trees, but they began to build a massive network of irrigation systems, high-tech irrigation systems, much further along than the rest of the world. Furthermore, it also just so happens that the water in the soil that they are irrigating there is custom tailored to produce amazing produce. It just needed the Jewish people to pump it out:

"There's a prevailing thought that says that it's hard to establish agriculture in the desert. But that's not necessarily so. When mentioning the desert, one thinks of dryness, heat and desolation. But it turns out that the desert can bloom, be full of life, and yield harvests of fine fruits and vegetables.

Actually, if you think about desert as desert then you probably think there is no water, but we find a huge aquifer under the desert which allowed us to use it and actually we can pump it out and make the desert bloom or green with a lot of agriculture.

It turns out the desert climate is good for agriculture, thanks to the ground water under the sand dunes. It's possible to do a lot of agriculture in the desert, for a few reasons. First, we have the perfect weather for agriculture. We can grow vegetables in the winter.

Second, we have the experience and the brackish water that will allow us to do that in a very easy way. Although the groundwater is somewhat salty, it turns out that this saltiness actually improves the fruit. We can produce sweeter and better vegetables.

What happens when you irrigate the fruits or the vegetables with brackish water is that the plant is in a very serious stress, he's suffering and he's producing less leaves and more fruits with less water inside and a lot of meat, and actually that makes it three times sweeter than usual vegetables."[12]

I'm sure it's just purely by chance that the water under Israel is custom tailored for amazing produce that is much larger and three times as sweet as other areas. Who would've thought that the desert could bloom again and produce such amazing quantities? It's almost like when God said this land was "a good land"

and a land "flowing with milk and honey" that it just needed the "right people" to get back there and make it come alive again. I wonder who that is? The Jewish people maybe?

There is even more. Israel also diverted the water from the Sea of Galilee and channeled it through sections of the deserts, which have allowed the deserts to literally begin to blossom with an abundance of flowers, even to the point where Israel is now a major exporter of flowers and ornamental plants.[13] Just like the Bible said! When? In the Last Days!

VII. Seventh End Time Prophecy Concerning the Jewish People - Israel Would Have a Powerful Military

Zechariah 12:6 "On that day I will make the leaders of Judah like a firepot in a woodpile, like a flaming torch among sheaves. They will consume right and left all the surrounding peoples, but Jerusalem will remain intact in her place."

Here's what's amazing about this prophecy. Outnumbered and against all odds, the Israeli forces have astounded the world by their victories over and over again during multiple wars. For instance, within hours of Israel's declaration of independence in 1948, Egypt, Syria, Jordan, Iraq, and Lebanon all invaded Israel. The combined population of those countries was at least 20 million at that time. Yet, Israel had fewer than 1 million. However, when all was said and done, the Jewish people not only won the war, they had expanded the size of Israel by 50 percent. Today Israel has one of the most powerful military forces in the world with full nuclear capabilities. Hands down, they are the most powerful force in the region.[14] Just like the Bible said! When? In the Last Days!

VIII. Eighth End Time Prophecy Concerning the Jewish People - Israel Would Be a Center of Conflict to the Whole World

Zechariah 12:2-3 "I am going to make Jerusalem a cup that sends all the surrounding peoples reeling. Judah will be besieged as well as Jerusalem. On that day, when all the nations of the earth are gathered against her, I will make Jerusalem an immovable rock for all the nations. All who try to move it will injure themselves."

In other words, don't mess with Israel! In 1948, when the Jewish people became a nation again, the very next day, the nations around them declared war with Israel and the fighting for control has never stopped. Also, it just so happens that Israel's location in the heart of the world's oil reserves makes it of great strategic significance to all the countries in the world. Then to make matters worse, the world's three largest religions have headquarters in guess where? Jerusalem! This is why daily you can turn on the news and read in all the newspapers of how Israel has indeed become an international global problem. It has become a center of world conflict, exactly like the Bible said would happen. When? In the Last Days!

Before we continue with Israel's prophetic signs, let us try to grasp the amazing prophetic significance of eight prophecies being fulfilled in just one entity, the Jewish people. So far we've seen that:

1. **Israel Would Return to The Land**
2. **Israel Would Become a Nation Again**
3. **Israel Would Be Brought Forth in One Day**
4. **Israel Would Be a United Nation Again**
5. **Israel's Currency Would Be the Shekel**
6. **Israel Would Blossom as a Rose in The Desert**
7. **Israel Would Have a Powerful Military**
8. **Israel Would Be a Center of Conflict to the Whole World**

Now listen to the odds of all these eight prophecies coming to pass in just one people:

"By using the modern science of probability, we find that the chance that any one entity might have lived down to the present time and fulfilled just eight prophecies is 1 in 10^{17}.

In order to help us comprehend this staggering probability, it can be illustrated by taking 10^{17} silver dollars and laying them on the face of Texas, which would be enough to cover the state two feet deep.

Now mark one of these silver dollars with a 'red X' and stir the whole mass thoroughly, all over the state. Blindfold a man and tell him that he can travel as far as he wishes, but he must pick up one silver dollar and say that this is the right one.

What chance would he have of getting the right one? Just the same chance that the prophets would have had of writing just eight prophecies and having them all come true in any one people."[15]

Now, I'm not a rocket scientist, but I'd say it's pretty obvious that there's no way the Jewish people fulfilled those eight prophecies by accident. It's almost like God's trying to get our attention or something. In fact, let's put the nail in the coffin. Let's turn the tables around. Let's see how the so-called psychics of the world do in comparison to the Bible:

"Amid hundreds of prophecies, Biblical prophets are not known to have made a single error. However, a study of the prophecies made by psychics showed that of the seventy-two predictions, only six were fulfilled in any way. However, two of these were vague and two others were hardly surprising, that the U.S. and Russia would remain leading world powers.

Another study of the top twenty-five psychics and seventy-two of their predictions revealed that 92% were totally wrong. And the remaining 8% could easily be explained by chance and general knowledge of circumstances. In fact, in 1993 the psychics missed every single unexpected news story like Michael Jordan's retirement and the flooding in the Midwest.

Among some of their false prophecies that year were that Kathy Lee Gifford would replace Jay Leno as host of The Tonight Show and the Queen of England would become a nun."[16]

Nevertheless, people will listen to them instead of the Bible! But there's even more. That eighth prophecy of **Israel Becoming a Center of Conflict for the Whole World** is actually leading to the fulfillment of another prophecy in the New Testament. The Apostle Paul mentioned this one:

1 Thessalonians 5:1-3 "Now, brothers, about times and dates we do not need to write to you, for you know very well that the day of the Lord will come like a thief in the night. While people are saying, 'Peace and safety,' destruction will come on them suddenly, as labor pains on a pregnant woman, and they will not escape."

According to this text, the Apostle Paul tells us one of the signs that we know we are getting close to the Lord's Return is when all of a sudden, you see people all over the planet crying out a specific phrase. Notice what that phrase was. It was "Peace and Safety." Not "Peace and Happiness," not "Joy and Prosperity," but specifically the phrase "Peace and Safety." Now pay attention because nothing is by chance in the Scripture. It just so happens that the Greek word there for "safety" is *asphaleia* and it literally means "security" as in "security from enemies or security from danger." So you literally could say in that text, "Peace and Security" and still be totally accurate. Now, take this Bible prophecy passage from Paul about "Peace and Security" being the exact phrase that people would be crying out for in Last Days; just prior to Jesus' Second Coming. Combine it with Israel coming back on the scene and becoming a "center of conflict for the whole world". Can anybody guess just what in the world the world's leaders are crying out for in regards to Israel right now? Specifically, Peace and Security! The exact phrase Paul said people would cry out for in the Last Days as this man shares:

"The very first time I heard the phrase "peace and security" used in a public speech was when then President Bush mentioned the phrase three times in a speech that closely followed the 9/11 attacks. He used it several more times during the rest of his administration, as did Condoleezza Rice, Dick Cheney, and General Wesley Clark.

Then Obama also used the phrase three times in a post-election speech in 2008. Since then the phrase has been used repeatedly by the former president, former Secretary of State Hillary Clinton (who used the terms twenty-three times in a twenty-minute speech), Israeli Prime Minister Benyamin Netanyahu, former U.N. Secretary General Ban ki-Moon, and various world leaders from not only the Far East and even the Middle East, but literally from around the world.

With the increasing use of that phrase found in the end times verse of 1 Thessalonians 5:3, we can see that we are approaching the fulfillment of end times Bible prophecy." [17]

Not "joy and prosperity" not "deliverance and happiness" but wonder of wonders it just happens to be the exact Biblical phrase right now that the Bible warned would come upon the scene in the Last Days, "peace and security". When you see people all over the planet specifically crying out that phrase, what did the Bible say would happen? Bang! Sudden destruction will come upon them and they will not escape! What more does God have to do to get our attention? The Lord's Return is getting close and we better wake up! Yes, we don't know the day or the hour, but what more does He have to do? We are clearly living in the Last Days!

IX. Ninth End Time Prophecy Concerning the Jewish People - Israel Would Rebuild the Temple

1. The Temple Will Be Rebuilt in Jerusalem

The first thing we know about this temple, according to Scripture, is that it will be rebuilt in Jerusalem:

Revelation 11:1-8 "I was given a reed like a measuring rod and was told, "Go and measure the temple of God and the altar, and count the worshipers there. But exclude the outer court; do not measure it, because it has been given to the Gentiles. They will trample on the holy city for 42 months. And I will give power to my two witnesses, and they will prophesy for 1,260 days, clothed in sackcloth." These are the two olive trees and the two lampstands that stand before the Lord of the earth. If anyone tries to harm them, fire comes from their mouths and devours their enemies. This is how anyone who wants to harm them must die. These men have power to shut up the sky so that it will not rain during the time they are prophesying; and they have power to turn the waters into blood and to strike the earth with every kind of plague as often as they want. Now when they have finished their testimony, the beast that comes up from the Abyss will attack them, and overpower and kill them. Their bodies will lie in the street of the great city, which is figuratively called Sodom and Egypt, where also their Lord was crucified."

According to our text, the Book of Revelation clearly reveals that a Jewish temple will be in existence during the time of the Tribulation. That's big news because the last Jewish Temple was destroyed in 70 AD by the Romans, which is precisely what Jesus prophesied would happen. The text also says that the Two Witnesses and the Antichrist will be associated with it and it all takes place in the Holy City where their Lord (Jesus) was crucified, which is undoubtedly of Jerusalem. Therefore, the Bible clearly says that in the Last Days, there will be a Rebuilt Jewish Temple in Jerusalem.

2. The Place Where the Antichrist Will Declare Himself to be god

The second thing we know about this Temple, according to scripture, is that this is where the Antichrist Will Declare Himself to be god:

2 Thessalonians 2:1-4 "Concerning the coming of our Lord Jesus Christ and our being gathered to Him, we ask you, brothers, not to become easily unsettled or alarmed by some prophecy, report or letter supposed to have come from us, saying that the day of the Lord has already come. Don't let anyone deceive you in any way, for that day will not come until the rebellion occurs and the man of lawlessness is revealed, the man doomed to destruction. He will oppose and will exalt himself over everything that is called God or is worshiped, so that he sets himself up in God's temple, proclaiming himself to be God."

Here we see the Last Days Jewish Temple will not only be rebuilt in Jerusalem, but halfway into the 7-year Tribulation, the Antichrist himself goes into that temple and declares himself to be god. Therefore, if you want to know how close we're getting to the 7-year Tribulation, i.e. the End of Time, you need to be looking out for signs of a rebuilt Jewish Temple. You can't have the Two Witnesses without it and you can't have the Antichrist without it. You have to have a Temple. Well guess what's happening right now? The Jewish People are rebuilding the Temple! It makes you wonder if the Antichrist isn't already alive and well on planet earth just waiting for it to be completed!

1. The First Way We Know the Jewish People Are Rebuilding the Temple – The Plans Are Made

So what is this proof that the Jewish People really are rebuilding the Last Days Temple that the Two Witnesses and the Antichrist will be involved with in the 7-tear Tribulation? The first way we know the Jewish People really are Rebuilding the Last Days Temple is that **The Plans Are Already Made** for the Temple. The Jewish People aren't just back in the Land again and established as a nation again, right now they are getting ready to rebuild their Temple again. Not a hundred years down the road, but right now! Here's an official announcement:

"'Now presenting, the greatest progress toward the rebuilding of the Holy Temple in modern history: Blueprints for the Holy Temple.'

In his recent USA speaking engagement tour, (January 2011), Rabbi Chaim Richman of the Temple Institute revealed to the public for the very first time detailed construction plans for the Chamber of Hewn Stone: the seat of the Great Sanhedrin which is a central component of the Holy Temple complex on the Temple Mount. These complete and highly intricate plans constitute the first stage of a historical undertaking of the Temple Institute: the drafting of blueprints for the entire Holy Temple complex.

These plans, drawn up by a top Israeli architectural firm hired by the Temple Institute, take into account the specific requirements of the Sanhedrin assembly hall, known historically as the Chamber of Hewn Stone. At the same time these plans incorporate modern technological infrastructure necessary to a twenty-first century facility: this includes internet ports, wireless communications systems, computer data storage, elevators, air conditioning, and underground parking. All these modern amenities, and many more, have been integrated into the Sanhedrin structure without compromising the integrity of the great assembly's physical or spiritual character.

No land can be prepared, no foundation can be laid, no wall can be erected without a detailed architectural plan first being drawn up, approved by engineers, and presented to the appointed site manager. The plans you are viewing on this page fulfill every requirement necessary for the immediate commencement of work on this aspect of the Holy Temple complex.

The Sanhedrin Chamber of Hewn Stone is but a single chamber in the northern wall of the Holy Temple. It was chosen as the initial focus of the blueprint project, not because of its architectural significance, per se, but because of its overwhelming spiritual significance to the world. The seventy elders of the Sanhedrin have been vested with the authority of the seventy elders whom God commanded Moshe to appoint in the desert:

Then HaShem said to Moses, 'Assemble for Me seventy men of the elders of Israel, whom you know to be the people's elders and officers, and you shall take them to the Tent of Meeting, and they shall stand there with you. I will come down and speak with you there, and I will increase the spirit that is upon you and bestow it upon them. Then they will bear the burden of the people with you so that you need not bear it alone.' (Numbers 11:16-17)

These elders are not only judges, but also teachers whose task is to ensure that 'for out of Zion shall the Torah come forth, and the word of HaShem from Jerusalem.' (Isaiah 2:3) This being said, it should also be noted that the Chamber of Hewn Stone sits in close proximity to the Ark of the Covenant, from which the sages draw Divine inspiration. We invite all souls who long for the

Holy Temple and seek a role in the historical undertaking that we have begun, to join us in our efforts."[18]

It sure appears that somebody is pretty serious about building a Temple in the Last Days! But there's a problem. Even though the Temple Institute has made the plans to do so, there's a position problem. The Muslim Dome of the Rock is sitting right where many believe the previous temple was and where the new proposed temple needs to be. So what are you going to do? First of all, this is why there is so much strife in Jerusalem today. It's not just a land issue but a spiritual issue. Strife or not, the Bible is clear, the end times temple will be rebuilt. So what are they going to do? How are they going to build it? Those plans aren't going to do any good if you don't have a place to build it.

Well, it just so happens, right now, there's a group of Jewish archaeologists who are saying that the actual site for the temple isn't where the Dome of the Rock is, but it's either to the North or the South of it, which means they could build the Temple right now even with the Dome of the Rock being where it is![19] So that's one possibility. However, there's still a strong group of Jewish supporters that say, "Oh no! It's exactly where the Dome of the Rock is." So again, now you're back to the original problem, what are you going to do? Well, some would say that maybe a stray missile with all that fighting going on over there will fix that in a hurry. Perhaps, even a supernatural earthquake from God will change things. Possibly a missile or bomb during the fulfillment of the Gog and Magog prophecy, where the surrounding nations including Russia from the North come against Israel and get totally annihilated by God will clear out the Temple area. Either way, a newly leveled landscape of the Dome of the Rock is not only plausible in our lifetime, but many scholars believe that it will occur as a result of a peace treaty made with the Antichrist himself, which is the very event that starts the 7-year Tribulation.

Daniel 9:27 "He will make a treaty with the people for a period of one set of seven, but after half this time, he will put an end to the sacrifices and offerings."

So here we see according to Daniel that the specific event that starts the 7-year Tribulation is when the Antichrist makes a treaty with the Jewish people. What's amazing is, if you're paying attention to the news, of all places, where in the world is everyone trying to make a peace treaty and with whom? Israel! In fact, some feel that the Antichrist with all his false miracles and fabulous charisma will be the only one to convince Israel to not only give up even more land, but the carrot he uses is the permission to rebuild the Temple. He knows how desperately they want one. So maybe after an unfortunate missile has rearranged the real estate of the Dome of the Rock, he strikes a 7-year deal with them, which starts the 7-year Tribulation, and they start building the Temple. Again, this is not only plausible, this is something that the Jewish people are wanting right now, not one hundred years down the road. They are ready to rebuild the Temple now!

2. The Second Way We Know the Jewish People Are Rebuilding the Temple – Priests Are Already Trained for the Temple

Which brings us to the second way we know the Jewish People really are Rebuilding the Last Days Temple is that **The Priests Are Already Trained for the Temple**. It just so happens in our lifetime, the Jewish People not only became a nation again and are getting ready to rebuild their Temple again, but thanks to modern technology, they've rediscovered the priestly line again. This is important because the Jewish People have been scattered all over the earth and haven't had a Temple since 70 AD. Therefore, the problem is, who knows who belongs to who or what tribe? The Bible clearly says that you have to be of the Priestly line to serve in the Temple. So what are you going to do? Well, believe it or not, they recently discovered the "Cohen" or "Priestly Gene" and so now thanks to modern technology the Jewish people know who is of the Priestly line again, as this article shares:

"Jewish tradition, based on the Bible, is that all Kohanim or Priests are direct descendants of Aaron, the original Kohen or High Priest.

Dr. Karl Skorecki considered a hypothesis: if the Kohanim are descendants of one man, they should have a common set of genetic markers. So 188 Jewish males were asked to contribute some cheek cells from which their DNA was extracted for study. Participants were from Israel, England and North America and they were asked to identify whether or not they thought they were a Kohen.

What they found was that there's a particular array of six chromosomal markers in actual Kohens that has come to be known as the Cohen Modal Haplotype or (CMH). It has now become the standard genetic signature of the Jewish priestly family.

In fact, date calculations based on the variation among Kohanim today yields a time frame of 106 generations from the ancestral founder of that line, some 3,300 years, the approximate time of the Exodus from Egypt, and of course the lifetime of Aaron the original High Priest."[20]

In other words, they know who's of the Priestly line and who's not, thanks to modern genetic technology discovered in our lifetime. It's almost like things are getting close! Furthermore, they not only know who's a priest and who's not, but they're already training them to serve in the Temple as this next report shares:

"Today is really a historical event for the Jewish people. It's the beginning of the work of the Third Temple, construction of the Third Temple. Here we are building a field school for Kohanim and Levites in order to teach them the work that they have to do in Jerusalem when the Temple will be rebuilt.

We are starting to build the replica of the Temple here that will serve as a school to educate the Kohanim, the priests, how to serve in the Temple. It will be an exact replica of the Temple. Today we are drilling the holes for the libations, the water and wine libations in the altar. They will learn exactly what they will have to do when the time comes and the Temple is rebuilt in Jerusalem, they will know exactly how to perform the service.

We've been waiting the last 2,000 years for the rebuilding of the Third Temple, and here it is for the first time. We're actually taking concrete measures in order to fulfill that dream and start the process of the Third Temple."[21]

Sounds to me like somebody's getting ready to build a Temple! But there's more. They not only know who the priests are, and they are not only training them, but they've actually built the stone altar for the Temple!

"Building a Holy Temple begins with the first stone. With this in mind, the Temple Institute has embarked upon building the mizbeach - the stone altar. On the 9th of Av, 5769, (July 30, 2009), the Temple Institute called upon every Jew who was willing to shed his mourning sackcloth, and roll up his work sleeves, and who was ready to curtail his participation in the traditional Tish'a b'Av afternoon custom of studying chapters of Torah which deal with the destruction of the Holy Temple, and to instead occupy themselves with the blood, sweat and tears of real-life preparation for the building of the Holy Temple and the renewal of the Divine service. In a word, to build a stone altar, one that can be placed in

the courtyard of the Holy Temple, and upon which the kohanim can bring the offerings.

This historical project actually began some months ago, just before the Passover festival, when a group of young men were brought to the Dead Sea, where they gathered together stones that would be used in the construction of the mizbeach - altar. The Dead Sea was chosen because it was upon its deserted shores that stones could be collected which had never been quarried or cut with metal blades or implements. Our sages point out that the Torah ban on dressed stones was intended to preserve the integrity of the altar as a place of peace, and tools made of metal, from which weapons of war are also manufactured, would undermine the ultimate purpose of making offerings on the altar, the purpose of making peace between man and God.

The stones were then individually wrapped in heavy plastic and sealed, thus guaranteeing their untainted integrity as they were transported to the community of Mitzpe Yericho, 20 kilometers northeast of Jerusalem.

Meanwhile, of particular concern was the unique nature of the cement to be used to hold the stones together. Temple Institute researchers paid a visit to the Finish glass factory near Yerucham to learn how to create a mixture which would remain as cool as possible under the altar's unremitting fires and protect the kohanim, whose work in the Holy Temple was always conducted barefoot. A formula was arrived at which would involve a mixture of sand, clay, tar, and asphalt.

Finally the appointed day of action arrived: this day was Tish'a B'av, the day the Second Temple was destroyed 1,939 years ago. What better day, and what better way to commemorate the past and to commence the future, than to begin the building of the great stone altar on the 9th of Av! The work began at 5:30 in the afternoon of the 9th, well into the twenty-five hour fast that had begun the night before. Despite the hunger and the accompanying fatigue, the volunteer participants were anxious and ready to get started.

Rabbi Yisrael Ariel, the founder of the Temple Institute, struck a deep chord when he pronounced, 'Today, Tisha B'av, is not just a time to mourn the destruction of the Temple. It is also a time to build.'

The Temple Institute director explained, 'We are building an altar of the minimum possible size so that we will be able to transport it to the Temple when it is rebuilt.' The altar, when completed, will stand 2 meters tall, 1 meter long, and 1 meter wide. Much smaller than the altar which stood in the Holy Temple courtyard. It will, nevertheless, fulfill the Torah requirements.

The rocks collected by the Dead Sea comprise 10 cubic meters and weigh several tons. Over 100 people were present at the event on the stifling hot afternoon. Yonaton Tzadok, one of the main organizers of the event, added a historical-spiritual perspective. 'The altar represents the return to our roots, to the time of creation when everything was pure. We have taken rocks from the Dead Sea, rocks never touched by human hands.'

To the surprise of many who had come simply to watch, they too were invited by Rabbi Ariel to take part and pour the tar onto the cornerstones. Rabbi Ariel first asked if there were any kohanim in the crowd, and invited them to start. A woman requested to also participate. 'Of course,' Rabbi Ariel responded, 'women are also commanded to build the Holy Temple!'

As the sun set, and the fast day was nearing its conclusion, Yonaton Tzadok called upon volunteers to return another day to complete the building of the altar. 'Carrying rocks and pouring tar is a lot of work,' he said. 'We could use a few hundred people to help.'"[22]

Then, as if that wasn't enough, for the first time in 2,000 years, the Jewish people started the Pesach (Passover) Sacrifice again and have declared, "We Are Ready!" In fact, during the sacrifice, one rabbi stated this:

"We see these crowds of hundreds and hundreds of people, from all over who came today to see this event. This is the basic command of the Torah for every Jew on Pesach, the Passover and how we need to bring our Passover offering. The very fact that we are here, we are saying to God, 'Here we are. We are ready. It's in our hands. We are ready to worship you as free people. We hope to do it in the next few years in the way it should be done in a Temple.'"[23]

For the first time in nearly 2,000 years, the Jewish People have once again reconstructed the actual stone altar that will be used in the coming Temple and are once again making the Passover sacrifices associated with the Temple. What more does God have to do? Remember, the Bible says that the Antichrist, halfway into the 7-year Tribulation, is going to put a stop to these very sacrifices that the Jewish people are starting to make again for the first time in 2,000 years. That's how close we are!

3. The Third Way We Know the Jewish People Are Rebuilding the Temple – Articles Are Already Made for the Temple.

But that's still not all. The third way we know the Jewish People really are Rebuilding the Last Days Temple is that **The Articles Are Already Made for the Temple**. Right now the Jewish people are not only making the plans and training the priests and doing sacrifices right now for service in this new Temple, but they've even reconstructed most of the clothing, the vessels, and the articles to be used in the worship of the new Temple.

The first golden Menorah since the destruction of the Holy Temple in 70 AD has been constructed. In fact, for the first time since it was removed by the Romans at the destruction of the Temple in 70 AD, the Golden Menorah has once again been returned to the Temple, as this article shares:

"In the spirit of the Maccabees who purified the Holy Temple and rekindled the golden menora, the golden menora which today stands in the Cardo, is moving this week closer to its intended destination - the Sanctuary of the Holy Temple itself - may it be rebuilt soon in our days.

The menora, the work of master craftsman Chaim Odem and a team of experts has been standing the past seven years in the ancient Cardo. The Cardo which is located in the Jewish Quarter of the Old City of Jerusalem, was a major commercial thoroughfare during the era of the Roman occupation of the land of Israel.

On one of the first nights of Chanuka 5768, (beginning December 4), the menora, with the aid of a robotic crane capable of climbing stairs, will be moved some 400 meters in the direction of the Temple Mount, home of the once and future Holy Temple. The new temporary home of the menora will be in the open plaza next to the Rabbi Yehuda Halevy stairs, which lead from the Jewish Quarter to the Western Wall plaza and the Temple Mount.

There it will be once again on display for the millions of pilgrims and tourists and passers-by each year as they head to and from the Western Wall and Temple Mount. Chanukat HaMenora, a rededication ceremony will take place on Rosh

Chodesh Tevet, (the new month of Tevet), the seventh day of Chanuka, (December 12). Rabbis and dignitaries will be in attendance.

From its new location the menora will be overlooking its ultimate destination - the location of the Sanctuary of the Holy Temple on the Temple Mount.

The menora was painstakingly crafted only after years of extensive research by the Temple Institute's full time staff of researchers. The conclusions upon which the construction of the menora was based took into account archeological evidence and, of course, the halachic (Jewish law) requirements of materials, dimensions, ornamental affects and manner of manufacture as first delineated in the Book of Exodus, and further explicated by Jewish sages throughout the millennia.

The menora weighs one-half ton. It contains forty-five kilograms of twenty four karat gold. Its estimated value is approximately three million dollars. The construction of the menora was made possible through the generosity of Vadim Rabinovitch, a leader of the Jewish community of Ukraine."[24]

They have also reconstructed the golden flasks needed for water libation, the silver shovel for removing ashes from the altar, the gold and silver-plated ram's horns to be blown in the Holy Temple, the silver trumpets to be used to announce Temple services and festivals, the harps and lyres and other musical instruments to be used for music in the Temple services, the wooden and golden lots to be used to determine which goat will be used for sacrifice, the golden altar of incense, the actual knives to be used to prepare the sacrifices to be offered at the Temple, the Table of Showbread, the Laver, the Incense Chalice, the three-pronged fork, the measuring cups, the copper vessel for meal offerings, the sickle, the Menorah cleaner and oil pitcher, the frankincense censer, the garments of the ordinary priests and the loom they are woven with, the spinning wheel with the colored threads arranged for the High Priest's garments, the golden bells for the hem of the High Priest's robe, and the garments for the High Priest, just to name a few.[25] In fact, they have even recently reconstructed the golden crown needed for the High Priest to serve in the Temple, as this article shares:

"Work has just been completed on the manufacture of the Golden Crown of the High Priest. This later version is much more accurate in its design, according to a historical account by the Jewish historian Josephus. The new crown took over a year to construct and cost around $30,000 to make.

The Temple Institute is an organization that is working towards the rebuilding of the Temple, and has already made many of the objects that were once used in its service. All the implements are constructed according to methods described in the Torah. The last ceremonial artifact to be completed was the blue Ephod of the High Priest.

The Temple Institute noted that work on the Golden Crown of the High Priest was completed just as the Israeli Prime Minister was in attendance at the Annapolis peace conference, offering to divide Jerusalem and hand the Temple Mount over to their enemies.

Another report states: The Temple Institute in Jerusalem announces the completion of the Tzitz, the High Priest's headplate - now ready for use in the Holy Temple. The tzitz is made of pure gold, was fashioned over the course of more than a year by the craftsmen of the Temple Institute, and is ready to be worn by the High Priest in the rebuilt Holy Temple in Jerusalem.

The words 'Holy for God' are engraved on the headplate, in accordance with Exodus 28:36. Rabbi Chaim Richman, International Director of the Temple Institute, explained to Arutz-7 that until it can actually be used, the tzitz will be on view in the Institute's permanent exhibition display, together with other vessels and priestly garments fashioned for use in the Holy Temple by the Institute.

'At present,' Rabbi Richman explained, 'people are in despair, and wonder if we're not dreaming futilely while around us our leaders are planning to give the country away. We say to them: It appears that those who went to Annapolis are the dreamers, thinking that their efforts to make peace will succeed, or that the public is with them in their efforts to give away our Jerusalem, our Temple Mount, and other national historic assets.'

'We are now approaching the holiday of Chanukah,' Rabbi Richman continued, 'which is the holiday that commemorates the re-dedication of the Holy Temple. We're not just building beautiful vessels; we're interested in granting God the dwelling place that He wants in this world; the Temple is not merely a building, but a way of bringing God into our lives in a very real way. And that is what we aim to do. This tzitz is God's Chanukah present to us, and our Chanukah gift to the Jewish People.'"[26]

As you can clearly see, almost everything is ready right now for the new Temple with the exception of one thing; a red heifer.

Numbers 19:1-4 "The LORD said to Moses and Aaron: This is a requirement of the law that the LORD has commanded: Tell the Israelites to bring you a red heifer without defect or blemish and that has never been under a yoke. Give it to Eleazar the priest; it is to be taken outside the camp and slaughtered in his presence. Then Eleazar the priest is to take some of its blood on his finger and sprinkle it seven times toward the front of the Tent of Meeting."

According to the Bible, the ashes of a pure red heifer are needed to perform the necessary purification and cleaning rituals that are a part of the service of the Temple. But the problem is, since the Temple was destroyed by the Romans in 70 AD, pure red heifers no longer exist. That is, until now. It started several years ago when all of a sudden red heifers started popping onto the scene. Even though some of the first ones ended up having slight blemishes, and were thus disqualified, it just so happens they're starting to appear on the scene again after all these years![27] That should get your attention! Then, even if it doesn't happen naturally, we just happen to be living in the days when for the first time in man's history, we could create a red heifer artificially through genetic engineering and cloning. But even so, God doesn't need the hand of man to help him out. Can you guess what was just born on the scene and is now being kept in hiding from the public? A pure red heifer and this one does qualify as this breaking news report reveals:

"I was listening to a show that aired today, it's called Temple Talk. It's hosted by Yitzchak Reuven and Rabbi Richman. They talk about the relationship between the golden calf and the mysterious red heifer, including a dramatic revelation, of a new red heifer alive and well in Israel in an undisclosed location. This is breaking news. Here's what they said:

'Because everyone is very interested in the status of the red heifer, people speculate, people remember the excitement of when a red heifer was born, people talk about it. And the reason for that of course, why there's such excitement anybody mentions a red heifer is because a lot of people know that there is a Jewish tradition, it's in the Mishna, that there were only nine red heifers throughout the entire history of the Jewish people. The ashes of those nine red heifers were enough to accomplish the process of cleansing for all the generations of the people of Israel.

And there is a tradition that the tenth red heifer is the one associated with the rebuilding of the Third Temple. That's why when there's a news report about a red heifer being born, people get very very excited. It's looked upon as some sort of wakeup call or something like that.

I wanted to share with our listeners far and wide the fact that there is definitely a kosher red heifer here in Israel right now. This is really breaking news. This should be on a scroll on the bottom of CNN or something.

We're not making a lot of noise about it, we're not taking out all sorts of ads, and we're certainly not disclosing the location, that's definitely not prudent and I'm not going to be sharing it with the United States embassy, absolutely not.

But you should know that there is definitely, in fact, I think there is more than one, but there is definitely at least one kosher red heifer here in Israel right now. So that is not what is impeding the process at all."[28]

What more does God have to do to get our attention? If we see for the first time in 2,000 years the Jewish People having the plans, the priests, the articles, and even the ashes of a red heifer to rebuild the end times Temple right now, then how much closer is the 7-year Tribulation which requires the rebuilt Jewish Temple for the Antichrist and the Two Witnesses to be a part of? We are so close it's not even funny, as this Jewish man warns:

"In 1981, Indiana Jones made his big-screen debut re-igniting world-wide interest in history's most hunted relic: The Ark of the Covenant. That same year, two real-life raiders went on their own search for the Ark. There were no Nazis and no snake pits - like the movie. Just two renegade Rabbis on a mission. Their search came to an end in Jerusalem.

'God signed, like with a pen, the location where the Ark of the Covenant was located. You can see it today even, on the rock,' said Gershon Salomon, Founder of Temple Mount Faithful.

Designed by God, created by Moses, and revered by the Israelites, from the Sinai Desert to the Temple of Solomon, the Ark of the Covenant was the place of meeting between God and man. In 586 B.C., Israel was conquered by the Babylonians. The Temple was raided by Nebuchadnezzar's army and the Ark disappeared from the pages of history.

'What happened, why did this most dramatic instrument of God's glory and power in human history suddenly vanish?' questioned Joel Rosenberg, Author of Dead Heat.

'All what we know is legends,' said Archaeologist Gabriel Barkay who believes the legends are what make so many people interested in finding the Ark. Those legends stretch all over the ancient world - starting with Nebuchadnezzar in Babylon.

In Israel, most Rabbis agree that when it comes to the Ark all roads lead back to Jerusalem. They say the Ark never left the city. To them, the so-called 'Lost Ark' was never really lost.

On June 7, 1967, Israeli troops recaptured Jerusalem in the Six-day War. The Western Wall was in Jewish hands and those hands were ready to dig. Archaeologists exposed parts of the wall that had been buried for 2000 years. Not all of the digging was done legally. In 1981, two of Israel's highest-ranking Rabbis, Shlomo Goren and Yehuda Getz picked up their pick-axes and started chiseling their way under the Temple Mount.

'And he knew that at the end of the gate he will come to the secret room where the ark of covenant is located,' said Salomon, who was also one of the paratroopers who liberated the Western Wall in 1967.

Salomon was there fourteen years later, the night Rabbi Getz opened a secret passage in the Wall and remembers their conversation.

'It was after midnight. And he called me and said to me, Gershon, come immediately, don't wait, your dream is going to be fulfilled.' 'What happened?,' I told him. 'The Messiah came?' And he told me, 'He is coming almost.'"

What came next was a subterranean slugfest according to Salomon. 'Arab demonstrations, you know? The Israelis are coming to build their temple underneath the dome of the rock.' At the end of the day, the passage to the Temple Mount was permanently sealed by Israeli Police.

'No doubt, I tell you. No doubt, we needed just two days more to come to the place where the ark of the covenant is located,' Salomon explained.

Scholars may not agree on the fate of the Ark but many of them agree on one thing: its discovery could set in motion another event that's been 2000 years in the making – the rebuilding of the Jewish Temple.

'Perhaps when it's time to build the third temple, the second temple treasures will be found. Why? Because in Ezra and Nehemiah, the Bible indicated that when it was time to build the second temple, God restored the treasures from the first temple which of course had been carted off to Babylon,' said Rosenberg. 'When it's time to build a third temple, the second temple's treasures would be found. Wouldn't that be dramatic?' he concluded.

'It is soon to come, I tell you, I promise you, and you check me. Test me. It will be in our lifetime,' added Salomon."[29]

X. Tenth End Time Prophecy Concerning the Jewish People - They Would Have a Relationship with the Antichrist

1. The First Thing We Know About the Jewish People's Relationship with the Antichrist – They Will Make a Peace Treaty with Him

Daniel 9:20-27 "While I was speaking and praying, confessing my sin and the sin of my people Israel and making my request to the LORD my God for his holy hill – while I was still in prayer, Gabriel, the man I had seen in the earlier vision, came to me in swift flight about the time of the evening sacrifice. He instructed me and said to me, 'Daniel, I have now come to give you insight and understanding. As soon as you began to pray, an answer was given, which I have come to tell you, for you are highly esteemed. Therefore, consider the message and understand the vision: Seventy 'sevens' are decreed for your people and your holy city to finish transgression, to put an end to sin, to atone for wickedness, to bring in everlasting righteousness, to seal up vision and prophecy and to anoint the most holy. Know and understand this: From the issuing of the decree to restore and rebuild Jerusalem until the Anointed One, the ruler, comes, there will be seven 'sevens,' and sixty-two 'sevens.' It will be rebuilt with streets and a trench, but in times of trouble. After the sixty-two 'sevens,' the Anointed One will be cut off and will have nothing. The people of the ruler who will come will destroy the city and the sanctuary. The end will come like a flood: War will continue until the end, and desolations have been decreed. He will confirm a covenant with many for one 'seven.' In the middle of the 'seven' he will put an end to sacrifice and offering. And on a wing of the temple he will set up an abomination that causes desolation, until the end that is decreed is poured out on him.'"

Now, this is the classic passage of Scripture we saw earlier that specifically tells us the exact event that starts the 7-year Tribulation in the Last Days. That event is when the Antichrist makes a "peace treaty" or covenant with the Jewish People. Not only that, the specific time frame about this covenant is that it's going to be specifically for seven years. Furthermore, as we saw earlier, who in the world is everybody right now wanting to make a peace treaty with? Israel! Little bitty tiny Israel! Not Russia. Not China. But little bitty tiny Israel. Why? Because they are fulfilling the prophecy that says one day they will become a source of worldwide conflict and it's leading to the fulfillment of this prophecy here from Daniel. One day, because of all this conflict, they're going to strike a relationship with, of all people, the Antichrist himself, and seek a peace treaty with him.

In fact, to make matters even more interesting, for the first time in 1,600 years we have the rebirth of the Jewish Sanhedrin, just a few years ago.[30] So now, we just happen to have the same ruling body once again alive on planet earth that rejected Jesus at His First Coming, to once again possibly make another horrific mistake, this time, a treaty with the actual Antichrist himself prior to Jesus' Second Coming!

So the question is, "Are there any signs the Jewish people are trying to make a peace treaty or covenant with other people around the world? Yes, of course. In fact, let me show you just a few of the attempts people and other governments around the world have attempted to make with Israel in our lifetime exactly like the Bible said would happen in the Last Days!

- UN Security Council Resolution 242, 1967
- Camp David Accords, 1978
- The Madrid Conference, 1991
- Israeli-Syrian Talks 1991
- Oslo Agreement, 1993
- Israel-Jordan Treaty of Peace, 1994
- Camp David, 2000
- Taba Talks, 2001
- Saudi Peace Plan, 2002
- Road Map Peace Plans, 2003
- Geneva Accord, 2003
- Sharm el-Sheikh Summit, 2005

- Franco-Italian-Spanish Middle East Peace Plan, 2006
- Israel-Hamas Ceasefire, 2008
- Direct Talks Peace Plan, 2010
- Israeli Peace Initiative, 2011[31]

Sure looks like somebody's trying to get a peace treaty going with Israel! Again, you have to understand the significance of this. One of these treaties, or maybe it's one that's even being hashed out behind the scenes even now, we don't know, but one of them is going to be signed with the actual Antichrist himself. Unlike all the other failed ones as we just saw, he alone is going to do what others have failed to do. However, it's not going to lead to peace in the Middle East, rather it's going to be the planet's worst nightmare. It's the very event that starts the 7-year Tribulation! So when you see this happen, Israel making treaties or covenants with other people around the world, you better wake up! It's a sign you're living in the Last Days!

2. The Second Thing We Know about the Jewish People's Relationship with the Antichrist – They Will Place Their Hope in Him

Romans 11:25-26 "For I do not desire, brethren, that you should be ignorant of this mystery, lest you should be wise in your own opinion, that blindness in part has happened to Israel until the fullness of the Gentiles has come in. And so all Israel will be saved, as it is written: 'The Deliverer will come out of Zion. And He will turn away ungodliness from Jacob.'"

Here we see just one of many examples in the Bible that clearly tells us that God is not finished with the Jewish people. They are currently under a temporary blindness until the amount of Gentiles or non-Jewish people that God wants saved, get saved. Then God's going to focus again on the Jewish people and He's going to rescue them and fulfill His promises to them. But until that time, the Jewish People are not only going to be blinded to the true identity of the Antichrist and even strike a relationship with him via a treaty, but apparently they're going to look upon him as some sort of savior and hope that he can do what everybody else has failed to do i.e. give them peace. So that's the question. Are there any signs that the Jewish people right now are expecting a messiah type figure to place their hopes in, in order to prepare their hearts to unfortunately receive the actual Antichrist? Yes! Check out their words for yourself:

- *"The most important event in the Messianic era will be the rebuilding of the Holy Temple. It is the act of building the Temple that will establish the identity of the Messiah beyond all shadow of a doubt. The Messiah will be a king over Israel, and a king can only be crowned by the Sanhedrin. The reason he will come to Jerusalem first is to be recognized by the Sanhedrin."*

- *"Chief Rabbi Berel Lazar believes the Earth will soon see the coming of a Messiah to judge all mankind. 'We know that he is very near at hand. The Messiah may well have been born already. The world today is in a state described by our sages as 'hevley mashiah,' that is, labor that precedes the coming of a Messiah. We are living on the verge of history. It can be felt everywhere.'"*

- *"Rabbi Yitzchak Kaduri called upon worldwide Jewry to return to Israel due to natural disasters, which threaten to strike the world. 'In the future, the Holy One, Blessed be He, will bring about great disasters in the countries of the world to sweeten the judgments of the Land of Israel. I am ordering the publication of this declaration as a warning, so that Jews in the countries of the world will be aware of the impending danger and will come to the Land of Israel for the building of the Temple and revelation of our righteous Mashiach (Messiah). The Mashiach is already in Israel."*[32]

Unfortunately, it looks like the Jewish people are not only showing signs of getting ready to sign a peace treaty with the Antichrist himself, but it sure looks to me like their hearts are awfully ripe to receive him as some sort of false messiah too. The point is, the Bible says when you see this happen, you better wake up! It's a sign you're living in the Last Days!

3. The Third Thing We Know About the Jewish People's Relationship with the Antichrist – He Will Demand Worship as a Man

Revelation 13:11-12,14-15 "Then I saw another beast, coming out of the earth. He had two horns like a lamb, but he spoke like a dragon. He exercised all the authority of the first beast on his behalf, and made the earth and its inhabitants worship the first beast, whose fatal wound had been healed. Because of the signs he was given power to do on behalf of the first beast, he deceived the inhabitants of the earth. He ordered them to set up an image in honor of the beast who was wounded by the sword and yet lived. He was given power to give breath to the image of the first beast, so that it could speak and cause all who refused to worship the image to be killed."

Here we see how the false prophet is actually going to dupe the whole world into worshiping the Antichrist. In fact, it says it twice there in that text that people will worship him, a mere man. Then he even adds a little pressure there and says if you don't do it; you're going to die! So that's the question. Do we see any signs of people's hearts being prepared to worship a man, specifically a political figure of a man because that's what the Antichrist is? Yes! In fact, this has been evidenced in the giant parades and humungous posters of Stalin or Mao Tse-tung being paraded through the streets of their countries as if it were some sort of worship service. Then, even more recently, we had the death of North Korea's President Kim Jong-il where, if you saw the videos, people were weeping hysterically bowing before his image. It was unbelievable. He was just a man. Yet, we here in America might be tempted to smugly reply, "That's just those people in communist countries! There's no way our hearts will ever do something like that! We'd never worship a political figure of a man!" Really? What I'm about to share is not only shocking, but it has nothing to do with politics. Rather, it has everything to do with Bible prophecy. Throughout this book, you're going to see examples of various Democrats and Republicans along with various leaders from around the world doing some dastardly deeds. So don't assume I'm picking on one party over another. Truth be told, I think they're both in it together. Not every single one of them, but a lot of them. Let's take a look at how America responded to our former President Barrack Obama. What I'm about to share with you is proof that yes, even here in America, we too are guilty of worshiping a political figure of a man, and so our hearts too are being prepared to worship the soon coming Antichrist. Let's look at that proof:

- A massive bust of Barack Obama that was made of steel and concrete, topped 20 feet and weighed roughly 12 tons was shipped in two pieces on the back of a truck to make its way along a 10-state, 40-city tour that was scheduled to conclude its journey just outside Mount Rushmore.

- An artist in Iowa created a piece of artwork depicting an inaugural parade with Barack Obama, riding on a donkey, making his own triumphal entry complete as adorers wave palm fronds along with a "Secret Service" escort.

- Another artist planned to unveil a portrait of Barack Obama in a Christ-like pose with a crown of thorns upon his brow at New York City's Union Square Park, marking the president's 100th day in office.

- Many Hollywood celebrities are praying to Barack Obama and pledging allegiance to him to help make "a change" as this article shares:

"In a new YouTube video produced by Oprah Winfrey's Harpo Productions, dozens of celebrities – television and movie actors, sports heroes, musicians and more – describe how they will pledge to 'be the change' and 'be a servant to our president.'

The video opens with a quote from President Truman, 'They say that the job of the president is the loneliest job in the world,' something the celebrities plan to alleviate for Obama by pledging to pitch in through several causes.

Throughout the video, the celebrities pledge to support local food banks, to smile more, to be better parents, to work with the charity UNICEF, to 'never give anyone the finger when I'm driving again,' to help find a cure for Alzheimer's, to meet neighbors, to use less plastic, to plant 500 trees, to 'be more green,' to turn the lights off and to 'free 1 million people from slavery in the next five years,' among dozens of other pledges.

The purpose of all this pledging is summed up in the video's grand finale. Actors Demi Moore and Ashton Kutcher begin the closing scene by saying, 'I pledge to be a servant to our president and all mankind.'

Then, as the scene pans out, the other celebrities join the chant: 'Because together we can, together we are, and together we will be the change that we seek.'

By the end of the mass pledge, the camera has panned back to a mosaic of faces that morphs into a picture of Barack Obama's face with the words, 'Be the change.'

And while several of the celebrities attempt to portray heartfelt emotion and others attempt to be funny in their pledges, tattooed celebrity Anthony Kiedis of the band Red Hot Chili Peppers may have been going for the shock effect. While kissing his own biceps, he declares, 'I pledge to be of service [kiss] to Barack Obama [kiss].'

Near the end of the video, the celebrities took turns looking into the camera and challenging, 'What's your pledge?'

Not surprisingly, viewer reaction and comments on the video have been widely mixed.

One poster who obviously disagreed posted the correct pledge, 'I pledge allegiance to the flag of the United States of America and to the Republic, for which it stands: one nation, under God, indivisible, with liberty and justice for all.'

- Then there are actually other videos of people on the Internet who are praying to Barack Obama as this next article shares.

"A newly publicized video shows leaders of a Chicago-based community organizing group called the Gamaliel Foundation held a rally shortly after President Obama's election and 'prayed' to him, seeking his intervention in their difficulties.

'Hear our Cry Obama. Deliver us Obama,' the organizers chanted as a single leader recited the organization's perceived problems, based on the philosophies of Saul Alinsky, the radical father of community organizing.

The video explains the event took place at a leadership conference just a few weeks after Obama's election in November.

The 'leaders' enter a room chanting, 'Everybody in, nobody out,' apparently referring to health care.

Then the chanter leads: 'We are here for the healing of the nation,' to which the crowd responds, 'Yes.'

'With the prophet Jeremiah we cry out, Is there no balm in Gilead?' continues the chanter. 'Is there no physician here. Why then has the health of thy poor people not been restored?'

The crowd responds: 'Hear our cry Obama.'

The chanter references the 'prophet Martin Luther King Jr.,' to which the crowd responds, 'Hear our cry Obama.'

The chanter then intones: 'From health care systems and industries that place profit over people,' and the people respond, 'Deliver us Obama.'

The chanter then references 'lobbying efforts' and 'greed and fear,' to which the crowd responds, 'Deliver us Obama.'"[33]

Yes, things have changed alright. Our hearts, even here in America, are now showing signs of worshiping a man; specifically a political figure of a man. The Bible says, when you see this take place, you better wake up! It's a sign you're living in the Last Days!

4. The Fourth Thing We Know About the Jewish People's Relationship with the Antichrist – He Will Demand Worship as a God

2 Thessalonians 2:1-4 "Concerning the coming of our Lord Jesus Christ and our being gathered to Him, we ask you, brothers, not to become easily unsettled or alarmed by some prophecy, report or letter supposed to have come from us, saying that the day of the Lord has already come. Don't let anyone deceive you in any way, for that day will not come until the rebellion occurs and the man of lawlessness is revealed, the man doomed to destruction. He will oppose and will exalt himself over everything that is called God or is worshiped, so that he sets himself up in God's temple, proclaiming himself to be God."

Now again, this is the text where we saw previously in the Last Days, the Antichrist is going to go up into the rebuilt Jewish Temple, halfway into the 7-year Tribulation, and declare himself to be god. But it's a good thing we don't see any signs of people worshiping a man as god! I mean, it's one thing to worship a political figure as a man, but no way would we worship a man as a god, right? Well, I wish I could say no. But unfortunately we do! In fact, there's a whole bunch of false teachings out there to choose from that actually encourage people to fulfill this particular piece of Bible prophecy. Let's take a look:

- **Environmentalism** says that all is god. "The philosophy of radical environmentalism is based in the religious belief of pantheism, that god is in all and all is god; that earth is our mother (Gaia); that all living things have equal value and that mankind has overstepped its bounds, even being a cancer on the rest of nature. As ardent environmentalist Al Gore states, 'God is not separate from the Earth.'"

- **Hinduism** says that all is god. "Hinduism worships multiple deities: gods and goddesses and [teaches] that all reality is a unity. The entire universe (including you and me) is seen as one divine entity just in different facets, forms, or manifestations."

- **Mormons** say you can become a god. "After you become a good Mormon, you have the potential of becoming a god. Then shall they be gods, because they have no end; therefore shall they be from everlasting to everlasting, because they continue; then shall they be above all, because all things are subject unto them. Then shall they be gods."

- **So-called Spirit Guides** say we are god. "Feel the millions of souls; the divine spark within each of them. We are here in your moment of realization; in the moment you come to meet with your divinity; in the moment when you finally accept, that which you truly are."

- **Supposed UFO Space Brothers** say we are god. "Love yourself among the ones who love you, allow their love to fill you but above all, feel your own love that you have for yourself. We feel very honored this day to sit before the humans who have chosen to be among the first to step into their divinity, to walk as complete divine beings clothed in human flesh.

- **Supposed Messages from Mary** say we are god. "God is all that is. Therefore, We are Prime Creator expressing Itself as us. We are not striving for perfection as we are already perfect. What we are striving for is to *remember* our perfection. We are not divided into parts. Since God is us, therefore, we are God."

- **Supposed Messages from Angels** say we are god. "It is nice to come and break bread...the bread of truth. God gives all of His creation freedom of choice to find themselves, to find their true ancestry of God-Goddess within them."

- **New Age** says we are god. One of the most ardent New Agers, Shirley Maclaine not only says she's god but made a movie, *"Out on a Limb"* encouraging everyone to do the same.

- **Wiccans** (witchcraft) says we are god within. "The existence of a supreme divine power is known as 'The One,' or 'The All'. 'The All' is not separate from the universe, but part of it and from 'The All' came the god and goddess and they are manifested in various forms in the universe. Divinity is within."[34]

- **The devil** says we can become gods. **Genesis 3:5** "For God knows that when you eat of it your eyes will be opened, and you will be like God."

Now, I not only find those statements kind of sickening, but I also find them kind of frightening. I mean, can you imagine the audacity of a mere man saying he's God? Talk about lightning bolt city! Besides, the Bible flatly denies the existence of any other gods:

Isaiah 43:10 "You are My witnesses, declares the LORD, Before Me no god was formed, nor will there be one after Me."

Isaiah 44: 6,8 "This is what the LORD says – I am the first and I am the last; apart from Me there is no God. Is there any God besides Me? No, there is no other Rock; I know not one."

Isaiah 45:5 "I am the LORD, and there is no other; apart from Me there is no God."

I think the point is obvious. There's a ton of false teachings out there encouraging people to worship a man as a god, even though the Bible clearly condemns it, right? It's all over the place. Remember, that's what the Antichrist is going to do! He's going to say, "Worship me as god!" But praise God, that's not going to happen to the Church! No way we're giving into that lie! Or are we? You tell me if even in the Church people aren't being encouraged to worship a man as a god, and therefore their hearts too are being prepared to receive the Antichrist as god! Check it out yourself:

- **Fredrick Price:** "God can't do anything in this earth realm except what we, the body of Christ, allow Him to do. So, if man has control, who no longer has it? God. Yes! You are in control!"

- **Benny Hinn:** "When you say, 'I am a Christian, you are saying, 'I am a little messiah walking on earth. That is a shocking revelation. May I say it like this? You are a little god on earth running around. Christians are "Little Messiah's and "little gods" on the earth. Say "I'm born of heaven, a God-man. I'm a God man. I am a sample of Jesus. I'm a super being. Say it! Say it!"

- **Paul Crouch:** "Somebody said – I don't know who said it – but they claim that you Faith teachers declare that we are gods. You're a god. I'm a god. Well, are you a god? I am a little god! I have His name. I'm one with Him. I'm in covenant relation. I am a little god! Critics, be gone!"

- **Kenneth Copeland:** "Jesus is no longer the only begotten Son of God. You are not a spiritual schizophrenic – half-God and half-Satan – you are all-God. You don't have a god in you. You are one. I say this with all respect so that it don't upset you too bad, but I say it anyway. When I read in the Bible where he [Jesus] says, 'I Am,' I just smile and say, 'Yes, I Am, too!'"

- **Kenneth Hagin:** "The believer is called Christ. That's who we are; we're Christ. You are as much the incarnation of God as Jesus Christ was.

- **Morris Cerullo:** "You're not looking at Morris Cerullo – you're looking at God. You're looking at Jesus."[35]

Now, who in their right mind would have thought that even in the Church people would be encouraged to worship a man as god, which is preparing their hearts to receive the ultimate false god, the Antichrist! When you see this taking place, the Bible says, you better wake up! It's a sign you're living in the Last Days!

5. The Fifth Thing We Know About the Jewish People's Relationship with the Antichrist – He Will Slaughter Two-Thirds of Them

Unlike the false teachers in the Church, the Jewish people will *never* go along with worshiping a man as God, maybe as a messiah to put their hopes in unfortunately, but not as a god. They know the Scripture too well, there is only One God. So, here's the problem. The Antichrist is not going to like this. He wants to be worshiped as god. So halfway into the 7-year Tribulation, he's not only going to go into the Temple and declare himself to be god, but apparently he's going to go after the Jewish people and annihilate them because they refuse to worship him as god. This is when the blinders come off and they realize the horrible mistake they made. In fact, Zechariah tells us how many of the Jewish people will be slaughtered:

Zechariah 13:8-9 "In the whole land, declares the LORD, two-thirds will be struck down and perish; yet one-third will be left in it. This third I will bring into the fire; I will refine them like silver and test them like gold. They will call on my name and I will answer them; I will say, 'They are my people,' and they will say, 'The LORD is our God.'"

Here we see some good news and some bad news. The good news is that the Jewish people will eventually lose their spiritual blindness and get right with God. But the bad news is that two-thirds are going to be struck down. Which means, if that were to happen right now, the current population of Israel is at about 8 million,[36] which means this slaughter alone will be over 5 million people. And when it happens, it's going to happen like a flood. This is what the Apostle John talked about:

Revelation 12:1-6,13-17 "A great and wondrous sign appeared in heaven: a woman clothed with the sun, with the moon under her feet and a crown of twelve stars on her head. She was pregnant and cried out in pain as she was about to give birth. Then another sign appeared in heaven: an enormous red dragon with seven heads and ten horns and seven crowns on his heads. His tail swept a third of the stars out of the sky and flung them to the earth. The dragon stood in front of the woman who was about to give birth, so that he might devour her child the moment it was born. She gave birth to a son, a male child, who will rule all the nations with an iron scepter. And her child was snatched up to God and to his throne. The woman fled into the desert to a place prepared for her by God, where she might be taken care of for 1,260 days. When the dragon saw that he had been hurled to the earth, he pursued the woman who had given birth to the male child. The woman was given the two wings of a great eagle, so that she might fly to the place prepared for her in the desert, where she would be taken care of for a time, times and half a time, out of the serpent's reach. Then from his mouth the serpent spewed water like a river, to overtake the woman and sweep her away with the torrent. But the earth helped the woman by opening its mouth and swallowing the river that the dragon had spewed out of his mouth. Then the dragon was enraged at the woman and went off to make war against the rest of her offspring – those who obey God's commandments and hold to the testimony of Jesus."

It's going to be such a horrible slaughter and happen with such ferocity and fierceness like a flood, that Jesus even warned you better run for your life and never look back!

Matthew 24:15-22 "So when you see standing in the holy place 'the abomination that causes desolation,' spoken of through the prophet Daniel – let the reader understand – then let those who are in Judea flee to the mountains. Let no one on the roof of his house go down to take anything out of the house. Let no one in the field go back to get his cloak. How dreadful it will be in those days for pregnant women and nursing mothers! Pray that your flight will not take place in winter or on the Sabbath. For then there will be great distress, unequaled from the beginning of the world until now – and never to be equaled again. If those days had not been cut short, no one would survive, but for the sake of the elect those days will be shortened."

Wow! That sounds pretty horrible! Good thing though there are no signs of this prophecy coming to pass! I mean, surely we've learned our lesson from WWII and all the evil atrocities Hitler did with the Holocaust, right? Unfortunately no. Not only can you go on the Internet and see a multitude of people, even children, from around the world declaring and calling for the death of the Jewish people again, even here in America when teenagers were asked if they even knew who Adolph Hitler was, the majority of them said they had no idea! As if that wasn't shocking enough, they were then asked if they would be willing to drive a bulldozer and bury Jews alive just to save their own life and the majority said yes! Here's the gut-wrenching proof:

"Evangelist Ray Comfort revealed that during the making of his dramatic pro-life film, '180,' he was sickened by the answers so many young people gave to a hypothetical question he asked them after describing a life and death, Holocaust-like scenario.

The 33-minute video released for free online, documents the responses of young adults to questions from Comfort about their stance on abortion, but also includes discussions on Adolf Hitler and the Holocaust in Europe.

While focusing on the responses given by several people with a pro-abortion stance, Comfort then transitions from talk about lives lost in the Holocaust to lives lost as the result of abortions in the U.S.

The hypothetical scenario Comfort described to those he interviewed for the film went like this:

It's 1943. A German officer has a gun pointed at you. He wants you to get into a bulldozer and drive it forward. In front of the bulldozer is a pit in which there are 300 Jews who have just been shot. Some of them are still alive. He wants you to bury them alive! If you don't do what he says, he is going to kill you and do it himself. If you do what he says, he will let you live. Would you drive it forward?

'I was surprised that so many said that they could bury another person alive. I felt sickened, but at the same time I don't know if I believed others when they quickly said that they would take the bullet, rather than do it,' said Comfort in a recent interview made available to The Christian Post. 'I guess it takes a lot of soul-searching. It certainly is a character-test for each of us.'

Comfort explained how the conversations with the people he interviewed at different outdoor Southern California locales began.

'I would begin an interview by asking the question 'Have you heard of Adolf Hitler?' If they said, 'No,' I had the difficult task of getting them on camera,' Comfort said. 'It was hard to hide my shock that anyone didn't know who Hitler was, and the moment they suspected that they should know about him they refused because they felt foolish. So there were a number of interviews I missed out on because of that.'

'Still, we were able to get 14 people on-camera, mainly university students, who didn't have a clue who Adolf Hitler was,' Comfort said. 'The swing from the Holocaust to abortion was fairly seamless because it came in the form of a question: 'How do you feel about abortion?'

Then came, 'Do you think it's a baby in the womb?' If they said that they thought it was a baby in the womb, I asked if they could think of any justification for taking its life. The only people who became angry were the two women who had painted their bodies silver. After one admitted that she couldn't kill Jews but other people should have the right to kill them, she must have realized what she had just said. She then became angry, and walked off. However, each of the others were genuinely moved by the interview.'

Comfort said the other surprising moments came when he discovered that so many people said that 'it was a baby in the womb, and yet they still said that terminating the pregnancy was a woman's choice.'

'After giving them some knowledge that made them change their minds, I realized that so many have been brainwashed and that all they need is information to give them another perspective.'"[37]

It's precisely because of this brainwashing procedure and lack of proper perspective that reports are now saying in regards to the rise of anti-Semitism that, "It's just as bad as it was in the 30's,"[38] you know, prior to WWII and what Hitler did. Who would have thought, even after all the recent atrocities Hitler did to the Jewish people, that another generation would arise and not only not know who Hitler is or what he did, but they'd actually lend a helping hand in getting rid of the Jewish people again! Are we living in the Last Days or what? We have got to wake up! Yet, even with all this amazing evidence pointing to the signs of Christ's soon return, some people still refuse to heed the warning and are headed for certain destruction, like this guy:

"Two local Pastors were fishing on the side of the road one day, and being Christians and all, they decided to make a sign that said, 'The End is Near! Turn yourself around now before it's too late!' and showed this sign to each passing car.

Well, one driver that drove by didn't appreciate the sign at all. So he shouted at them, 'Leave us alone you religious nuts!' and he kept on driving.

Then all of a sudden there was a big splash, so they looked at each other, and the one Pastor said to the other, "Do you think we should've just put up a sign that says, 'The bridge is out?'"[39]

Now, that guy didn't want to listen to the warning did he? In fact, he thought that the people who were saying it were a bunch of wackos. Yet the Bible says that this skeptical attitude would be commonplace in the end times.

2 Peter 3:3-4 "First, I want to remind you that in the Last Days there will be scoffers who will laugh at the truth and do every evil thing they desire. This will be their argument: 'Jesus promised to come back, did he? Then where is he? Why, as far back as anyone can remember, everything has remained exactly the same since the world was first created.'"

I hope you're not one of those scoffers who wake up one day and realize too late that you've been left behind. And you know what? So does God. Because He loves us, He has given us the warning sign of **The Jewish People** to show us that the 7-year Tribulation is near and Christ's Coming is rapidly approaching. Jesus Himself said this:

Luke 21:28 "When these things begin to take place, stand up and lift up your heads, because your redemption is drawing near."

Like it or not, we are headed for *The Final Countdown*. We don't know the day or the hour. Only God knows. The point is, if you're a Christian, it's time to get serious and get motivated about who we are and what we're called to do as Christians. It's high time we Christians speak up and declare the good news of salvation to those who are dying all around us. But please, if you're not a Christian, give your life to Jesus today, because tomorrow may be too late! Just like the Bible said!

Chapter Two

Modern Technology

"One day a guy needed to get a ride home in a taxicab, so he hailed one down and hopped into the back seat. Well, on the way home, the passenger tapped the taxicab driver on the shoulder to ask him a question.

But at this, the taxicab driver screamed bloody murder, lost control of the car, nearly hit a bus, went up on a footpath, and stopped just inches from a shop window.

For a second everything went quiet in the cab, then the driver said, 'Look buddy, don't ever do that again. You scared the daylights out of me!'

The passenger apologized and said he didn't realize that a little tap on the shoulder could scare the guy so much.

The driver calmed down and replied 'Hey listen, I'm sorry, it's not really your fault. You see, today is my first day as a taxicab driver – for the last 25 years, I've been driving a hearse!'"[1]

Now, how many of you would say that taxicab drivers fear was justified once you understand the whole context here? He was scared out of his wits, wasn't he? However, he's not alone. The Bible says one day *the whole planet* is going to be *scared out of their wits* just like that driver at the Rapture of the

Church! The Bible says their hearts will actually "fail them with fear," or in other words, they'll be dropping like flies with massive heart attacks all over the place because they are so terrified! That's because they just entered the 7-year Tribulation and it's no joke!

The time of the Tribulation is not a party. It's an outpouring of God's wrath upon a wicked and rebellious planet. In fact, Jesus said in Matthew 24 that it would be a time of greater horror than anything the world has ever seen or will ever see again. He also said that unless that time of calamity is shortened, the entire human race would be destroyed. But God is not only a God of wrath; He's a God of love as well. And because He loves us, He has given us many warning signs so that we would know when the Tribulation was near and Christ's Second Coming was rapidly approaching. Therefore, to keep people from experiencing the ultimate surprise of being left behind, we're going to continue taking a look at *The Final Countdown*.

In the last chapter we looked at the **tenth sign** on *The Final Countdown*, which was **The Jewish People**. There we saw that God lovingly foretold us that when we see the Jewish people returning to the land, becoming a single united nation with a powerful military, blossoming as a rose in the desert with a currency of the shekel, preparing to rebuild the temple, and even developing an unfortunate relationship with the Antichrist, this would be an indicator we are in the Last Days.

But that's not the only sign that God has given us. The **ninth sign** on *The Final Countdown* is none other than **Modern Technology**. So just what are these specific prophesies being fulfilled today concerning Modern Technology, revealing that we could be in the Last Days?

I. First End Time Prophecy Concerning Modern Technology - There Would Be a Great Increase of Travel and Knowledge.

Daniel 12:4 "But you, Daniel, keep this prophecy a secret; seal up the book until the time of the end. Many will rush here and there, and knowledge will increase."

Many scholars see this passage as strictly referring to people rushing here and there, increasing their knowledge of prophecy in the Last Days. Which is exactly what we see today, do we not? Then there are those who see this passage strictly referring to people traveling all over the earth with an explosion of information like never before. Which is also exactly what we see today, do we not? Therefore, I think that it's not necessarily one or the other, but actually both.

1. First Way Modern Technology Reveals We Could be in the Last Days – Increase of Travel

So, specifically, just what kind of Modern Technology has arisen to enable this prophecy to come to pass? When Daniel wrote down the words of this prophecy, the mode of travel had been basically the same for thousands of years. It's only *in this last century alone* that we've seen a major change in transportation.

For instance, the fastest that mankind could travel for thousands of years was about 30 mph via horseback. From Adam to Alexander the Great to Abraham Lincoln, transportation pretty much stayed the same.[2] For instance, at the turn of the 20th century in New York, the major traffic concern was dead horses! Each year there were about 15,000 horses dying from exhaustion, beatings, or accidents. Believe it or not, they had their own air pollution too from a million pounds of manure produced every day! People quickly learned to keep their windows closed during the summer. But by and large, the major means of transportation for thousands of years was the horse.[3]

That is, until now. *All in the last century alone*, we have gone from the horse to the horseless carriage; the car. We've gone from a top speed of 30 mph to literally hundreds of mph. In just a few decades, we now rush here and there an average of 14,000 miles per year, with an estimated 1 Billion cars on the road by 2025.[4]

Oh, but that's only by land. Thanks to the invention of the airplane, which also occurred in the last century, the world has become a much smaller place. For instance, the first flight by the Wright brothers was only 120 feet. Had they flown from the back of a Boeing 747 they wouldn't have even made it to first class. The first plane had limited seating. But a Boeing 747 can carry more than 400 passengers, fly 8,300 miles without refueling, has 6 million parts, 171 miles of wiring, 5 miles of tubing and a tail the size of a six-story building.[5]

Because there are so many people traveling today, the industry is making it even easier and faster to rush here and there, just like the Bible said would happen. For instance, you can not only order your tickets online, but also print boarding passes from your own computer. In addition, for those of you who worry about your loved ones flying, worry no more. Thanks to the Internet, you can follow a flight in transit, graphics and all, observe the speed and altitude it's traveling, and be told when it has arrived.[6] Not just the Internet, but now you can even do this on your cell phone. You don't even need to be at a computer anymore, it's with you wherever you go! Isn't that convenient! In fact, they're now combining this ability to travel on Land and Air to where you can really rush here and there in your own flying car:

"In 1900, Henry Ford markets his first automobile. In 1903 the Wright brothers have their first flight at Kitty Hawk. In 1949 Molt Taylor invents the Aerocar. In 2004 the FAA creates the Light Sport Aircraft category. In 2009, the 'Transition' flying car passes its first flight test. In 2010, the next generation design of the Transition is released to the public.

We've always dreamed about having a flying car, and here it is. The idea of combining the automobile with the airplane is no longer a fantasy. Celebrated by news media around the world as the modern day flying car, the Transition represents a safer and more practical approach to personal air travel.

It sounds like science fiction but before long Britain will have its first car-planes. American company Terrafugia has developed a new model which drives on the road with wings folded before opening them to take off as a light aircraft. The Terrafugia Transition has a top speed of 185 mph in the air and can be parked in the garage at home.

The Transition costs around $280,000 and the first deliveries were expected in 2012. The car-plane offers a unique opportunity to drive to the airport and take off in the same vehicle – and perhaps to avoid traffic jams.

Aircraft have looked essentially the same for the past 50 years. Transition really is the next step in the evolution of aircraft. The transition can convert between flying and driving almost instantly; you just get in the cockpit, push a couple of buttons and the wings fold up.

Although it has been dubbed "a flying car," the Transition is really an airplane that can legally and safely be driven on roads and highways and parked in your single car garage. The Transition's a really fun flying car to drive; it's got a lot of power, it's got a well-tuned suspension, and it's very responsive.

The Transition flies like a really nice airplane. I've flown 20 to 30 different airplanes in my career and the Transition is by far the easiest airplane to land. It's smooth, controllable and very stable. The Transition is designed to fly like any other sport aircraft, but it provides a unique capability to land and continue your trip on the ground safely, no matter what the weather is like.

Pilots who get behind the controls for the first time will feel at ease in the Transition's comfortable and user-friendly interior. The control panels are touch screen interfaces, designed to be intuitive and easy to use. There's also just one GPS navigation system that combines both your road maps and your aviation charts.

The Transition is fueled by super unleaded gas, which is cheaper and more environmentally friendly than aviation fuel." [7]

Furthermore, because of this new travel technology, you can go down to your local store and get fresh crabmeat from Thailand, or have a thoroughbred horse shipped to you from New Zealand. You can now get fresh flowers from South America, a genuine New York City pizza delivered anywhere in the world, and send a package from Japan in the afternoon to have it in Washington by the next morning. [8]

However, the friendly skies are not the only place we like to rush here and there. You see, the airplane paved the way for *space travel*. Now we can fly around the planet in eighty minutes. [9] In fact, pretty soon, you don't even have to be an astronaut anymore to go into space. Thanks to Virgin Airlines, or should I say Galactic Airlines, we'll soon be going into space:

"Sir Richard Branson and New Mexico Governor Susana Martinez dedicated the 'Virgin Galactic Gateway to Space.' Looking skyward, more than 800 guests marveled at Virgin Galactic's commercial space vehicles as they soared through the skies of southern New Mexico during the dedication ceremonies of Virgin Galactic's new home at Spaceport America. The flights of WhiteKnightTwo and SpaceShipTwo were the highlight of a spectacular ceremony which featured the dedication of the Sir Norman Foster-designed building and announcements of new scientific and educational customers for the world's first commercial space line.

'Today is another history-making day for Virgin Galactic,' said Sir Richard Branson. 'We are here with a group of incredible people who are helping us lead the way in creating one of the most important new industrial sectors of the 21st century. We've never wavered in our commitment to the monumental task of pioneering safe, affordable and clean access to space, or to demonstrate that we mean business at each step along the way.'

Branson and his children, Sam and Holly, who will be the first commercial passengers on SpaceShipTwo, brought the event to a spectacular conclusion by officially naming the world's first purpose-built spaceline terminal as the 'Virgin Galactic Gateway to Space' while rappelling together from the roof of the striking new building.

'I trust that will be the first of many safe landings at Spaceport America! What an absolute joy to celebrate the naming of the Virgin Galactic Gateway to Space with Governor Martinez!' said Sir Richard, as the family touched the ground.

The Virgin Galactic Gateway to Space, a combined terminal and hangar facility, will support up to two WhiteKnightTwo and five SpaceShipTwo vehicles. In addition, The Gateway will house all of the company's astronaut preparation and celebration facilities, a mission control center, and a friends and family area. There is also space committed to public access via the planned New Mexico Spaceport Authority's Visitor Experience.

The iconic 120,000 square-foot building, which meets LEED Gold standards for environmental quality, was designed by world-renowned United Kingdom-based Foster + Partners, along with URS Corporation and local New Mexico architects SMPC. The trio won an international competition in 2007 to build the first private spaceport in the world. Built using local materials and regional construction techniques, the facility is sustainable with few additional energy requirements due to the use of a range of sustainable features including geothermal heating and cooling.

New Mexico Governor Susana Martinez participated in the dedication ceremony with U.S. Congressman Steve Pearce, representing New Mexico's 2nd District.

'New Mexico has a long tradition of pioneering innovation in aerospace and related technologies,' said Governor Martinez. 'We already possess an impressive array of facilities and expertise in advanced technologies. Spaceport America and the opening of the Virgin Galactic Gateway to Space significantly deepen those capabilities and strengthen our global position as a powerhouse supporter of the space industry. Our partnership with Virgin Galactic is a perfect example of how government and private industry can work together to drive economic growth and science education.'

Virgin Galactic CEO and President George Whitesides said the company continues to make excellent and unequalled progress, under the motto 'safety is our North Star.' Whitesides remarked, 'Flight testing by prime contractor Scaled Composites is progressing very well, with 30 SpaceShipTwo flights and 75 WhiteKnightTwo flights to date. We are also recruiting aggressively and assembling a highly talented and accomplished workforce focused on safe commercial operations led by Vice President of Operations Mike Moses, who will run our efforts at the spaceport.'

In addition, the company is taking steps to expand its mission beyond commercial space tourism. The company announced last week that it had been awarded a contract under NASA's Flight Opportunity Program for research flights to a potential value of $4.5m. During the ceremony, it was announced that new flight reservations have been made by research and education institutions to support research initiatives and inspire students. Purdue University, Space Florida, the Challenger Center for Space Science Education and Southwest Research Institute were recognized as the most recent participants in this new growth area for Virgin Galactic.

'For me, my children and our ever growing community of future astronauts, many of whom are with us today, standing in front of the Virgin Galactic Gateway to Space as it glimmers majestically under the New Mexican sun brings our space adventure so close we can almost taste it,' said Sir Richard.

Present for the dedication ceremony were over 150 Virgin Galactic customers from 21 countries who have already made deposits to fly to space. A total of over 450 future astronauts worldwide have signed on to join Virgin Galactic for a voyage into space."[10]

Now, for those of you who don't like flying and yet still want to go into space, they've even thought of that one too! Other researchers are working on what's called a "Space Elevator." That's a device that uses carbon-technology that suspends a massive line anchored to earth all the way up into outer space, and it will be able to transport us into space *via an elevator* all the way into the upper atmosphere:

"The main problem with space travel is cost. To put you in orbit around the planet earth costs about $10,000 a pound. Once you're outside the first 100 miles you coast, you coast all the way out to Pluto. So if the first 100 miles is the only

problem, why not have a space elevator where you simply hit the up button and you ascend up a cable into outer space. Although this idea seems impossible, I can start by saying that our technology is increasing exponentially, meaning that we learned more in the last 12 years than in the past 200 years. You still don't believe? What if I tell you that Japan's Obayashi Corp. has announced plans to build a space elevator by 2050?

In 1959 a Russian scientist, Yuri N. Artsutanov, suggested using a geostationary satellite as the base from which to deploy the structure downward. By using a counterweight, a cable would be lowered from geostationary orbit to the surface of Earth, while the counterweight was extended from the satellite away from Earth, keeping the cable constantly over the same spot on the surface of the Earth. But building a compression structure from the ground up proved an unrealistic task as there was no material in existence with enough compressive strength to support its own weight under such conditions, until now.

For a century, we thought that this idea of a space elevator was ridiculous. Now we have a new game changer; Carbon Nanotubes. Carbon Nanotubes are a form of carbon with a cylindrical nanostructure. These cylindrical carbon molecules have unusual properties, which are valuable for nanotechnology, electronics, optics and other fields of materials science and technology. It is stronger than steel, and have electrical properties that rival the best semiconductors, yet they have a diameter smaller than hair. Carbon Nanotubes will be able to withstand the tension of traveling at enormous velocities in outer space as the space elevator rotates with the planet earth. It is the strongest substance known to science and it will suspend a space elevator without breaking. Theoretically the main challenges have been negotiated.

To build a space elevator, first we need to use a space shuttle to carry reels holding a thin inner-layer cable of carbon nanotubes into orbit. The 22 thousand mile cable would then be unrolled with the free end being snaked down from orbit and attached to an anchoring barrage in the ocean to keep some flexibility. To stabilize the upper-end of the cable, an artificial 'asteroid' would be attached to act as a counterweight, this counterweight could also be a space station itself with house labs, living space, and photovoltaic panels that could transmit electricity back to the ground. With the initial inner cable in place, automated 'climbers' would then begin adding additional strengthening layers of cable from the ground up. The elevator would get energy by using a laser-beamed power.

Total construction time is estimated at three to five years. It could open up the universe for the average person."[11]

As well as a whole new set of fears! How many of you are afraid of elevators? Wait till you see that one. It's going to be your worst nightmare! But that's still not all. We not only went to the moon and back in rockets, but now our eyes are on the planet Mars. Keep in mind that this is *in the last century alone*! Do you get the feeling that things are being sped up? Somehow, Star Trek doesn't sound so foreign anymore, does it? Speaking of which, did you know that even *teleportation is no longer a myth*? In the past couple of years, scientists have successfully teleported light particles over a few miles.[12] It would appear as if nothing is holding us back from being able to rush here and there, wherever and whenever we want. That is of course, except God. The sad thing is that this explosion of modern travel technology has made us arrogant and overconfident like the Edomites of long ago who also tried to escape the boundaries of Almighty God:

Obadiah 1:3-4 "The arrogance of your heart has deceived you, You who live in the clefts of the rock, In the loftiness of your dwelling place, Who say in your heart, Who will bring me down to earth?' Though you build high like the eagle, Though you set your nest among the stars, From there I will bring you down," declares the LORD."

Even if we can one day arrogantly boast that we don't need God because we can rush here and there, even to the edge of the stars, God will one day, just like the Edomites, bring us down. When? In the Last Days.

2. Second Way Modern Technology Reveals We Could be in the Last Days - Increase of Knowledge

When Daniel wrote down the words of this prophecy, the amount of retrieving and sharing knowledge was severely limited. We didn't even see the invention of the printing press until a few centuries ago. However, look at us today! *All in the last century alone*, just like the Bible said, we are experiencing nothing short of an information explosion! In fact, let's take a look at some information on information:

- The total store of human knowledge is now doubling every 8 years.

- 80% of all the scientists who have ever lived are alive today.

- Every minute 2000 pages are added to man's scientific knowledge.

- The scientific material produced in 1 day would take 1 person 5 years to read.

- About 1/2 million new books are published every year.

- Since 1970 computer technology has developed so fast that if the auto industry had developed at the same rate, you would today be able to buy a Rolls Royce for three dollars and you could fit 8 of them on the head of a pin!

- Speaking of Rolls Royce's and "head of a pin"; thanks to nanotechnology we can now construct motors that fit on the head of a pin, thousands of them via a new emerging technology called nanotechnology as this article shares:

"Nanotechnology is the new technology that has emerged whereby scientists can now manipulate matter on an atomic and molecular scale. It is considered a key technology for the future and various governments have invested billions of dollars in its future. The USA has invested 3.7 billion dollars through its National Nanotechnology Initiative followed by Japan with 750 million and the European Union 1.2 billion.

Nanotechnology may be able to create many new materials and devices with a vast range of applications, such as in medicine, electronics, biomaterials, and energy production. Most applications are limited to the use of first generation passive nanomaterials which includes titanium dioxide in sunscreen, cosmetics, surface coatings, and some food products; Carbon allotropes used to produce gecko tape; silver in food packaging, clothing, disinfectants and household appliances; zinc oxide in sunscreens and cosmetics, surface coatings, paints and outdoor furniture varnishes; and cerium oxide as a fuel catalyst.

Further applications allow tennis balls to last longer, golf balls to fly straighter, and even bowling balls to become more durable and have a harder surface. Trousers and socks have been infused with nanotechnology so that they will last longer and keep people cool in the summer. Bandages are being infused with silver nanoparticles to heal cuts faster. Cars are being manufactured with nanomaterials so they may need fewer metals and less fuel to operate in the future. Video game consoles and personal computers may become cheaper, faster, and contain more memory thanks to nanotechnology.

Nanotechnology may have the ability to make existing medical applications cheaper and easier to use in places like the general practitioner's office and at home. Nanorobotics centers on self-sufficient machines of some functionality operating at the nanoscale. There are hopes for applying nanorobots in medicine. A new breed of nanobots is being designed to assist doctors by going where no surgeon or technology has gone before.

Working at the scale of molecules, these micro-machines are taking their cues from bacteria and the way in which they find their way around the human body. If they are successful, they could bring about a new type of molecular surgery and a different perspective to our own inner space.

The engineers and scientists working on the development of these nanobots – the size of only a few molecules – believe they could reach liquid parts of the body difficult or impossible to get to using today's medical practices, precisely delivering drugs to areas such as the eyeball cavity or arteries in the heart.

They might sound like the stuff of science fiction, but at their most basic level these medical micro-robots are man-made protein 'machines' that produce movement through chemical reactions.

Dr. James Friend, senior lecturer in the Department of Mechanical Engineering at Monash University in Australia, is developing a nanobot propelled by a tiny rotor motor measuring about five-millionths of a meter. A simple injection would place the tiny machine into the body and it would swim to its intended target.

'We aim to provide doctors with a means to avoid major surgery and extend the capabilities of doctors to diagnose and treat patients. The powerful micro-motor will have its own power supply and be able to perform tasks by remote control,' said Friend. [13]

Think that's wild? Check out these stats on the explosion of information technology published in 2009:

- A weekday edition of any major newspaper has more information than the average person living in the 17th century would have come across in a lifetime.

- Thanks to the Internet, 1,000's of international papers are at your fingertips.

- Every day, the equivalent of over 300 million pages of text is sent over the Internet with millions of sites.

- About 1/2 of all medical knowledge is outdated every 10 years and in some scientific fields, such as biotechnology, the cycle is less than 6 months.

- There are now wristwatches that wield more computing ability than some 1970s computer mainframes.

- Ordinary cars today have more intelligence than the original lunar lander.

- Did you know that 25% of India's population with the highest IQ's is greater than the total population of the United States. Translation: India has more honors kids than America has kids.

- The Top 10 in-demand jobs in 2010 did not exist in 2004. We are currently preparing students for jobs that don't yet exist using technologies that haven't been invented in order to solve problems we don't even know are problems yet.

- 1 out of 8 couples married in the U.S. last year met online.

- We are living in exponential times. There are 31 Billion searches on Google every month. In 2006, this number was 2.7 Billion.

- Around 90 trillion emails were sent through the Internet in 2009 with an average of 30 million emails per day by 1.4 billion email users worldwide (Jan 2010). Over the last 12 months over 100 million people have become new email users.

- There are 1.83 billion Internet users worldwide. Projection for 2012 is 2.10 billion. There was an 18% increase of Internet users since the previous years (08-09). The U.S. Internet of 2015 will be at least 50 times larger than it was in 2006. Global Internet traffic is expected to increase 5 times from 2008 to 2013.

- Bing estimates there are more than 1 trillion pages of content on the Internet. That's almost 150 pages per person alive. The number of websites in 2009 was 234 million. 47 million alone were added in 2009.

- If Facebook were a country, it would be the third largest in the world just below China and India and above the United States. Facebook tops Google for weekly traffic in the U.S.

- Social media has overtaken pornography as the #1 activity on the web. What happens in Vegas stays on Facebook, Twitter, and YouTube.

- YouTube is the second largest search engine in the world. While you read this, 100 plus hours of video will be uploaded to YouTube. In fact, more video was uploaded to YouTube in the last two months than if ABC, NBC, and CBS had been airing new content 24 hours a day 7 days a week 365 days a year since 1948 which was when ABC started broadcasting.

- The first commercial text message was sent in December of 1992. Today, the number of text messages sent and received everyday exceeds the total population of the planet.

- Years it took to reach a market audience of 50 million:
  - Radio 38 years.
  - TV 13 years.
  - Internet 4 years.
  - iPod 3 years.
  - Facebook 2 years.

- The number of internet devices in 1984 was 1,000. 1992 - 1,000,000. 2008 - 1,000,000,000. The average online viewer watches 12.2 hours of online video each month.

- The mobile device will be the world's primary connection tool to the Internet in 2020. The computer in your cell phone today is 1 million times cheaper, and 1,000 times more powerful, and about 100,000 times smaller, than the 1 computer at MIT in 1965. So what used to fit in a building, now fits in your pocket.

- Two to three new Twitter accounts are activated every second. Twitter averages 50 million tweets per day. Ashton Kutcher and Britney Spears have more Twitter followers than the entire populations of Sweden, Israel, Switzerland, Ireland, Norway, and Panama.

- Adults spend 15 plus hours a week on the Internet. Broadband access will grow from 55% to 90% in 2012. 35% of the global work force will be mobile by 2013.

- There are about 540,000 words in the English language. About 5 times as many as during Shakespeare's time. Wikipedia has more than 14 million articles written by 75,000 contributors in 260 languages viewed by 684 million viewers.

- It is estimated that 4 exabytes (4.010^{19}) of unique information will be generated this year. That is more than the previous 5,000 years.

- The amount of new technical information is doubling every 2 years. For students starting a 4-year technical degree this means that half of what they learn in their first year of study will be outdated by their third year of study.

- NNT Japan has successfully tested a fiber optic cable that pushes 14 trillion bits per second down a single strand of fiber. That is 2,660 CDs or 210 million phone calls every second. It is currently tripling every six months and is expected to do so for the next 20 years.

- By 2013, a supercomputer will be built that exceeds the computational capabilities of the human brain. Predictions are that by 2049, a $1000 computer will exceed the computation capabilities of the entire human species.[13]

These facts are from a few years ago, so you can imagine the impact today! So what does all this mean? It looks like we're experiencing some sort of information explosion like the Bible said would happen in the Last Days! In fact, as you just saw with those statistics, experts are saying that the technology is growing so fast that we are headed for a serious danger called, *singularity*.[14] This is the term to describe the point where the technology grows so fast that it actually spawns a type of super intelligence that far exceeds any kind of human intelligence and then it begins to take over, which, experts are saying could happen very soon, "The human era will be ended." Machines will take over. Now, here's the point. The Bible says, when you see these things take place, you better wake up! It's a sign you're living in the Last Days!

3. Third Way Modern Technology Reveals We Could be in the Last Days - Increase of Unrest

2 Timothy 3:1,7 "But mark this: There will be terrible times in the Last Days. Always learning but never able to acknowledge the truth."

The Bible also warned that in the Last Days, not only would we be traveling like never before and acquiring information like crazy, but we would also see *an increase of unrest*. Why? Because we would become a people who are always learning yet are never able to acknowledge the truth, leaving us in a frustrated and restless state. Is this not exactly what has happened to our society? We are being told today that the more we acquire this new technology, the more time it will save us, so we can spend even more time rushing here and there. Then, if that wasn't bad enough, we are being told that the more we can learn from this increase of information, the more peace it will supposedly produce in our lives. But is this true? Have we really saved more time and created more peace in our lives with all this new technology? Absolutely not! We have actually become a society on the brink of disaster! This is exactly what the secular experts are saying. Even though we have the most highly funded educational system in the world, we are producing the most confused, ignorant and violent children ever.[15] Rates of depression have been doubling every ten years and suicide is the third most common cause of death among young adults in North America. Fifteen percent of Americans have had a clinical anxiety disorder and serial killers are now commonplace.[16] How can this be? It's simply because we are always learning yet never able to come to the truth! The truth is that the more we fill our lives with so-called timesaving devices, the more rushed we feel. In fact, we are in so much of a rush that "we tap our fingers while waiting for the microwave to zap our instant coffee."[17] These devices that are supposed to save us so much time so that we can rest more, are actually making us more restless. In fact, one researcher made this comment. See if it sounds familiar:

"This century's mad dash of innovation has produced the most frantic human era ever. We phone. We fax. We page. We e-mail. We race from one end of life to the other, rarely glancing over our shoulders. Technology, mass media and a desire to do more, do it better and do it yesterday have turned us into a world of hurriers.

Stop and smell the roses? No more. Instead, we have a world of 7-day diets, 24-hour news channels, 1-hour photo, 30-minute pizza delivery, 10-minute facials, 2-minute warnings, and Minute Rice. Fast food. Fast computers. Fast cars in fast lanes. DVD players with 5 fast-forward settings. Sound bites and the rat race and instant coffee. Get rich quick. Live fast, die young, leave a good-looking corpse.

Run on empty. Just do it. Places to go, people to meet, planners to fill, files to download, bills to pay, planes to catch, frozen dinners to nuke, web sites to surf, kids to pick up, stress to manage, and speeding tickets to pay." [18]

One researcher stated, "It's significant that we call it the Information Age. We don't talk about the Knowledge Age. Our society is basically motion without memory, which of course is one of the clinical definitions of *insanity*." [19] We have advanced beyond our wildest dreams technologically, *yet we are still spiritually bankrupt about the true meaning of life*. It's all because we have been tricked and seduced by a restless rat race society. The problem of being in a hurry all the time is that you never take the time to stop and think about what is most important in life. Therefore, you will never find the truth. But just in case there was a teensy weensy little bit of time left in the day after running like a restless rat all day, there's a stranger out there who steers us away from God, like this man recognized:

"A few months before I was born, my dad met a stranger who was new to our small Tennessee town. From the beginning, Dad was fascinated with this enchanting newcomer, and soon invited him to live with our family. The stranger was quickly accepted and was around to welcome me into the world a few months later.

As I grew up I never questioned his place in our family. In my young mind, each member had a special niche. My brother, Bill, five years my senior, was my example. Fran, my sister, gave me an opportunity to play 'big brother' and develop the art of teasing. My parents were complementary instructors – Mom taught me to love the Word of God, and Dad taught me to obey it.

But the stranger was our storyteller. He could weave the most fascinating tales. Adventures, mysteries and comedies were daily conversations. He could hold our whole family spellbound for hours each evening. If I wanted to know about politics, history, or science, he knew it all. He knew about the past, understood the present, and seemingly could predict the future.

The pictures he could draw were so life like that I would often laugh or cry as I watched. He was like a friend to the whole family. He took Dad, Bill, and me to our first major league baseball game. He was always encouraging us to see the movies and he even made arrangements to introduce us to several movie stars. My brother and I were deeply impressed by John Wayne in particular.

The stranger was an incessant talker. Dad didn't seem to mind but sometimes Mom would quietly get up, while the rest of us were enthralled with one of his stories of faraway places, go to her room, read her Bible and pray. I wonder now if she ever prayed that the stranger would leave.

You see, my Dad ruled our household with certain moral convictions. But this stranger never felt obligated to honor them. Profanity, for example, was not allowed in our house—not from us, from our friends, or adults. Our longtime visitor, however, used occasional four letter words that burned my ears and made Dad squirm.

To my knowledge the stranger was never confronted. My Dad was a teetotaler who didn't permit alcohol in his home, not even for cooking. But the stranger felt like we needed exposure and enlightened us to other ways of life. He offered us beer and other alcoholic beverages often. He made cigarettes look tasty, cigars manly, and pipes distinguished.

He talked freely, probably too much, too freely, about sex. His comments were sometimes blatant, sometimes suggestive, and generally embarrassing. I know that my early concepts of the man-woman relationship were influenced by the stranger.

As I look back, I believe it was the grace of God that the stranger did not influence us more. Time after time he opposed the values of my parents. Yet he was seldom rebuked and never asked to leave.

More than thirty years have passed since the stranger moved in with the young family on Morningside Drive. He is not nearly so intriguing to my Dad as he was in those early years. But if I were to walk in my parent's den today, you would still see him sitting over in a corner, waiting for someone to listen to him talk and watch him draw his pictures.

His name? We always just called him 'TV'"[20]

Do we not see what is happening to us? All this Modern Technology, this explosion of travel and information, is not only a sign we are living in the Last Days that ends up creating a restless rat race society, but it ensures that in the Last Days we don't even take the time to seek out the One Who Alone could give us rest and that is God! Instead, we spend our time with TV, the Internet, texting, cell phones, YouTube, Facebook, Twitter, and a whole slug of other things that are supposed to save us time and give us peace; but they don't! It's a spiritual trap! You cannot grow spiritually watching 3 hours of TV a day versus 3 minutes of the Bible a day![21] You don't pray to God but you socialize on Facebook? That's a trap! It's taking away whatever time you have left in the day after running the rat race to spend time with God, when of all times, in the Last Days, we're going to need Him the most! Don't you see it? It's so obvious that even the devil admits it. This short story brings to light the way the enemy tricks us:

"One day the devil called a worldwide convention of his evil demons and said this. 'We can't keep the Christians from going to heaven, but we can keep them from forming an intimate relationship in Christ. If they gain that connection with Jesus, our power over them is broken. So here's what we do.

Let's steal their time, so they can't gain any strength in Jesus Christ. Let's distract them by keeping them busy in the nonessentials of life and invent unnumbered schemes to occupy their minds. We'll over stimulate their minds so that they cannot hear that still small voice.

We'll entice them to play the radio or cassette player whenever they drive, to keep the TV, the DVD player, and their CD's going constantly in their homes.

And we'll see to it that every store and restaurant in the world plays music constantly jamming their minds to break that union with Christ.

We'll fill their coffee tables with magazines and newspapers and pound their minds with the news twenty-four hours a day. We'll invade their driving moments with billboards and flood their mailboxes with junk mail, sweepstakes, mail order catalogues and every kind of newsletter and promotional offering promising false hopes.

We'll even get them to be excessive in their entertainment or recreation and send them to amusement parks, sporting events, concerts, and movies so they'll return exhausted, disquieted and unprepared for the coming week.

And even when they meet for spiritual fellowship, we'll involve them in gossip and small talk so that they leave with troubled consciences and unsettled emotion. Why, we'll crowd their lives with so many things that they have no time or energy to seek power from Christ.

It was quite a convention in the end. And the demons went away eagerly causing Christians everywhere to get busy, busy, busy and rush here and there. Don't forget what 'busy' means. B-eing U-nder S-atan's Y-oke. Has the devil been successful at his scheme? You be the judge."[22]

I'll say it one last time. The problem of being in a hurry all the time is that you never take the time to stop and think about that which is the most important in life. Because of that, it's not only a sign that you're living in the Last Days, but that you've been lassoed by Satan's yoke and therefore you will never find the truth because you're just too busy. Wake up! Instead of worshiping the One and Only True God, we have bowed to the idol of technology. The sad thing is that the truth about life is right before us, if only we'd stop long enough to listen. We don't need to travel halfway across the world for truth. In fact, we don't even need that latest computer gizmo to understand it, nor do we need to spend a dime to receive it. Why? Because the truth about a restful life has been right under our noses all the time, in the words of Jesus Christ:

Matthew 11:28 "Then Jesus said, 'Come to me, all of you who are weary and carry heavy burdens, and I will give you rest.'"

Please don't be fooled into thinking that by rushing here and there and by increasing your knowledge, you will find rest. If you do, you will not only remain restless, but you may one day wake up to find yourself in the greatest time of unrest the world has ever known, the 7-year Tribulation and it's coming much sooner than you think!

II. Second End Time Prophecy Concerning Modern Technology - There Would Be a Great Increase of Bible Fulfillment

For the past 100 years or so people have been mocking Christians and Christianity and saying that nothing ever changes with statements like, "You Christians keep saying that the Lord is coming back, real soon, any day now, but nothing ever changes. Why is this time so different? Why should I listen to you now?" Well, that's the importance of understanding what's going on with Modern Technology. For the first time in human history we have the technology to pull off the events that are mentioned in the 7-year Tribulation. Which means for the first time, the stage really is set. Everything *really is* ready to go. There's nothing technologically holding it back from occurring. That's why you should listen. That's why you should pay attention this time.

So what are these passages being fulfilled with Modern Technology today; showing us we really are living in the Last Days?

1. The First Bible Passage Being Fulfilled in Minute Detail – The Death of the Two Witnesses

Revelation 11:1-9 "I was given a reed like a measuring rod and was told, 'Go and measure the temple of God and the altar, and count the worshipers there. But exclude the outer court; do not measure it, because it has been given to the Gentiles. They will trample on the holy city for 42 months. And I will give power to my two witnesses, and they will prophesy for 1,260 days, clothed in sackcloth.' These are the two olive trees and the two lampstands that stand before the Lord of the earth. If anyone tries to harm them, fire comes from their mouths and devours their enemies. This is how anyone who wants to harm them must die. These men have power to shut up the sky so that it will not rain during the time they are prophesying; and they have power to turn the waters into blood and to strike the earth with every kind of plague as often as they want. Now when they have finished their testimony, the beast that comes up from the Abyss will attack them, and overpower and kill them. Their bodies will lie in the street of the great city, which is figuratively called Sodom and Egypt, where also their Lord was crucified. For three and a half days men from every people, tribe, language and nation will gaze on their bodies and refuse them burial."

Now, once again, you have to take a look at this passage in its historical setting to understand its prophetic significance. Imagine what it must have been like when the Apostle John was writing this nearly 2,000 years ago. It must have seemed like an incredible fantasy for the whole planet to simultaneously watch two dead bodies, rejoice over their death and even send gifts to each other. But guess what? It's not fantasy anymore! Due to the advent of television and global satellite technology, we can simultaneously watch anything we want, anywhere we want, around the world. Which means, this passage is being fulfilled before our very eyes. We have the technology *right now* to watch the death of the Two Witnesses for 3½ days for the first time in the history of mankind! This is why you should listen this time. That's why you need to pay attention when people say Jesus is coming back real soon. We have the technology to pull off this passage for the first time ever!

Furthermore, we not only have the technology to observe the death of the Two Witnesses during the 7-year Tribulation, but we even have the platform being built for the first time in human history to watch their death. Believe it or not, plans are being made *right now* to build for the first time in human history, a Global Television Network to broadcast these kinds of events, for a "Global Ruler." Remember, it's a "Global Ruler" called the Antichrist that is allowed to overpower the Two Witnesses and kill them:

"In an article entitled, 'Global Television for Our Future Global Leader,' UN Watchdog Cliff Kincaid reported, 'Surprise and even shock were among the reactions to my recent column about how elite members of the World Economic Forum (WEF) meeting in Davos, Switzerland, were considering a proposal for a new global television network to usher in a state of 'global governance.''

He said the media proposal is to create 'a new global network' with 'the capacity to connect the world, bridging cultures and peoples, and telling us who we are and what we mean to each other.'

He says, 'Isn't it nice that we might have a TV network telling us 'who we are?' And 'what we mean to each other?' Perhaps we will learn that we are global citizens. Perhaps a global leader of some sort will tell us that. Who might that be? Kincaid says this story smacks of George Orwell's 1984.

Several prominent U.S. media figures signed on to the alarming and controversial proposal that envisions itself to become 'a genuine, global voice.'

The council declared that it is, 'Championing a new global, independent news and information service whose role is to inform, educate and improve the state of the world – one that would take advantage of all platforms of content delivery from mobile to satellite and online to create a new global network.'

Kincaid said although he's no Biblical scholar, he wonders about the end-times implications of such a channel. 'Clearly they're talking about this global order, the new world order, global taxes and now global TV put at the service of some kind of global ruler of the world,' he continues. 'I don't know whether that would be the anti-Christ or not.'"[23]

Nonetheless, just in case you miss the up and coming soon to be Global News Broadcast for the death of the Two Witnesses, it just so happens that Google just launched a new program allowing you to get a bird's eye view of all places, the streets of Jerusalem, that you can view on your computer or even your cell phone. Here's the announcement:

"After months of consultations with Israeli security officials, Google has launched its popular Street View service in the country's three largest cities.

The new Street View provides images of ordinary life, contested areas and religious sites in the Holy Land. Due to security issues, areas around several sensitive sites, such as the military headquarters in Tel Aviv and the prime minister's residence in Jerusalem, are blurred out.

Google Street View is available in more than 30 countries. It was held up in Israel by concerns that images of its streets could be used by terrorists. The Islamic Jihad militant group in Gaza, for instance, has boasted that it used Google Earth, which gives birds-eye views and some street-level pictures of sites around the world, to aim rockets at Israel.

Last August, after a panel of government ministers met for six months to draft security guidelines, Israel announced it had reached an agreement with Google.

The service was quietly launched late last week and officially unveiled Sunday. The images are obtained by specialized cameras mounted on vehicles.

Israel is the first Middle Eastern nation to display its cities and streets online. Iraq's National Museum is also available on Street View.

Pictures online Sunday showed typical street scenes — bicycles chained to the gates of apartment gardens in Tel Aviv, tourists sunbathing on Haifa's beaches, and the crowded cobblestone Via Dolorosa, the path that Jesus is said to have walked before his crucifixion in Jerusalem's Old City.

Tel Aviv Mayor Ron Huldai brushed off security concerns about Tel Aviv, a city that was hit hard by suicide bombings on buses and in restaurants during the Palestinian uprising a decade ago.

He said militants know the city well enough without the Google service. 'Tel Aviv-Jaffa is a target anyway,' Huldai said Sunday.

He noted that other urban military installations, like the Pentagon outside Washington, also were left off Street View.

Despite Google's enthusiasm, not all Israelis were happy.

Retired Lt. Col. Mordechai Kedar, who served for 25 years in Israeli intelligence, said the service would be a boon to militants seeking to attack Israel.

'They will use it daily,' Kedar said. 'Every day Street View is online, it's causing damage.'

Google Israel's country manager, Meir Brand, said additional cities will soon join the first three, including Beersheba, Nazareth and Eilat."[24]

What did the text say? Their bodies will lie *in the street*! Apparently, with Google's help, people won't have any trouble finding out what street that is! Based on the current evidence, I'm thinking we're getting pretty close to having a Global Television Network that's apparently being built for a Global Leader who's going to broadcast the death of the Two Witnesses and who even throws in a Global Google App for your cell phone just to make sure you don't miss the show! This is not by chance. It's all happening in our lifetime *now*. Tell me we're not getting close. In addition, what else did the text say? What did these people *do* as they were watching this event for 3½ days on their phone or TV? Let's take a look at the text:

Revelation 11:10 "The inhabitants of the earth will gloat over them and will celebrate by sending each other gifts, because these two prophets had tormented those who live on the earth."

Now again, think about this from the Apostle John's perspective 2,000 years ago. It must have blown his mind. How could people not only watch the death of two guys from around the world *simultaneously*, but how in the world are they going to be able to *celebrate* and *send each other gifts around the world in 3½ days*? They didn't even have the Pony Express back then. Well, it's not a surprise anymore! As we already saw, we now have, for the first time in man's history, *a global distribution network*! Thanks to this rise of Modern Technology we have a Global Transportation system that's hooked up to a Global Communications system that's linked to a Global Supply Chain system that's overseen by a Global Trade and Commerce system that allows us to go down to our local store and get fresh crabmeat shipped to us from Thailand, or have a thoroughbred horse shipped to you from New Zealand. Or get fresh flowers all the way from South America or have a New York City pizza delivered anywhere in the world, and be able to what? Send a package from Japan in the afternoon and have it arrive in Washington the next morning, *which includes* a celebratory package sent by someone who's gloating over the death of the Two Witnesses that they're viewing on their phone or TV within 3½ days for the first time in mankind's history. In fact, thanks to the recent advent of the Internet, you don't even have to go to the store anymore. You can just send that celebratory gift with the click of a mouse or even the touch of a finger on your cell phone! Why should people listen when others warn them about the soon return of Jesus Christ? Because never before in the history of mankind have we had the technology to pull these passages off *but we do now*! That's why people need to listen!

2. The Second Bible Passage Being Fulfilled in Minute Detail – The Deception of the False Prophet

Revelation 13:11-13 "Then I saw another beast, coming out of the earth. He had two horns like a lamb, but he spoke like a dragon. He exercised all the authority of the first beast on his behalf, and made the earth and its inhabitants worship the first beast, whose fatal wound had been healed. And he performed great and miraculous signs, even causing fire to come down from heaven to earth in full view of men."

Here we see the classic passage that tells us how the False Prophet is actually going to dupe people, the whole world, into worshiping the Antichrist. Notice what it was. He's going to *cause fire* to come down from heaven, or in other words, the atmosphere, in full view of men. However, it's all going to be a bunch of chicanery. This is what the Apostle Paul reiterates in this passage.

2 Thessalonians 2:9 "The coming of the lawless one will be in accordance with the work of satan displayed in all kinds of counterfeit miracles, signs and wonders."

So here we see that these so-called miracles, even causing fire to come down from heaven in full view of men, are *counterfeit*. In other words, it's a fake; it's a phony; it's manufactured and not a true miracle. So that's the question. "Do we see any kind of technology on the planet *right now* that could help the False Prophet pull off this phony miracle of causing fire to come down from heaven?" Yes. It's called HAARP and it's not the kind that angels play:

"It is no coincidence that the United States began building its own mysterious array of antennas in Feb 1992. They are located in Gakona, Alaska. The project is called HAARP. HAARP is the High Frequency Active Aurora Research Project, originally a joint effort of the Air Force and Navy in cooperation with a number of academic institutions.'

It is today the world's largest radio broadcasting station, but it's not designed to broadcast for human ears. It uses a unique patented ability to focus the energy coming out of the antennae field and injects that energy into a spot at the top of the atmosphere in a region called the ionosphere.'

HAARP is comprised of 180 antennas approximately 72' feet tall, linked together to function as one giant steerable antennae. Steerable, because it can aim millions of watts of ELF waves into one tiny patch of the atmosphere.

The amount of the energy we are talking about here is 3.6 million watts. To give you an idea of what that is, the largest legal AM radio station here in America is 50,000 watts. HAARP is 72,000 of these AM stations (50,000 watts each) injecting their entire output into a spot 12 miles across by about 2½ miles deep by about 90 miles up.

This is where HAARP is pointing, it's an area located roughly 300 miles from Anchorage. The US military says that HAARP is merely being used to study the physical and electrical properties and behavior of the ionosphere for both civilian and defense purposes. However, another theory has surfaced, that the intense energy being beamed into the sky by HAARP is actually heating up the atmosphere causing weather changes.

HAARP is being used for weather modification. The military's own record proves it. They've admitted it within their own documents and yet they still deny it to the public. Dr Brooks Agnew has researched the ELF wave technology for the past thirty years and is convinced HAARP's effect on the ionosphere does alter the weather.

HAARP is one of several ELF wave transmitters located all over the globe. The United States own, and operates three of them. One in Gakona, AK, one in Fairbanks, AK and one in Arecibo, Puerto Rico. Russia has one near Vasilsursk, and the European Union has one near Tromso, Norway.

Working in tandem, these transmitters could potentially alter weather anywhere in the world. Changing the jet streams course entirely. Triggering massive rainstorms or droughts. Even hurricane steering would be possible by heating up the atmosphere and building up high pressure domes that could deflect or change the course of hurricanes.

The US government is firm in its position that HAARP is just an atmospheric research facility, but is it more than a coincidence that since going online experts have reported strange weather anomalies including massive floods, hurricanes, and earthquakes.

HAARP went online in 1994 and construction continued until 2007. There are reportedly a total of 5 known ionic heaters, including HAARP, in the world today. There are possibly 20 other ionospheric heaters in existence all over the world today. There's no conclusive proof that any of them are used as weather weapons, although they do have the ability to manipulate the ionosphere.

That brings us to something else. In December 2001, scientists at Ames Research Center in Palo Alto, CA made a discovery. In studying more than 100 earthquakes with magnitudes of 5.0 or greater, they found that almost all of them are preceded by electrical disturbances in the ionosphere. Could there be a connection to HAARP or a facility like it?

Doctor Agnew experienced the power of ELF waves firsthand back in the 1980's. He was hired by an energy company to locate oil and gas using the same kind of ELF waves at much lower frequencies to carry out his search. It's a process called earth tomography. But during one particular incident, Dr Agnew believes his use of HAARP-like ELF waves accidentally triggered an earthquake.

'It was in the spring of 1987, we arrived in Roseburg, Oregon to use our ELF technology to search for oil and gas. Setting up that day, we had a little bit different results than we expected because the instant we energized it, there was between a 4 to 4.5 earthquake on the Richter scale earthquake that occurred. We were so amazed about what seemed to be cause and effect. We get to an area that has a high propensity for earthquakes in an area known as a Mega Thrust Fault Line of the Pacific Northwest. We turn it on, and an earthquake occurs.'

When HAARP's broadcast array in Gakona, Alaska sends pulses of ELF waves into the ionosphere, the waves get reflected back down and pass through the earth and the ocean. If 3.6 million watts of ELF waves were purposely or accidentally aimed at an already unstable fault line, it could, according to Dr Agnew, cause a tremendous earthquake.

Conspiracy theorists believe HAARP is responsible for triggering earthquakes in enemy territories like Iran, China, and rogue parts of Afghanistan over the past 3 years.

But HAARP's startling potential doesn't end there. Some say it's linked to a strange phenomena occurring in our skies, that is, chemtrails. In recent years, peculiar cloud formations have been appearing in our skies all over the world, increasing in frequency. I think most of us in North America have wondered at these plumes crisscrossing the sky in grid patterns, parallel rows and the now familiar X's. Many of us have wondered what these trails are.

While highly speculative, some researchers suggest these strange cloud formations are another agent of weather warfare. They first appear to be simply contrails, coming from high flying jet airplanes. But these trails linger in the sky for many hours. Some even for an entire day, forming an artificial cloud. The theory is that chemtrails are being used in conjunction with HAARP. By spraying metal oxides in the air above enemy territory skies, then directing ELF waves to heat those metal oxides, the temperature of the sky is raised to more than 100 degrees Fahrenheit. Preventing the accumulation of water vapor, which would otherwise form clouds and produce rainfall.

The ELF waves that HAARP produces, bounce off the ionosphere and are able to curve around the earth over the horizon to the ground, making any point on the globe well within reach. Imagine the effects of chemtrails on the battlefield, causing extended droughts in enemy countries. Drying up their resources. Forcing surrender.

Just as terrifying is another form of weather being weaponized. Rain that can trigger devastating floods and wipe cities clean off the map. If you can make it rain, you can have a profound effect on the battlefield. One of the critical elements of launching a weatherized battle is being able to control rain and unleash floods.

In history there is a chilling example of a flood that may have been accidentally triggered by weather weapons. August 15, 1952 near the small town of Lynnmouth, England, a massive rainstorm strikes. The rivers swell. Scores die. It's estimated that 250 times as much rain fell in a period of 24 hours as normally fell in an entire month. The EastLynn and West Lynn Rivers flood their banks. According to the BBC, 90 million tons of water swept down into the town of Lynnmouth, 35 people were killed, bodies washed out to sea and were never found. Trees are uprooted forming dams behind bridges creating walls of water that carry huge boulders into the village destroying shops, hotels and homes.

Was this just a freak act of nature? The prevailing theory is that it may have been a British military experiment gone bad as they had been known to be conducting cloud seeding tests around that same time. Allegedly, early in the morning on Aug 15th 1952, some witnesses reported seeing Royal Air Force jets flying in the area. Disappearing from sight at times, flying high above the cloud bank. Were they on a routine training mission or as some people speculate, were they dumping payloads of Silver Iodide into the clouds.

Silver Iodide is one of the most common chemicals used for cloud seeding. It forces the tiny ice crystal that make up the cloud to fuse together. Once enough tiny ice crystals fuse together they become heavy and fall to the earth in the form of rain. And On that fateful day in August 1952, rain fell in record amounts. Did the Royal Air Force embark on daring cloud seeding experiments without public knowledge?'

Some people reported seeing aircraft undertaking strange maneuvers. It subsequently confirmed that there was an experiment code-named 'Operation Cumulus which was indeed an attempt at weather modification. Interestingly, many of the documents relating to Operation Cumulus, have disappeared and are not available from the National Archives.

A little over a decade later, the U.S. military conducted experiments to bring weather to the battlefield. In October 1966, the Vietnam war was in full swing. U.S. military scientists were devising a way to slow down enemy forces using the weather. The US employed a ground breaking military directive called Project Popeye. Project Popeye was a weather modification program that involved cloud seeding, and the idea behind it was to produce or exaggerate the monsoon rains which are traditional in that region.

Experiments were carried out beforehand with the military aircraft dropping silver iodide crystals in clouds over the Laos panhandle above the SeKong River Valley. Fifty cloud seeding runs were conducted. 82% of the clouds seeded produced rain within a brief period of time. The goal of Operation Popeye was to extend the monsoon season and create and inordinate amount of rainfall by seeding clouds over the Ho Chi Min Trail. The Ho Chi Min Trail was a primary supply route by which the North Vietnamese army supplied its troops by operating combat forces in South Vietnam as well as supplying the Viet Cong. So it was the most significant logistical center of gravity to the North Vietnamese and it was an important objective for the United States and Vietnam alllies to try to interrupt that supply line cutting off those supplies to the enemies.

Operation Popeye's objectives were to soften road surfaces on the Ho Chi Min Trail, cause landslides along roadways and wash out river crossings. The military had their own catch phrase as a result of this program and it was 'make mud not war'. They flew over 2,600 missions from a period of 1966 to 1972 and it is believed that it did exacerbate the amount of rainfall and probably extended the monsoon season by 30-45 days.

Operation Popeye showed that weather can be brought to the battlefield as rain. But can it be weaponized in the form of a hurricane? Some say it already has. August 23rd 2005, the National Weather Service is tracking an unassuming storm forming over the Bahamas. A storm this size rarely damages building or takes lives, in fact at this point it's simply known as Tropical Depression 12. But that will change. It will unexpectedly grow into the mother of all storms. A category 5 hurricane, with winds up to 175mph. Its name: Hurricane Katrina.

When Katrina slams into the Gulf Coast of the United States, it will become one of the deadliest disasters in U.S. History. Costing 81 billion dollars in property damage and claiming more than 1,800 lives. Like other hurricanes of that era Katrina showed some very peculiar movements never before seen in a major hurricane. During the 2005 hurricane season there were some very strange and amazing anomalies which should not have happened. One of the things was that many of the hurricane tracts were almost straight lines, and hurricanes don't go in straight lines.

Some people believe Katrina hit where it hit, with the power that it struck, because of Russian or Chinese weather control experiments. Just before coming onshore Katrina did an abrupt 90 degree turn hard left and went down the beach for a substantial ways before coming onshore. So we have speculations that our enemies have been throwing hurricanes at us. We were being 'bombarded, attacked' with the weather. To direct and control a hurricane gives you power at least equivalent to nuclear weapons. A hurricane could be an ultimate weapon of war.

The very next year after Katrina, something strange happened. According to the National Weather Service, not a single hurricane made landfall in 2006. Could the U.S. military be using HAARP to fend hurricane attacks? A regular high pressure zone above the Southeastern United States points to this conclusion according to Jerry Smith. This high pressure dome has never existed before; it has never been seen to have a high pressure dome parked over the southeastern United States within the entirety of a hurricane season. It has NEVER happened before. And it has happened 3 years in a row now.

This high pressure dome worked like the rubber bumpers on a pinball machine. Every hurricane, like a pinball hit it and bounced off safely going back out to sea. The coincidental date of HAARP being completed and this buffer being in effect, I think is very telling.

Today, nations still deny weaponizing weather, but there are suggestions to the contrary. The US Air Force Report 'Weather as a Force Multiplier: Owning the Weather in 2025' outlines the military's desire to exploit and manipulate the weather for the purpose of war by 2025. According to one of the most harrowing lines in the report 'Weather modification is a force multiplier with tremendous power that could be exploited across the full spectrum of war fighting and environments.'

The 2025 report on the weather was essentially a military analysis of 'what could we do?'. Whether it was to create rainfall or create drought conditions, the idea was by 2025 we would be able to manipulate virtually every aspect of weather. The rationale for this is really the ultimate war. If you never have to fire a round and nobody ever knew who launched the fight; this is what weather warfare offers militaries around the world.

With the deadline of 2025 quickly approaching, the future of weather warfare is cause for concern. The worst case scenario is that satellite based weapons systems will turn the earth's weather on its head. It could rain in the desert and create a heat wave in the Artic. If an enemy could change the jet stream over in North America it could plunge North America into an ice age.

Fifty years from now geophysical manipulation of the planet could be the weapon of war. Where it is not bombs and bullets; it is earthquakes, it's tidal waves, manipulation of weather systems. Those become the future of warfare. When we talk about weather warfare, we are talking about death technology. This has nothing to do with enhancing life. The aim of weather warfare is catastrophic environmental destruction and horrific loss of life.

In the future, he who can control the weather will probably control the earth."[25]

Now, wait a second, we have the technology in different places around the world to control the weather or even make an earthquake? Yes, it would appear so. It's called HAARP. In fact, one thing they left out was that this same technology could be used to create a type of *death ray* that could be beamed over the atmosphere and then down anywhere on the planet to an intended target:

"Plasma physicist Bernard Eastlund explains that it is possible for a HAARP beam to take a part of the atmosphere and push it up further.

Earth Tomographer Brooks Agnew says that they are not paying attention to the ionosphere while it is being held 80 miles out into space by this high energy beam. He says during that time, the ionosphere is heating up and creating energy that can discharge back down the radio beam and strike the earth with 100 times the energy released from a thunderbolt.

He further explains that once a 'solar tap' is formed, and the ionosphere actually discharges, the electrons and energy will come from all over the ionosphere and will strike the ground in a bolt which is a hundred times greater than any lightning bolt imaginable, and it will not strike one time, but rather 30-40 times per second until there is no longer any energy to flow from the ionosphere through that tap.

Also when it strikes the ground it will vaporize the ground, water, or whatever it happens to hit, like three or four Mt. Saint Helens Volcanoes going off each second that the bolt discharges."[26]

So if you put all this together with our above passages, imagine the level of deception and chicanery of the False Prophet, what he has at his fingertips. In essence he could state, "If you don't worship the Antichrist like I tell you to, I'll cause a hurricane to take out your country. I'll cause an earthquake to really mess you up. I'll cause *fire to come down from heaven*, i.e. I'll send a death ray with HAARP and take you out!" Only he won't tell people it's HAARP! The whole time it's phony, it's a counterfeit, exactly like the Bible said would happen, in the Last Days, during the 7-year Tribulation. Now, as if that wasn't wild enough, there's one other interesting side effect of this new HAARP technology. It also has the strange ability to send a beam down that can adversely affect the human brain:

"Jean Manning is a journalist who stumbled into a strange world when she started asking questions about alternative energy sources and heard the story of an early 20th century inventor named Nicholas Tesla. Tesla is almost a cult hero, and an overlooked genius, and he has so many inventions that are at the basis of technologies that we have today.

Tesla talked about this 'Tesla shield' around the planet and talked about particle beam weaponry, something called the 'death ray'. Death ray? Jean wasn't sure where all this was leading until 'Mr. X' called again. And he said, 'The maniacs are actually going to do it, up in Alaska.'

Zap incoming missiles, disrupt global communications and engineer the weather. And ready? There's one more. Some people believe the technology being tested here could be used for sinister projects involving humans. Radio waves messing around with people's brain waves.

The human mind is subject to being affected by radio frequency energy and that's what this device is. In other words, you can move the moods of large populations using this kind of technology.

Scientists have been experimenting with radio frequencies on animals' brains for decades and the military has followed it all very closely. Especially, once it found that the Russians were on to it.

It was all kept a deep dark secret by the two superpowers. Back in the 60's the Soviets began zapping the American Embassy in Moscow with a low frequency beam. No one knows for sure what they were up to but one theory is that they were trying to mess with people's central nervous systems and one report did say the diplomats got depressed a lot.

Just think of all the nifty applications against the enemy. Why blow people up when you can drive them crazy. From documents dating back into the early 80's we see that military had discussed the possibilities of mind control through radio-frequency energy.

A 1982 Air Force report called Radio Frequency Energy, a major new research initiative, said that our 'RF' energy can 'disrupt normal purposeful behavior.' A 1987 military report called for more research on RF energy as a nonlethal weapon, pointing out that most of the existing technology is classified and, sure enough, in 1993 there was a big conference at Johns Hopkins University. Here, the entire conference was classified but the agenda was not. Weapons using extremely low radio frequency or ELF were listed as 'a very attractive option.'

Is it just a coincidence that there's been all of this talk and that HAARP will be experimenting with this? Is that all just coincidence?

ELF waves produced from HAARP, when targeted on selected areas, can weather-engineer and create mood changes affecting millions of people. The United States is bathed in this magnetic field, so everyone can be affected and mind-controlled. The entire artificial ground wave spreads out over the whole of the USA like a web.

In 1963, Dr. Robert Beck explored effects of external magnetic fields on brainwaves showing a relationship between psychiatric admissions and solar magnetic storms. He exposed volunteers to pulsed magnetic fields similar to magnetic storms, and found a similar response. US 60 Hz electric power ELF waves vibrate at the same frequency as the human brain. UK 50 Hz electricity emissions depress the thyroid gland.

Dr. Andrija Puharich experimented discovering that:

A. **7.83 Hz** (earth's pulse rate) made a person feel good, producing an altered-state.
B. **10.80 Hz** causes riotous behavior
C. **6.6 Hz** causes depression.

The question is could they-would they? We believe they can and we believe they will. It happens to be in Alaska. It happens to be now."[27]

So why would you want a technology to alter the human brain to make people feel agitated or put people into a state of euphoria? Well, if you couple this with another new technology called, "The Voice of God Weapon" or "Sonic Projector" which is put out by DARPA or the Defense Advanced Research Projects Agency, then you can have some serious deception going on. These are weapons that can actually beam the sounds of someone speaking into a microphone at your head without you seeing or hearing where it came from and it actually sounds like the voice is coming *from inside your head*:

"Imagine a weapon that creates sound that only you can hear. Science fiction? No, this is one area that has a very solid basis in reality. The Air Force has experimented with microwaves that create sounds in people's heads (which they've called a possible psychological warfare tool), and American Technologies can 'beam' sounds to specific targets with their patented HyperSound (and yes, I've heard/seen them demonstrate the speakers, and they are shockingly effective).

Now the Defense Advanced Research Projects Agency is jumping on the bandwagon with their new 'Sonic Projector' program. The goal of the Sonic

Projector program is to provide Special Forces with a method of surreptitious audio communication at distances over 1 km.

Here's the question of the day: if the military were to beam voices into somebody's head, what would they say?" [28]

Now add to that what this article shares:

"Lightning guns, heat rays, weapons that can make you hear the voice of God. This is what happens when the war on terror meets the entrepreneurial spirit.

'This is very clandestine,' Pete Bitar whispered, as his red Dodge Caravan idled in the parking lot of a Burger King near Fort Belvoir. 'They called last week, and they wanted delivery this week.'

It did feel a little clandestine, if a bit unlikely. Yet there, in the Burger King parking lot, a small transaction in America's war on terror was about to take place. In the minivan were Bitar, the president and founder of Xtreme Alternative Defense Systems (XADS), Edward Fry, the company's research coordinator, and George Gibbs, of Marine Corps Systems Command, who two years ago plucked Bitar's obscure company out of its paper existence and provided it with more than half a million dollars in Pentagon funding.

Bitar had battled start-up disappointments and even ridicule – not to mention January cold and Beltway rush-hour traffic – to seal his first Pentagon deal. The procurement order had gone through so quickly that the Indiana-based Bitar, who was in town for a conference, agreed to make his final delivery at the Burger King to avoid the hassle of getting onto the Virginia Army base.

Bitar flipped open a case containing his first sale: the 'dazzler,' one in a line of about a half-dozen 'nonlethal' weapons that XADS is marketing to the military. It looked like an executive pen: slick, green and flecked with gold. But the pen was really a green laser designed to disorient and temporarily blind an enemy. Sale price: $1,100 apiece.

Supercharged versions of commercial laser pointers, dazzlers are the lowest-tech of Bitar's weapons, and they're not what initially caught the Pentagon's eye. Rather, it was his concept for a gun that could shoot bolts of artificial lightning to paralyze, but not kill, an enemy, like a 'Star Trek' phaser set on stun. Bitar learned that the Pentagon was seeking ideas for a taser gun. It was like being struck by lightning. He dusted off his decade-old idea and, in 2002, was granted a contract to develop his lightning gun.

Gibbs, the Marine Corps official who first funded Bitar, has a fondness for edgy ideas. A chemical engineer and longtime proponent of nonlethal weaponry, Gibbs funds other offbeat projects, such as Medusa, an attempt to develop a weapon that uses low-power microwaves – believed to cause an audible buzzing in subjects' heads – to make people think God is speaking to them. Another such weapon would use beams of energy to make people dizzy and lose their balance.

But ideas are what Bitar overflows with. His latest is to use ultrasonic waves in the dazzler not to just blind enemies, but also to convey messages into their heads, similar to Gibbs's Medusa project. Hearing voices from God is a 'big thing' in Arab culture, according to Bitar. 'We flash-blind them. And, while their eyes are shut, you could send a recorded message or deep guttural voice that echoes in the inside of their head. They're looking around, 'Hey, did you hear that?'

Bitar laughed. 'That's the psych warfare side of this thing.'
XADS had also added a new acoustic weapon called 'Screech', which true to its name emits an ear-piercing shriek designed to disperse crowds and cause headaches, Bitar said.

Bitar's technology is based on a technique pioneered more than 100 years ago by the eccentric Serbian inventor Nikola Tesla. The 'StunStrike' uses an electrical charge to break down the air in front of the weapon to create a path for sparks generated by a 'resonant transformer,' better known as a Tesla coil. Unlike a typical Tesla coil, however, Bitar's invention uses electronics to tune and direct the spark stream.

'We can tune it all the way down so it feels like broom bristles, and all the way up to knock you down,' Bitar informed a group of gawkers.

However, Bitar noticed that foreign militaries were the most interested in his weapons, and officials from Asia, the Middle East and Europe had all visited his booth. 'It's kind of weird, especially because when it comes to weapons, you'd rather arm your own country than someone else,' he said.

He shrugged and added, 'A customer is a customer.'" [28]

Now, put all this together with what this article revealed:

'No one ever notices what's going on at a Radio Shack. Outside a lonely branch of the electronics store, on a government-issue San Diego day in a strip mall where no one is noticing much of anything, a buff man with thinning, ginger hair and preternaturally white teeth is standing on the pavement, slowly waving a square metal plate toward people strolling in the distance. 'Watch that lady over there,' he says, unable to conceal his boyish pride for the gadget in his giant hand. 'This is really cool.'

Woody Norris aims the silvery plate at his quarry. A burly brunette 200 feet away stops dead in her tracks and peers around, befuddled. She has walked straight into the noise of a Brazilian rain forest – then out again. Even in her shopping reverie, here among the haircutters and storefront tax-preparers and dubious Middle Eastern bistros, her senses inform her that she has just stepped through a discrete column of sound, a sharply demarcated beam of unexpected sound. 'Look at that,' Norris mutters, chuckling as the lady turns around. 'She doesn't know what hit her.'

Norris is demonstrating something called HyperSonic Sound (HSS). The aluminum plate is connected to a CD player and an odd amplifier – actually, a very odd and very new amplifier – that directs sound much as a laser beam directs light. Over the past few years, mainly in secret, he has shown the device to more than 300 major companies, and it has slackened a lot of jaws.

As Norris continues to baffle shoppers by sniping at them with the noises he has on this CD (ice cubes clanking into a glass, a Handel concerto, the splash of a waterfall), some are spooked, and some are drawn in. Two teenage girls drift over from 100 feet away and ask, in bizarre Diane Arbus-type unison, 'What is that?'

Norris responds with his affable mantra – 'In'nat cool?' – before going into a bit of simplified detail: how the sound waves are actually made audible not at the surface of the metal plate but at the listener's ears. He doesn't bother to torment the girls with the scientific gymnastics of how data are being converted to ultrasound then back again to human-accessible frequencies along a confined column of air.

*'See, the way your brain perceives it, the sound is being created right here,'
Norris explains to the Arbus girls, lifting a palm to the side of his head. 'That's
why it's so clear. Feels like it's inside your skull, doesn't it?'*

*In the years Norris has demonstrated HSS, he says, that's been the universal
reaction: the sound is inside my head. So that's the way he has started to
describe it.*

*Just to check the distances, I pace out a hundred yards and see if the thing is
really working. Norris pelts me with the Handel and, to illustrate the
directionality of the beam, subtly turns the plate side to side. And the sound is
inside my head, roving between my ears in accord with each of Norris's turns.*

*The applications of directional sound go quite a bit beyond messing with people
at strip malls, important as this work may be. Norris is enthusiastic about all of
the possibilities he can propose and the ones he can't.*

*Imagine, he says, walking by a soda machine (say, one of the five million in
Japan that will soon employ HSS), triggering a proximity detector, then hearing
what you alone hear – the plink of ice cubes and the invocation, 'Wouldn't a
Coke taste great right about now?'*

*Or riding in the family car, as the kids blast Eminem in the back seat while you
and the wife play Tony Bennett up front. Or living in a city where ambulance
sirens don't wake the entire neighborhood at 4 a.m. Or hearing different and
extremely targeted messages in every single aisle of a grocery store – for
instance, near the fresh produce, 'Hey, it's the heart of kiwi season!'*

*A sampling of the companies that are in active talks with A.T.C. includes Wal-
Mart, McDonald's, Dolby Laboratories, both Coca-Cola and Pepsi, major TV
networks and film studios, cell phone makers and museums all over the world, to
say nothing of the world's big-ticket speaker manufacturers.*

*The U.S.S. Carl Vinson and the U.S.S. Winston S. Churchill are now equipped
with A.T.C. speakers, and the Navy has expressed interest in outfitting every
carrier in the fleet.*

*'The L.A.P.D. wants to try it on high-crime alleys,' Norris says. 'The Army might
use HSS for decoy troop movements. And Disney is nuts about it!'*

Even Florida Power and Light has been given a taste. It seems endangered canaries have been sparking themselves to death on power lines and could do with some warning.

Not surprisingly, people who've heard of HSS have responded variously. On any given day, Norris might receive 17 e-mail messages from a company in Hong Kong begging to manufacture HSS – and several from civilians who think he's either a genius or a psychopath. One man recently wrote to insist that Norris 'be jailed' if he fields this product (curiously, sending this demand to Norris). And a woman wants to secretly install HSS in her lover's car or golf bag so that she may continually transmit a message deep into his head: Marry Donna...Marry Donna.

Scientists at NASA once got wind of an offhand remark he had made about wireless receivers and flew him to Texas; they'd been having trouble with boom microphones slipping around inside space helmets. 'Suddenly I hear these words coming out of my mouth,' Norris recalls: 'Well, I can give you a one-piece system so you won't need a boom mike at all. The sound can come through the bones in your head!' And the NASA guys were, like, 'Yeah. Right.' Thirty days later, Norris had a prototype, which the space agency grabbed with both hands. Norris translated the concept into an 'all-in-your-ear headset' that came to be called Jabra.

In reality, HIDA is both warning and weapon. If used from a battleship, it can ward off stray crafts at 500 yards with a pinpointed verbal warning. Should the offending vessel continue to within 200 yards, the stern warnings are replaced by 120-decibel sounds that are as physically disabling as shrapnel. Certain noises, projected at the right pitch, can incapacitate even a stone-deaf terrorist; the bones in your head are brutalized by a tone's full effect whether you're clutching the sides of your skull in agony or not. 'Besides,' Norris says, laughing darkly, 'grabbing your ears is as good as a pair of handcuffs.'

Most of the sounds under military consideration are classified, but some are approved for public consumption. One truly harrowing noise is that of a baby crying, played backward, and combined with another tone.

'HIDA can instantaneously cause loss of equilibrium, vomiting, migraines – really, we can pretty much pick our ailment,' he says brightly.

Norris prods his assistant to locate the baby noise on a laptop, then aims the device at me. At first, the noise is dreadful – just primally wrong – but not unbearable. I repeatedly tell Norris to crank it up (trying to approximate battle-strength volume, without the nausea), until the noise isn't so much a noise as an assault on my nervous system. I nearly fall down and, for some reason, my eyes hurt. When I bravely ask how high they'd turned the dial, Norris laughs uproariously. 'That was nothing!' he bellows. 'That was about 1 percent of what an enemy would get. One percent!' Two hours later, I can still feel the ache in the back of my head.

So unlike sound that travels on radio waves and has to be converted by your stereo's receiver, you simply need to be standing in the path of an HSS beam in order to hear the sound.'"[28]

So if you put all this together, HAARP and the Voice of God weapon and other internal sound devices, then it just so happens you have precisely the instruments the Occult believes are needed for the ultimate deception in the Last Days. In order to get people around the world to worship and receive the Antichrist. Here's what they are waiting for:

"The occult believes that once all the world's religions come together, (and they're expecting it soon) a religious leader will be chosen to be earth's religious spokesman and this spokesperson will then encourage all the people of the world to accept a new world leader, who will suddenly appear on the scene.

Interestingly enough, the occult is in agreement that none of this can fully take place until the people who will never go along with this One World Religion are out of the way. Can anyone guess who that might be? That's right! Christians!

In fact, they say that these people who are restraining or holding things up won't necessarily die, but will somehow mysteriously disappear, or in their words, 'Elect to leave this dimension as if going to another room.'"

Hey, that sounds like the Rapture of the Church, doesn't it?

"The occult also believes once these people leave this earth, the new world leader will take his rightful place over the world. And then, and only then, will it be possible to build a combination Temple-Church-Mosque in Jerusalem, which will then finally break the Middle East log jam, which just so happens to sound

like what the Antichrist is going to do with Israel by signing a peace treaty that starts the actual 7-year Tribulation.

They also believe that just minutes before the Antichrist arises, some supernatural sound will be heard and spiritually felt by everybody on the planet simultaneously. At no other moment in world history will so many people be impacted at once. This action is designed to get everyone looking around as to what caused this sound."

In fact, it just happens there's a recent flood of reports all over the world of people saying how they are hearing all kinds of strange sounds from the sky as this man shares:

"We have all heard about the strange sounds being heard around the world. The best that anyone can figure is they started about mid-2011 and have escalated since the beginning of 2012.

They are being reported in virtually every part of the globe, Canada, Asia, Europe, Central and South America and the USA. They are being reported as loud rumblings, tornado like, groaning, low pitch roar, rushing air or water, scraping of metal, loud freight train, trumpets, deep vibrations, they last for one or two minutes or they can go on for days. While most are a low type rumble some are a loud bang or a series of loud booms that last for minutes or hours.

Some have actually called it a 'skyquake'. They have reportedly set off car alarms, freaked out dogs, cats, farm animals and they certainly have made mainstream media news reports. Some say it is coming from the sky while others claim it's coming from the earth. It seems that almost everyone rules out a mechanical sound such as planes, trains or helicopters.

Speculation is running rampant, things people have put forward, Pole Shift, Atmospheric anomalies, the start of UFO Disclosure, HAARP (High Frequency Active Aurora Research Program), Government diversion to divert attention, End Times fast approaching, etc.

The quantity of the reports is overwhelming, the reasons given for these strange noises runs the gamut from plausible to bizarre and the truth is no one really knows what is actually causing this phenomenon. If you speak with those that have heard these strange sounds there is no doubt in your mind that they are real. Until the mystery is solved we can only sit back and listen!"[29]

Could this be the False Prophet's practice run? The Occult continues with their belief system:

"Then with everyone's attention aroused, images of Antichrist will appear simultaneously over the entire earth speaking to mankind, each in his own language. The 'signs and wonders' will have begun.

Here the Antichrist will appear as a man to a man and a woman to a woman. He will appear as a white to a white, as a black to a black, as an Indian to an Indian, etc. It makes no difference whether you are viewing him in person or on Television. Thus, 'He will show that he is all things to all people.'"[30]

We don't have the technology to create a massive vision in the sky to dupe people, do we? Yes, we do. In fact, some would say some pretty massive ones have already appeared in China:

"ITN, a broadcast network in Britain, posted video last week of a stunning mirage in East China that features a city skyline, replete with what appear to be buildings and trees, but in fact, the images were just an elaborate optical illusion.

The amazing mirage appeared over Huanshan City East China at dusk on Thursday. Following a heavy downpour, the spectacular images of mountains, buildings, and trees appeared in the thin mist above the Xin'an River.

The phenomenon began about 5:00pm local time to the amazement of passersby. One lady who witnessed the event stated, 'It's really amazing. It looks like a scene in a movie, in a fairy land.'

This is not the first time mirages like this have been reported in China. In 2006, China Daily, an English language newspaper, posted four images of what it said were mirages off the coast of Eastern China's Shandong province.

Although residents say that similar sites have been seen lately, most agreed that this one had been the most spectacular."[31]

Talk about deception! What did the above texts say? In the Last Days the False Prophet is going to use false signs and wonders, and counterfeit miracles, to dupe the world into worshiping the Antichrist. Why should people listen when they are warned about the soon return of Jesus Christ? Because never before in the history of mankind have we had the technology to pull off what's mentioned in these passages, *until now*! That's why people need to listen.

3. The Third Bible Passage Being Fulfilled in Minute Detail – The Death and Demands of the Antichrist

Revelation 13:14-15 "Because of the signs he was given power to do on behalf of the first beast, he deceived the inhabitants of the earth. He ordered them to set up an image in honor of the beast who was wounded by the sword and yet lived. He was given power to give breath to the image of the first beast, so that it could speak and cause all who refused to worship the image to be killed."

Here we see the rest of the infamous passage concerning the False Prophet and the Antichrist. It tells us the ultimate goal of the False Prophet's deception; to get people to worship the Antichrist or to be killed. Then, at some point, the Antichrist is going to die or "appear" to die, because remember his tactics as we already saw are characterized by counterfeit signs, wonders, and miracles. He's a liar and deceiver. So after this death or "alleged" death, the False Prophet is going to set up an image or likeness of the Antichrist that can actually speak and cause all who refuse to worship it, the Antichrist, to die!

So that's the question; Do we see any kind of technology on the planet that could help fake the death of the Antichrist and create some sort of life-like talking image that can interact with people, even causing their death? Yes! In fact, it's a combination of several new technologies that have arisen on the planet for the first time in man's history that are being put together to pull it off.

The first new technology that makes it all possible is **3-D Holograms**. Believe it or not, we now have the ability to broadcast a life-like 3-D image of anyone anywhere on the planet. In fact, they're getting so commonplace now they're even being used in news broadcasts. The following news reports are various examples of hologram technology being used today:

"Holy holograms, was that Princess Leia on CNN during election night? No, it was just Jessica Yellin, a CNN correspondent. CNN beamed her image from Chicago to the CNN press center in New York City, where Wolf Blitzer and the rest of the team were covering election returns.

Yellin, who claimed she was the first person to be beamed in a 'hologram' on live TV, explained for the audience how this was done. She said she was standing in a tent outside of the Obama headquarters in Chicago where the CNN crew had set up 35 high-definition cameras in a ring. She stood in the center of this ring and the cameras picked up her every movement and transmitted the image in 3D to the studio in New York.

At one point during his interview with Yellin, Blitzer commented that he felt bringing Yellin into the studio via hologram created a more intimate setting for their interview.

Whatever technique CNN used, there's no doubt that it looked cool and it conjured up some futuristic thoughts of Star Trek and Star Wars." [32]

"Telstra, the Australian phone company, used a hologram earlier this year to beam its chief technology officer from Melbourne to a business meeting about 460 miles away in Adelaide. Cisco Systems has also used holograms in demonstrations to talk about its telepresence products." [32]

"Environmental enthusiast Prince Charles has delivered a speech to a green energy conference in Abu Dhabi – as a hologram. He may not be known as the most modern of men, but the Prince of Wales' concern for the planet has catapulted him straight into the 21st Century.

He was keen to prove his green credentials by noting that if he had chosen to appear in person, his long-haul flight would have emitted around 15 tons of carbon dioxide, the greenhouse gas which is causing global warming.

So he appeared as a hologram to congratulate Abu Dhabi for its plans to harness the power of natural resources to create a new zero carbon city called Masdar.

As the 3D image vanished, he left the audience with the words: 'I am now going to vanish into thin air, leaving not a carbon footprint behind!'

The speech by the 3D version of Charles was recorded in person at Highgrove last year, using technology from British multimedia firm Musion.

Prince Charles is not the first famous figure to use the technology.

David Beckham recorded a message in LA, appearing as a hologram in London. Richard Branson has also given virtual speeches, as did Al Gore during his Live Earth concerts last year.

But the most exciting thing is that those behind the technology have already tried out a live hologram – in other words, they have the technology to make people appear as a hologram in real time from anywhere in the world.

Mr O'Connell said: 'There has been one successful test which carried a full High Definition signal 11,000 miles from San Jose in America to Bangalore in India. The hologram that appeared was very similar to the one of Prince Charles, but it could interact with the crowd and the people on stage via special screens. I think that is the future for this technology.'" [32]

"Tupac Shakur (who died in 1996) appeared in concert at the Coachella music festival Sunday night, wowing audiences who watched his image rap with Snoop Dogg.

And now, the Wall Street Journal is reporting (with the puntastic headline "Rapper's De-Light") that the late rapper, despite having died in a shooting years ago, may be going on tour.

The team pulled together Tupac's performance by looking at old footage and creating an animation that incorporated characteristics of the late singer's movements.

AV Concepts president Nick Smith told the Journal that the company had used the technology to digitally resurrect some deceased executives – though he gave no details on that.

Over at MTV, writer Gil Kaufmann questioned whether the success of the virtual Tupac would set a trend, particularly for performances including multiple artists. The potential for a surprise appearance from a beloved celebrity performer could be a draw for audiences." [32]

What? You mean to tell me we have the technology *right now* to beam an image of a person, even a dead person, or world leader that's not even alive? Wouldn't that come in handy for the death or "alleged" death of the Antichrist? In addition, we can not only have a 3-D image of someone interacting with us anywhere on the planet, but now people are starting to interact with these images themselves, almost in a state of *worship*, like with this Japanese Anime character:

"Everyone gets a little obsessed with famous musicians now and then, but things get really weird when the famous musician is actually just a piece of software. Hatsune Miku is a rising star in Japan and abroad, singing catchy J-pop that matches her blue-green hair. She's also a virtual avatar created by Crypton Media using Yamaha's Vocaloid voice synthesizer.

That hasn't stopped her from amassing a legion of fans who really love her work. I mean really love it. Check out the crowd frantically waving glow-sticks and singing along with Hatsune Miku as she appears via a '3D hologram' on stage. Thanks to Klas Klazon for pointing us to these awesome HD clips of her work.

If you want to know more about Crypton's Hatsune Miku and similar Vocaloid based characters check out my earlier coverage. I'm not sure I'm a big fan of 'her' music, but Hatsune Miku certainly has star talent.

In the HD clips you can really see how eager the fans are, and how well they know her music. The mid-range shots of the crowd with Miku in the background also show how great her 'hologram' appears live on stage.

The high definition quality only goes to show that Hatsune Miku, and other virtual rockers on the rise, can hold their own against their real-world counterparts. Who knows, maybe these software singers will grow to dominate the world of music. After all, human pop stars already seem like they were created in a science lab, why not just take the next step?"[33]

That's not only wild, but if you supplant that character with the Antichrist's image, it sure looks like people on the planet right now are ready to do what that Antichrist says, "Worship me and my image!" Furthermore, you can now carry on an *intelligent conversation* with this image and even *touch it* for some serious interaction:

"Lionhead Studios showed a video demonstrating a virtual child called Milo. Able to recognize facial expressions and vocal emotions, Milo chatted with real-life demonstrator Claire.

Milo also threw her a pair of goggles (which she automatically grabbed for and then 'put on'). Later, Milo grabbed a piece of paper that Claire held in front of the camera for a mere instant. Another aspect saw Claire splashing around virtual water in real-time.

Studio founder Peter Molyneux boasted that these were concepts even science fiction writers haven't been able to dream up, and that the technology is here, now.

Now it was finally my turn, and luckily I got a chance to experience the best part – direct speech with Milo. Molyneux asked me to say my name clearly in front of the screen and then take a step back. I did both and then when Peter asked me to take a step forward and I did, Milo immediately recognized me – 'Oh, Hello Jeremy!' Milo said before hopping out of his swing and walking up to greet me. Next he quipped, 'I see you're wearing blue today,' in reaction to the blue shirt that I had on. I could hear the sound of impressed acknowledgments from the people standing behind me right afterwards.

'Say something funny and see how he reacts,' Molyneux said, but under the pressure of suddenly saying something witty I choked up and said something about Milo's shirt being nice and that the drawing on it kind of looked like a backwards Yoda. Yeah, I know, not funny at all, but what was cool is that Milo recognized this and had a bit of a grimace on his face before turning his attention elsewhere.

And with that we were out of time. Even so, the potential for this game and how you could ultimately interact with the character is very high, and I'm excited to see where it goes next." [34]

Then add to this the advancement of "touchable" holograms!

"Researchers at Tokyo University have come up with a technology that is a first and significant step away from the mouse and keyboard – touchable holograms.

Up until now, holography has been for the eyes only, and if you'd try to touch it, your hand would go right through. But now we have a technology that also adds the sensation of touch to holograms.

The technology consists of software that uses ultrasonic waves to create pressure on the hand of a user 'touching' the projected hologram.

Researchers are using two Wiimotes from Nintendo's Wii gaming system to track a user's hand.

The technology was introduced at SIGGRAPH, an annual computer graphics conference, and has so far only been tested with relatively simple objects.

But its inventors have big plans for touchable holograms in the future.

For example, it's been shown that in hospitals, there can be contamination between people due to objects that are touched communally. But if you can change the switches and such into a virtual switch, then you no longer have to worry about touch contamination. This is one application that's quite easy to see.

Touchable holograms could be used for a wide variety of things. Everything from light switches to books with each appearing when needed, and then disappearing when not.

And holograms could replace the need for making new interfaces for technology, since they could be changed without having to make a new physical product."[34]

Is this what the Antichrist is going to do? Combine this Milo technology with the touchable hologram technology and voila! You have to reach out and literally touch the hand of the Antichrist's image and kiss it as a sign of your devotion or worship? Then if you don't, you're going to die? Either way, as you can see, the point is *for the first time in mankind's history*, we have the technology to pull it off! But what about the Antichrist's death or "alleged" death. Do we have the technology to "fake" or "give the appearance" of something like that going on? Yes! Believe it or not, *for the first time in man's history*, scientists believe they can actually now download a person's brain into a computer and thus preserve it theoretically for life! Therefore, if you combine that technology with the advancements being made in *robotics*, you can come up with a pretty life-like image:

"It's a conservative statement to say that by 2025 we'll be able to look inside your brain, see everything that going on. All the interneural connections, all the synaptic clefts, all the neural transmitter strings in creating a huge database and

copying down every detail and then reinstantiate that information in a neural computer of sufficient capacity and create basically a copy of the thinking process that takes place in your brain.

But that's one scenario but it's really an existence proof to show that we can tap the secrets of intelligence that exist in the human brain. Once we've scanned that information we can also understand and see how it's organized and improve on it. We can extend it, we can make the memory a thousand times bigger, we can make it faster, we can expand the perceptual capabilities.

To transfer your mind to a computer, this seems to be the ultimate dream of many scientists. To liberate us from our old body that is becoming obsolete in this technological world. We then would go on living as free spirits in cyberspace. So in a way, I might wind up living as a short cut of my own artificial intelligence that allow us to have machines with human minds. I'm hoping we can fit it on a CD-Rom that's 600 megabytes. I bet that's what we need to copy a person. So it's a difficult time to predict what these new humans will be like. I think it's important to include the third component which is the virtual, along with the artificial and along with the flesh but how that mixture goes together in a co-operative verses a competitive way. It's hard to predict. It's very interesting. It's a great time to live in.

Reality and virtual reality are beginning to merge. We will be able to inject a certain number of nanobots into our bodies where they will locate our brain cells and copy their functioning. With no effort we'll get a new copy of our consciousness that will then send a software copy to a computer where more copies can be made. Or our consciousness will be allowed to merge with others' souls in software programs. Then we will be ready to leave this planet and start the exploration of the universe."[35]

Now, remind me again, why people should listen when they are warned about the soon return of Jesus Christ? That's right! Because never before in the history of mankind have we had the technology to pull off this kind of intimate detail mentioned in all these passages; the *image* of the Antichrist or even his *pseudo-death*, that is, until now. That's why people need to listen!

Please, if you're reading this and you're not a Christian, don't be fooled into thinking that by *rushing here and there* and by *increasing your knowledge*, you'll find rest. If you do, you will not only remain restless, but you may one day wake up to find yourself in the *greatest time of unrest* the world has ever known, the 7-year Tribulation, just like the Bible said. When? In the Last Days. Believe it or not, even with all this amazing evidence pointing to the signs of Christ's soon return, some people still refuse to admit the truth and are in certain danger, like these people:

"One day a group of Florida senior citizens were sitting around talking about their ailments when one person said, 'My arms are so weak I can hardly hold this cup of coffee.'

'Yes, I know.' Replied another. 'My cataracts are so bad I can't even see my coffee.'

Then the person with the loudest voice of the group piped in, 'Oh yeah, well it's gotten to where I cannot hear anything anymore.'

Then a fourth person nodded weakly in agreement, 'I know what you mean, I can't turn my head because of the arthritis in my neck.'

'Well, that's nothing,' claimed another 'my blood pressure pills make me dizzy.'

'You think that's bad," said another person, 'Why I can't even remember what I'm doing half the time. If I don't make myself a note I forget what I am trying to do in the first place.'

Then an old wise man of the group winced and shook his head saying, 'I guess that's the price we pay for getting old.'

Then there was a short moment of silence and one woman cheerfully announced, 'Well, it's not that bad. Thank goodness we can all still drive.'"[36]

Now those people didn't want to admit the truth. Because of this they were not only a danger to themselves but to other people as well. Yet the Bible says that this refusal to admit the truth would be commonplace in the Last Days, just like it was with Noah.

Matthew 24:37-39 "When the Son of Man returns, it will be like it was in Noah's day. In those days before the Flood, the people were enjoying banquets and parties and weddings right up to the time Noah entered his boat. People didn't realize what was going to happen until the Flood came and swept them all away. That is the way it will be when the Son of Man comes."

I hope you're not one of those who are too busy partying and acting like nothing will ever change. If you are, you might wake up one day and discover that *you've been left behind*. And you know what? God doesn't want you left behind. Because He loves us, He has given us the warning sign of **Modern Technology** to show us that the 7-year Tribulation is near and that Christ's Coming is rapidly approaching. Jesus Himself said this:

Luke 21:28 "When these things begin to take place, stand up and lift up your heads, because your redemption is drawing near."

Like it or not, we are headed for *The Final Countdown*. We don't know the day or the hour. Only God knows. The point is, if you're a Christian, it's time to get busy. There's a war going on and each of us needs to find something to do to serve the Lord while we still can. It's high time we Christians speak up and declare the good news of salvation to those who are dying all around us. But please, if you're not a Christian, give your life to Jesus today, because tomorrow may be too late! Just like the Bible said!

Chapter Three

Worldwide Upheaval

If there's one thing I've learned in Christian ministry over the years, it's got to be this truth. Being a Pastor definitely comes with its moments of surprise, like this Pastor's letter reveals:

"As a bagpiper, I play many gigs. Recently, I was asked by a funeral director to play at a graveside service for a homeless man. He had no family or friends, and so the service was to be at a pauper's cemetery in the far corner of town, way out in the back country.

Well, I was not familiar with the backwoods of our town, so I got lost; and being a typical guy; I didn't stop and ask for directions. So I finally arrived an hour late and I noticed the funeral director had evidently left and the hearse was nowhere in sight.

But then I noticed the diggers and the crew were still there, and they were eating lunch. So, I felt bad and apologized to the men for being late, and I went to the side of the grave and looked down, and the vault lid was already in place. I didn't know what else to do, so I started to play.

The workers put down their lunches and began to gather around. I played my heart and soul out for this man with no family and friends. I played like I've never played before for this homeless man.

As I played 'Amazing Grace,' the workers began to weep. They wept, I wept, we all wept together. When I had finished, I packed up my bagpipes and started for my car. Though my head was hung low, my heart was full.

And as I was opening the door to my car, I heard one of the workers say, 'I never seen nothin' like that before, and I've been putting in septic tanks for twenty years.'"[1]

How many of you would say that Pastor had a serious rude awakening? Believe it or not, he's not alone. The Bible says one day *the whole planet* is going to be in for a *rude awakening* at the Rapture of the Church and they're going to be changing their tune real quick! That's because they just entered the 7-year Tribulation and it's no joke! For those of you who don't know, the 7-year Tribulation is not a party. It's an outpouring of God's wrath on a wicked and rebellious planet. In fact Jesus said in Matthew 24 it's going to be a "time of greater horror than anything the world has ever seen or will ever see again. And that "unless that time of calamity is shortened, the entire human race will be destroyed."

Though praise God, God's not only a God of wrath, He's a God of love as well. Because He loves us, He's given us many warning signs to show us when the Tribulation is near and Jesus Christ's Second Coming is rapidly approaching. Therefore, in order to keep people from experiencing the ultimate bad day of being left behind, a serious rude awakening, we're going to continue in our study, *The Final Countdown*. So far we've already seen how the **tenth sign** on The Final Countdown was **The Jewish People**. Then in the last chapter we saw how the **ninth sign** was **Modern Technology**. There we saw that God lovingly foretold us that when we see across the world an **Increase of Travel**, an **Increase of Information**, an **Increase of Unrest**, an **Increase of Bible Fulfillment** with the **Death of the Two Witnesses**, **The Deception of the False Prophet**, and **The Death and Demands of the Antichrist,** showing us that we really have for the first time in mankind's history the technology to pull off all the things mentioned in the passages we saw, it's a clear indicator from God, *we're living in the Last Days*.

The **eighth sign** on The Final Countdown is none other than **Worldwide Upheaval**. In other words, the planet is really going to get messed up before Jesus comes back:

Matthew 24:1-8 "Jesus left the temple and was walking away when His disciples came up to Him to call His attention to its buildings. Do you see all these things? He asked. I tell you the truth, not one stone here will be left on another; every one will be thrown down. As Jesus was sitting on the Mount of Olives, the disciples came to Him privately. Tell us, they said, when will this happen, and what will be the sign of Your coming and of the end of the age? Jesus answered: Watch out that no one deceives you. For many will come in My name, claiming, I am the Christ, and will deceive many. You will hear of wars and rumors of wars, but see to it that you are not alarmed. Such things must happen, but the end is still to come. Nation will rise against nation, and kingdom against kingdom. There will be famines and earthquakes in various places. All these are the beginning of birth pains."

I. First Sign of Worldwide Upheaval - Increase of Famines

According to the Bible, one of the first signs to indicate that we are headed for Worldwide Upheaval and hence living in the Last Days is that there would be an Increase of Famines. Now, the scoffer would look at this passage and sarcastically state, "Famines are no big deal, we've always had famines." Granted yes, that is true. Though not like we see today! *In the last century alone*, we have seen nothing short of an explosion of *worldwide famines* like never before. The World Health Organization estimates that while 1/3 of the world is well-fed, another 1/3 are under-fed and the final 1/3 is starving to death right now. Just in the 1990's alone, 100 million children starved to death and a total of 4 million people will die this year alone. This means that by the time you are done reading this chapter, about 200 people will have died due to food shortages.[2]

The question is, how can there be such an increase of worldwide famine when we are living in the most technologically advanced era ever? Well, some are caused by war, embargoes, government corruption or economic debt. But it's also caused by overzealous environmentalists who have stirred up restrictions on the usage of fertilizers, which is one of the reasons why 12,000 square miles a year of Africa is now turning into desert.[3] That doesn't sound like saving the earth to me!

Speaking of deserts, the Africans are not the only ones with this problem. So are the Chinese. Today as we speak, China is losing 4,000 square miles of land to deserts each year. About 1/3 of their total land has now been covered by desert in the form of massive drifting sand dunes.[4] Just one of their famines killed an estimated 20-43 million people![5] In fact, throughout the world, a land area bigger then the state of Texas is becoming desert every single year.[6] No matter what people try to do to reverse it, the deserts just keep on coming. So guess what? So will the famine. In fact, let's take a look at some statistics on global famine which bring to light just how bad it really is right now:

- In the Asian, African and Latin American countries, well over 500 million people are living in what the World Bank has called "absolute poverty."

- Every year 15 million children die of hunger.

- For the price of one missile, a school full of hungry children could eat lunch every day for 5 years.

- Throughout the 1990's more than 100 million children died from illness and starvation. Those 100 million deaths could have been prevented for the price of ten Stealth bombers, or what the world spends on its military in two days!

- One in twelve people worldwide is malnourished, including 160 million children under the age of 5.

- The Indian subcontinent has nearly half the world's hungry people. Africa and the rest of Asia together have approximately 40%, and the remaining hungry people are found in Latin America and other parts of the world.

- Nearly one in four people, 1.3 billion live on less than $1 per day, while the world's 358 billionaires have assets exceeding the combined annual incomes of countries with 45 percent of the world's people.

- 3 billion people in the world today struggle to survive on US $2/day.

- In 1994 the Urban Institute in Washington DC estimated that one out of 6 elderly people in the U.S. has an inadequate diet.

- In the U.S. hunger and race are related. In 1991 46% of African-American children were chronically hungry, and 40% of Latino children were chronically hungry compared to 16% of white children.

- The infant mortality rate is closely linked to inadequate nutrition among pregnant women. The U.S. ranks 23rd among industrial nations in infant mortality. African-American infants die at nearly twice the rate of white infants.

- One out of every eight children under the age of twelve in the U.S. goes to bed hungry every night.

- Half of all children under five years of age in South Asia and one third of those in sub-Saharan Africa are malnourished.

- In 1997 alone, the lives of at least 300,000 young children were saved by vitamin A supplementation programs in developing countries.

- Malnutrition is implicated in more than half of all child deaths worldwide - a proportion unmatched by any infectious disease since the Black Death.

- About 183 million children weigh less than they should for their age.

- To satisfy the world's sanitation and food requirements would cost only US $13 billion - what the people of the United States and the European Union spend on perfume each year.

- The assets of the world's three richest men are more than the combined GNP of all the least developed countries on the planet.

- Every 3.6 seconds someone dies of hunger.

- It is estimated that some 800 million people in the world suffer from hunger and malnutrition, about 100 times as many as those who actually die from it each year.[7]

Now, as gut-wrenching as that is, believe it or not, it's projected to get even worse. As a recent news headline put it "There are fears over our *global food supply*". Wheat prices have gone through the roof, countries are suffering their worst droughts on record, food shortages have been the worst in the last 30 years, which has spawned riots in many different countries, and 800,000 children are expected to die just in the Horn of Africa alone![8]

Lest you think it's not going to hit here in America you're wrong! I quote, "Drought is spreading across 14 states from Florida to Arizona. In Texas, where the drought is worst, virtually no part of the state has been untouched." "The U.S. Department of Agriculture designated all 254 counties in Texas as natural disaster areas."[9] In fact, here's a photo revealing just how fast it's spreading across America.

Drought conditions

Dry/moderate ━━━━━━━━━━━ Exceptional

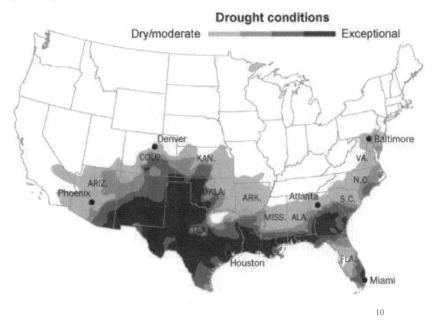

[10]

Looks like its spreading here in America just like China. As one person stated, "This is quite serious." And another person stated, "We are headed for a *global crisis*...one that would match the current one in the banking sector,"[11] only this one has to do with *food*.

As bad as this is *right now*, believe it or not, it's nothing compared to what's coming. Remember what Jesus said. All these signs of famine are just the beginning of birth pains, which means the "big one" is yet to come! Pay attention to the verbiage Jesus is using here. Ladies, how many of you quickly found out that the closer you arrived to the actual birth of your child that the pain got even worse and more intense until the actual birth of your child? It's called *birth pains* for a reason and that's the exact same verbiage Jesus is using here. Which means, all these famines that we see right now, as bad as they are, are nothing compared to what is coming. They're just *a small tiny contraction* compared to the big one that's coming down the pike. The Bible tells us what that will be like:

Revelation 6:5-6 "When the Lamb opened the third seal, I heard the third living creature say, "Come!" I looked, and there before me was a black horse! Its rider was holding a pair of scales in his hand. Then I heard what sounded like a voice among the four living creatures, saying, "A quart of wheat for a day's wages, and three quarts of barley for a day's wages, and do not damage the oil and the wine!"

According to this text in the Bible, we see that the famine conditions during the first half of the 7-year Tribulation are going to be so bad that the whole world is going to be on some sort of global food distribution program just to stay alive. Only this time, to get your food you have to work for it. A quart of wheat was given for one day's work, or you could get three quarts of barley for a days work. Now, barley back in the day was basically poor man's food. It was pretty much animal food with low nutritional value. Therefore, the Bible is telling us that this famine in the 7-year Tribulation is so bad, that a person could either work a day and feed themselves with somewhat normal food, or they could work a day and feed a family of three with animal food just to stay alive. For those of you who might be having a hard time conceptualizing what this might be like, let's see how the following family is surviving today, and you tell me if we're not getting close to what the Bible talks about:

"Twelve million people are affected by this severe drought and this famine. 600,000 or more children are acutely malnourished. This is really like teetering on the brink of life or death.

The center of this crisis is the Horn of Africa which include Somalia, Ethiopia and Kenya. Where it's worst right now is in Somalia. This is the most significant humanitarian crisis in the world today. The largest refugee camp in the world is growing day by day because of people who are escaping their country because of instability and a simple lack of food and water.

This happens family by family. One mom and dad waking up in the morning and realizing there's nothing left, and they have to go. These families are setting out on a road trip usually on foot and they're doing it in the most hazardous environment you can imagine. They are at risk of wild animals, banditry, people who don't wish them well, and it's scary.

There is a family that stands out in my mind and is a reflection of what's really happening. They have a son about three years old who became so desperate that he ate dirt just to have something in his belly. This is what parents have to deal with in the middle of nowhere where their child dies. [12]

Now, the general rule in Biblical interpretation is that anything we can come up with in our minds to try to explain a text, usually pales in comparison to the actual reality. So put yourself in that family's shoes. *Right now*, they are eating dirt to stay alive. As bad as that is, it pales in comparison to the actual famine conditions during the 7-year Tribulation. Which means, one day, if you refuse to accept Jesus Christ as your Personal Lord and Savior, your family is going to end up *worse* than that one! As you can clearly see, the world is being *shriveled* like never before. Although we may have always had famines, *nothing like we see today*. As bad as it is now, it's just a birth pain, a little one, a tiny one, compared to the big one that's coming down the pike. Exactly like the Bible said would happen, when you are living in the Last Days.

II. Second Sign of Worldwide Upheaval – Increase of Earthquakes

Matthew 24:3,7,8 "As Jesus was sitting on the Mount of Olives, the disciples came to him privately. Tell us, they said, when will this happen, and what will be the sign of your coming and of the end of the age? There will be famines and earthquakes in various places. All these are the beginning of birth pains."

Again, the scoffer would look at this passage and sarcastically state, "Earthquakes are no big deal, we've always had earthquakes." Granted yes, that is true. We've always had earthquakes, but not like we see today! *In the last century alone*, we have seen nothing short of an explosion of *worldwide earthquakes* like never before, and the ground is *cracking up* all over the planet! As a recent environmental article explained, "Scientists are sounding the alarm: Mysterious cracks are appearing all across the planet!" Here are the facts:

- *South America – Scientists don't know what to think about South America busting at the seams. In Southern Peru, there suddenly appeared a huge crack almost 2 miles long and nearly 330 feet wide. Scientists are confused with this fact and cracks also appeared in neighboring Bolivia.*

- *Iceland – Lake Kleifarvatn in Iceland is disappearing due to a giant crack that appeared in the earth. The crack leads directly into the lake and disappears beneath the water. "If you put your ear to the ground, you can hear the lake draining. It sounds like water going down the drain of a sink."*

- *Africa – A 1,640 foot long giant crack appeared in Africa in just a few days that normally would take years to form. Scientists believe this tear in the earth's continental crust could eventually isolate Ethiopia and Eritrea from the rest of Africa.* [13]

Lest you think it won't hit here in America:

- *Michigan – One day the land was flat and filled with trees shooting straight into the air. Twenty-four hours later there's a 600-foot-long crack, 4-feet deep twisting its way through the woods - and those vertical trees are now pointed 30 degrees left and right where the earth has mounded 15 feet high. No, it's not a disaster movie; it's what happened Monday at the home of Eileen Heider on Bay de Noc Road in Birch Creek.*

Heider was sitting in her recliner watching TV at about 8:30 that morning. "The chair shook for a few seconds and I thought the spring in the chair went," she said. Heider heard a noise at the same time. She checked her chair and around the house inside and out but couldn't find anything unusual.

Heider wasn't alone. A neighbor across the road told her she heard a boom while taking a shower and that her husband was leaning against the washing machine and said he felt it move, even though it wasn't running.

Another neighbor said he heard a boom and closed his window thinking it was thunder but then noticed the sky was clear.

The next day Heider's friend, Doug Salewski, found a hole in the ground and a 200-yard crevasse a short ways away which wasn't there before. Heider went to investigate and said the crack was three-feet wide and about five-feet deep in spots. "The trees on one side are kind of tilted and on the other side are tilted the opposite way." she said.

Heider called authorities and Michigan State Trooper, Paul Anderson, from the Stephenson Post came out to take a look. "There's no gas line or anything, I have no answers to it," he said. "It heaved the ground 10 to 15 feet. I mean the ground used to be flat and now it's just heaved, it heaved the entire ground." Anderson said he'd follow up with phone calls to geologists at Michigan Tech. [13]

I wonder if that's what's going to happen to the U.S. Are we going to crack right down the middle like in Ethiopia? Lest you think that's not possible, you need to realize that the ground is not only cracking up all over the planet, but the earthquakes are getting *bigger*, all over the planet:

EARTHQUAKES 6.0 OR GREATER

From 1000 AD to 1800	21	(800 Years)
From 1800 to 1900	18	(100 Years)
From 1910 to 1929	4	(20 Years)
From 1930 to 1949	9	(20 Years)
In 1950's	9	(10 Years)
In 1960's	13	(10 Years)
In 1970's	51	(10 Years)
In 1980's	86	(10 Years)
From 1990 to 1994	Over 100	(5 Years)

EARTHQUAKES IN GENERAL

December 26th, 2006	454	(1 Week just in the U.S.)
February 13th, 2008	1,100	(1 Week just in the U.S.)

If those facts on the massive rise of earthquakes were not apparent enough for you, then maybe the following chart from the USGS will help get the point across.

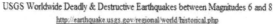

USGS Worldwide Deadly & Destructive Earthquakes between Magnitudes 6 and 8
http://earthquake.usgs.gov/regional/world/historical.php

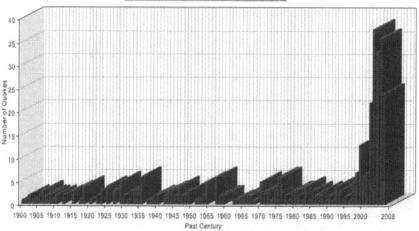

14

Once you look at the facts, I think it's pretty obvious that earthquakes really are on a serious rise. In addition, keep in mind that although earthquakes last for only a few seconds or minutes, the trail of devastation lasts a long time. For instance, because of this massive rise of earthquakes, each year they produce billions of dollars worth of damage, they kill 1000's and 1,000's of people (one quake alone killed 255,000)[15] they make hundreds of thousands of people homeless and it's getting worse. This sudden "increase of severe earthquakes has led scientists to predict that *we are entering a new period of great seismic disturbances.*"[16] Where have I heard that before? In fact, one quake expert stated, "The earth is cracking up! There is no doubt that something is seriously wrong. There have been too many strong earthquakes."[17] They're also predicting that the death tolls from earthquakes are only going to skyrocket due to the massive exodus of people who are moving out of the rural areas and into the big cities. The problem with this is that many of the cities just happen to be built right on top of fault lines. Therefore, scientists are now saying that we are entering a time when fatalities from quakes totaling over three million will not be uncommon.[18] This is also due to another side-affect from earthquakes, and that is landslides, which are another major cause of loss of life.

Again, remember what Jesus said. These are nothing compared to what is to come. All these signs of *earthquakes* and even *landslides* caused by earthquakes are just *the beginning of birth pains*, which means the "big one" is yet to come! It's chump change compared to the one the Bible says is coming soon:

Revelation 6:12-14 "I watched as he opened the sixth seal. There was a great earthquake. The sun turned black like sackcloth made of goat hair, the whole moon turned blood red, and the stars in the sky fell to earth, as late figs drop from a fig tree when shaken by a strong wind. The sky receded like a scroll, rolling up, and every mountain and island was removed from its place."

Wow! Did you catch that? Every mountain and island was removed from its place! That's a serious disturbance! In fact, you can laugh and scoff all you want, but the Bible is clear. If you refuse to accept Jesus Christ as your Personal Lord and Savior *right now*, you are headed for a reality just like that. Again, remember the Biblical rule. Anything we can come up with in our minds or even on a movie screen to try to explain it, pales in comparison to the actual reality. I think it's abundantly clear that our world is being *shaken* like never before. Yes, we may have always had earthquakes, but nothing like we see today. As bad as it is now, it's just a birth pain, a little one, a tiny one, compared to the big one that's coming down the pike. Exactly like the Bible said would happen, when you are living in the Last Days.

III. Third Sign of Worldwide Upheaval - Increase of Pestilence

Luke 21:7,11 "Teacher, they asked, when will these things happen? And what will be the sign that they are about to take place? There will be great earthquakes, famines and pestilences in various places, and fearful events and great signs from heaven."

Again, the scoffer would look at this passage and sarcastically state, "Pestilence is no big deal, we've always had outbreaks of diseases."[19] Granted yes, that is true. Though not like we see today! *In the last century alone*, we have seen nothing short of an explosion of *worldwide pestilence* like never before. For instance, even as recently as 1918, we had the infamous Influenza outbreak that killed anywhere from 50-130 million people worldwide.[20] The reason why it spread so fast worldwide was it just so happens that we had for the first time in mankind's history a *global transportation system* that helped transport it like never before, which means Modern Technology is actually helping the spread of pandemics.

Yet, even with a recent example as that, in 1979, the U.S. Surgeon General still made this bold arrogant announcement, "It is time to close the books on infectious diseases." So was he right in his prediction? Absolutely not! By the 1990's, instead of fading out of existence, *infectious diseases had gone ballistic.* We've all heard of the AIDS virus but did you know that millions of people have it worldwide and it's growing like wildfire daily? Did you know that in 1998 the combined wars in Africa killed 200,000 people but AIDS killed *10 times more* than that?[21] Did you also know that 75% of all HIV infections are now being spread via heterosexual contact?[22] But AIDS isn't the half of it. Diseases that were once considered conquered such as tuberculosis, (which they're projecting 10 million might die of it by 2015)[23] malaria, cholera, diphtheria and even the black plague are coming back and they're coming back with a vengeance![24]

But the question is, how can there be such an increase of worldwide pestilence when we're living in the most medically advanced era ever? Well, other than scientific experimentation, biological warfare and population control, it's actually due to *an overuse of antibiotics.* Because we have saturated ourselves with so many antibiotics, *the diseases are now mutating* and becoming resistant to all medication. Now we have SARS, Ebola Virus and the Avian Bird Flu, just to name a few! In fact, one strain of the Avian Bird Flu from Cambodia that just came out has an 85% mortality rate![25] And new ones are cropping up all the time! This has alarmed the medical community so much that they have stated, "The emergence of bacteria strains that cannot be killed by the current arsenal of antibiotics could become a public health threat *worse than AIDS.*"[26]

In fact, at a meeting of the American Association for the Advancement of Science in 1994, scientists there announced that they see us heading towards, *"nothing short of a medical disaster."*[27] The terms they are using today to describe this "medical disaster" are things like, *Super Bugs, Super Flu,* or *Viral Storm* to describe the trend of diseases that are spiraling out of control. In a recent article from the BBC News entitled, "Europe Losing Super Bugs Battle," they stated, "The World Health Organization says the situation has reached a critical point. We could be dealing with the *nightmare scenario* of a worldwide spread of untreatable infections,"[28] like these news reports reveal:

"The fear of a devastating new virus leaping from animals into humans and spreading across the globe is not just the stuff of Hollywood movies like Contagion. In 2002, 8000 cases of SARS came from a virus in bats. In 2009, Swine Flu-the H1N1 virus- originated in pigs and killed 18,000 people. And then there's AIDS. 60 million people have been infected with HIV, the virus that causes AIDS. 25 million have died.

Dr. Richard Besser ABC NEWS Chief Health & Medical Editor: You know David, this is a problem that keeps me up at night, these bugs are getting stronger and there aren't any new drugs coming quickly.

All this incredible connectivity of humans - the flights and the boats - that are connecting all of us. So if one of the new diseases emerges here, it can go everywhere.

Dr. Besser: The most concerning thing to me is that in less than 24 hours after I was in the jungles of Cameroon looking for the next pandemic virus, I was at a baseball stadium in Cooperstown N.Y. watching my son playing Little League, and if I were infected with the next contagion I could have spread it to 5000 people from 22 states.

It would have just gone all over the world so quickly. Imagine a deadly disease carried across continents by millions of free-flying agents. That's the fear factor behind the so called bird-flu.

Dr Marc Siegel: The difference between bird flu and the other health scares is that in this case-the worst case scenario- being influenza, it is worse than in some of the other scares.

Dr Marc Siegel has been investigating the mechanisms of this disease as it progresses through Asia, China, the Pacific Islands, Africa and Europe.

Dr. Siegel: There's been by the way, several outbreaks of avian influenza, highly pathogenic avian influenza in the United States. It just hasn't been talked about much because it's been controlled.

The terms bird flu and avian influenza actually refer to a group of illnesses caused by a large number of different viruses, all of the same species; Influenza Type A. The "A" by the way, does not stand for Avian, meaning birds. One sub-species of Influenza A, caused by the particular virus that scientists label H5N1, has proven particularly deadly among people who handle birds.

It's killed nearly 2/3^{rds} of those who've been diagnosed. Hardest hit, Indonesia and Vietnam. There's currently no natural immunity and no effective vaccine. H5N1 makes so many different animal species sick, over such a wide area, that some health professionals are concerned about a worldwide human *pandemic.*

Dr. Siegel: A recent AP poll said that 35% of the people surveyed felt that they or someone they knew was going to contract this bird flu. The virus's ability to crossover into the human population is by no means unique. All flu originates in birds. Every year, the yearly human flu outbreak was originally, way back when, an avian flu.

Dr. Siegel: Our emphasis should be on trying to control this better in birds, doing more thorough testing of birds, more surveillance in birds, a better strategy for birds and much more money towards looking at this in birds."[29]

As bad as the Avian Bird Flu and all the other Superbugs and Super Viruses spiraling out of control are *right now*, remember what Jesus said. That's nothing compared to what's coming down the pike! All these signs of *pestilence* are just *the beginning of birth pains*, which means the "big one" is yet to come! Here's how the Bible describes it:

Revelation 6:7-8 "When the Lamb opened the fourth seal, I heard the voice of the fourth living creature say, "Come!" I looked, and there before me was a pale horse! Its rider was named Death, and Hades was following close behind him. They were given power over a fourth of the earth to kill by sword, famine and plague, and by the wild beasts of the earth."

The Bible clearly tells us that during the first half of the 7-year Tribulation, one fourth of the earth, approximately *two billion people,* will be dying in one shot. Could that really happen? Yes, it not only can, *it will* and plagues or pestilence will play a big part in that. Which means, if you refuse to accept Jesus Christ as your Personal Lord and Savior right now you are headed for a reality just like that! What's the Biblical rule again? Anything we can conceptualize in our minds pales in comparison to the actual reality. In other words, what you just read is chump change compared to what's really coming to our planet very soon.

IV. Fourth Sign of Worldwide Upheaval - Increase of Wars

Matthew 24:3-8 "As Jesus was sitting on the Mount of Olives, the disciples came to Him privately. Tell us, they said, when will this happen, and what will be the sign of Your coming and of the end of the age? Jesus answered: Watch out that no one deceives you. For many will come in My name, claiming, I am the Christ, and will deceive many. You will hear of wars and rumors of wars, but see to it that you are not alarmed. Such things must happen, but the end is still to come. Nation will rise against nation, and kingdom against kingdom. There will be famines and earthquakes in various places. All these are the beginning of birth pains."

Right after the warning of deceit from Jesus, *the very first sign* He told us, to know we're living in the Last Days was *wars and rumors of wars*, nation against nation and kingdom against kingdom. Once again, the scoffer would look at this passage and sarcastically state, "Wars are no big deal, we've always had wars." Granted yes, that is true. But not like we see today! *In the last century alone*, we have seen nothing short of an explosion of *worldwide wars* like never before.

For instance, more people have been killed by wars in the previous century then at any other time of mankind's history.[30] In fact, prior to WWI, war had never been universal. Yet, not only have we had two of them, but after WWII, which was supposed to be the war to end all wars, there have been *more than 150 major wars*.[31] In 1993 alone there were a record of 29 major wars being fought.[32] However, that record was soon to be broken because two years later in 1995 there were 71.[33] In fact, the whole world is gearing up like never before for more war. Furthermore, speaking of the rise of wars and the armies that go along with them, *in this century alone*, we can see *for the first time in mankind's history* the possible fulfillment of several other passages of Scripture when it comes to Bible Prophecy.

1. The First Passage Coming Alive due to the Increase of Wars – The Gog and Magog Prophecy

Ezekiel 38:1-6 "The word of the LORD came to me: "Son of man, set your face against Gog, of the land of Magog, the chief prince of Meshech and Tubal; prophesy against him and say: 'This is what the Sovereign LORD says: I am against you, O Gog, chief prince of Meshech and Tubal. I will turn you around, put hooks in your jaws and bring you out with your whole army – your horses, your horsemen fully armed, and a great horde with large and small shields, all of them brandishing their swords. Persia, Cush and Put will be with them, all with shields and helmets, also Gomer with all its troops, and Beth Togarmah from the far north with all its troops – the many nations with you."

What you just read is just a portion of the classic passage of Scripture that deals with the Gog and Magog prophecy. It shows how in the Last Days, a confederation of nations will come against Israel, attack Israel and try to annihilate Israel. However, number one, they are the ones who are going to get annihilated by God because He's going to protect Israel. Number two, the key to understanding who these nations are and just how close we are to the fulfillment of this particular Last Days prophecy is seen when you take a historical look at their modern-day identity:

"The eyes of the world are fixed on the Middle East. Every day the papers of all major countries carry lead stories about Israel, Iran, Syria, Lebanon, Egypt, Saudi Arabia, Iraq, Pakistan and other Middle East nations. Further, it is evident to all that the nation of Israel is increasingly under fire both politically and militarily.

The militant Shiites in Iran are openly boasting that they are racing to develop nuclear weapons with the explicit announced goal of wiping Israel from the face of the earth.

Many believe that the Middle East is about to explode and drag the world into one of the most difficult and terrifying conflicts in world history. The prophets in the Old Testament predicted just such a situation will occur. 2,600 years ago, God revealed specific information to the prophet Ezekiel about a group of nations that would come together and attack Israel in the Last Days. Bible scholars refer to this attack as the Ezekiel 38 War. Do we see any evidence that the nations Ezekiel spoke about are threatening Israel today?

The Islamic world is what is going to basically come together and align themselves to try to destroy the Jewish state, with one exception. Russia is mentioned in the book of Ezekiel Chapter 38, in verse 2 it talks about Magog. Gog in the land of Magog. Now Gog would be the person, Magog would be the particular state that it was talking about and according to Biblical geography Magog would be that land mass north of the Caspian and Black Seas, which is Russia today.

Then in verse 2 it says Meshech and Tubal. Down in verse 6 it says Gomer and Togarmah. When traveling in Turkey recently I picked up an ancient Turkish map. In biblical times Turkey was actually divided into four parts – Meshech, Tubal, Gomer and Togarmah. So now we're talking about Russia and Turkey.

There in verse 5, it says Persia. Until 1936 there were three nations we know today that were known as Persia. Those nations we know today are Afghanistan, Pakistan and Iran.

Continue on in verse 5, Ethiopia or Cush in some translations. That would be Ethiopia, Somalia and Sudan.

Then in verse 5 again it says here in my Bible, Libya or maybe in another translation Put. That's modern day Libya.

You also have to coordinate this with Daniel Chapter 11:40-45 where it talks about the King of the North. Earlier in Chapter 11 you find out that area is what we know as Syria today and the King of the South would be Egypt today.

Then going over to the book of Psalms Chapter 83, it talks about a list of nations. It mentions the Ishmaelites. Well that's modern day Saudi Arabia. In verse 5 it talks about Tyre. That's modern day Lebanon.

So now we are seeing a list of Arab nations, with the exception of Russia, who will form this coalition to come against Israel in the Last Days."[34]

So let me get this straight. In the Last Days, Russia will work together with Turkey, Afghanistan, Pakistan, Iran, Ethiopia, Somalia, Sudan, Libya, Syria, Egypt, Saudi Arabia, and Lebanon to destroy Israel? If you put that Biblical truth together with what's going on in the news *right now*, you can clearly see that the Gog and Magog prophecy is on the cusp of being fulfilled for the very first time in mankind's history. Sounds to me like we need to get motivated!

2. The Second Passage Coming Alive due to the Increase of Wars – The Judgment of God on People Coming Against Israel

If you continue in the Gog & Magog prophecy throughout Chapter 38 and on into Chapter 39, you'll see that even though Israel currently only has a population of just under 8 million people, the Muslim nations surrounding them have a combined population of 100's of millions of people, yet God totally wipes Israel's attackers out! Once again the lesson is clear, don't mess with Israel because God's not done with them. But let's get down to some specifics when it comes to the Hand of God coming down upon people who dare mess with His chosen people Israel.

Zechariah 14:12 "This is the plague with which the Lord will strike all the nations that fought against Jerusalem: Their flesh will rot while they are still standing on their feet, their eyes will rot in their sockets, and their tongues will rot in their mouths."

Some people would say that this passage is referring to just some sovereign act of God where He supernaturally causes a plague that instantly removes people's flesh while they're standing. It could be. I personally don't want to be there to find out. However, with the modern weaponry that we see today, what does that graphic description sound like to you? Kind of like a nuclear holocaust doesn't it? It might even be from a biological weapon. But either way, *in this last century alone*, we can get a real good idea can't we? And speaking of nuclear warfare, as of the year 2000, just between the U.S. and Russia, we now have enough nuclear bombs to destroy the planet *six times over!*[35] But that's not the half of it. *Right now*, even small countries all over the world have their own supply of nuclear weapons and it's only increasing each year. Many already believe that it's not a matter of if but when and where the next nuclear strike will be. What happens after that, no one knows for sure, but it sounds like a WWIII or Gog and Magog scenario. Speaking of Gog and Magog, there's another judgment of God after that battle that's being fulfilled before our very eyes, in the following passage.

Ezekiel 39:1,4-5,9-10 "Son of man, prophesy against Gog and say: 'This is what the Sovereign LORD says: I am against you, O Gog, chief prince of Meshech and Tubal. On the mountains of Israel you will fall, you and all your troops and the nations with you. I will give you as food to all kinds of carrion birds and to the wild animals. You will fall in the open field, for I have spoken, declares the Sovereign LORD. Then those who live in the towns of Israel will go out and use the weapons for fuel and burn them up – the small and large shields, the bows and arrows, the war clubs and spears. For seven years they will use them for fuel. They will not need to gather wood from the fields or cut it from the forests, because they will use the weapons for fuel."

As you can clearly see, the nations that come against Israel at the time of the Gog and Magog prophecy are going to lose. They are going to get annihilated by God *and* the Israelites are going to get to burn their weapons for fuel for seven years! First of all, seven years is a long time which tells you how many people came against them and just how many weapons they left behind. But there's a problem. When Ezekiel wrote this prophecy, the weapons of his day, bows, arrows, clubs, shields and spears were made of wood so you could expect to burn them. However, today our weapons are made of metal. You can't burn them like weapons of old that were made of wood. So how are you going to fulfill this passage? Well, it just so happens that Russia, who is arming many of these nations in this prophecy, is using a new substance in their weapons called *lignostone*. And lignostone, "is a special kind of wood that's stronger than steel, is very elastic and it burns better than coal."[36] So here's the point. You make your weapons out of that stuff, lignostone, and it's not only going to burn, but it's going to burn really well...you know, make for a great fuel for seven years! Isn't that wild? Every aspect of this prophecy is coming to pass!

3. The Third Passage Coming Alive Due to the Increase of Wars – The 200 Million Man Army

Revelation 9:15-16 "And the four angels who had been prepared for this hour and day and month and year were turned loose to kill one-third of all the people on earth. They led an army of 200 million mounted troops – I heard an announcement of how many there were."

Some would say that this passage is just referring to a demonic host of 200 million that will be released to kill 1/3 of mankind. It could be. I personally don't want to be there to find out. However, with the explosion of the world population, can you guess just who it is that has *already gone on record* stating they have a literal 200-million-man army? That's right! China.[37] In fact, one columnist wrote that an interesting side-effect of our recent economic crash is "80% of China's military build-up is being funded by the interest on the debt America owes the Chinese communist government."[38] Then another interesting business venture by China could very well be fulfilling this prophecy.

Revelation 16:12,14 "The sixth angel poured out his bowl on the great river Euphrates, and its water was dried up to prepare the way for the kings from the East...to gather them for the battle on the great day of God Almighty."

Here we see the Kings of the East, people like China, who are going to be gathered in the Last Days for the Battle of Armageddon that takes place in the Valley of Megiddo outside of Jerusalem. To get there, they're going to be crossing the River Euphrates, which runs through Turkey, Iraq, Syria, etc. Here's the point. Can anyone guess who's building a giant high-speed railroad system *right now* in that area? China! I quote, "China is signing a $2 billion dollar deal to build a railway line in Iran, in the first step of a wider plan, to tie the Middle East and Central Asia to Beijing. That line would give the central Asian states vital access to Iran's port of Chahbahar on the shores of the Persian Gulf, and could also eventually give China a vital overland freight route to Europe."[39] And dare I say, it would also give them a fast, cheap and efficient way to make it right on time for the Battle of Armageddon!

4. The Fourth Passage Coming Alive Due to the Increase of Wars – The Running into Mountains for Protection

Revelation 6:12-17 "I watched as he opened the sixth seal. There was a great earthquake. The sun turned black like sackcloth made of goat hair, the whole moon turned blood red, and the stars in the sky fell to earth, as late figs drop from a fig tree when shaken by a strong wind. The sky receded like a scroll, rolling up, and every mountain and island was removed from its place. Then the kings of the earth, the princes, the generals, the rich, the mighty, and every slave and every free man hid in caves and among the rocks of the mountains. They called to the mountains and the rocks, "Fall on us and hide us from the face of him who sits on the throne and from the wrath of the Lamb! For the great day of their wrath has come, and who can stand?"

So here we see that the people in the 7-year Tribulation are actually going to try to hide from the wrath of God, which is impossible, but they still try anyway. The point is they're going to try to hide of all places *in the mountains, the caves* and *among the rocks*. What's wild is that little do people know that thanks to the rise of wars and the military inventions that come along with them, *for the first time in mankind's history* we have the ability to do just that, try to hide away in mountains. They're called D.U.M.B's and yes it's dumb to try to hide away from God's wrath, but that's not what it stands for. It's an acronym that stands for Deep Underground Military Bases and they're all over the world, just like the text says:

"D.U.M.B.'s or Deep Underground Military Bases are not only reported to be in various places throughout the United States, but literally all over the world by different countries. They are made possible thanks in part to massive high-powered tunnel boring machines.

In fact, some of them are reported to actually be 'nuclear powered' and can not only literally 'melt' solid rock leaving behind glass-like walls, but they

can also drill a tunnel seven miles long in just one day. Due to these
technological abilities, some of these underground facilities are reported to be 42
levels deep and are between 2.66 and 4.25 cubic miles in size. They are basically
large whole cities underground. Other reports say that they are connected by
high-speed magneto-leviton trains that have speeds up to Mach 2.

As to why these bases are being built underground; there are many
different explanations. One report says that most of them are being built away
from geotectonic areas because they know that catastrophe is coming."[40]

You can run and hide all you want from God, even in those amazing
technological accommodations, but God's got a bunker buster that'll blow even
that away. It's called His wrath! One breath from His nostrils and you're toast no
matter how far you try to hide underground! There's only one way to escape it.
It's through Jesus. Only He can save you from the wrath to come. But as you
guys can see, our world is being *shot to pieces* like never before. Yes, we may
have always had wars, but nothing like we see today. Exactly like the Bible said
would happen, in the Last Days.

V. Fifth Sign of Worldwide Upheaval - Increase of Signs in the Sky

Luke 21:7,10-11 "Teacher," they asked, "when will these things happen? And
what will be the sign that they are about to take place?" Then He said to them:
"Nation will rise against nation, and kingdom against kingdom. There will be
great earthquakes, famines and pestilences in various places, and fearful events
and great signs from heaven."

Yet another sign Jesus gives us as an indicator we're living in the Last
Days is when all of a sudden you see an increase of weird things or signs going
on in the sky or atmosphere. So that's the question. "Do we see any signs of
weird things going on in the sky or our atmosphere, showing us that the return of
Jesus Christ is imminent?" Yes! Just a few!

1. The First Sign from the Heavens – The Rise of Solar Activity

Revelation 16:1,8-9 "Then I heard a loud voice from the temple saying to the
seven angels, 'Go, pour out the seven bowls of God's wrath on the earth.' The
fourth angel poured out his bowl on the sun, and the sun was given power to
scorch people with fire. They were seared by the intense heat and they cursed the

name of God, who had control over these plagues, but they refused to repent and glorify Him."

Here we see that in the second half of the 7-year Tribulation the *sun* is going to become so hot that people across the planet are going to literally get seared and curse the Name of God. So that's the question, "Do we see any *signs in the sky* that *the sun* is going to get hotter anytime soon?" Yes! In fact, all kinds of weird things are going on with the sun recently! For instance, there have been massive mega solar flares, huge massive sunspots, a solar tornado on the sun's surface that was 125,000 miles high, which is about half the distance between the earth and the moon, as well as all kinds of solar storms going off on the sun that experts are saying are getting ready to, "Hit the earth with the force of 100 million hydrogen bombs."[41] Clearly something's going on and the experts are saying, "It's not looking good. It's going to mess up the planet," as this report from a few years ago declares:

Charles Payne: *Should we be worried about increasing solar activity? Michio Kaku is here. Professor, should we be worried about these flare ups or is it when we're talking about it this morning, we all agreed, it has this Y2K feeling, like it could happen, but if it doesn't, we're going to spend a lot of money for nothing.*

Michio Kaku: *Well we had a wakeup call just two weeks ago, giant Auroras – Northern Lights as far as Michigan and Wisconsin and that's a warm up. A warm up for 2012-2013 when we have the sun's spot cycle. Every 11 years the North Pole and the South Pole flip, releasing a burst of radiation BUT every 100 years or so a monster tsunami from the sun emerges, which could literally cause trillions of dollars in property damage. It could paralyze the economy of the planet earth.*

Guest Panelist: *But not from a physical perspective.*

Michio Kaku: *Physical perspective yes. In 1859 we had a gigantic solar storm, which knocked out telegraph wires back then, 150 years ago. If that had happened today, it would knock out almost all our satellites, knock out power stations, there would be food riots around the country because refrigeration would stop, airplanes would probably crash without radar. It would paralyze the planet earth."[42]*

Sounds to me like if you're paying attention to the news, the experts are clearly declaring that the sun is capable and getting ready to do something pretty horrible. Again, remember the Biblical rule, as bad as that is, as bad as that damage he said would happen as a result of the sun flaring up, it's still nothing compared to what is to come. Jesus says it's just a birth pain, a tiny one compared to what is getting ready to be unleashed on the planet. That's precisely why He's given us these signs in the sky to show us it's getting close and we better get ready.

2. The Second Sign from the Heavens – The Rise of an Asteroid Impact

Revelation 8:2,8-9 "And I saw the seven angels who stand before God, and to them were given seven trumpets. The second angel sounded his trumpet, and something like a huge mountain, all ablaze, was thrown into the sea. A third of the sea turned into blood, a third of the living creatures in the sea died, and a third of the ships were destroyed."

Now we see prior to the sun getting turned up in the last half of the 7-year Tribulation that another event in the sky takes place. An *asteroid*, i.e. *a huge mountain all ablaze*, is thrown into the sea. So that's the question, "Do we see any sign in the skies that we're under any threat of a giant asteroid smashing into the earth any time soon?" Yes! In fact, there's been all kinds of warnings for many years. Even Hollywood's getting in on the act by making all kinds of movies about this looming danger. Scientists are saying it's not just a matter of "if" but "when" we get struck by an asteroid and the damage they say would be absolutely inconceivable. Quote, "If a space rock were to hit the earth the damage would be devastating. The amount of destruction would depend if it hit land or ocean, (and our text says it's going to hit the ocean). Regardless of the impact location, loss of human, animal, and plant life on a grand scale would take place, particularly if it impacted a big population area." [43] "The shockwaves from that would create huge tsunami waves, destroying both coastlines and inland areas,"[43] not to mention all the ships in the surrounding area, like 1/3rd of the ships from around the world.

In fact, I believe God's given us a birth pain view of this Last Days tsunami caused by an asteroid impact, with the 2011 tsunami event in Japan. Let's take a look at what this "birth pain" did to the ships and inland areas:

"The March 2011 tsunami in Japan sent 5 million tons of debris into the Pacific Ocean. While about 70 percent of it sank off shore, more than a million tons is

still floating east – everything from ghost trawlers to lost Harley Davidsons.

The tsunami was caused by a 9.0 magnitude earthquake that was the largest earthquake to hit Japan in recorded history and the seventh biggest earthquake in the world since records have been kept.

Male reporter commenting from helicopter footage: *'Images even more terrifying emerge from the same Pacific coasts. The huge tide appears to just eat everything in its path. Look at the road. Look how tiny the cars are. (As tsunami wave engulfs the roadway) One of the worst earthquakes ever in Japanese history. In fact, it's the 7th most powerful earthquake in history, none of the other six were in areas as populated as this.'*

Female reporter responds: *'Look at these pictures, we can see something is ablaze there on the ground as this very strange wave of mud and debris with boats included and cars and all sorts of things. It's when you see something like this unfold before your very eyes that you get the idea that there's nowhere to run when you have something like that coming so fast towards you. Of course it appears to be very slow when you're looking from above but if you're on the ground and that is moving at such a fast speed, you can see the boat there, unbelievable!'*

Hundreds of flights to Japan were cancelled due to the earthquake and tsunami, affecting many people. As of April 8th, 2011 the Japanese National Police Agency has officially confirmed 12,915 deaths, 4,711 injured, and 14,921 people missing across eighteen prefectures, as well as over 125,000 buildings damaged or destroyed.

The earthquake started a tsunami warning for Japan's Pacific coast and other countries, including New Zealand, Australia, Russia, Guam, Philippines, Indonesia, Papua New Guinea, Nauru, Hawaii, Northern Marianas and Taiwan. The tsunami warning issued by Japan was the most serious on its warning scale.

Kyodo news agency has reported a four-meter-high tsunami hit with waves carrying buildings and cars along as they traveled inland. In some areas the waves reached 10 km inland. In fact, a wave two meters (6.5 feet) high reached California, after traveling across the Pacific Ocean at a speed of 500 kilometers (310 miles) per hour. A man in California was drowned after being swept into the ocean while trying to take a photograph of the tsunami wave.

In response to the great disaster, Emperor Akihito directly addressed his subjects in a television broadcast. This was the first time any emperor used television in this way."⁴⁴

Again, keep in mind the Biblical rule and our context. What did Jesus say? As bad as what you just read really was, it was just a *birth pain*, a tiny one compared to what's coming. One day, an asteroid is going to hit the earth that is so big, it's not just going to mess up one tiny area in one little country, but it's going to wipe out 1/3ʳᵈ of the sea creatures and destroy 1/3ʳᵈ of the ships around the world.

VI. Sixth Sign of Worldwide Upheaval - Increase of Volcanic Activity

Revelation 6:12-14 "I watched as he opened the sixth seal. There was a great earthquake. The sun turned black like sackcloth made of goat hair, the whole moon turned blood red, and the stars in the sky fell to earth, as late figs drop from a fig tree when shaken by a strong wind. The sky receded like a scroll, rolling up, and every mountain and island was removed from its place."

Now, we've already seen this passage a couple of times, but I want to point out another item that we skipped over, and that is this. Notice what happened right after this great earthquake which was mentioned there occurred. The *sun turned black like sackcloth* and the *moon turned blood red*. In other words, after this earthquake, the sun is going to become darkened during the daytime and at night the moon is going to take on a reddish hue. So here's the point. Many experts believe this passage is to be taken literally because *for the first time in mankind's history*, thanks to the science of seismology, we now know this fits the perfect description of an after-effect of an earthquake. It's called a **Volcanic Eruption**!⁴⁵ We now know that when a volcano erupts, it spews forth massive amounts, literally tons of volcanic ash into the air. This in turn darkens the sunlight, almost like something's covering it like maybe sackcloth *and* at night the moon takes on a reddish color. Where have I heard that before? It fits the text perfectly! Mystery solved!

So that's the question. "Do we see any signs of Volcanic Activity increasing on the planet to show us we're getting closer to this giant one going off in the 7-year Tribulation?" Yes! In fact, if you've been paying attention to the news, *volcanoes are on the rise all over the world*! There's been the recent ones in Iceland, Costa Rica and Ecuador, that sort of made the news, but that's the tip of the iceberg. What they haven't been telling you is there's all kinds of volcanoes going off *right now* all over the world in Europe, Africa, Central America, the Caribbean, the Pacific Islands, Indonesia, Japan, South America, the Philippines, and even in Antarctica![46]

In fact, one of big ones that's supposed to be going off anytime now here in the United States, is the infamous Yellowstone Caldera or *Super Volcano*, that experts are saying, "Would explode with a force 1,000 times more powerful than Mount St. Helens, spewing forth lava and ash into the sky that would fan out and dump a layer of toxic air and ash 10 feet deep up to 1,000 miles away, turning 2/3rds of the U.S. into an uninhabitable wasteland, forcing millions to flee."[47] That almost sounds like that Volcano in Revelation Chapter 6! In fact, it might be much closer than many people realize, or want to admit, as this article shares:

"The oldest, most famous national park in the United States sits squarely atop one of the biggest volcanoes on Earth. Yellowstone's volcano is not extinct. To an unsettling degree, it is very much alive.

There are volcanoes, and then there are supervolcanoes. The latter have no agreed-on definition—the term was popularized in a BBC documentary in 2000—but some scientists use it to describe explosions of exceptional violence and volume.

The U.S. Geological Survey applies the term to any eruption ejecting more than 1,000 cubic kilometers (240 cubic miles) of pumice and ash in a single event— more than 50 times the size of the infamous Krakatau eruption of 1883, which killed more than 36,000 people.

Volcanoes form mountains; supervolcanoes erase them. Volcanoes kill plants and animals for miles around; supervolcanoes threaten whole species with extinction by changing the climate across the entire planet.

No supervolcano has erupted in recorded human history, but geologists have pieced together what an explosion must have been like. First, a plume of heat wells up from deep within the planet and melts rock just beneath the crust of the Earth, creating a vast chamber filled with a pressurized mix of magma, semisolid rock, and dissolved water vapor, carbon dioxide, and other gases.

As additional magma accumulates in the chamber over thousands of years, the land above begins to dome upward by inches. Fractures open along the dome's edges, as if burglars were sawing a hole from beneath a wooden floor. When the pressure in the magma chamber is released through the fractures, the dissolved gases suddenly explode in a massive, runaway reaction.

'It's like 'opening the Coke bottle after you've shaken it,' says Bob Christiansen, a U.S. Geological Survey scientist who pioneered research on the Yellowstone volcano in the 1960s. With the magma chamber emptied, the surface collapses. The entire domed region simply falls into the planet, as though the Earth were consuming itself. Left behind is a giant caldera, from the Spanish word for 'cauldron.'

The 'hot spot' responsible for the Yellowstone caldera is rooted deep in the Earth, and the tectonic plate above it is moving southwest, ghostly calderas from the more ancient explosions are strung out like a series of gigantic beads across southern Idaho and into Oregon and Nevada, the subsequent lava flows forming the eerie moonscapes of the Snake River Plain.

The last three super-eruptions have been in Yellowstone itself. The most recent was a thousand times the size of the Mount St. Helens eruption in 1980, which killed 57 people in Washington.

But numbers do not capture the full scope of the mayhem. Scientists calculate that the pillar of ash from the Yellowstone explosion rose some 100,000 feet, leaving a layer of debris across the West all the way to the Gulf of Mexico.

Pyroclastic flows – dense, lethal fogs of ash, rocks, and gas, superheated to 1,470 degrees Fahrenheit – rolled across the landscape in towering gray clouds.

The clouds filled entire valleys with hundreds of feet of material so hot and heavy that it welded itself like asphalt across the once verdant landscape. And this wasn't even Yellowstone's most violent moment.

An eruption was more than twice as strong, leaving a hole in the ground the size of Rhode Island. In between, was a smaller but still devastating eruption. Each time, the whole planet would have felt the effects.

Gases rising high into the stratosphere would have mixed with water vapor to create a thin haze of sulfate aerosols that dimmed sunlight, potentially plunging the Earth into years of 'volcanic winter.'

For all their violence, the supervolcanoes have left little behind beyond a faintly perceptible sense of absence. The Yellowstone caldera has been eroded, filled in with lava flows and ash from smaller eruptions and smoothed by glaciers.

Peaceful forests cover any lingering scars. The combined effect makes it almost impossible to detect, unless you've got a good eye, or a geologist whispering in your ear.

'You're seeing two-thirds of the entire caldera,' says Bob Smith. 'The size is so immense that people don't appreciate it.' Smith is a University of Utah geophysicist and a prominent expert on the supervolcano at Yellowstone.

We're standing atop Lake Butte, an overlook at the east end of Yellowstone Lake, one of the best places to see the caldera. But I don't see it. I can see the lake spread out for miles beneath us and a few little hills to the north – old lava domes.

But I can't follow the caldera rim visually because much of it is beneath the lake and because of the sheer scale of the thing – roughly 45 miles across. I see only distant mountains on the horizon on either side and between them, to the west, the 'unmountains,' the emptiness where the land swallowed itself in the course of a few days.

The park roils with geysers, fumaroles, mud volcanoes, and other hydrothermal activity. Half the geysers on the planet are in Yellowstone. The hydrothermal features change constantly in temperature and behavior, with new ones popping up in the forests, spewing clouds of steam visible from airplanes, exuding vapors that have been known to kill bison on the spot.

In spite of this 'most violent gaseous ebullition,' the volcano beneath Yellowstone was long thought to be extinct, or at least in its dying days. Indeed, after federal surveys in the late 19th century, the volcanic nature of Yellowstone received little scientific scrutiny for decades.

Then in the late 1950s, a young Harvard graduate student, Francis 'Joe' Boyd, became intrigued by the presence of a welded tuff – a thick layer of heated and compacted ash, which he realized was a sign of pyroclastic flows from an explosive, geologically recent eruption.

In 1965 Bob Christiansen found a second distinct welded tuff; the next year he and his colleagues identified a third. They determined that the three tuffs were the result of three distinct eruptions. Each created a giant caldera, with the most recent eruption largely burying signs of the previous two.

Then one day in 1973, Bob Smith and a colleague were doing some work on Peale Island, in the South Arm of Yellowstone Lake, when Smith noticed something odd: Some trees along the shoreline were partially submerged and dying.

He had worked in the area back in 1956 and was planning to use the same boat dock as on the earlier trip. But the dock was also inundated. What was going on?

Intrigued, Smith set out to resurvey benchmarks that park workers had placed on various roads throughout the park beginning in 1923. His survey revealed that the Hayden Valley, which sits atop the caldera to the north of the lake, had risen by some 30 inches over the intervening decades.

But the lower end of the lake hadn't risen at all. In effect, the north end of the lake had risen and tipped water down into the southern end. The ground was doming. The volcano was alive.

Smith published his results in 1979, referring in interviews to Yellowstone as 'the living, breathing caldera.'

Then in 1985, heralded by a 'swarm' of mostly tiny earthquakes, the terrain subsided again. Smith modified his metaphor: Yellowstone was now the 'living, breathing, shaking caldera.'

In the years since, Smith and his colleagues have used every trick they can devise to 'see' beneath the park. Gradually, the proportions and potential of the subterranean volcanic system have emerged.

At the shallowest level, surface water percolates several miles into the crust, is heated, and boils back up, supplying the geysers and fumaroles. About five to seven miles deep is the top of the magma chamber, a reservoir of partially melted rock roughly 30 miles wide.

Basaltic magma is trapped inside the chamber by denser, overlying rhyolitic magma, which floats on top of the liquid basalt like cream on milk.

By looking at the way sound waves created by earthquakes propagate through subsurface rock of varying densities, the scientists have discovered that the magma chamber is fed by a gigantic plume of hot rock, rising from the Earth's upper mantle, tilted downward to the northwest by 60 degrees, its base perhaps 400 miles below the surface.

When the plume pumps more heat into the chamber, the land heaves upward. Small earthquakes allow hydrothermal fluids to escape to the surface, easing the pressure inside the chamber, which causes the ground to subside again.

After the 1985 earthquake swarm, Yellowstone fell eight inches over the course of a decade or so. Then it rose again, faster this time. Since 2004, portions of the caldera have surged upward at a rate of nearly three inches a year, much faster than any uplift since close observations began in the 1970s.

The surface continues to rise despite an 11-day earthquake swarm that began late in 2008, causing a flurry of apocalyptic rumors on the Internet.

'We call this a caldera at unrest,' Smith says. 'The net effect over many cycles is to finally get enough magma to erupt. And we don't know what those cycles are.'

So, the colossal question: Is it going to blow again? Some kind of eruption – perhaps a modest one like Mount Pinatubo's in the Philippines, which killed 800 people in 1991 – is highly likely at some point.

The odds of a full, caldera-forming eruption – a cataclysm that could kill untold thousands of people and plunge the Earth into a volcanic winter – are anyone's guess; it could happen in our lifetimes."[48]

Now that's just *one* Super Volcano going off. As horrible as that is, taking two-thirds of the U.S. with it, the Bible says that's chump change compared to what's coming! Again, remember, the Biblical rule. Anything we can dream up in a movie screen pales in comparison to the actual reality. Especially when you put it together with another piece of information we now know thanks to modern seismology. The following is a global map of all the *current active volcanoes* that we know exist around the planet. Notice where the USGS has them positioned:

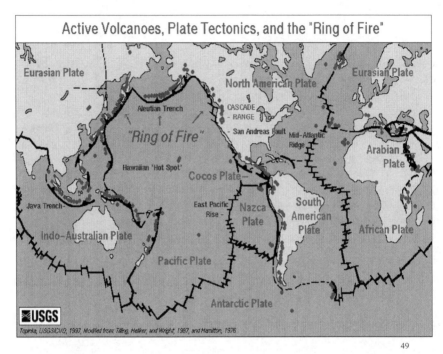

As you can see, all the dots, the volcanoes, are lined up *right on top of all the fault lines around the earth.* So now, *for the first time in mankind's history,* guess what we can see? When that earthquake goes off in Revelation Chapter 6, the one that removes every mountain and island from their place, *all those fault lines are going to get adjusted,* which will then proceed to trigger off not just one volcano, but most likely *all those volcanoes are all going to go off all at the same time all over the world*! What would that do? I bet it would cause, "the sun to turn black like sackcloth and the moon turn blood red," all over the planet! We are getting so close it's not even funny!

VII. Seventh Sign of Worldwide Upheaval - Increase of Global Catastrophes

Joel 2:30-31 "I will show wonders in the heavens and on the earth, blood and fire and billows of smoke. The sun will be turned to darkness and the moon to blood before the coming of the great and dreadful day of the LORD."

In other words, you don't want to be there! Here we see in this text that God will not only show us signs *in the sky* that He's getting ready to judge us, but He's also going to give us signs *on the earth*. So that's the question, "Do we see any signs that the earth is also going through some weird aberrant behavior letting us know that God's getting ready to judge us real soon? Yes!

1. The First Sign of Global Earth Catastrophes – The Rise of Weird Weather

Job 37:5-6 "God's voice is glorious in the thunder. We cannot comprehend the greatness of his power. He directs the snow to fall on the earth and tells the rain to pour down."

According to the Bible, I think it's pretty obvious Who in the world is the ultimate weatherman? It's not mother nature, it's Almighty God! He's the One in control over the *weather*, and it's not just the *rain* and *snow*. Let's look at some other weather He's also controlled in the past.[50]

1. Caused the world to FLOOD: Genesis 7
2. Caused FIRE from heaven upon the cities: Genesis 19
3. Caused plagues of HAIL, THUNDER and LIGHTNING in Egypt: Exodus 9
4. Caused the WIND to divide the Red Sea: Exodus 14
5. Caused the SUN to stand still: Joshua 10
6. Caused DEW to form on Gideon's fleece: Judges 6
7. Caused a WHIRLWIND to carry Elijah to heaven: 2 Kings 2
8. Caused RAIN in answer to Samuel's prayer: 1 Samuel 12
9. Caused a STORM to confuse the Philistine army: 1 Samuel 7
10. Caused DARKNESS at the crucifixion: Matthew 27

The reason why I bring this up is because most people, even Christians, think when it comes to the weather, it's just some naturalistic cause or explanation. They have no idea that it might actually be a *wakeup call* from Almighty God! He controls the weather and the Bible says, sometimes He uses it for Judgment. So that's the question. "Do we see any signs of *weird weather* on planet earth lately that might very well be a wakeup call from God, letting us know His Judgment is just around the corner? Yes! Scientists are not only *right now*, "Warning the world to prepare for Extreme Weather," but listen to this, "2010 through 2011 brought extreme weather not only to the United States but to the entire world. Record-setting rain triggered massive floods and mudslides from Australia to Mexico; bulb-shattering blizzards brought minus temps across most of North America." Another person stated, "Earthquakes, heat waves, floods, super typhoons, blizzards, landslides, and droughts, killed at least ¼ million people in 2010 alone – the deadliest year in more than a generation. In fact, more people have been killed worldwide by natural disasters *in 2010 alone* than have been killed in terrorism attacks in the past 40 years combined."[51] That's still the tip of the iceberg:

"The global impact of natural disasters took a turn for the worse in 2010 with an increase in fatalities and economic damage, according to a report released Tuesday. There were 385 natural disasters worldwide in 2010 alone that killed more than 297,000 people, affected over 217 million others and caused $123.9 billion dollars in economic damages, according to the Annual Disaster Statistical Review. The number of victims increased from 198.7 million in 2009 to 217.3 million in 2010. In fact, just two of the mega-disasters that occurred in 2010 made it the deadliest year in at least two decades."

Lest you think this really isn't a trend of things getting worse, you need to observe the following statistics:

- In 2009, there were 1,146 tornadoes in the United States.
- In 2010, there were 1,282 tornadoes in the United States.
- In 2011, there were 1,691 tornadoes in the United States.

Believe it or not, as shocking as those statistics on the rise of tornadoes were, the weather is projected to get even worse as this next report shows:

"In just the first half of 2011, the world experienced so many natural disasters that it was the most expensive year ever for property damage.

The year 2011 began with a flood in Australia so vast it turned an area almost twice as large as Texas into a disaster zone.

The first half of 2011 saw thousands of lives lost to natural disasters and made it the most expensive on record in terms of property damage.

In January, earthquakes hit Argentina, Chile, Iran, Pakistan, Tajikistan and Tonga. In February, they hit Burma, the Pacific Islands and the big one, in Christchurch, New Zealand.

The quake struck at midday. Buildings were toppled. Scores were buried under rubble and 181 died. Survivors who crawled from collapsed office buildings were stunned.

One woman who appeared dazed, said of her office building, 'It just came down. Like, right down.'

The monster earthquake of 2011 in Japan was like something out of a science fiction movie. From 20 miles under the surface of the Pacific, the quake created a wall of water 130 feet high that traveled six miles inland, causing cars and boats to bob like toys.

It was a quake so powerful it moved the island of Honshu eight feet. More than 15,000 people died and nearly 5,000 are still missing.

Then in a terrible twist, after the quake knocked out power at the Fukushima nuclear plant, the tsunami washed out its backup generators, the last line of defense against overheating. It would be the world's first triple meltdown, spreading radiation over a wide area.

It was the worst disaster to afflict Japan since World War II.

The world was still in shock when the southern and eastern United States experienced the worst rash of tornadoes in recorded weather history. The 2011 'Super Outbreak' included four EF-5 tornadoes, and led to almost 350 deaths and more than $6 billion in insured losses.

Then just weeks later on a Sunday afternoon in May, a mile-wide multiple vortex EF-5 tornado plowed through Joplin, Mo., obliterating parts of the city, killing 159 people and causing an estimated $2 billion in insured losses.

The insurance industry was left reeling. Americans were in shock.

Vinson Synan, author of 19 books and the dean emeritus at Regent University in Virginia Beach, Va., says the unprecedented string of calamities is forcing many Americans to ask, 'Why?'

'It's a sobering thing, for even natural man to face up to natural disasters that don't make any sense at all. And to hit randomly in the world, and may hit you,' Synan said. 'And the question, in the back of their minds – 'What does this mean?'

'So I think it brings people to question the ultimate end of everything,' he explained.

And unfortunately, the world's worst disasters could still be ahead, like a category five hurricane making a direct hit on a large American city.

Experts have studied other disaster scenarios that many Americans do not know about. For example, geologists have warned that heavy rains on Mount Rainer in Washington State could cause a deadly 40-mile mudslide moving at 60 mph, filled with rocks and trees.

Some fear the collapse of the giant volcanic mountain Cumbre Vieja in the Canary Islands could send an 80-foot high tsunami slamming into the east coast of the United States at 600 mph.

And along the Mississippi, a catastrophic quake at the giant new Madrid fault would cause utter devastation to America's heartland, changing the course of the mighty Mississippi, and causing the ground to roll like the ocean, as it did in 1811 and 1812.

Many Americans might think they live in one of the safest periods in world history. But do they? Why have so many natural disasters struck the planet in recent years, and what does it mean?

'It brings people to question the ultimate end of everything. Even the natural man who doesn't even know God, is saying 'Something bad is happening,' It's getting worse and worse,' Synan told CBN News." [52]

In fact, lest you think this is just a flash in the pan, observe the following chart that catalogues the clear rise of Natural Disasters:

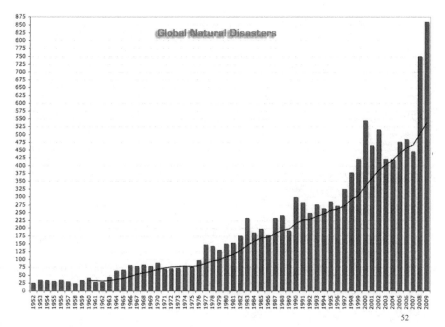

52

I think the point is obvious. God's trying to get our attention. In fact, it's almost like He's trying to send us a signal that He's not too pleased with us, and His judgment is just around the corner.

2. The Second Sign of Global Earth Catastrophes - The Rise of Plagues

The **first plague** that very well could be a sign of God's Judgment coming upon us is **The Rise of Animal Deaths**.

Exodus 9:1-3,5-6 "Then the LORD said to Moses, Go to Pharaoh and say to him, 'This is what the LORD, the God of the Hebrews, says: Let my people go, so that they may worship me. If you refuse to let them go and continue to hold them back, the hand of the LORD will bring a terrible plague on your livestock in the field – on your horses and donkeys and camels and on your cattle and sheep and goats. The LORD set a time and said, Tomorrow the LORD will do this in the land. And the next day the LORD did it: All the livestock of the Egyptians died."

I think it's pretty apparent in the above text that one of the things God does as an act of His judgment; He'll judge you by taking out your animals. Now the point is, I don't know if you've noticed or not, but that's exactly what's going on *right now* all over the world! There's a ton of *weird mass animal deaths* all over the world and it makes you wonder, is this a sign from God that He's about to judge us? Here's the ominous report:

"As you're likely aware, there's been a pretty bizarre spate of mass animal deaths reported around the world. First, it was the thousands of birds that fell from the sky in Arkansas on New Year's Eve. Some 100,000 fish also washed up on the shores of a river 100 miles away. Birds fell from the sky in Louisiana and Kentucky, too. Two million fish washed up dead in Chesapeake Bay. 50 birds fell from the sky in Sweden. 100 tons of fish washed ashore in Brazil. 40,000 crabs were found dead in England.

All of this carnage has left people around the world wondering the same thing: What is going on? Unfortunately, there's no good answer."

But once again, that's just the tip of the iceberg. It's not just birds dying off, falling from the sky, it's all kinds of animals dying off, all over the planet, all at the same time, in mass quantities. In fact, here's a list of animal deaths from around the world that occurred in just one month's time:

- Hundreds of dead seals washed ashore in Canada
- 200 cows found dead in Wisconsin
- 100 dead carp found in U.K.
- 730 African grey parrots died during flight
- 300 grackles found dead on a highway in Alabama
- Thousands of gizzard shad fish washed up near Chicago
- Countless fish found dead in U.K. brook
- 100 starlings found dead on highway in California
- Dozens of dead starlings turn up in Romania, blamed on "drunkenness"
- More than 1,000 dead turtle doves found in Italy
- 40,000+ dead Devil crabs washed ashore in the U.K.
- Hundreds of dead birds fall to ground in Kentucky
- Hundreds of dead birds found on highway in Texas
- Hundreds of dead snapper washed up on New Zealand beaches
- Up to 100 jackdaw birds found dead in Sweden
- Several dead manatees found dead on Florida coast
- Thousands of dead fish washed up on creek bank in Florida

- Hundreds of dead fish found on St. Clair River in Canada
- Hundreds of blackbirds dead in Louisiana
- Thousands of dead octopuses washed ashore on Portugal beach
- Two million dead fish washed up in Chesapeake Bay, MD
- 100 tons of dead fish washed ashore in Brazil
- 100,000+ dead drum fish found in Arkansas river
- 5,000+ birds found dead in Arkansas
- 70 bats found dead in Tucson, AZ
- Scores of dead fish washed ashore in a lake in Haiti
- Hundreds of dead starfish, jellyfish washed ashore in South Carolina
- Ten tons of mostly dead fish found in fishing net in New Zealand
- 100+ dead pelicans drop in North Carolina, unknown causes
- Thousands of dead fish turned up in bay in Philippines
- Dead fish washed ashore at lake beach in Indiana
- Thousands of dead fish washed ashore on Florida beach
- Thousands of dead barramundi fish washed up in Australia[53]

It's almost like God's trying to give us a wakeup call. What did the above text say? "If you don't turn around, if you don't do what I say, Egypt, and stop rebelling against Me, I'm going to take out your livestock!" What more does God have to do? We're living in the Last Days and we need to get right with Him *now*!

The **second plague** sent by God that very well could be a sign His judgment is getting ready to come upon us is **The Rise of Insects**.

Exodus 8:16,21 and 10:12 "Then the LORD said to Moses, Tell Aaron, Stretch out your staff and strike the dust of the ground,' and throughout the land of Egypt the dust will become gnats. If you do not let my people go, I will send swarms of flies on you and your officials, on your people and into your houses. And the LORD said to Moses, Stretch out your hand over Egypt so that locusts will swarm over the land and devour everything growing in the fields."

Now again, I think it's pretty clear that when God wants to judge a nation, He'll not only take down their livestock, but He'll also flood them with *insects*. Massive invasions of them! So that's the question. "Do we see any signs of *massive insect invasions* across the world as a sign that God is getting ready to judge us just like He did with Egypt? Yes! Here's the proof:

"Of all things, believe it or not, a massive stink bug invasion is occurring in 29 states of the U.S. and is spreading at an alarming rate. These dime-sized brown bugs are crawling into homes over windowsills, through door crevices and between attic vents in such numbers that homeowners talk about drowning them in jars of soapy water, suffocating them in plastic bags or even burning them with propane torches. Get used to it, experts say – the invasion is only going to get worse.

And that's because they have no natural predators in the United States and pesticides don't work effectively. In fact one person commented on how bad it is, 'I literally have made homemade chili and had to throw it out because there were stink bugs in it.' In fact, they went on to say, 'I have had people refuse to come over for dinner because they knew about my stink bug problem.'" [54]

Another article shared how another insect invasion of saltmarsh caterpillars was so bad in the South that a farmer used a roller to crush the worms crawling across a road between his fields, causing a slick road surface, and not just saltmarsh caterpillars, but grasshoppers, sugar cane beetles and armyworms are showing up in high numbers in the South which caused one entomologist to report, 'This year's insect situation is getting weirder and weirder.' [54]

In fact, researchers are now saying that three more insect invasions are getting ready to converge on the South. That is the Japanese beetle, emerald ash borer and the gypsy moth. Complete infestation is expected to occur within the next 2 to 25 years. [54]

Now keep in mind, this is occurring not just in the United States but in various places all around the world. Just like in the Biblical accounts, people are experiencing the worst locust invasion they've seen in decades:

"A plague of biblical proportions, as locusts invade South Wales in Australia. The swarms could cost billions in Aussie dollars in damage to the agriculture industry. Some have predicted that the area affected could be the size of Spain."

"Swarms of locusts, that are once again inundating parts of the state. Hundreds of thousands of the insects are eating through paddocks and even farmhouse doors.

Sarah Abo: 'A blanket of locusts covering a farmhouse in the state's mid-north. This home video recorded early this month shows hundreds of thousands of the little pests which have reached pupa stage.'

Property owner Paul Smart: 'Never been this thick. Not around house and through yards; it's just moved like the ground was alive.'"

"Triggered by the rains, an all devouring army of LOCUSTS! Millions emerge from eggs buried in the sand gathering into columns which may stretch for 10 kilometers. At this stage they can't fly, only hop, but it doesn't hinder their progress. These sweeping hoards devastate any new growth in their path. After 5 weeks of steady munching the infantry becomes airborne. These breeding swarms can cover up to 80 kilometers a day."

"Oh my, there's an absolute invasion. There's one on the window right here. (girl crying in the background) Oh my, Oh my here they come, here they come!"

"Portions of southern Russia are under attack courtesy of millions of locusts. The weather recently has been particularly good for locust production and it shows in this video from the country's Dagestan region. Locusts have taken over thousands of acres of land in Dagestan over the past two weeks as well in other areas within the Russian caucuses.

Last month, the U.N.'s Food & Agriculture Organization said it will help numerous countries in Eastern Europe and central Asia in an attempt to save farmland from a locust crisis said to be threatening the food security of some 20 million people. The Food Agency has also indicated that it will start a 5 year program to save more than 60 million acres of cultivated farmland from the giant grasshoppers." [54]

"Large swarms of locusts have laid waste to vast tracts of Northwest China's Xinjiang Uygur autonomous region, with authorities expecting the plague to worsen as the weather heats up.

The locust plague began in the pastureland of the Ili River Valley and Taer Basin in late April, said Wang Xinchang, an official with the animal husbandry bureau in Tacheng Prefecture, on Tuesday.

'Locusts have infested nearly 100,000 hectares of pastureland in Tacheng Prefecture,' he said.

As the summer heat persists, the situation might still worsen next month. 'At least 400,000 hectares of pastureland could become infested,' he said.

Xinjiang's regional headquarters of locust and rodent control said an estimated 15.7 million hectares of pastureland would suffer from the locust plague this summer.

The local governments in Ili and Tacheng have stepped up monitoring of the plague and have launched a pesticide spraying campaign to stop it spreading. Xinjiang has more than 100 kinds of locusts, one of the major menaces to the health of its grassland. It has a history of using chickens, ducks and other birds to fight the insects." [54]

"Locust plague hits eastern Australia. Swarms of locusts have been ravaging crops in a vast section of eastern Australia following recent floods in the region. They have infested a huge area of eastern Australia roughly the size of Spain.

Chris Adriaansen, head of the Australian Plague Locust Commission, said the quick-breeding creatures had hit from Longreach in Queensland in the northeast to Melbourne and Adelaide – about 500,000 square kilometres (190,000 square miles).

'What we've got certainly is a very large and widespread infestation,' he told AFP. 'It's simply a reflection of the fact that we've had widespread rain across that entire area.'

Adriaansen said some swarms covered areas as large as 300 square kilometres, and with about 10 locusts per square metre, 'that's a lot of locusts.'

Local media said the insects had already wiped out thousands of hectares (acres) of crops and were also damaging grazing areas and gardens in the key agricultural area.

'One farmer has about 400 hectares (1,000 acres) which will have to be resown,' an agronomist in the town of Forbes, Graham Falconer, told public broadcaster ABC. 'The locusts are doing considerable damage.'

Adriaansen said the insects, which had destroyed some early planned cereal crops but mostly fed on pasture, were set to multiply in coming months as their offspring hatch.

'Come the middle of September through to October across that entire inland area...we expect there to be some very large infestations again,' he said.

Swarms are expected in southern Queensland and northern New South Wales, areas which last month were flooded after heavy rains broke almost a decade of drought." [54]

"U.S. states brace for invasion of cicadas as they hatch after 13 years underground. Even at this very moment, billions of the winged insects are crawling from their exoskeleton cages, ready to suck the sap out of every plant, tree and bush that gets in their way.

But they are here to breed, laying eggs in the twigs and branches of trees as they call out to mates with their deafening song. The red-eyed army has already reached the southern states of America, prompting many farmers to cover their crops with heavy protective netting.

'There are billions of them in the trees,' Greta Beekhuis told USA Today from her home in Pittsboro, North Carolina. 'The sound of the cicadas is clearly audible over the line. 'When I drove from my house to the grocery store, I ran over thousands of them. They're everywhere. The air is just thick with them.'

There have been reports of mass-hatchings in South Carolina, Georgia, Mississippi, North Carolina and Arkansas. But now the inch-long insects are heading north, desperate to continue their breeding frenzy." [54]

It sure looks like there's a rise of insect invasions going on all over the planet. Could it be God's way of getting our attention, just like He tried with Egypt? I kind of think so!

The **third plague** sent by God that very well could be a sign of His Coming Judgment is **The Rise of Hail**.

Exodus 9:22,25 "Then the LORD said to Moses, stretch out your hand toward the sky so that hail will fall all over Egypt – on men and animals and on everything growing in the fields of Egypt. Throughout Egypt hail struck everything in the fields – both men and animals; it beat down everything growing in the fields and stripped every tree."

One last time, *yet another* instrument that God will apparently use as an act of His Judgment is *hail*. So that's the question. "Do we see any signs of *an increase of hail storms* all across the planet as a sign that God might very well be getting ready to judge us real soon? Yes! Observe the following report:

"Recently 40 people were killed in China due to a violent hour-long hailstorm in their Northwest region. It "wreaked havoc" on all of the county's 18 townships and affected more than two thirds of its 450,000 residents. Roads were blocked, houses collapsed, and farmland was destroyed."

Furthermore, there have been recent indications that the hail storms are not only getting much more ferocious as was the case there in China, but they are also getting much more numerous. So much so that they are actually creating rivers. Here's an actual transcript of a recent news broadcast in Texas:

"I have to tell you I have never ever, ever, ever seen what you're about to show.

Pete Dellkus Chief Meteorologist: 'Yeah, let's take a look at this video right now. I want you to check this out and you can see we had anywhere between two and four feet of hail. Two to four feet deep in hail and then it all started to melt.'

(A river of melting hail is shown flowing just like a raging river)

This was north of Amarillo, it was just to the south of Dumas. Look at the hail piled up over there on the right side of the screen. I mean this is absolutely amazing stuff courtesy KVII, an ABC affiliate up in Amarillo.

Check out some of these pictures right here. That's not water; that's just hail that started to fall right there on Highway 287 that runs north out of Amarillo. It started to fall on this truck - got just trapped - it stopped because of the enormity of the hailstones and just the sheer mass of it all.

Look at these pictures right here. It looks like something you'd see in the winter time. I have another picture I want to show you and you can see that it's 287 Northbound. That's just amazing stuff.

This comes courtesy of the National Weather Service in Amarillo. That firefighter, has a four-foot pile of hail there next to him."

A four-foot pile of hail? Wow! In fact, hailstorms are not only getting more ferocious and numerous, they're also getting bigger. Recently a small town in South Dakota experienced a massive hailstorm that, "punched holes through the tops of buildings and left dents in the ground as large as coffee cans" as this next report reveals:

"This immense hole [shows a massive hole in a roof] by a hailstorm of Biblical proportions with rocks of ice pounding into cars and homes. Holes were punched in the tops of buildings, and for Les Scott he'll never forget what it sounded like.

Les Scott: 'Guys throwing bricks at the house and there was many of them. It was scary.'

Scott watched as massive hailstones pummeled the ground. Today the divots are still visible, some as large and deep as coffee cans but when the hail stopped, a certain stone grabbed his attention.

Scott: 'I just happened to see this one fall and the only reason I went out and got it because it had all of these fingers sticking out of it, and I thought, well that's weird and I'll go get that one.'

Scott originally wanted to make a daiquiri out of the hail but he decided to contact the national weather service instead. Today they were in Vivian. They carefully took out the stone from the freezer and placed it in a cooler with dry ice. The next stop was at the post office where the hail had a date with the federally certified scale. Moments later the hail weighed in at 1.9375 lbs.

Officially we know where records have been kept this will be the U.S. record and the World record for weight. So it's very impressive.

The finder said the ice chunk could have been even bigger but with no power to keep the freezer going it had shrunk by 5 centimeters."[55]

A *two-pound* hailstone? How many of you would say that would cause some serious damage? Yet once again, that's just a baby one compared to what's coming to this planet! Remember the Biblical rule. All of this, all of these global catastrophes is just *a birth pain*. Which means, these two-pound hailstones, they're actually baby ones! Here's how big the hail is going to get in the 7-year Tribulation!

Revelation 16:17,21 "The seventh angel poured out his bowl into the air, and out of the temple came a loud voice from the throne, saying, It is done! From the sky huge hailstones of about a hundred pounds each fell upon men. And they cursed God on account of the plague of hail, because the plague was so terrible."

Now let's put all this into perspective. Here you see a picture of the *two-pound* hailstone:

I think we can agree that this size of a hailstone smashing into us from the sky would give us the worst headache in our life. In fact, it would probably take our head clean off!

However, here's what's mind-blowing. Our text says you need to multiply this two-pound hailstone by fifty! The head smashing hailstones that God is going to sending on the planet during the second half of the 7-year Tribulation are going to be one hundred pounds each! How big is that? Does this mean that the people on the earth during that time will be pummeled with hailstones the size of the next photo?

Giant 100-Pound Hail

Can you say ouch? Imagine living in a time when a hailstone the size of a Volkswagen Beetle was falling from the sky, tons of them, millions if not billions or trillions of them? No wonder Jesus warned about the coming 7-year tribulation! People can laugh and scoff all they want, but unless they accept Jesus Christ as your Lord and Savior *now*, that's what they're going to get! Believe it or not, even with all this amazing evidence pointing to the signs of Christ's soon return, some people are still having a hard time receiving the truth, like this story reveals:

"A man goes to the White House and asks to see President Obama.

So the Marine on duty quickly informs the guy that Barack Obama is no longer the President, and then asked him to please leave.

So the man goes away. But the next day the same guy comes back to the White House and asks to see President Obama again.

So the marine on duty reminds him that Obama is not the President, and to please go away.

So the man goes away. However, the next day, the same guy comes back again, and again the same Marine is on duty.

So the man asks to see President Obama, and at this the Marine finally loses his patience so he yells back, 'WHY DO YOU KEEP COMING HERE ASKING FOR OBAMA? BARACK OBAMA IS NOT THE PRESIDENT ANYMORE!!"

At this the man smiles and says, 'I know, I just like hearing it.'"[56]

Now that guy just couldn't get enough of the good news, could he? However, as we all know, there are some people out there who are still having a hard time receiving this good news. What's interesting is that this attitude is actually reminiscent of what the Bible said would happen in the Last Days. The Scripture says at that time many people in the world will also have a hard time receiving the truth about Christ's return and will instead be living in a dream world acting like nothing will ever change. In fact, it's described as the same unfortunate attitude that was on the planet in Lot's day.

Luke 17:28-30 "And the world will be as it was in the days of Lot. People went about their daily business – eating and drinking, buying and selling, farming and building – until the morning Lot left Sodom. Then fire and burning sulfur rained down from heaven and destroyed them all. Yes, it will be 'business as usual' right up to the hour when the Son of Man returns."

I hope you're not one of those who are living your life like it's "business as usual." Because if you are, you might wake up one day and discover that *you've been left behind.* And you know what? God doesn't want you left behind. Because He loves us, He has given us the warning sign of **Worldwide Upheaval** to show us that the 7-year Tribulation is near and that Christ's Coming is rapidly approaching. Jesus Himself said this:

Luke 21:28 "When these things begin to take place, stand up and lift up your heads, because your redemption is drawing near."

Like it or not, we are headed for *The Final Countdown.* We don't know the day or the hour. Only God knows. The point is, if you're a Christian, you need to realize that we are going to be dead a lot longer than we are alive. Therefore, let's not waste our lives on temporary things, but let's strive for those things that are eternal. It's high time we Christians speak up and declare the good news of salvation to those who are dying all around us. But please, if you're not a Christian, give your life to Jesus *today*, because tomorrow may be too late! Just like the Bible said!

Chapter Four

The Rise of Falsehood

"Three guys named Al, Wes, and Kenny decided to go fishing out at Lake Mead and everything was going fine until Al noticed that Kenny forgot to tie the boat off to the side of the lake there, and so the boat was gone! It had disappeared! It had totally floated away!

To make matters worse, it was getting late and they were on the complete opposite side of the lake, they had no water, and they had no idea how they were going to cross it!

So Al, being a Christian and all, he decided to kneel down on his knees and begin to pray. Here's what he said, 'Lord give me the power and strength to cross the lake.'

So suddenly, Al became very strong and swam across Lake Mead.

At this Wes thought, 'Well hey, if it worked for Al, it'll work for me.' So Wes knelt down and prayed, 'Lord give me the skills and the strength to cross the lake.'

So Wes built a canoe and rowed himself across the lake.

Naturally Kenny thought, 'Man, if it worked for both Al and Wes, I know it'll work for me. So Kenny knelt down and prayed, 'Lord give me the wisdom and knowledge to cross Lake Mead.'

So Kenny turned into a woman and walked across the bridge."[1]

How many of you would say that those three men learned the hard way that sometimes the way out of your predicament is right smack dab in front of your face? It was there the whole time and yet they still missed it! Yet, believe it or not, the Bible says one day *the whole planet* is going to miss the way out of a horrible predicament called the 7-year Tribulation. Even though calling upon the Name of Jesus, the way out, was right smack dab in front of their faces the whole time, they refused to accept Him as their Lord and Savior and thus sealed their fate. For those of you who don't know, the 7-year Tribulation is not a joke and it certainly is not a party. It's an outpouring of God's wrath on a wicked and rebellious planet. In fact, Jesus said in Matthew 24 it's going to be a "time of greater horror than anything the world has ever seen or will ever see again. And that "unless that time of calamity is shortened, the entire human race will be destroyed."

But praise God, God's not only a God of wrath, He's a God of love as well. And because He loves us, He's given us many warning signs to show us when the Tribulation is near and Jesus Christ's Second Coming is rapidly approaching. Therefore, in order to keep people from experiencing the ultimate bad day of being left behind, a serious mistake, we're going to continue in our study, *The Final Countdown*. So far we've already seen how the **tenth sign** on The Final Countdown was **The Jewish People**. The **ninth sign** was **Modern Technology**. Then in the last chapter we saw how the **eighth sign** was **Worldwide Upheaval**. There we saw that God lovingly foretold us that when we see an **increase** of **Famines**, **Earthquakes**, **Pestilence**, **Wars** and rumors of wars, **Signs in the Sky** with an **increase** of **Volcanoes**, **Global Earth Catastrophes**, and **Plague-like Activity** just like in Egypt, it's a clear indicator from God, *we are living in the Last Days*.

The **seventh sign** on *The Final Countdown* is **The Rise of Falsehood**.

I. First End Time Prophecy Concerning the Rise of Falsehood - There Would be an Increase of False Christs

Luke 21:5-8 "Some of His disciples were remarking about how the temple was adorned with beautiful stones and with gifts dedicated to God. But Jesus said, 'As for what you see here, the time will come when not one stone will be left on another; every one of them will be thrown down.' 'Teacher,' they asked, 'when will these things happen? And what will be the sign that they are about to take place?' He replied: 'Watch out that you are not deceived. For many will come in my name, claiming, 'I am he,' and, 'The time is near.' Do not follow them.'"

So right out of the gates from the lips of Jesus, one of the biggest and most obvious signs to indicate when we were in the Last Days is when there would be *an increase of False Christs*. Granted, throughout history we've had a few people here and there claiming to be Jesus. That's pretty commonplace. What's not common is how, *in the last century alone*, there has been a literal explosion of people claiming to be the Messiah. For instance, one such person is the recently deceased **Reverend Sun Myung Moon** of the Moonies who has tons of followers. He not only claimed to be the "messiah" and the "lord of the universe" but he even stated that Jesus followed him:

"Jesus Christ is trying to follow me, my footsteps, all the way. He stayed in Paradise, because he did not marry. But I gave him marriage. Don't you want to meet the wives of Buddha, Confucius and Muhammad? They sent letters of gratitude to me from the spirit world. They pledge that even if their religion disappears, they will follow me."

As if that wasn't weird enough, believe it or not, Mr. Moon actually was crowned "messiah" in one of our senate buildings. One article shared the following shocking information:

"You probably imagine your congressman hard at work in the Capitol debating legislation, making laws – you know, governing. But your newspaper probably didn't tell you that one night in March, members of Congress hosted a crowning ritual for an ex-convict and multibillionaire who dressed up in maroon robes and declared himself the Second Coming.

On March 23, the Dirksen Senate Office Building was the scene of a coronation ceremony for Rev. Sun Myung Moon, owner of the conservative Washington Times newspaper and UPI wire service, who was given a bejeweled crown by Rep. Danny K. Davis, D-Ill. Afterward, Moon told his bipartisan audience of Washington power players he would save everyone on Earth as he had saved the

souls of Hitler and Stalin – the murderous dictators had been born again through him, he said.
In a vision, Moon said the reformed Hitler and Stalin vouched for him, calling him 'none other than humanity's Savior, Messiah, Returning Lord and True Parent.'

Then a Jewish Rabbi declared that Rev. Moon is the true messiah and blew his horn. And it wasn't just Jews, but also Muslims, Evangelicals, mainline Protestants, Hindus, assorted other faiths, and just about everyone."[2]

That's not all. You could also check out the **Jesus of Siberia** who *right now* has thousands of his own disciples who think he is Jesus because after all he walks around in a crimson robe and has long brown hair. His devotees say that he "radiates incredible love and speaking to him is like an electric shock or like bells ringing." In case you doubt, he has stated, "It's all very complicated. But to keep things simple, yes, I am Jesus Christ." Here's what one reporter exposed:

"Reporter Mary Garofalo: While Christians all over the world prepare to celebrate the birth of Jesus Christ, some believe he's alive right now. Where? Within the deep wilderness of northern Russia. Come along tonight for a truly unique story about a man they call Jesus of Siberia.

It looks like a scene right out of the Sermon on the Mount. We traveled many kilometers through a bug infested forest to reach this isolated village in Siberia, this most northern part of Russia. Here we meet "jesus" or Visserion as they also call him. Unbelievably, 15 years ago this "jesus" was Sergei Torop a small town Siberian policeman, but now he believes he is the son of god reincarnated.

Sergei "jesus": People will decide for themselves. Is His way for them or will they choose something else. But everything has a price.

Thousands in this village believe this is Jesus Christ. These are not misfits or lunatics. These are mostly professionals who abandoned lives in Europe to follow the man they call Jesus. Not long ago, Linetta was a Lithuanian diplomat serving at the European Union headquarters in Brussels, then she saw Visserion speaking.

Linetta: I cried, I began to cry – the feeling was unbelievable it was like I'm at home in love."[3]

For those who don't want to travel that far, today in Pennsylvania you could visit **What's Your Name**. The reason why people call him that is because when they ask him, "What's your name," he will only reply back, "What's Your name?" *Sounds like an annoying version of the messiah to me.* Yet he has thousands of people visiting him who state, "I was in his presence for an hour and felt unbelievable." People have had varied reactions to his appearance, including the following:

Policeman: When somebody comes into town without any shoes, dressed in a robe in the wintertime carrying a Bible – well obviously that's someone to keep an eye on.

News Reporter: Townspeople believe that he'll walk out of town never to return again.

Person: There is something wrong with this man, he's over the edge.

Priest: My first reaction was who is this kook.

Another priest: You have this hope. He's something like Francis of Asissi.

Lady driver: He is a blessing from God to all of us.

Another woman: He's a prophet, you know. [4]

In addition, believe it or not, the following quote came from "What's Your Name?" himself:

"Subconsciously there is a tremendous struggle with what I'm doing." [4]

Oh, but maybe Pennsylvania's Messiah is a little too homespun for you and you need a *real Jesus* with a *real accent*, because we all know according to the movies that Jesus spoke with a British accent, right? Yes, I'm joking! However, for those who need that sort of Messiah, **David Shayler**, the self-proclaimed **MI5 Messiah**, due to the fact that he's a former MI5 British secret agent, is here to help you out. Let's take a look at his audacious claims:

"David Shayler stated in an interview, 'I am the messiah and hold the secret of eternal life. It all came about quite suddenly. First I started meditating, then I learned how to channel the 'light,' and the more research I did into Freemasonry, the Knights Templar, Kabbalah the more convinced I became that I was the Christ,' speaking of the Messiah consciousness which He says is within each one of us.

'I was, though, crucified with a crown of thorns and nails then incarnated as Astronges, a Jewish revolutionary put to death by the Romans at around the end of the last century BC.'

The last decade has been a tough one for the former MI5 officer. 'It was in June that a psychic channeled the spirit of Mary Magdalene and anointed me the messiah and, finally, my whole life made sense.'

He also claims he can affect the weather, prevent terrorist attacks and influence football results. It was back in April that he performed what he calls his first and greatest miracle - securing his beloved team Middlesbrough a place in the UEFA Cup Final.

'It was the quarter-final against Basle and we were 3-0 down after the first leg and needed four goals in the second match to win. I sat there, said to the creator, 'give me a sign' and meditated – which is tricky at a football match, because every instinct is to abuse the ref and the opposition and, instead you have to shower them with unconditional love. But I managed to focus and we played like we'd never played before, winning 4-0.'

He did it again in the semi-final, against Bucharest. 'Again we were 3-0 down, again I meditated and, bang, we won – a real miracle.' So what about the final, when Middlesbrough lost 4-0 to Seville?

'Ah, interesting question,' he says, looking sheepish. 'I got drunk and it turns out it doesn't work if you're drunk. You can't focus.'"[5]

Oh, but for those who still need a Messiah with an accent yet has more power than just supposedly affecting sporting results, Australia is here to help you out. His name is **John Miller**, here are his claims:

"An ordinary Australian making an extra claim. AJ Miller says he's Jesus Christ. We first found him spreading his message in Australia. But now this self-proclaimed son of god has taken his mission to the world. Dannem Hitchcock caught up with AJ deep in the heart of Texas.

AJ: I am going to have to say I'm Jesus. I certainly don't want to be Jesus.

Hitchcock: His name is Allen John Miller or AJ, a former I.T. worker from Queensland's Bible Belt. He claims he's Jesus Christ back from the dead to spread a message he calls 'the divine truth.'

AJ: And remember that it has been prophesied in the bible and other places that I was going to do this, that I was going to return.

Hitchcock: AJ is currently on a worldwide tour. We traveled to the American state of Texas to find him. We went in with a local Christian who read about the seminar on the internet. The room is small but it's full. AJ is front and center, to his right is his girlfriend Mary. Not any Mary, but Mary Magdalene who witnessed the crucifixion. This century she has the handycam duty.

AJ: Usually before we give a talk we talk to our spirit friends about what they feel are the issues you are facing.

Hitchcock: AJ believes, after death, he and Mary were in the spirit world. A world he remains in contact with. It's a message the faithful have from all over the U.S and to here.

AJ: (Speaking of the locations of people attending the meeting that day) Florida and California, Philadelphia, New Mexico, Washington, South Carolina, Texas.

Hitchcock: The spirits say they want them to change the way they live. To love more, to become self-sufficient, to prepare for cataclysmic events such as the ones in the movie 2012. Huge natural disasters from which he will emerge as the savior. His followers have financed his current world trip. From Australia to Greece, England, Dallas TX and back to the U.K."[6]

Oh, but there's more! For those who want a Messiah even bigger than Pennsylvania or Australia or even the British Secret Service can offer, you can check out **Lord Maitreya** of whom thousands of people *all over the world* consider him to be Jesus. His appearance is supposed to have spawned "healing springs," "weeping and bleeding statues," and even "divine messages inscribed by the seeds within fruit and vegetables." Lest you think nobody will ever fall for this baloney, believe it or not, CNN has actually broadcast commercials for him on air announcing his coming. Here's the transcripts of those commercials:

"If the Christ or Buddha returned today, would you recognize him? The one awaited by all major religions is come when we least expected it. He is ready to emerge openly very soon. Look for a bright star shining in the sky night and day, as a sign of his public emergence.

Imagine a world free of war, poverty and injustice. Where sharing and cooperation replace greed and competition. Where peace, born of justice prevails. In the midst of today's chaos, is this new world possible? Now in our midst, we have help of an extraordinary kind, expected by every major faith. He awaits but our invitation. Maitreya, the world teacher is now among us"[7]

Now as amazing as all these accounts are of false messiahs, these guys are not the only ones claiming to be the Christ. *Right now* here in the United States alone there are an estimated 10,000 people claiming to be Jesus.[8] In fact, one of the most audacious ones is a guy named Jose Luis de Jesus Miranda who also recently passed away. However, listen to what he has his followers do:

"Reporter: In a tattoo parlor in trendy South Beach sat the daughter of the man who claims to be God.

Jo Ann De Jesus: Jesus is back. He's here to teach us that we should reign in life, that there is no sin and today we're honoring him with a symbol.

Reporter: Jo Ann De Jesus is one of several dozen members of a religious sect called Chrisienda en Gracia or 'Growing In Grace'. They were tattooed on their arms, ankles and even their necks with 666 – the Biblical sign of the Antichrist. Why? Because their spiritual leader says he is the Antichrist. Not the embodiment of evil but rather the second coming.

Jose Miranda: 666 – Antichrist means do not put your eyes on Jesus Christ of Nazareth put it in Jesus after the cross.

Reporter: And that's you?

Jose Miranda: That's me.

Reporter: And he says the word Antichrist is a bad translation of a word that actually means the 'new' christ, the second coming. Puerto Rican born Jose Luis De Jesus Miranda founded the sect 20 years ago in a warehouse outside of Miami.

Jose Miranda: You receive it, you accept it and confess it and it's done unto you.

Reporter: The charismatic 61 year old De Jesus claims millions of followers, most in Latin America. His sect does have hundreds of churches, cable TV stations and says it brought him 1.4 million dollars in donations last year and he boasts of a rapidly growing presence in the United States. In an interview with us in September he declared:

Jose Miranda: I do greater things than Jesus of Nazareth, much greater.

Reporter: Now sporting his new tattoo –

Jose Miranda: 6 - 6 - 6 three presents.

Reporter: De Jesus says those expecting the second coming of Christ on a cloud with angels have misinterpreted what Jesus Himself said.

Jose Miranda: He said it! You won't see me anymore because he will come in another body – which is me.

Reporter: De Jesus preaches that heaven can be found here on earth, simply by following him. There is no sin and there is no hell and that's part of the reason why he is attracting so many followers. But marking your body with 666 seems an unusual way to show you're a Christian."[9]

Now, it's one thing for a person to claim to be Jesus Christ, but to have tens of thousands of people across the world falling for it, even to the point where they're tattooing 666 on their bodies as a sign of allegiance? This is a clear sign *from the real Jesus* that we are living in the Last Days! Furthermore, every year in Jerusalem, a strange phenomenon is occurring that has been dubbed, *the Jerusalem Syndrome* where tens of thousands of people are having delusions of being a Biblical character or Jesus Christ Himself.[10] The sad thing is how most people on our planet have no idea that they are actually being prepared by these false christs to one day worship and follow the ultimate false christ, that is the Antichrist, who will also say he is a god during the 7-year Tribulation.

2 Thessalonians 2:3-4 "Don't let anyone deceive you in any way, for that day will not come until the rebellion occurs and the man of lawlessness is revealed, the man doomed to destruction. He will oppose and exalt himself over everything that is called God or is worshipped, so that he sets himself up in God's temple, proclaiming himself to be God."

As we've seen before, the Bible clearly says that during the 7-year Tribulation the Antichrist will not only actually proclaim himself to be god, but the people of the world will actually worship him as god. This is precisely what we're already seeing people do *right now* across the world. There's a massive increase of people worshipping mere men, false messiahs, as god. This shows us according to the words of Jesus, the One and Only Real Messiah, that we are living in the Last Days!

II. Second End Time Prophecy Concerning the Rise of Falsehood - There would be an Increase of False Myths

Now, this is important because you might be thinking, "Well come on now! Who in their right mind would ever listen to these goobers who are claiming to be Jesus Christ? I mean, this is ludicrous! All you have to do is read the Bible and see that's not the way Jesus is coming back! These guys are imposters!" Well yes, if you were to say that, you're right! Here's how the Bible says Jesus is going to come back and it's not going to be like those imposters:

Matthew 24:26-27 "So if anyone tells you, 'There he is, out in the desert,' do not go out; or, 'Here he is, in the inner rooms,' do not believe it. For as lightning that comes from the east is visible even in the west, so will be the coming of the Son of Man."

How can you get any clearer than that? When Jesus comes back He's not going to secretly appear in the desert in Australia. He's not going to appear in a rented room in some Holiday Inn in Pennsylvania asking people, "What's your name?" And He certainly isn't going to encourage people to tattoo 666 on their bodies and say that the Mark of the Beast is a good thing and there is no sin and there is no hell! No! The Bible says just as lightning shows up and is visible from the East to the West, so will be the coming of the Son of Man! In other words, it's going to be a global event that everyone's going to see and there will be no mistaking it! Everyone will know it's the One and Only real Jesus and it's not going to be done in secret, and neither does He need CNN to announce it!

But again, this is precisely the point. Again, who in their right mind would ever fall for one of these false christs, let alone the Antichrist, when the True Christ's appearance is so plain in the Biblical text? Well, that's precisely the problem. The Bible says in the Last Days that people won't be following after the Biblical text anymore, instead they're going to be chasing after *strange myths*.

2 Timothy 4:1-4 "In the presence of God and of Christ Jesus, who will judge the living and the dead, and in view of his appearing and his kingdom, I give you this charge: Preach the Word; be prepared in season and out of season; correct, rebuke and encourage – with great patience and careful instruction. For the time will come when men will not put up with sound doctrine. Instead, to suit their own desires, they will gather around them a great number of teachers to say what their itching ears want to hear. They will turn their ears away from the truth and turn aside to myths."

So here we see the sad reality of the Church in the Last Days. The Bible says that the status of the Church is not going to get better and better as the appearing of Jesus Christ gets closer and closer, as some would falsely state. Rather, Churches will purposely hire Pastors to tickle their ears with non-convicting sermons, i.e. of things they want to hear, and stroke them with comments of how wonderful they are, instead of the truth. In fact, it says that it gets so bad in the Church they will actually turn away from the truth, i.e. the Bible, and instead follow after myths, or literally things made up! So here's your answer. This is why people, even in the Church, are falling for these goobers who would have the audacity to claim to be Jesus Christ. They refuse to listen, heed, study the Bible and instead would rather run after things that are made up. In fact, let me give you just a small dose of proof revealing how people all over the planet, many claiming to be Christians, are seeking the truth outside the scope of the Bible. Now, it might sound like a small thing, but once you go outside the parameters of the Bible, you open up Pandora's Box and come up with all kinds of wacked out heresy, like these guys did:

"Reporter: The cars and trucks rush up and down Interstate 35 every day. A number of Christians have come to believe because of recent prophecies, dreams

and visions that I-35 is the highway spoken of in Isaiah 35:8 'and a highway will be there; it will be called the way of holiness.' Jeff Baldwin college and career pastor at Dallas's Heartland Ministries.

Jeff Baldwin: There have been very specific cities given in these prophetic words to say 'go to these cities and cry out for holiness and purity and I'll come down and invade' and all those cities were along the 35 corridor.

Reporter: And now dozens of Midwest ministries have linked arms to pray these prophecies are soon fulfilled and they've set aside 35 days to concentrate on I-35.

Cindy Jacobs: We have seventeen 24 hour prayer rooms going on.

Reporter: Two of the main organizers are prophetic intercessors Cindy Jacobs and Heartland senior pastor Steve Hill famous for his evangelizing in the Brownsville revival.

Cindy Jacobs: What do we expect to see? We expect laws to be changed in cities. We expect righteous leaders. We expect a movement and a reformation that will literally sweep the face of the earth.

Jeff Baldwin: There's something happening. There is a shift in the heavenlies. I believe we are moving angels and demons right now."[11]

Yes, I agree there's a whole new shift taking place. A shift from the Bible! Can you believe that? Personally, I'm glad I live next to I-15 instead of I-35, because if I ever had to fast like those people, apparently I would only have to do it for 15 days! In fact, I did a little research and I discovered that there is a verse in Isaiah 15, because that's the highway where I live here in Las Vegas and according to these people, this must be a word for the Church here in Vegas. It says there, "Every head is shaved, and every beard is cut off." So don't you see? This is a clear sign from God that if we all go to the store and buy some razors and shave ourselves that He's going to come to Las Vegas and bring revival! It's right there in the text! Now, obviously I'm joking, but do you see what happens when people, even professing Christians, engage in this type of behavior? Once you veer outside the scope of Scripture, you can make *anything sound spiritual.* In addition, this same unbiblical mentality also leads to all kinds of so-called "secret signs" from God, including so-called *appearances of Jesus Christ.* What

I'm about to share with you is absolute proof that people re turning away from God's truth and have turned aside to myths. The above passage is being fulfilled. Starting off with *Jesus on a French Fry*:

- **Jesus on a French Fry:** A local woman in the California capitol says she was cooking dinner for her husband when she suddenly noticed the crispy crucifix. Adding she has never seen anything like it in her 88 years on the planet. No word on whether Jesus Christ on a French fry will follow the path carved by Jesus Christ on an oyster, Jesus Christ on a fish-stick and Jesus Christ on a pierogi, all winding up on Ebay.

- **Jesus on a Chip:** The lady saw the discovery of the chip as a sign that the family is doing something right, and perhaps as an indication that they need to stop smoking. "This strengthens my faith," she said. "It makes me believe even more."

- **Jesus on a Cheeto:** The man said, "I was fixin' to eat it, when I saw the image. I don't think the heavenly choir actually started singing, but in my mind they did."

- **Jesus on a Bruise:** The girl commented that she thought it was a sign that, "Jesus wants us to ride around in cars with boys; He's telling us it's okay and that I need a cooler cell phone."

- **Jesus on a Cell Phone:** The message that I got was that He was telling me He was with me. Just to be sure it wasn't a hoax, they checked to see if the image had come preloaded with the phone, or had been sent to her. Apparently it was a truly divine miracle.

- **Jesus on a XBOX 360:** This XBOX 360 package has an image that resembles Jesus on the back. I did not alter the package in any way. This is a natural occurrence of something beyond my understanding.

- **Jesus on a Pulpit:** Jubilee Fellowship Church members say you can see the face of Jesus on their pulpit. After it was re-varnished, someone from the Church noticed the profile of what they believe is Jesus Christ.

- **Jesus on a Closet Door:** The guy said, "My old closet door has a very curious wood grain pattern in it, that many people over the years have said looks exactly like Jesus Christ holding out His hands."
- **Jesus on an Iron:** Speaking of doors, right behind a door, one woman says she found Jesus on an iron. Mary Jo Coady says, "Jesus is on my iron. You see his head there, his hair, his eyes, his nose. Last Sunday, the door was shut. I opened the door and I looked down and I see this image staring at me and I was like...my first reaction was an image of Jesus looking at me. I was like okay you're crazy, I looked at it again – he's still there. It'll be a reminder that things are going to be good and get better.

- **Jesus on a Guitar:** Jeff Hoyer told the Ludington News, "I've been here for 27 years and I've never seen anything close to that. The face is so clear. It reminded me of the Shroud of Turin and we know who that was."

- **Jesus on a Tree:** Recently, while attempting to find solace against an imminent foreclosure, a couple discovered that an image of Jesus had appeared in a knothole in their tree. The couple believes that this is a sign that something good is coming their way.

- **Jesus on a Rock:** The lady said she was riding on a bus looking out the window when she saw it. Her friend believes that the image is there to watch over them. Another friend says since the lady needs a kidney, the image is a sign she will be okay.

- **Jesus on a Ceiling Stain:** Dominique Sartin, a staff member of Body Shoppe said, "I think it's a silhouette and kind of a partial beard." She said if it had leaked a little more, it would be a beard on the other side too. They're looking at selling it on Ebay.

- **Jesus on a Shoe:** An individual in Southeast Kansas noticed a strange stain on the tongue of his new shoes. Upon further inspection, it was the image of Jesus Christ. The shoe has been listed on Ebay, with a portion of the proceeds to go to Church ministries.

- **Jesus on a Lava Lamp:** The man said, "I had been going through a tough time and was praying for a divine sign from God that I was not alone and that all would work out fine." After the revelation of the lava lamp, he said his life turned around.

- **Jesus on a Pita Bread:** One day a New Zealand gentlemen woke up to cook some pita bread. Oddly enough one piece looked like the face of Jesus. He said, "I was tempted to eat it, but for some reason, I didn't."

- **Jesus on a Rotten Potato:** Renee said she had been looking for an excuse to get out of making potato salad. "I was hesitant about making the potato salad because sister Frankie makes the potato salad at Church. And I said, 'Lord, if it's not for me to make the potato salad then send me a sign.'" She got her sign right off the bat with the first potato she split in half.

- **Jesus on Everything:** Jesus on a Dog Door, Jesus on an X-Ray, Jesus on a Moth, Jesus on a Cat, Jesus on a Wheel, Jesus on a Pretzel, Jesus on a Spoon, and who could forget…

- **Jesus on a Beer Bottle:** The man said, "When I saw it I got goose pimples. I have no doubt it is the face of Jesus. You can even see his beard and hair." The article said, "The devil is constantly at work to stop these signs from spreading. It ended up getting collected by a barmaid when no one was paying attention and thrown away."

- **Jesus on a Toilet Seat:** Lest you think that God doesn't care about us people here in Las Vegas, recently a woman shared how Jesus sent all of us here in Vegas an encouraging word on her toilet seat." [13]

"Reporter: Yes, you can call it the royal flush. Magdalena Nelson's guest bathroom screams 'I love Las Vegas.'

Magdalena: I get a little choked up because it's so silly and so funny but it really just made my day. It really made my day.

Reporter: And by that she's referring to what she says appeared while she was cleaning.

Magdalena: The face of Jesus came out.

Reporter: Take a look, do you see it? Look closer. (flushing sound)

Magdalena: I said holy ****. I went from every angle and I looked and I looked

and I called my boyfriend in and it was there.
Reporter: What did you think when your girlfriend said I see Jesus in a bumper sticker on her toilet.

Boyfriend: I thought it was ridiculous, I thought she was crazy.

Reporter: But once he looked closer he says he now sees the image as plain and clear. So you think that there is something to it?

Boyfriend: I hope so, it's helped us feel better. We kinda been going through tough times and it's brought us up a little bit and our spirits up that day.

Reporter: And now they say praying to the porcelain god has taken on a whole new meaning. Ever since Magdalena discovered the sign on Thursday, she said this bathroom is literally off limits to the family. Magdalena says she'll protect the image as long as she can and however it got there she believes timing is everything.

Magdalena: So when I saw that it was just, "Bing!" okay. We're gonna be alright no matter what. The economy is in the toilet but I think we're gonna be alright." [12]

Well there you have it. Everything is going to be fine here in Vegas. Jesus just appeared on a toilet seat! I mean, what more proof do you need? Excuse me? Do you see what happens when you start going down this route? But it gets even worse:

"50 people looking for a solar image of Mary lose their sight. 'At least 50 people in Kottayam district have reportedly lost their vision after gazing at the sun while looking for an image of Virgin Mary.

Though alarmed health authorities have installed a signs to counter the rumor, curious onlookers, including foreign travelers, have been thronging the venue of the 'miracle.'" [13]

So let me get this straight. You'll burn your eyeballs out looking at a supposed vision of Virgin Mary but you won't spend one blink of an eye reading the Bible! Still others will get all elated about supposedly finding Jesus on a bruise or a piece of toast or even a toilet seat but you don't ever get excited about reading the Word of God? How could this be? Well, if people would read the Bible they would discover the answer. The Bible says in the Last Days, just prior to Christ's return "People will gather around them a great number of teachers to say what their itching ears want to hear and they will turn their ears away from the truth and turn aside to myths." That's why! It's all a sign from God that we really are living in the Last Days!

III. Third End Time Prophecy Concerning the Rise of Falsehood - There Would be an Increase of False Teachings

Matthew 24:3-4,10-11,23-25 "As Jesus was sitting on the Mount of Olives, the disciples came to Him privately. 'Tell us,' they said, 'when will this happen, and what will be the sign of your coming and of the end of the age?' Jesus answered: 'Watch out that no one deceives you. At that time many will turn away from the faith and will betray and hate each other, and many false prophets will appear and deceive many people. At that time if anyone says to you, 'Look, here is the Christ!' or, 'There he is!' do not believe it. For false Christs and false prophets will appear and perform great signs and miracles to deceive even the elect – if that were possible. See, I have told you ahead of time.'"

So now we see that the very first thing Jesus mentions to indicate when we are living in the Last Days is that it would be a time of *great, massive deception*. In fact, so much so, He repeatedly warned about it over and over again in that passage. He said this *deception* is promoted by false Christs and false prophets with their *false teachings* and it's so powerful that it comes close to even deceiving the elect. Therefore, Jesus warned us, "I've told you ahead of time!" In other words, we need to be on our guard and see to it that *no one* deceives us in the Last Days with their false teachings. So that's precisely what we're going to do now. We're going to take a look at several different false teachings out there that have specifically appeared on the planet in these Last Days that are not only a sign we're living in the Last Days like Jesus said, but are also single-handedly helping to usher in the Antichrist's kingdom.

1. The First False Teaching in These Last Days – The False Teaching of Evolution

A false teaching has arisen in these Last Days, to help usher in the Antichrist's kingdom; the **False Teaching of Evolution**. Evolution not only undermines everything we believe in as Christians from page one forward of the

Bible, but as we will see it's also going to be used in the Last Days to justify the murder of billions of people on the planet, explain away the Rapture of the Church from the planet and get us to think being left behind on the planet is actually a good thing. But let's first demonstrate just how much of a lie, a false teaching, evolution really is.

The First Way We Know Evolution is a Lie and a False Teaching in the Last Days is from the Evidence of Intelligent Design

Romans 1:18-20 "The wrath of God is being revealed from heaven against all the godlessness and wickedness of men who suppress the truth by their wickedness, since what may be known about God is plain to them, because God has made it plain to them. For since the creation of the world God's invisible qualities – His eternal power and divine nature – have been clearly seen, being understood from what has been made, so that men are without excuse."

In other words, nobody's going to stand before God and say, "I just didn't have enough evidence you were real." Rather, as God clearly stated in that passage, there's tons of evidence of His existence in everything He made, that is, His creation. This is the argument of Intelligent Design, which basically states that if you see design in something, then logically, it implies a designer.

For instance, what if I were to tell you my watch with about twelve moving parts slowly evolved in an empty field across the street from my office over millions and billions of years from the rain and erosion beating down on the rocks and interaction with sticks and mud and I just happened to be walking by and picked it up? If I really stated that as a fact, or even a supposed theory, what would you say? You'd say the cheese has slid off my cracker. Why? Because a watch can't design itself. Watches are made by watchmakers. Somebody had to design it!

So here's the question. Then why is it acceptable for an evolutionist to say that, not just a watch, *but our whole world and all of life* did evolve by chance? Whose cheese is sliding off of whose cracker? Now, it's one thing to think this, promote this, believe this, or even teach this, but the Bible says this is suppressing of the truth about God's existence and is precisely why *the wrath of God* is being revealed from heaven!

Therefore, let's take a look at some of the evidence that God has left behind for us in His creation showing us that He really does exist, so as not to fall for the lie of evolution:

DESIGN OF THE HUMAN BODY

OUR INTERNAL ORGANS: Did you know our kidneys contain approximately 280 miles of tubes and they filter 185 quarts of water a day from our blood?

Did you know the heart pumps 5,000 gallons of blood a day and beats approximately 100,800 times a day or 2 billion 500 million times in an average lifetime?

Did you know our bodies make about 2 to 10 million blood cells every second and if you lined up the red blood cells in one person's body end to end they'd go around the equator 4 times?

OUR BRAINS: Did you know that the average brain weighs about 3 pounds and yet contains 12 billion cells, each of which is connected to 10,000 other brain cells making 120 trillion connections! The brain controls hearing, sight, smell, speech, eating, resting, learning, and stores so much memory data that by the age of 40, it would take the Empire State building full of computers just to store the same amount of information.

OUR DNA: Did you know the DNA molecule in our bodies is the most complex molecule in the universe? Its code is so unbelievably complex that if you typed it all out, it would create enough books to fill the Grand Canyon 40 times.

In fact, your body has 50 trillion cells with each cell having 46 chromosomes but if you took all of the chromosomes out of your body, they'd only fill up 2 tablespoons! If you stretched them out and tied them all together, one person's chromosomes would reach from the earth to the moon and back, FIVE MILLION times!

DESIGN OF THE ANIMALS

THE GIRAFFE: Charles Darwin believed that the giraffe was just a regular animal that grew a longer neck because it needed to reach the higher branches for food. But the question is, "Could a giraffe evolve a longer neck?" You be the judge.

First of all, the neck of the giraffe is about 6 feet long, which means that just bending over, it could explode its brain from the pressure. So how does it stay alive?

Well, it just so happens the giraffe has the most powerful heart in the animal kingdom. It's 2 feet long, weighs 25 lbs. and has walls 3 inches thick. But that's not all. It also comes equipped with 4 safety features to keep its brain from exploding while bending over to take a drink of water.

One, the giraffe has in his jugular veins a series of one-way check valves that immediately close as soon as the head is lowered.

But this puts way too much blood in the carotid artery, so what's it do? Well, two, that extra blood is immediately pushed into a special spongy tissue that's located near the brain which absorbs all the excess blood. But this could cause a rupture in the brain, so what does it do?

Well, three, it produces a fluid in the brain that acts as a counter pressure to prevent the rupture from occurring.

Then four, just to make sure there's no other rupture anywhere else along the way, the walls of the giraffe's arteries just happen to be thicker than any other mammal.

Question, "How could this ever evolve like Charles Darwin said? And at what stage of development could the giraffe survive unless all of these features were fully functioning all at the same time?"

DESIGN OF THE BIRDS

THE WOODPECKER: Did you know that woodpeckers don't just peck on trees to look for food and make homes, but they do so at a rate of 15-16 times a second, which is a rate of fire twice as fast as a machine gun, meaning they're head travels twice the speed of a bullet?

This means the force of stress on its head is equivalent to 1,000 times the force of gravity or more than 250 times the force an astronaut experiences when taking off in a rocket!

So how does the woodpecker keep from beating its brains out?

Well, it just so happens, the woodpecker's skull is extra-reinforced with bone. Then it just so happens the bill is stronger than most birds. Then it just so happens this keeps its head and beak from being smashed to bits at the very first peck.

But what about the brain? How does it survive the impact?

Well in most birds, the beak is joined to the cranium, which surrounds the brain. But it just so happens, the beak of the woodpecker is separated by a sponge-like tissue that acts as a shock absorber which scientists say is far better than anything man has ever come up with.

Then just to make sure, the woodpecker also comes with special muscles that pull the brain case away from its beak every time it strikes a blow. For even more protection, the woodpecker comes with neck muscles that keep its head perfectly straight. This really comes in handy because if its head varied even the slightest, it would rip its brain right off the skull!

Keep in mind, it does this year in, year out, thousands of times every day!

Then, if that wasn't amazing enough, the woodpecker also comes with a very unique and very long tongue to get its food. But where does the woodpecker put such a long tongue when there's not enough room in its beak?

Well, it just so happens the tongue of the woodpecker is anchored and stored in its right nostril when not in use. But when he does use it, it emerges from the right nostril, splits into two halves, then each half passes underneath the skin over one side coming around the back of the skull and then underneath the beak and then enters a hole in the beak where the two halves come back together again. All that just to stick its tongue out!

Question, "How could this pecking ability and tongue ever evolve? And at what stage of development could the woodpecker survive unless all of these features were fully functioning all at the same time?"

DESIGN OF CELLS & BACTERIA

THE CELL: Did you know each tiny cell is a literal factory containing an elaborate network of interlocking assembly lines, each of which are composed of large protein machines bristling with high-tech machinery?

In fact, on the outside of each cell are sensors, gates, pumps and identification markers while the inside is jam-packed with power plants, automated workshops and recycling units. They even have miniature monorails that whisk materials from one location to another.

And that's why it's been said that even the most advanced, automated modern factory, with all its computers and robots all coordinated on a precisely timed schedule, is LESS complex than the inner workings of a single cell.

Apparently that's also why the so-called simplest of all cells, the paramecium, is actually more complex than the space shuttle. Which by the way, is the most complex machine man has ever built!

In fact, it's now known that the DNA molecule is 45 trillion times more efficient than the silicon megachip, which by the way, was made by teams of designers.[14]

This is precisely why, when observing this kind of information and much more revealing God's Intelligent Design in His creation, that other researchers have stated that thinking all this came about by random chance of evolution is about as *intelligent* as saying, "If given enough 'time' and 'chance' a Scrabble factory could explode enough times, until the letters eventually landed to perfectly spell out the book *War and Peace*." Or that, "A tornado can whip through a junkyard leaving behind a perfectly formed Boeing 747." And, "Not just you, but you and your entire extended family are more likely to win the lottery every week for 100 years than it is for a single bacterium to ever form by chance!"[15] In other words it's impossible! Common sense and the facts tells us that *creation was designed by God*! In fact, even the scientists are starting to admit it:

Charles Townes a Nobel Prize winner for Physics said: "The more we know about the cosmos (the universe) the more they seem inexplicable without some aspect of intelligent design. And for me that inspires faith."

Alan Sandage a winner of the Crawford prize in astronomy said: "I find it quite improbable that such order came out of chaos. There has to be some organizing principle. God to me is a mystery but is the explanation for the miracle of existence."

Werner Arber a Nobel Prize winner for Medicine said: "Although a biologist, I must confess I do not understand how life came about. The possibility of the existence of a Creator, of God, represents to me a satisfactory solution to this problem."

George Greenstein astronomer said: "Is it possible that suddenly, without intending to, we have stumbled upon scientific proof of the existence of a Supreme Being? As we survey all the evidence, the thought insistently arises that some supernatural agency must be involved."

Tony Rothman physicist said: "When confronted with the order and beauty of the universe and the strange coincidences of nature, it's very tempting to take the leap of faith from science into religion. I am sure many physicists want to. I only wish they would admit it."[16]

In other words, "I wish they'd stop lying!" Why? Because any person knows that design in something implies a designer. And that Designer is God! He's loves us and He's given us no excuse to not know about His existence! He's left behind plenty of proof for us in His Creation. Unfortunately, it's being suppressed by a lie called evolution in the Last Days.

The Second Way We Know Evolution is a Lie and a False Teaching in the Last Days is the Evidence of a Young Creation

Simply put, we have been seriously lied to when it comes to the age of life. This is because *time* is the Achilles heel of evolution. They have to have millions and billions of years in order for their lie to work. The problem is, just like the rest of their belief system, their version of time is also a lie! Not so surprisingly, the Bible disagrees with them. Here's how long we've been here according to Jesus.

Mark 10:1-9 "Jesus then left that place and went into the region of Judea and across the Jordan. Again crowds of people came to Him, and as was His custom, He taught them. Some Pharisees came and tested him by asking, 'Is it lawful for a man to divorce his wife?' 'What did Moses command you?' He replied. They said, 'Moses permitted a man to write a certificate of divorce and send her away.' 'It was because your hearts were hard that Moses wrote you this law,' Jesus replied. 'But at the beginning of creation God made them male and female. For this reason a man will leave his father and mother and be united to his wife, and the two will become one flesh. So they are no longer two, but one. Therefore what God has joined together, let man not separate.'"

So here we see the Bible clearly informing us that when Jesus was answering a question concerning marriage, He went right back to the very first account of the very first man and woman, that is, Adam and Eve. They were literal people by the way, not figurative as some would say. Now, notice what Jesus said there about this very first marriage. He said it was the very first marriage because it was *at the very beginning of creation*. From the lips of Jesus Himself, He declared that the literal account of Genesis was the actual beginning point of time. Therefore, the point is, if you start with the account of Adam and Eve and you add up the dates in the Bible you arrive at an estimated age of about 6,000 years. I know it sounds kind of odd at first, but that's because we've been lied to by evolution. Evolution does not teach what our Lord Jesus taught, that a literal creation began with a literal Adam and Eve just a few thousand years ago. Rather they say, "We came from the 'goo' to the 'zoo' to 'me and you' over millions and billions of years." But the question is, "Is this true? Is it accurate? Is evolution's time scale based on hard scientific data? No! In fact, it's just another one of their lies to try to prop up their false teaching. For proof of this, let's take a look at the *supposed dating methods* they use to arrive at their dates, and you tell me if they don't have some serious problems.

The **first method** is called the **Geologic Column**. If you'll recall from secular school, that's the supposed *column of dirt*, that by the way, only exists in the textbooks because it appears nowhere on earth in its complete form. Nonetheless, it's the supposed proof revealing eras of evolutionary life forms evolving into other life forms through different periods of time like the so-called Cambrian period, the Devonian period, the Jurassic period, etc. This is one of the methods evolutionists use to give them their much-needed millions and billions of years. They say each of these "dirt" or "rock layers" contain "index fossils" and based upon what "rock layer" these "index fossils" are found in, this is supposed to tell us how old they are. For instance, if it's found in the Jurassic Layer it's supposed to be around 200 million years old. But if the "index fossil" is found in the Cambrian Layer it's supposed to be 500 million years old. Now, that's nice if you want to believe that, but my question is, "What scientific data do you have to back that up? How do you know in the first place that those layers are 500 million years old? Was there a date attached to the dirt there? How do you know?" Well, believe it or not, they say it's because of the "index fossils." But stop and think about it. There's a *major* problem here. How can you date the "fossils" by the "rocks" and then turn around and say you date the "rocks" by the "fossils"? That's circular reasoning and believe it or not they even admit it:

J.E. O'Rourke, America Journal of Science: "The procession of life was never witnessed, it is inferred. The rocks do date the fossils, but the fossils date the rocks more accurately."

Niles Eldredge, (American Museum of Natural History of New York) "And this poses something of a problem. If we date the rocks by their fossils, how can we then turn around and talk about patterns of evolutionary change through time in the fossil record?"

J.E. O'Rourke, Journal of Science: "The intelligent layman had long suspected circular reasoning in the use of rocks to date fossils and fossils to date rocks. The geologist has never bothered to think of a good reply, feeling that the explanations are not worth the trouble as long as the work brings results."

Dr. Donald Fisher, state paleontologist for New York, was asked by Luther Sunderland, *"How do you date fossils?"* His reply: *"By the Cambrian rocks in which they were found."* And Sunderland then asked him if this was not circular reasoning, and Fisher replied, *"Of course, how else are you going to do it?"*[18]

That's supposed to be science? This is how you arrive at your dates of millions and billions of years? What a joke! What a lie! But you might be thinking, "Well, wait a second. Don't they have other dating methods like carbon dating, and potassium argon, and all those other methods they say *prove* we've been here for millions and billions of years?" Yes, as a matter of fact they do. So let's take a look at those results, those other so-called dating methods and you tell me if we're dealing with an exact science here:

• New wood from actively growing trees has been dated at 10,000 years!

• The new lava dome from Mount St. Helens was formed in 1986. In 1997 five specimens were taken from this dome at five different locations and subjected to conventional Potassium-Argon dating. The results indicated ages of less than ½ to almost 3 million years old, all from an 11-year old rock.

- Mortar from an Oxford Castle in England gave an age of 7,270 years. The only problem was the castle was built about 800 years ago.

- Lunar soil collected by Apollo 11 gave ages by different methods from 2.3 billion to 8.2 billion years all from rocks in the same location!

- Shells from living snails were carbon dated as being 27,000 years old.

- A freshly killed seal was carbon dated as having died 1,300 years ago!

- One part of a mammoth carbon dated at 29,500 years and another part at 44,000. Now that's one slow birth! How many of you ladies would like to give birth for 14,500 years?

- One part of a frozen mammoth was 40,000 years, another part was 26,000 years and the wood immediately around the carcass was 9-10,000 years.

- For years the KBS tuff, named for Kay Behrensmeyer, was dated using Potassium Argon at 212-230 Million years. But then a human skull was found in 1972 under the KBS tuff making it look like modern humans were around 212 million years ago instead of 2.9 million years as they teach. If the skull had not been found no one would have suspected the 212 million year dates as being wrong. But immediately seeing the dilemma, 10 different samples were retaken from the KBS tuff and were dated as being .52-2.64 Million years old, way down from 212 million. But even the "new and improved" dates still show a 500% error![18]

In other words, *not one* of those dating methods would even be close to being accurate *and they know it*. In fact, they even admit that the dating results can be tampered with very easily:

H.C. Dudley: "Aside from other contamination problems, everything hinges on unchanging decay rates. H.C. Dudley noted five ways they could change. He actually changed the decay rates of 14 different radioisotopes by means of pressure, temperature, electric and magnetic fields and stress. He also cited research by Westinghouse laboratories which changed the rates simply by placing inactive iron next to radioactive lead."

L.A. Rancitelli: "As much as 80 percent of the potassium in a small sample of an iron meteorite can be removed by distilled water in 4.5 hours."

Frederick B. Jueneman: "Just one catastrophe, such as a worldwide flood, would throw all the dating clocks off. Immense contamination of all radioactive sources would occur."[19]

So basically what they're saying is that the Biblical Flood of Noah would guarantee that *not one* of their dating methods would even come close to being accurate. That starts to explain why evolutionists would make insane comments like the following:

J.B. Birdsell in his book Human Evolution said: "In the last two years an absolute date has been obtained for the Ngandong beds, above the Trinil beds and it has the very interesting value of 300,000 years plus or minus 300,000 years."[20]

Yes, that is interesting, isn't it? Absolute date? Feel free to repeat after me, "Liar! Liar! Pants on fire!" So this leads us to what I believe is a common sense question, "Why? Why would the evolutionists do this when the *scientific evidence* points to the contrary? The evidence actually supports the Biblical account of God's existence, yet they persist. They're obviously intelligent, so why?" Well, believe it or not, it has nothing to do with the *facts*. It has to do with the *flesh*; that is, sin. The Bible states that this is exactly what would happen in the Last Days.

2 Peter 3:3-7 "First of all, you must understand that in the Last Days scoffers will come, scoffing and following their own evil desires. They will say, Where is this 'coming' He promised? Ever since our fathers died, everything goes on as it has since the beginning of creation. But they deliberately forget that long ago by God's word the heavens existed and the earth was formed out of water and by water. By these waters also the world of that time was deluged and destroyed. By the same word the present heavens and earth are reserved for fire, being kept for the day of judgment and destruction of ungodly men."

So you mean to tell me that in the Last Days scoffers would come who would deliberately forget the facts about God's creation just so they could continue to live out their evil desires? Could that really happen? As you can see it's not only happening before our very eyes *but* the Bible says it's a clear sign you're living in the Last Days! Which means our society today is the Last Days society of scoffers and mockers that make fun of Jesus' Second Coming and the lie of evolution is helping to produce it! In fact, if you press them hard enough, the evolutionists will actually admit they really are deliberately suppressing the truth of God's existence just to satisfy their own lusts in the Last Days:

George Wald states, "When it comes to the origin of life there are only two possibilities: creation or spontaneous generation. There is no third way. Spontaneous generation was disproved one hundred years ago, but that leads us to only one other conclusion, that of supernatural creation. We cannot accept that on philosophical grounds; therefore, we choose to believe the impossible: that life arose spontaneously by chance."

Arthur Keith, author of twenty books defending evolution, wrote, "Evolution is unproved and unprovable. We believe it because the only alternative is special creation, and that is unthinkable."

Huxley, said "I suppose the reason we all jumped at the Origin (Darwin's Origin of Species) was because the idea of God interfered with our sexual mores."[21]

Excuse me? The idea of God interferes with your sexual mores? To think this whole time, we've been told that evolution is based on hardcore facts of science. However, by their own words, you can see it has *nothing* to do with science and *everything* to do with sin! These men are the prophesied scoffers the Bible said would come in the Last Days who would choose to "deliberately forget" or basically "be dumb on purpose" just so they could go on living out their sinful desires. Exactly like the Bible said would happen in the Last Days! When you think of how much this evolutionary lie is being crammed down our throats day in and day out all across America and around the world, it's not only unbelievable, it's downright un-American. I didn't say that. Our Founding Fathers did in the Declaration of Independence:

"We hold these truths to be self-evident that all men are created equal, that they are endowed by their *Creator* with certain unalienable Rights, that among these are Life, Liberty and the pursuit of Happiness."

Let me translate that founding phrase for you. "If you as an evolutionist don't want to believe in a Creator God like the rest of us, and if you want to be dumb on purpose, then maybe it's time you go create your own country somewhere else and leave ours alone!" Please, if you're reading this and you're not a Christian then heed the evidence you just read, admit the facts; you've been lied to. God is real and you need to *reverse your thinking* like this person before it's too late:

Ephesians 2:1 "As for you, you were dead in your transgressions and sins, in which you used to live when you followed the ways of this world."

Reverse Your Thinking

I will live my life according to these beliefs:

God does not exist

It's just foolish to think

That there is an all knowing God with a cosmic plan

That an all-powerful God brings purpose to the pain and suffering in the world

Is a comforting thought however

It

Is only wishful thinking

People can do as they please without eternal consequences

The idea that

I am deserving of hell

Because of sin

Is a lie meant to make me a slave to those in power

"The more you have, the happier you will be"

Our existence has no grand meaning or purpose

In a world with no God
There is freedom to be who I want to be

But with God

Life is an endless cycle of guilt and shame

Without God

Everything is fine

It is ridiculous to think

I am lost and in need of saving

And that's how I thought…before Christ opened my eyes…changed my heart…and reversed my Thinking.

I am lost and in need of saving

It is ridiculous to think

Everything is fine

Without God

Life is an endless cycle of guilt and shame

But with God

There is freedom to be who I want to be

In a world with no God

Our existence has no grand meaning or purpose

"The more you have, the happier you will be"

Is a lie meant to make me a slave to those in power

Because of sin

I am deserving of hell

The idea that

People can do as they please without eternal consequences

Is only wishful thinking

It

Is a comforting thought however

That an all powerful God brings purpose to the pain and suffering in the world

That there is an all knowing God with a cosmic plan

It's just foolish to think

God does not exist

I will live my life according to these beliefs:

Ephesians 2:4 "Because of His great love for us, God Who is rich in mercy, made us alive with Christ even when we were dead in transgressions."[22]

The Third Way We Know Evolution is a Lie and a False Teaching in the Last Days is from the Evidence of a Special Creation

Genesis 1:24-28 "And God said, 'Let the land produce living creatures according to their kinds: the livestock, the creatures that move along the ground, and the wild animals, each according to its kind.' And it was so. God made the wild animals according to their kinds, the livestock according to their kinds, and all the creatures that move along the ground according to their kinds. And God saw that it was good. Then God said, 'Let us make mankind in our image, in our likeness, so that they may rule over the fish in the sea and the birds in the sky, over the livestock and all the wild animals, and over all the creatures that move along the ground.' So God created mankind in his own image, in the image of God he created them; male and female he created them. God blessed them and said to them, 'Be fruitful and increase in number; fill the earth and subdue it. Rule over the fish in the sea and the birds in the sky and over every living creature that moves on the ground.'"

Here we see the Bible informing us that after God made the animals, He made mankind. But not only that, it also says that He made mankind specifically in His image. Now, here's the problem. What does evolution teach? Do they say we were specially created in the image of a special God for a special purpose? No! They say we were created in the image of an ape and that we have no special existence at all! No wonder our world is so hopeless. Think of what the lie of evolution is telling people. They say you are nothing, you came from nothing, and you have no future! That's hopeless! Evolution not only denigrates mankind and actually reduces us to a mere animal, but it teaches the exact opposite of what God says. They don't say God created us after the animals, they say we actually came from an animal. So again, the logical question is, "What evidence do the evolutionists have to back this up? It's one thing to believe this faulty history and promote it, but what *hardcore scientific evidence* do you have that proves that we came from an ape instead of Adam? Well, believe it or not, they don't have any! We've been lied to yet again! For proof of that, let's take a look at the so-called mechanisms of evolution and you tell me if this whole idea of a random chance existence is a bunch of baloney!

THE LIE OF APE MAN

Nebraska Man: In 1922, scientists discovered a fossil in Nebraska that was reported to be 1 million years old and it was heralded as the "missing link" in human evolution and used in the Scopes Monkey trial for proof. The only problem was that it was actually found to be just a mere tooth and that of a pig! Eager evolutionists built a whole imaginary society and lifestyle around this single pig tooth! They built the entire Nebraska man out of plaster of Paris and imagination and then they even built him a wife. You have to be pretty good to know what his wife looks like from only his tooth!

Piltdown Man: For more than 50 years we were led to believe that this ancient creature was another supposed ancestor of modern man and considered the second most important fossil proving evolution. The only problem was that it was a fraud! The original discoverers took a human skull and an ape's jaw bone, filed them down and made them fit together. Then they treated them with acid to make them look old and then buried them in a gravel pit. Voila! "discovered" Piltdown man.

Neanderthal Man: Neanderthal man is the first supposed ape-man ancestor found back in Darwin's day. A professor in 1908 declared that the Neanderthal man was an ignorant knuckle-dragging ape-like man because of the low eye brow ridges and his stooped over posture. However, it was discovered that Neanderthal man was just as human as us and his stooped over posture was caused by arthritis and rickets. He was bent over, not because he was slowly evolving coming up, he was an old man with arthritis slowly going down!

Lucy: Lucy is one of the more recent finds of a supposed ape-man evolution example that has been almost universally accepted without question. But the problem is what scattered bones that were found were assembled from totally different locations. The knee joint was found a mile and a half away from the rest of the skeleton and yet was labeled in *National Geographic* as "Lucy's Knee." As one man remarked, "How fast was that train going when it hit that monkey?" Then they said Lucy was becoming a human due to the fact that an ape has a straight femur, yet Lucy's knee was angled to the side like a human's. However, although monkeys that walk on the ground do have a straight femur, monkeys that climb trees have an angled femur. All this shows is that she was a tree-climbing monkey as opposed to one that walked on ground. Furthermore, as if that wasn't bad enough, the St. Louis Zoo put up a display of Lucy with human feet on her. Guess how many foot bones were found. Zero! Pure propaganda! As it turns out, Lucy was just a tree climbing monkey and some feel there might even be some still alive today in Sumatra down near Vietnam.

THE LIE OF NATURAL SELECTION

Peppered Moth: One of the most popular proofs of so-called "natural selection" is a species of moth in England called the "peppered moth" that comes in light and dark varieties. Supposedly, the light colored moths started out being the dominant ones, but due to pollution, the black ones became more dominant because they were camouflaged by the black soot. The birds ate the light colored ones. But years later when anti-pollution laws were enforced, the black ones lost their camouflage and the birds ate them which caused the light ones to become dominant.

The whole "story" was made up by a guy named H.B. Kettlewell and at first his experiments seemed very straightforward. He even took photographs of the light and dark moths resting on tree trunks during the daytime with birds eating the less camouflaged ones. He even described it as, "The most striking evolutionary change ever actually witnessed in any organism." Or was it? Nope! It was another lie!

First of all, after 25 years only 2 moths were seen in their natural habitat. Then it was discovered that peppered moths don't even rest on tree trunks in the daytime like the pictures showed. Instead, they turned out to be night fliers and they hide under leaves. So to get the "desired" pictures, Kettlewell and others trapped the moths, raised them in a laboratory, and then took some dead ones and some live ones and either pinned or glued them to the trees. In fact, some of the live ones were so sluggish they had to warm them up on the hood of their car to "liven" them up just so the birds would eat them!

THE LIE OF EMBRYOLOGY

Ernst Haeckel: The idea of embryology began in the late 1800's with a German evolutionist named Ernst Haeckel. He said that as a fertilized egg develops to form an embryo, it actually repeats its supposed evolutionary history. So Haeckel actually examined and drew pictures of fish, frogs, chickens, pigs and human embryos side by side and said there was a remarkable similarity between their stages of development.

The only problem with all those pictures and diagrams of embryos that Haeckel used for proof of his theory, was they were fakes! As it turns out, Haeckel was an accomplished artist as well as an anatomist. Therefore, he faked the drawings to "make" his theory appear to be true!

Believe it or not it was exposed as a fraud as early as 1874. Haeckel was convicted of this fraud by his own university where he taught, was charged with fraud by five professors and was considered an utter disgrace for the rest of his career.

Yet amazingly, Haeckel actually said this in his defense, "Other evolutionists had committed similar offences." Makes you wonder what else they're lying about![23]

In fact, this lack of proof for their theory has gotten so bad for the evolutionists, they just keep pumping out the lies like it's no big deal. Then they even have the audacity to yell back at us when we question, "How dare you question us! We smart. You dumb dumb!" Speaking of which, another one of their dumb lies that they use to try to prop up their lie for evolution is called **Sequential Ordering**. This is the premise where they put the bones of dead things they find in the dirt in a certain order to supposedly prove evolution. Yet, if you think about it, when you find a bone in the dirt, all you know about it is that it died. You don't know anything else. You don't know if it had any kids let alone what kind of kids. Therefore, you can put any kind of bones in any kind of supposed order you want but it still doesn't prove a thing! Now, to show you how goofy this sequential ordering idea really is, let's apply that very same logic to the ordering of other items, and you tell me if it's something worthwhile to explain our origin let alone the origin of anything else:

"Just because you can arrange animals in a certain order doesn't prove a thing. Even if you find them buried in a certain order, that doesn't prove a thing. If I get buried on top of a hamster, does that prove he's my grandpa?

I've been doing a lot of research on the evolution of the fork. I've pieced together fragmentary evidence for years. I believe after intensive research, the knife evolved first and then slowly evolved into the spoon. It took millions of years with great geological pressures that squeezed, dished it out and widened it a little bit. Then slowly, erosion cut grooves into the end and turned it into the short tine fork. And then very slowly over millions of years, the grooves got longer and wider until it turned into the long tine fork. I knew I had the right order, but I felt like I had a missing link, particularly between spoons and forks. You see, spoons are rounded and have no grooves but forks are squared and grooved. That's two jumps in one. Even punctuated equilibrium can't do that. So I knew I had a missing link but I couldn't find it.

Until one day I'm flying in an airplane on US Air, 30,000 feet off the ground, and a stewardess walked down the aisle and handed me the missing link! I don't think she knew what she had, but my trained scientific eye picked it up. I said, 'This is it!' Then later that day I went to get some chicken for lunch and found another one. There they are folks, the missing links...sporks!

So now the evolution of silverware is becoming complete. All I need to do is apply for a 10 million dollar grant and I think I can wrap this up. I've found a lot of evidence since then. I've been gathering data on this for a long time. I've even found some mutants along the way (melted plastic forks). They didn't quite make it for some reason.

You know, it was very interesting though. As soon as people found out that I was doing research on the evolution on the fork, everybody wanted to become famous. They sent me all their data from all over the country. Even some lies got sent to me. One of them was an obvious fake. It was a fork head on a spoon handle. It didn't get by me though. This is a cutthroat business. This fossil business is dangerous you know; you have to watch them. But I caught it right away. It's not in my museum. The rest of them are though.

Now look, you can arrange letters in order and try to prove something if you want. You can turn a cat to a cot to a dot to a dog making one letter change at a time. If you play around for a while, you can turn yourself into a fool. Doesn't take long either!"[24]

How many of you are going to take a closer look at your silverware next time you go out for lunch? Hey, you might find a missing link, maybe it's a piece of sausage on the end of your fork! I was personally thinking about messing with the evolutionist's minds by having my wife bury me on top of my two wiener dogs. Hopefully she'd do it after I was dead. But seriously, maybe you're starting to think what I'm thinking, "If all you have is lies to support your theory Mr. Evolutionist, then maybe it's time to get a new theory!" Furthermore, "Why would you deliberately want to lie to people?" Well, as we already saw, the Bible gave us the answer! It's a sign you're living in the Last Days. "In the Last Days, scoffers would come who would not only mock and scoff at God's existence, but they would actually 'deliberately forget' the *genuine proof* of God's existence and make up a bunch of baloney stories, including Ape-man, Natural Selection, Embryology and a whole host of other lies just so they could live out their ungodly desires." That's not only the answer to the evolutionists' lying behavior, but it's also the answer as to why the wrath of God is coming!

The Fourth Way We Know Evolution is a Lie and a False Teaching in the Last Days is from the Evidence of a Judged Creation

Matthew 24:36-39 "No one knows about that day or hour, not even the angels in heaven, nor the Son, but only the Father. As it was in the days of Noah, so it will be at the coming of the Son of Man. For in the days before the flood, people were eating and drinking, marrying and giving in marriage, up to the day Noah entered the ark; and they knew nothing about what would happen until the flood came and took them all away. That is how it will be at the coming of the Son of Man."

Now, even though we clearly don't know the exact day or hour when Jesus is coming back. Still, Jesus, out of love, gave a clue as to how we can know when it's getting close. Notice what clue He uses. He tells us about a *literal guy* name Noah who *literally entered* into a *literal ark* that was *literally filled with animals* to escape a *literal judgment* upon the world. Yet, here's the problem. What does evolution teach? Do they say, "Oh yes, there was a literal guy named Noah who literally survived on a literal ark with literally all the animals in the world to escape a literal judgment"? No! They not only *mock the account of Noah*, which is calling Jesus a liar, but they flat out call it a *myth*. In fact, they usually say something like, "Well, you mean to tell me that all the animals in the world could fit on that Ark? Are you kidding me? That's a bunch of baloney!" Really? Well, first of all, if you read the Bible you'll see that Noah didn't need to bring two of every single living thing that was on the planet, like the skeptics want to say. Rather, he only had to bring two of every *kind*. Not two of every *species* but two of every *kind*. This means he didn't need to bring two of every single species of dog, he just needed two of the dog kind, a male and a female, that's it. Then, the Bible says Noah only had to bring the *air-breathing land animals*, not the water ones. So that would seriously reduce the number required. However, I agree, even after that, that's *still* a lot of animals to squish into that boat! So let's put it to the test. Could Noah's ark, with its dimensions, have contained enough space to hold two of every *kind* of *air-breathing land animal* on the planet? Yes! Unlike the evolutionists, we don't make up our stories! They are based on facts. Let's take a look at that evidence.

First of all, the ark was not a ship with sloping sides, it was a large barge, so it had a larger carrying capacity. If you do the math with the dimensions given to us in the Bible:

Genesis 6:14-16 "So make yourself an ark of cypress wood; make rooms in it and coat it with pitch inside and out. This is how you are to build it: The ark is to be 450 feet long, 75 feet wide and 45 feet high. Make a roof for it and finish the ark to within 18 inches of the top. Put a door in the side of the ark and make lower, middle and upper decks."

So, if you do the math the ark would have had over 100,000 square feet of floor space and a total cubic volume of 1,518,000 cubic feet, which is equivalent to about 569 modern railroad stock cars. Therefore, researchers agree that there was plenty of room on the ark to hold two of every kind of air-breathing land animal. In fact, there was room to spare. They have actually discovered that on the high side, no more than 35,000 individual animals needed to go on the ark because the average size of animal is about the size of a sheep, and even the few large ones like elephants don't need to be represented by the giant older ones but rather the much smaller, younger ones. Even so, researchers decided to pad this number anyway to be generous. So they assumed an incredibly high amount of 50,000 animals to be put on the ark, 15,000 more than what was required, and here's what they found. Using the railroad cars for comparison, they noted that the average double-deck stock car can accommodate about 240 sheep. So if you do the math that means all of the 50,000 animals can be carried on only 208 of the 569 railroad cars which is only about 37% of the ark. This would leave an additional 361 cars or enough to make about 5 trains of about 72 cars each to carry all of the food and all the baggage plus Noah's family of eight people."[25]

As you can see, based on the evidence, there was plenty of room on the ark to hold those animals with room to spare. There's no need to mock, there's no need to scoff! The facts are, the Flood of Noah is a literal account of the first judgment from God to warn about the coming next judgment from God! Besides, flip it around. Have you ever thought about what evolutionists teach? They want to mock and scoff at us and the Biblical account and say something like, "You mean to tell me that all the dogs in the world came from two dogs on Noah's ark? You're crazy!" Really? Have you ever stopped to think of what you teach? I have no problem with two dogs over the last 4,500 years producing all the dogs we see today. Just one litter can produce different sizes and different colors. Extrapolate that over a few thousand years and there's no problem. Yet I have a problem with what you the evolutionist are saying and that is that we all came from a rock, as this man points out:

"I was speaking in a college in Boston one time and this Preacher called all the colleges and universities around Boston for a debate with me. So when I got

there I got my charts out and I said 'Now folks, I believe the Bible.' Nobody cheered. I said, 'I believe about six thousand years ago God made everything. The world's not millions of years old. And two thousand years ago Jesus came.' And I gave them the basic Bible story.

Then I told them what they believe because most of them don't know what they believe, you have to tell them. I said, 'You guys believe that twenty billions years ago there was a big bang where nothing exploded and produced everything. Then you say 4.6 billion years ago the earth cooled down, made a hard rocky crust, it rained on the rocks for millions of years, turned them into soup and the soup came alive three billion years ago. And this early life form found somebody to marry.' Boy now that's a good trick! And I continued, 'Then it found something to eat of course and then slowly evolved into everything we see today.'

One professor was kind of getting upset at about this time. I seem to do that to them. He said, 'There are hundreds of varieties of dogs in the world.' I said, 'Yes sir, you're right about that.' He said, 'You mean to tell me that you believe that all these dogs came from two dogs off of Noah's Ark? You expect me to believe that?'

I said, 'Sir, would you look at what you're teaching your students? You're teaching your students that all the dogs in the world came from a rock!'

Then I had one lady come to me after a debate one time. She was steaming down the aisle. Boy, she was mad! She walked up and said, 'Tonight, you said we believe that we came from a rock. We do not believe that.'

I said, 'Well maam, calm down for just a minute. Do you believe in evolution?' She said, 'Yes I do. I'm a professor here at the university.' I said, 'Well, will you please tell me then where we came from?' She said, 'We came from a macro molecule.' I said, 'Where did that come from?' She said, 'From the oceans. From the pre-biotic soup.' I said, 'Where did that come from?' She said, 'Well, it rained on the rocks for millions of years...'

And then she paused and you could see that it was slowly dawning on her that, 'I really do believe that I came from a rock, don't I?' I replied, 'Yes mam, you do. You ought to be proud of it. But be careful not to step on Grandpa whatever you do!'"[26]

Me personally, I think I'll stick to the Biblical account of two dogs on Noah's ark. I don't have enough faith to believe in evolution! Apparently, I'm not that religious! But seriously, as you can see, there's no need to mock and scoff at the Biblical account of Noah. It's not only factual, it's much more feasible than evolution. And remember, this is the clue from Jesus as to how close we're getting to the Last Days! "As it was in the Days of Noah *literally* so shall it be at the Coming of the Son of Man *literally*!" In other words, He's telling us that He *literally* judged this planet once and He's *literally* getting ready to do it again! We better be ready!

The **fifth way** we know evolution is a lie and a false teaching in the Last Days, is from the **Evidence of a Fearful Creation**. The Bible clearly tells us that one of God's most awesome and fearful creations that He ever made was the *dinosaur*. Yes, God made the dinosaur too! I didn't say that. He did.

Genesis 1:24-25 "And God said, 'Let the land produce living creatures according to their kinds: the livestock, the creatures that move along the ground, and the wild animals, each according to its kind.' And it was so. God made the wild animals according to their kinds, the livestock according to their kinds, and all the creatures that move along the ground according to their kinds. And God saw that it was good."

So here we see that God created all the land animals on day six. It's right there in black and white. Therefore, common sense tells us that this would obviously include the dinosaurs. They lived on the land too, didn't they? Furthermore, this would also mean as we already saw that Noah's flood must have been the event that's responsible for wiping them out. What did we just witness? The flood took out all the air-breathing land animals and that has to include the dinosaurs! Here's the problem. What does evolution teach? Do they teach that God made the dinosaurs and then wiped them out with the flood at the first judgment? No! They say they came from a rock and died out 70 million years ago. So once again, the question is, "Okay, it's one thing to believe that, but what *hardcore scientific data* do you have to back it up?" Believe it or not, the answer is *none*! In fact, when you do look at the actual evidence it clearly agrees with the Biblical account.

First of all, scientists not only find tons and tons of dead things around the world, but they find so many of them that they've actually given them a name. They call them fossil graveyards. These graveyards not only contain tons and tons of fossils, but they find them all jumbled up and thrown together in a completely disordered mass, exactly like you'd expect to find in a "sudden" violent flood. In fact, the pictures of these dinosaur graveyards often show people chiseling out a backbone of an animal that has no legs, head, tail or rib cage attached to it with no teeth marks on the bone, and next to it is another backbone of another animal all bent up and twisted. It's just a bunch of parts and pieces!

This shows us that these animals were not torn apart by scavengers but rather, they are the remains of a swirling mass of rotting animal parts that were deposited at the flood. In fact, one person stated, "We have huge, mass graves where dinosaur fossils are jumbled together like flotsam after a flood." Gee, I wonder which flood that was? Another researcher stated, "At this spot in Wyoming the fossil hunters found a veritable gold mine of dinosaur bones. The concentration was so remarkable; they were piled in, like logs in a jam." Sounds like flood words to me! Yet, even with all this clear-cut evidence that a worldwide flood is what wiped out the dinosaurs, the evolutionist will still "deliberately forget" and come up with all kinds of wild and crazy stories to the contrary. Here's just a few of them:

- The sun became either too hot or too cold for dinosaurs.
- The world's climate became either too dry or too wet.
- A supernova exploded nearby, spraying the earth with radiation.
- A passing comet poisoned the earth with chemicals.
- Earth's magnetic field reversed, and incoming radiation killed them.
- An asteroid plunged into the earth and that's what destroyed them.

But wait a second, common sense tells us that if this were true, then why did this asteroid, comet, radiation, whatever, only kill the dinosaurs and not the rest of life?

- Mammals ate the dinosaur eggs
- Dinosaurs turned into birds and flew away!
- New narcotic plants evolved (Drugs killed them?)
- The inability of dinosaurs to experience slow wave sleep
- They were killed by volcanoes
- Poisonous gases
- Parasites
- Slipped discs
- Mass suicide
- Constipation

- Shrinking brain (they got really dumb)

Speaking of "really dumb" one man observing these theories rightly stated, "It is obvious that evolutionists don't know what happened and are grasping at straws."[27] Or can I translate that for you? You will "deliberately forget" and turn a blind eye to the evidence. Coming up with all kinds of wacked out and crazy stories, including back problems or constipation is what took out the dinosaurs, just as long as it *doesn't* agree with the Biblical account. Why? Because the Bible said this was going to happen in the Last Days! "In the Last Days, scoffers would come and they'd not only mock and scoff at God's existence, but they would 'deliberately forget' the proof of His existence and His First Judgment so we would all be blindsided and not prepared for the Second Coming Judgment!"

IV. Fourth End Time Prophecy Concerning the Rise of Falsehood - There Would be an Increase of False Prophets

2 Peter 2:1-3 "But there were also false prophets among the people, just as there will be false teachers among you. They will secretly introduce destructive heresies, even denying the sovereign Lord who bought them – bringing swift destruction on themselves. Many will follow their shameful ways and will bring the way of truth into disrepute. In their greed these teachers will exploit you with stories they have made up. Their condemnation has long been hanging over them, and their destruction has not been sleeping."

In other words, you don't want to be in their camp! According to the Bible, another thing the Apostle Peter tells us we need to be on the lookout for *in the future*, is not only a rise of skepticism and scoffing towards God in the Last Days, but also to look out for *false prophets* who introduce *false teachings in the Church*, right? He also noted that these false teachings by these false prophets are *destructive heresies* that specifically *deny Jesus Christ*, the way to heaven, with stories they have made up! This fits in line perfectly with what Jesus already said in Matthew 24, "Watch out that no one deceives you." Why? Because, as we saw, the Last Days are going to be full of *deceit, deceit, deceit*! That's why He said, "See, I've told you ahead of time." Now, the Apostle Peter warns about it to!

So let's do that. Let's give ourselves a heads up advanced warning about all these false prophets and their false teachings that have appeared on the scene in these Last Days so we don't fall for it too. What I'm about to share with you are many of the false teachings that have been promoted by false prophets, all starting roughly at about the same time during the turn of the Last Century from the mid-to-late 1800's and on into the early 1900's. Tell me this isn't something the enemy would do, especially in the Last Days. The timing is impeccable. The devil knows that his gig is up! He knows that he's lost! Jesus defeated him! He's the biggest loser! It's done! It's over! But he's so evil that he's seeing how many people he can take with him into the Lake of Fire. Therefore, if you were the devil and you wanted to take people with you into the Lake of Fire and you were "that close" to pulling off the Antichrist's kingdom, what would you do? You'd make sure you keep people away from the truth that's only contained in the Bible because that's the only book on the planet that exposes what you're up to in minute detail! So what better way to cover up your evil plans, your dastardly deeds, than to do what the Bible says you're going to do, *introduce destructive heresies in the Church* not the world, and *steer people away from the truth*! This is the very tool satan uses in these Last Days to cloud the issue of God's truth and keep people off track of what's really going on so they join him in the Lake of Fire.

1. The First False Teaching Being Promoted by False Prophets in the Last Days – The Lie of Mormonism

Now all I know is that somebody's done a brilliant PR job for Mormonism because the impression that most people have in our country concerning Mormons is that they are synonymous with Christianity. The problem is, as you will see, it is not! Even though they may *use* Christian terminology and *say* they're the "Church of Jesus Christ" of Latter Day "Saints," when you look at the facts of what they actually believe and teach, they're definitely not Christian and they're definitely not saints! You tell me if this belief system is synonymous with true biblical Christianity:

"Mormonism teaches that trillions of planets scattered throughout the cosmos are ruled by countless gods who once were human like us. They say that long ago on one of these planets, to an unidentified god and one of his goddess wives, a spirit child named Elohim was conceived. This spirit child was later born to human parents who gave him a physical body. Through obedience to Mormon teaching, and death and resurrection, he proved himself worthy and was elevated to godhood as his father before him.

Mormons believe that Elohim is their heavenly father and he lives with his many goddess wives on the planet near a mysterious star called Kolob. Here the god of

Mormonism and his wives, through endless celestial sex produced millions of spirit children.

To decide their destiny, the head of the Mormon gods called a great heavenly council meeting. Both of Elohim's eldest sons were there. Lucifer and his brother Jesus. Lucifer became the devil and his followers the demons. Sent to this world, they would forever be denied bodies of flesh and bone. Those who remained neutral in the battle were cursed to be born with black skin. This is the Mormon explanation for the Negro race.

Early Mormon prophets taught that Elohim and one of his goddess wives came to earth as Adam and Eve to start the human race. Thousands of years later, Elohim in human form, once again journeyed to earth from the star base Kolob. This time to have sex with the virgin Mary in order to provide Jesus with a physical body.

After Jesus Christ grew to manhood, he took at least 3 wives - Mary, Martha and Mary Magdalene. Through these wives the Mormon Jesus, for whom Joseph Smith claimed direct descent, supposedly fathered a number of children before he was crucified. [28]

Yup, that's so much like Christianity, I don't know why you'd ever doubt. Excuse me? God had multiple wives, Jesus' brother was satan, having black skin is a curse, and you can become a god, what? How could people ever fall for that boloney? That's *a story you made up*! Here's the reason why. It's a sign we're living in the Last Days! The Bible says, the enemy, in the Last Days, is going to introduce destructive heresies *in the Church* with stories made up including the planet Kolob! The devil will introduce a *pseudo-fake-false-Christianity* just to keep people away from the truth, which is exactly what the false teaching of Mormonism is doing!

2. The Second False Teaching Being Promoted by False Prophets in the Last Days – The Lie of Jehovah's Witnesses

Now wait a second! It says, "Jehovah" and we're supposed to be "witnesses." I mean, surely these guys are Christian? Wrong! Once again, just because you use Christian terminology doesn't mean you're Christian! Jehovah's Witnesses not only teach that Jesus was the archangel Michael and that He didn't rise from the dead physically, but they also state that the Holy Spirit is not alive;

he is mere force. Just like Mormonism, they say you have to work your way to heaven. That is clearly *not* Christianity! Jesus Christ is the Son of God, He did rise from the dead and the Holy Spirit is alive, and you don't work your way to heaven. Salvation is a gift from God based on the work of Jesus Christ alone on the cross! To make matters worse, little do people know that this *pseudo-Christian group* called Jehovah's Witnesses got their so-called truth from a short order cook in Ohio! Don't believe me? They even admit it:

"One member, David Riccaboni remembers his long time service at the Society's headquarters printing the Watchtower magazine. He is seen in the 1953 film 'New World Society in Action.'

Dave Riccaboni: One thing that impressed me as a Jehovah's Witness was our willingness to admit our mistakes. I thought that was great at the time. I knew the Society had been wrong in the past when they set dates for the end of the world. And I saw the major changes in their doctrine and I felt – sometimes I felt upset – but I was taught from the time I was a little child that this is the way Jehovah revealed 'new light' to the organization.

The Bible produced by the Jehovah's Witnesses called the New World Translation has caused quite a stir. Their 'Proclaimers' book claims that it is a literal translation that faithfully presents what is in the original writings and that the entire translation committee were spirit anointed Christians.

Joan Cetnar: My late husband, Bill Cetnar was at the Watchtower headquarters doing work on the New World Translation. Former president Fred Franz was mainly responsible for the translation work. He was neither a Hebrew nor a Greek scholar and only had two years of college. There were no scholars. I know because I knew them all personally. The so called translation was written to reflect their own peculiar doctrine and the 'Proclaimers' book is not telling the truth when it says this is a fresh translation from the original Greek.

Dave Riccaboni: The only original Greek I knew was George Gangas of the secretive translation committee, and he was no scholar, that's for sure, because he, himself told me that before he came to Bethel he was a short order cook in Columbus, Ohio."[29]

Excuse me? That's your source of truth? Your scholars for your "new translation" were short order cooks from Ohio with no training? How could people ever fall for such boloney? That's *a story you made up*! Well, here's the reason why. It's a sign we're living in the Last Days! The Bible says, the enemy, in the Last Days, is going to introduce destructive heresies *in the Church* with stories that people made up! In other words, He's going to introduce *a pseudo-fake-false-Christianity* just to keep people away from the truth and that's exactly what Jehovah's Witnesses are doing!

3. The Third False Teaching Being Promoted by False Prophets in the Last Days – The Lie of Christian Science

Now hold on here. It says "Christian" and we all love "science." Surely they support God's truth? Wrong! Again, just because you use Christian terminology doesn't mean you're a Christian! Christian Science not only teaches that Jesus was *not* the Messiah *nor* God, but they have the audacity to say that God is Father-Mother, and that Jesus' work on the cross was *not* sufficient to cleanse us from sin, because after all, they say there is no sin and there is no devil![30] What? That's not Christianity! That's *a lie from the devil.* Who is real, by the way, and he is using Christian Science in the Last Days to steer people away from the truth, exactly like the Bible said would happen!

4. The Fourth False Teaching Being Promoted by False Prophets in the Last Days – The Lie of Seventh Day Adventism

Wait a second. It's says "Seventh Day" and we believe in a "seven day creation" and it mentions "Adventism" and we believe in the "Advent of Jesus Christ." Surely they're Christian? Wrong! Just because you use Christian terminology doesn't mean you're Christian! Seventh Day Adventists also believe that Jesus is the archangel Michael, just like Jehovah's Witnesses, and then they say our sins will ultimately be placed on *satan*, not Jesus on the cross. Furthermore, they even say that hellfire is *not* eternal, the soul is *not* immortal, and worshipping on Sunday is the sign of the Mark of the Beast![31] Excuse me? That's not Christianity! It's a sign you're living in the Last Days. The Bible says in the Last Days people are going to *make stories up* and *introduce destructive heresies* to keep people away from the truth! This is exactly what Seventh Day Adventism is doing! It's another *pseudo-fake-false-Christianity* to steer people away from the truth in the Last Days!

5. The Fifth False Teaching Being Promoted by False Prophets in the Last Days – The Lie of the Charismatic Fringe

Just a minute. It says "charismatic" and isn't it good to be "charismatic" for the Lord? I've even heard people say that I personally have more "charisma" than a "bag full of cats!" Surely that's good? Well yes, having "charisma" *for the Lord* and *His Word* is good. But not when you use that so-called "charisma" to steer people *away from His Word*. This is what the Charismatic fringe does. They seek a so-called "Word from God" *outside* the actual "Word of God," the Bible, and once you go down this route you just opened up Pandora's Box! You can make anything appear to be true! Including, Mormonism, Jehovah's Witnesses, Christian Science, Seventh Day Adventists and a whole host of other false teachings. Why? Because they all say the same thing! They all have the same premise as the Charismatic fringe. *They got a new Word from God.* This destroys any grounds to counter the faulty belief systems of these other false teachings because you're doing the same thing they're doing. That is, seeking truth outside the Bible! Do you see the problem? Once you go outside the Bible, you can make anything appear to be true, including *the destructive heresies* that are going to be introduced into the Church in the Last Days!

6. The Sixth False Teaching Being Promoted by False Prophets in the Last Days – The Lie of the New Age Movement

It is my opinion that the false teachings of the New Age Movement are single-handedly preparing people *right now* **to accept** a *One World Religion*, a *One World Government*, and a *One World Ruler* the Bible says would come in the Last Days. This is due to the fact that the New Age Movement is a mixture of all religions where nothing is wrong and everything is right, except of course, Christianity. To show you what I mean, let's take a look at some of their beliefs:

"First of all, the New Age Movement began around 1875 (Notice the timing of the date. Right in line with the other Last Days false teachings we just saw) with the false teachings of a lady named Helena Blavatsky who was part of an occult group called, the Theosophical Society. They espoused the abolishment of Christianity, Judaism and Islam, and the promotion of unity between the rest of the world's religions. They claimed that their teachings were revealed by 'spirit' or elemental guides (demons) and they emphasized the evolution of a self-deified, master aryan society, and a one world "new age" religion and social order.

Later in the 1920's these teachings were picked up and promoted by another false teacher named Alice Bailey who formed the 'Lucifer Publishing Company' to help print and promote these ideas. Step by step they plotted the coming of a 'new age' with instructions and plans for the institution of a 'new world order.' Bailey established the symbol of a 'rainbow' as their identification sign and discussed extensively the plans for a religious war, forced redistribution of the world's resources, mass planetary initiations and theology for a new world order, world-wide disarmamen, and elimination of obstinate religions. She even discussed the sacredness of the new world leader's number, 666." [32]

In fact, here's a short bullet list of their core beliefs:

- **All is god: the earth, man, animals, and plants.** [32]

    Really? The Bible says that was the original lie that satan used back in the Garden of Eden and there is only one God.

    Genesis 3:4-5 "'You will not surely die,' the serpent said to the woman. 'For God knows that when you eat of it your eyes will be opened, and you will be like God, knowing good and evil.'"

    The following is a video excerpt describing this serious false teaching being promoted in New Ager Shirley MacLaine's movie, 'Out on a Limb.'

    "Shirley MacLaine was Time Magazine's poster girl for the New Age Movement in the 1980's. MacLaine starred in the biographical mini-series 'Out on a Limb' based on her journey in New Age belief. The series has been called 'The most talked about mini-series of all time.' The title 'Out on a Limb' refers to the risk involved in seeking the fruit of 'the Tree of Knowledge.'

    John Heard's character, David Manning, states in the movie: 'Mayan told me to tell you one thing if you had a hard time with this. She said in order to get to the fruit of the tree you have to go out on a limb.'

    Mayan is a spirit guide sending a message to MacLaine. A message that is repeated throughout the series.

    David Manning: 'I am god.'

    MacLaine: 'I am god.'

Manning: 'I am god.'

Manning and MacLaine in unison: 'I am god...I am god...I AM GOD! I AM GOD! I AM GOD!'"

- **Each one of us have the ability to become 'the Christ' or 'the Christ-consciousness.** [32]

Really? Jesus specifically warned about this phrase as a sign we're living in the Last Days.

Matthew 24:3-5 "As Jesus was sitting on the Mount of Olives, the disciples came to him privately. 'Tell us,' they said, 'when will this happen, and what will be the sign of Your coming and of the end of the age?' Jesus answered: 'Watch out that no one deceives you. For many will come in My Name, claiming, 'I am *the Christ*,' and will deceive many."

- **Man is destroying the earth along with the animals and plants. Unless he changes his ways, 'Mother Earth' will be forced to destroy humanity. Christianity is the biggest culprit destroying the earth by teaching that man had dominion over the earth when the earth is a living being.** [32]

Really? First of all, the Bible says we are to 'rule' over the earth which is not synonymous with 'abuse.' We are to be wise 'stewards' of it. Nobody is promoting pouring toxic waste into our water supply. Secondly, there's a major difference between being a 'steward' of the earth and a 'worshiper' of the earth, which is what New Age promotes. In fact, the Bible says, this is why the wrath of God is coming.

Romans 1:18-25 "The wrath of God is being revealed from heaven against all the godlessness and wickedness of men who suppress the truth by their wickedness. They exchanged the truth of God for a lie, and worshiped and served created things rather than the Creator – Who is forever praised. Amen."

- **There is no such thing as sin and no need to repent and be saved.** [32]

Really? The Bible says in **Romans 3:23,6:23** "For all have sinned and fall short of the glory of God, For the wages of sin is death, but the gift of God is eternal life in Christ Jesus our Lord."

- **Jesus is but one of many great teachers such as Buddha, Muhammad or Confucius.** [32]

Really? The Bible says Jesus *alone* rose from the dead!

Acts 13:34,35 "The fact that God raised Him from the dead, never to decay. You will not let your Holy One see decay."

Buddha, Muhammad and Confucius *are decaying* because they're dead!

- **Mankind should seek direction directly from 'the spirit world' via a psychic, a channeler, a palm reader, astrology, angels, space aliens, dead relatives, meditation, etc.** [32]

Really? The Bible says this is an abomination to God!

Deuteronomy 18:9-12 "When you enter the land the LORD your God is giving you, do not learn to imitate the detestable ways of the nations there. Let no one be found among you who sacrifices his son or daughter in the fire, who practices divination or sorcery, interprets omens, engages in witchcraft, or casts spells, or who is a medium or spiritist or who consults the dead. Anyone who does these things is detestable to the LORD."

Yet that's precisely what New Agers do. They contact actual demons for their teachings, as this report shows:

"This man channels a spirit calling itself "Bashar" who seems to hold his audience spellbound as he tells them they are equal to the Creator of the Universe.

"Bashar": That's why all are made in the image of the infinite Creator and what that means is you are all infinite creators.

Jack Purcell has become one of the more popular channelers possessed by a spirit named "Lazaris."

"Lazaris": Indeed, it's a pleasure to be talking with you. And. Uh. Well, shall we begin? Where you'd like to begin?

Lazaris tells the listener that God is already within man and that if man wants to find God he only needs to find himself.

Jane Roberts was a new age pioneer who channeled a spirit known as "Seth". Roberts sold more than a million copies of her books and has inspired many.

Rick Stack: Clearly the main message that Seth is trying to say is that people are gods in training.

Some may find it interesting that the name Seth is synonymous with the Egyptian god Set. And in the realm of the occult, Set is one of the infernal names of satan." [32]

- **All religions (except orthodox Christianity) are of equal merit.** [32]

  Really? Jesus said in **John 14:6** "I am the way and the truth and the life. No one comes to the Father except through Me."

- **In order for the world to be at peace and harmony there must be a New World Order, universal monetary system, world authority on food, health, and water, universal tax, military draft, one world leader, and the abolishment of Christianity.** [32]

  Now, wait a second. New Agers don't really believe that, do they? Yes, they do! Listen to them for yourself:

  "A magazine called the Omega Letter says, 'There is only one obstacle to world unity -- Christianity.'

  It goes on to say, 'Christianity claims 'supernatural knowledge' and 'divine revelation' and therefore, should not be tolerated.'

  Gus Hall the former leader of the Communist party in America said, 'I dream of a time when the last Congressman is strangled to death on the guts of the last preacher and since the Christians love to sing about the blood, why not give a little bit of it.'

Jesus said 'Yea, the time cometh, that whosoever killeth you will think that he doeth God a service. And these things they do unto you, because they have not known the Father, nor Me. But these things have I told you, that when the time shall come, ye may remember that I told you of them" John 16:2-4.'"[32]

That sure sounds like Jesus' other warning in Matthew 24 where He said, "See I've told you ahead of time." In other words, you need to be prepared! However, you might be tempted to think that nobody in their right mind is ever going to fall for this baloney, especially the annihilation of Christians. We're supposed to be a Christian Nation after all. Yet, this is all part of the seduction. As we already saw, in today's society, apparently anyone can just claim to be a Christian and somehow that makes you one. Which means the person sitting next to you in the pew may be the end of you because they may not even be a true born again Christian in the first place. Just *saying* you're a Christian and going to a Church service doesn't make you one! Furthermore, the New Age Movement is also *secretly introducing their lie* right under people's noses! As this quote explains:

"Today, the New Age movement appears to be a loose knit group of innocent organizations with ambiguous goals or leadership. But beneath the surface there is a definite, organized, secret leadership and strategy which guides the vast movement."[33]

That's why as of 1995, New Agers represented 20% of the population of the United States making them the third largest religious group.[34] So the question is, "How are they able to get so many converts here in America? Again, we're supposed to be a Christian Nation?"

1. The First Way New Age is Seducing People - Promotion Through a Hollywood Mogul

Believe it or not, thanks to Hollywood, the New Age Movement not only has the largest Church in the world, but their false teachings are being promoted every single day on TV. It's right under people's noses and yet most people don't even realize they are being indoctrinated into it. Let's see if you can guess who the Hollywood Mogul doing this deceptive work is:

"Have you heard about the largest church in the world? The first service was March 3, 2008 with an attendance of over 300,000. The attendance now is over 2 million and they conducted the first ever mass trance on March 17, 2008. What do they teach?

- *Who you are requires no belief.*
- *Heaven is not a location but refers to the inner realm of consciousness.*
- *The man on the cross is an archetypal image. He is every man and every woman.*

The leader's website teaches these lessons:

- *My mind is part of God's. I am very holy.*
- *My holiness is my salvation.*
- *My salvation comes from me.*
- *Let me remember that there is no sin.*
- *Do not make the pathetic error of "clinging to the old rugged cross."*
- *The only message of the crucifixion is that you can overcome the cross.*

Have you heard of this church? Or maybe its leader? **Oprah Winfrey**.

Years ago she denied Jesus is the only way. Today she has turned her millions of adoring fans over to new age doctrine. Christians are letting this into their homes and are being deceived.

Christians are confused...

Kelly (Afton, Illinois): In reading books such as Tolle, it's really opened up my eyes to a new way of thinking, a new form of spirituality that doesn't always align with the teachings of Christianity. So my question is to you Oprah, how do you reconcile these spiritual teachings with your Christian beliefs?

Oprah: I reconciled it because I was able to open my mind about the um-the absolute, indescribable hugeness of that which we call god. I took God out of the box, because I grew up in the Baptist Church and there were, you know, rules and belief systems and doctrine. I believe that God is love and that God is in all things and so that when the search for something more than doctrine-uh-started to stir within me.

Oprah to Tolle: The essence of all consciousness isn't something to believe. God Is.
Tolle: Yes, yes.

Oprah: God is. And God is a feeling experience not a believing experience.

Tolle: That's right.

Oprah: And if your religion is a believing experience. If God for you is still about a belief, then it's not truly God. "[35]

Excuse me? Some to this day wonder why I call her, "Oprah-Wan-Kenobi." It's because she's one of the biggest New Age Priestesses on the planet, next to Shirley MacLaine, who by the way, Oprah has had on her show multiple times! So as you can see, even Christians are being seduced when they *voluntarily indoctrinate* themselves into New Age teachings by watching her program, or dare I say, attend her Church services on TV every day! It's not just mind-blowing and seductive, it's a sign we're living in the Last Days! The Bible says in the Last Days, false prophets would come and *introduce destructive heresies in the Church* and *steer people away from the truth*, which would include, "The Oprah Wan Kenobi Show!"

2. The Second Way the New Age Movement is Seducing People - Promotion of a Healthy Earth

Of course, I'm talking about the **Environmental Movement**. Little do people realize that the tenets of environmentalism have their roots in the occult beliefs of the New Age Movement. Here's what God has to say about it.

Romans 1:18-25 "The wrath of God is being revealed from heaven against all the godlessness and wickedness of men who suppress the truth by their wickedness, since what may be known about God is plain to them, because God has made it plain to them. For since the creation of the world God's invisible qualities – His eternal power and divine nature – have been clearly seen, being understood from what has been made, so that men are without excuse. For although they knew God, they neither glorified Him as God nor gave thanks to Him, but their thinking became futile and their foolish hearts were darkened. Although they claimed to be wise, they became fools and exchanged the glory of the immortal God for images made to look like mortal man and birds and animals and reptiles. Therefore, God gave them over in the sinful desires of their hearts to sexual impurity for the degrading of their bodies with one another. They exchanged the truth of God for a lie, and worshiped and served created things rather than the Creator – Who is forever praised. Amen."

Now again, we've already seen how this passage tells us one of the reasons why the wrath of God is being revealed from heaven. It is because people have the audacity to *worship the earth*, a created thing, rather than the Creator. As we saw, this just so happens to be one of the major false teachings of the New Age Movement. Let's take a look at that again:

- *All is god: the earth, man, animals and plants.*

- *Man is destroying the earth along with the animals and plants. Unless he changes his ways, 'Mother Earth' will be forced to destroy humanity. Christianity is the biggest culprit in destroying the earth, by teaching that man has dominion over the earth when the earth is a living being.*[36]

Again, the Bible says we are to "rule" over the earth but that's not synonymous with "abusing" the earth. We are to be "wise stewards" of the earth and nobody, even Christians, are promoting that we pour toxic waste into our water supply. That's a bunch of baloney! That's a straw man argument. Secondly, there's a major difference between being a "wise steward" of the earth and "worshiping" the earth, which is what New Age espouses. I restated all of that to make the following point. The average person today thinks that they are helping to *save the earth* when in reality they are helping to spread the beliefs of the New Age Movement.

The First Way Environmentalism is Promoting the New Age Movement - Promotion of Earth Worship

Think about it. Does not the environmental movement believe that the earth, plants and animals are sacred, almost to the point of worship? Yes. Do they not say that man and Christianity are the biggest culprits for the destruction of the earth? Yes. What is that? New Age teaching. Just like the New Age Movement is using "Oprah-Wan-Kenobi" in Hollywood to promote their lies, so too, they're using Environmentalism to do the same! Now, for those of you who think the environmental movement doesn't really worship the earth. Observe the following transcript from a video, unveiling the behavior of radical environmental extremists, called *Earth First*:

"Video begins with Earth First group in the woods.

Then (Weeping heard in the distance)

(Group seen sitting on the forest floor all weeping and crying)

Commentator: Deep in the woods in North Carolina an extremist eco-group called Earth First for Whales In Violation of American Nature.

Woman from the group crying and screaming: 'I WANT TO MOURN THE LOSS OF ALL THE OLD GROWTH TREES I SEE AND TELL THEM THAT WE LOVE THEM AND THAT WE DON'T WANT THEM TO DIE. THAT WE ARE SOME PEOPLE HERE WHO DO CARE. SO I WANT YOU TO KNOW THAT TREES – THAT WE CARE!'

Syndee L'ome Grace: 'I think that we are deeply hurting in America. I think we are deeply craving answers. I think we've lost our identity as we have evolved into technology and into industrialized society. Bring me to this cathedral [woods]. Bring me to these guys [trees]. Bring me to this rock that has the most incredible life. That makes me feel alive.'"[37]

For those of you who think this kind of behavior is reserved only to the lunatic fringe and would never penetrate Christians, believe it or not, this article headline reads, "Earth Worship is on the Rise among Evangelical Youth."[38] Why? Because they're promoting it in Hollywood, which evangelical youth watch and they're promoting it in the school system, which evangelical youth attend. For even more proof, check out the "new" Pledge of Allegiance they came up with for schools. You tell me if this isn't promoting earth worship:

"Kids are singing with their hands to their hearts:

'I pledge allegiance to the earth to care for land and sea and air. To cherish every living thing with peace and justice everywhere.

I pledge allegiance to the earth to care for land and sea and air. To cherish every living thing with peace and justice everywhere.

With peace and justice everywhere.'"³⁹

What happened to going to school to learn reading, writing, and arithmetic? It gets even worse. A new U.N. document has recently been proposed to, "Give Mother Earth the Same Rights as Humans." This would include bugs, trees, and all other "natural things."⁴⁰ It sure would appear that all this promotion of New Age lies through Hollywood and the Environmental Movement is working like a charm. It's now being spread across the world via the United Nations. Speaking of which, little do people know that this may very well be one of the reasons why people around the world will refuse to repent and get saved during the 7-year Tribulation.

Revelation 9:20 "The rest of mankind that were not killed by these plagues still did not repent of the work of their hands; they did not stop worshiping demons, and idols of gold, silver, bronze, stone and wood – idols that cannot see or hear or walk."

You mean to tell me that people will be *worshiping wood* in the Last Days instead of getting right with God? As we just saw, people are *already* doing just that by the promotion of New Age in the environmental movement. It's a sign we're living in the Last Days!

The Second Way Environmentalism is Promoting the New Age - Promotion of Global Worship

This too happens to be another major false teaching of the New Age Movement. Let's take a look at that again:

- *All religions (except orthodox Christianity) are of equal merit.*

- *In order for the world to be at peace and harmony there must be a New World Order, universal monetary system, world authority on food, health, and water, universal tax, military draft, one world leader, and the abolishment of Christianity.⁴¹*

Now, here's the point. Does not the environmental movement likewise promote a return to more "earth-centered" religions and a global movement to unify people in order to save the earth? Yes. They too say we need to submit ourselves to some form of drastic global control because unless we do the planet will expire and so will we! Aaaahhhh! In fact, one of the biggest environmental groups, the Sierra Club, has gone on record as stating this:

"Turn to the traditions of ancient cultures such as Buddhist meditations and Native American Hopi rituals in order to 'reaffirm our bond with the spirit of the living earth. The more you contact the voice of the living earth and evaluate what it says, the easier it will become for you to contact it and trust what it provides.'"[42]

That sure sounds like New Age teaching to me! Now, there's nothing wrong with having a healthy earth. However, the problem is when you place the earth before man, and begin to worship it above God. That's why the wrath of God is coming! We've seen that many times already. Unfortunately, Hollywood once again is helping to promote this One World Worship as well. The following is an excerpt from an interview by Caryl Matriciana with actor James Coburn:

"Caryl: 'Mr Coburn, why should we care about Earth Day or Mother Earth?'

James Coburn: 'Mother Earth is our mother. She's the mother goddess. She's the one we should be praising rather than raping. I mean all of these people here today are here for one reason. Because they are concerned about what's happening and about what mankind is doing to the earth. I mean the negative emotions we carry around a lot of us is another contributor with all peace to the moon.

But what we need to do is to be true to ourselves be true to mother earth. Mother earth is going to be bountiful. She's going to give us everything we need. She has for a long time. We've lost our way. The pagans used to know how to do it, and the Indians-some of them remember how to do it. The earth is a living organism. We're killing the one we love the most- and she loves us. We've got to praise our mother goddess."[43]

Looks to me like he's promoting a new form of worship, a "global" worship. How much more proof do we need before we wake up and realize that there's a hidden agenda behind *Earth Day* and the environmental movement! It has nothing to do with recycling, nothing to do with being a responsible citizen, and nothing to do with properly disposing of your trash. I'm not against those things in principle but there's much more going on here than meets the eye! It's being used as a platform to indoctrinate people into a New Age lie, the acceptance of a One World Religion. Now, for those of you who are still having a hard time believing that the environmental movement really is being used by the New Age Movement to promote a One World Religion, *even in the Church*, I've got proof. You tell me if the world is not being prepared to all worship the same thing and it's not God! Here's another transcript, this time from Fox News:

"Fox News: What Would Jesus Drive? America's Newsroom-Reporter: Bill Hemmer.

Bill Hemmer: What would Jesus drive? Huh? Environmental evangelism. It is the new way to raise awareness about global warming. Our Fox Religion Correspondent Lauren Greene joins us with more on that. Hi! Good morning. Who's pushing Christian green lines?

Lauren Green: Hey! Well a lot of people, it really is across the board theoretically speaking or religiously speaking. Here are the top green religious people according to Live Earth.

We've got Rev. Joel Hunter. He's a senior pastor at Northland Church in Longwood, Florida. He was actually offered Head of the Christian Coalition but turned it down because he wanted to focus on issues such as poverty and environmental protection.

Then Norman Hobble is a theology professor out of Australia. He edited something called the Earth Bible.

Then of course there's Pope Benedict XVI and yesterday he issued a statement that said, 'The people of faith must listen to the voice of the earth or risk destroying its very existence.'

We also have the Archbishop of Canterbury-Rowan Williams-head of the Anglican Church and of course the Buddhist leader the Dalai Lama.

But one thing you should add to this list is the National Evangelical Association because two years ago it issued a letter to 50,000 member churches which means it's 30 million evangelicals saying that, 'We affirm that God-given dominion is a sacred responsibility and that government has an obligation to protect its citizens from the effects of environmental degradation.'

So it's a big movement all across the board."[44]

Yes, I'd say it's a big movement alright. It's a big movement to push for a One World Religion, even in the Church, just like the New Age Movement wants. Wow! An *Earth Bible*? As one article stated, "Green guru, James Lovelock, warned last week that 'The Green Religion' is now taking over from the Christian religion and 'a Green Bible is now available at your local Christian bookstore!'"[45] Perhaps that's why one guy stated, "Maybe it won't be long before recycling, carbon-foot reductions and riding bicycles to work become the new religious duties of the faithful."[45] You know, something we can all agree on! Now, here's the point. Little do people realize they are being prepared via the environmental movement *to explain away the earth's catastrophes* that will take place during the 7-year Tribulation.

Revelation 8:7,9,11 "Hail and fire mixed with blood were thrown down upon the earth, and one-third of the earth was set on fire. One-third of the trees were burned, and all the grass was burned. And one-third of all things living in the sea died. One-third of the water bitter, and many people died because the water was so bitter."

Now, it's obvious that this passage of Scripture is speaking of the judgment of Almighty God during the second half of the 7-year Tribulation. However, the average environmentalist is being brainwashed with this lie:

"Climatic shifts, droughts, floods, acid rain and pollution, earthquakes, and volcanic eruptions. Although severe, these changes will pave the way for a cleansing of the earth and a new relationship between earth and man.

This will be the Day of Purification. Trees will die. Cold places will become hot. Hot places will become cold. Lands will sink into the ocean and lands will rise out of the sea.

All the suffering going on in this country with the tornadoes, floods and earthquakes is carried on the breath of Mother Earth because she is in pain. This battle will cleanse the heart of people and restore our Mother Earth from illness, and the wicked will be gotten rid of."[46]

Can you see how people are being prepared *right now* to come to the wrong conclusion concerning the earth catastrophes that will come one day to the planet? People during the 7-year Tribulation will actually think that these horrible catastrophes are a *good thing*. It's all because they are being seduced by the New Age Movement and their promotion of a Healthy Earth via the environmental movement.

The Third Way Environmentalism is Promoting the New Age Movement – Promotion of Female Worship

This is yet another unfortunate behavior that will take place during the 7-year Tribulation.

Revelation 17:3-6 "Then the angel carried me away in the Spirit into a desert. There I saw a woman sitting on a scarlet beast that was covered with blasphemous names and had seven heads and ten horns. The woman was dressed in purple and scarlet, and was glittering with gold, precious stones and pearls. She held a golden cup in her hand, filled with abominable things and the filth of her adulteries. This title was written on her forehead: MYSTERY BABYLON THE GREAT THE MOTHER OF PROSTITUTES AND OF THE ABOMINATIONS OF THE EARTH. I saw that the woman was drunk with the blood of the saints, the blood of those who bore testimony to Jesus."

Here we see the classic passage concerning the Woman who Rides the Beast, who is the Antichrist, and how during the 7-year Tribulation she will actually be hunting down the people of God to the point where she is even drunk with their blood. It is speaking in regards to the Last Days One World Religion movement that has a *female* figurehead. Now, can anybody guess what the New Age Movement, environmentalism, and even the feminist movement are pushing for *right now*? You got it! A *female worship* of a *female deity*! We already saw how the New Age Movement and environmentalism not only encourage us to worship "Mother Earth" instead of "Father God," but they've also joined hands with feminism who is also radically promoting this female worship! They call it "Goddess Worship" and according to them, *it's alive*! The following is an excerpt from a video featuring Zsuzsanna Budapest, Gathering the Goddesses:

"The women's movement today is being called the women's spirituality movement in great part and that's because of concentrating on areas of social and political reform but it's looking high and fast at spiritual reform. Women are gathering today in circles just as their 1960 counterparts did in consciousness raising circles.

But now they're not just knocking down that door to a man's world asking for entrance, instead they're looking at the myths, spiritual beliefs, religion, values-everything that runs our culture. Everything that feeds our souls.

We're going to take a look at the 'women's spirituality movement' as it's been called, by the women participating in it who are weaving new stories of a returning goddess. They believe she's back on the planet-alive and well-and she can do a lot for you."

(Camera pans to a "goddess" made of fruits, flowers, plants)

Woman heard in the background: 'THE GODDESS IS ALIVE!'

Group of women respond in 'MAGIC IS AFOOT!'

A woman again shouts: 'THE GODDESS IS ALIVE!!'

Group again responds: 'MAGIC IS AFOOT!'

(Women dancing & clapping in a circle to sounds of beating drums)
Woman #1: 'What the goddess means to me is wholeness and peace'

Woman#2: 'The goddess means to me, my internal strength. She has come to me and shown me the beauty that is within myself'

Woman #3: 'The goddess is my voice. She is my self-empowerment. She's my self-respect. As a result my life is really undergone some major transformations not only creatively but in the pathway that I have now started to take and I have the works of Zsuzsanna Budapest to thank for that'

"THE GODDESS IS ALIVE!"
"MAGIC IS AFOOT!"
"THE GODDESS IS ALIVE!"
"MAGIC IS AFOOT!"[47]

Nearly 2,000 years ago, the Apostle John warned us in the Book of Revelation that in the last days the false One World Religion would be a *feminine worship*. As you just witnessed, it's happening now and it's being promoted through the lie of the feminist movement. Most people have no clue that feminism has nothing to do with equal rights and equal pay. In their own words, they just admitted it really has everything to do with getting rid of the male patriarchal God and replacing it with a female one. In fact, this horrible lie is even infecting the Church! What I'm about to share with you are all quotes from people *inside the Church*. I don't know if they're real Christians or not, but the point is they're *in the Church* and here's some of the *destructive heresies* they're teaching.

- *Mary Daly, who considers herself to be a Christian feminist, says this about traditional Christianity: "To put it bluntly, I propose that Christianity itself should be castrated." The primary focus of the 'Christian' feminist is to bring an end to what they perceive as male-dominated religion by 'castrating' the male influence from religion. Daly continued by saying, "I am suggesting that the idea of salvation uniquely by a male savior perpetuates the problem of patriarchal oppression."*

- *Herchurch.org is the website for Ebenezer Lutheran Church in San Francisco. On Wednesdays they open their sanctuary for the "Christian Goddess Rosary." They say that, "the exclusive emphasis of God as Father supports a domination structure that oppresses and subordinates women." They also encourage people to pray the "Hail Goddess Prayer" that states, "Hail Goddess full of grace. Blessed are you and blessed are all the fruits of your womb. For you are the MOTHER of us all."*

- *Another person stated, "I think that if you want to in your personal devotions address God as 'Mother' I don't have a problem with that."*

- *Paul Smith in his book,* Is it Okay to Call God Mother *"I believe it is important to call God, 'Mother' as well as 'Father' in public worship."*

- *Richard and Catherine Kroeger authors of "Women Elders…Called by God?" said, "There is a good Biblical reason, then, to speak of God as both Father and Mother, both 'she' and 'he'."*

- *Jann Clanton author of, "God, A Word for Girls and Boys" says "Masculine God language hinders many children from establishing relationships of trust with God. In addition, calling God "he" causes boys to commit the sin of arrogance…Calling the Supreme power of the universe "he" causes girls to commit the sin of devaluing themselves. For the sake of "these little ones" we must change the way we talk about God."*

- *And one of the hottest book and now films being promoted in the Church right now is called, "The Shack" If you look at it, it's not only openly New Age in doctrine and teaching, but it actually presents God as a woman![48]*

So much for equal rights and equal pay! Sounds to me like somebody's got a hidden agenda in there; seducing people to worship a female deity in the Last Days instead of a male deity. Again, nearly 2,000 years ago, the Apostle John warned us that this behavior would be a sign we're living in the Last Days. When you see this rise of a *female worship* instead of a male patriarchal worship paving the way for a One World religion, this *Woman that Rides the Beast*, you better watch out! She's going to be drunk with the blood of the saints! You don't want to be around! You better get saved now and avoid the whole thing!

3. The Third Way the New Age Movement is Seducing People - Promotion of a Healthy Body

Of course, I'm talking about the **Vegetarian Movement**. Now again, just like with environmentalism, I am not against people deciding to go down this route in principle either, i.e. become a vegetarian. If you want to eat veggies for the rest of your life, then that's up to you. However, what you need to realize is the vegetarian movement is also being used to promote the occult beliefs of the New Age Movement. Here's what God has to say about it.

1 Timothy 4:1-5 "The Spirit clearly says that in later times some will abandon the faith and follow deceiving spirits and things taught by demons. Such teachings come through hypocritical liars, whose consciences have been seared as with a hot iron. They forbid people to marry and order them to *abstain from certain foods*, which God created to be received with thanksgiving by those who believe and who know the truth. For everything God created is good, and nothing is to be rejected if it is received with thanksgiving, because it is consecrated by the word of God and prayer."

Now, if you've ever wondered why we Christians pray before our meals; here it is. What's also in this passage is another characteristic of people in the Last Days. They are actually going to follow *demonic teachings* that *forbid people to marry* (Sounds like the Roman Catholic Church) and *forbid people to eat certain kinds of foods.* If you think about it, this is exactly what the vegetarian movement is saying we need to do *right now*! In fact, if they would have their way they would even *order us* not to eat certain foods just like the text says. Yet, the Bible says it's perfectly fine to eat all kinds of food, including meat.

Genesis 9:2-3 "The fear and dread of you will fall upon all the beasts of the earth and all the birds of the air, upon every creature that moves along the ground, and upon all the fish of the sea; they are given into your hands. Everything that lives and moves will be food for you. Just as I gave you the green plants, I now give you everything."

Colossians 2:16 "Therefore do not let anyone judge you by what you eat or drink."

So even though God clearly says it's okay to eat all kinds of food, including meat, the vegetarian movement preaches the exact opposite. They *do judge* us by what we eat, telling us we need to *restrict ourselves from certain food*, the very thing the Bible said would happen in the Last Days! The average person today thinks they're helping to *save the animals* by becoming a vegetarian, when in reality they are helping to spread the beliefs of the New Age Movement. Once again, let's refresh our memory of some of the basic tenants of the New Age Movement:

- *All is god: the earth, man, animals, and plants.*

- *Man is destroying the earth along with the animals and plants. Unless he changes his ways, "Mother Earth" will be forced to destroy humanity. Christianity is the biggest culprit in destroying the earth by teaching that man has dominion over the earth when the earth is a living being.*[49]

So if you're paying attention, you can see how this is exactly what the vegetarian movement *also* teaches. Do they not believe that the earth, plants and especially animals are *sacred*, almost to the point of *worship*? Yes. In fact, even though as we saw, the Bible says we are to give thanks for *every food product*, they mock this command from God to give thanks for all food by trying to convince us eating meat is bad! Here's just one obvious example from a commercial by PETA or People for the Ethical Treatment of Animals:

"A PETA Thanksgiving. Large family gathered around the dining room table.

Dad to young daughter: 'Say grace hun?'

Young daughter: 'Sure. Dear God, thank you for turkey we're about to eat and for the turkey farms where they pack them into dark and tiny little sheds for their whole lives. Thank you for when they burn their feathers off while they're still alive and for when turkey gets kicked around like a football and killed by people who think it's fun to stomp on their little turkey heads and special thanks for all the chemicals and dirt and poop that's in the turkey we're about to eat. OH! And thank you for rainbows. Amen.'

Message on screen: 'This Thanksgiving, Be Thankful You're Not A Turkey. Go Vegan. PETA'"[50]

Don't you feel bad now? Don't eat that turkey. Don't give God thanks for that kind of food. Become a vegetarian and save the turkeys! Don't you see the seduction going on here? I'm not for the inhumane treatment of animals. I'm definitely not agreeing with some of the ways corporations raise turkeys and that there couldn't be some adjustment to their practices. Yet, that's not what's going. on here! Just like with environmentalism, vegetarianism has also become a smoke screen to lead you down a *bad spiritual path*. In fact, one such group is called SERV. The Society of Ethical Religious Vegetarians.[51] That's your clue that they're ultimately trying to lead you down a *spiritual* path. They're *religious* vegetarians! They say that man and Christianity are the biggest culprits in the destruction of the earth via the eating of animals, which is right out of a page of New Age teaching. They also just so happen to promote a global movement to unify people in order to save the animals, and of course save the planet. That too is New Age through and through! In fact, these vegetarians are totally blunt about this agenda. Here's what your average vegetarian is being taught today:

"We need an interfaith effort to gain a more humane, just, peaceful and environmentally sustainable world. We believe that applying spiritual values to scientific knowledge encourages plant-based diets, with major benefits to humans, animals and the environment.

It is essential that there is a major shift toward vegetarianism to end diseases, horrible mistreatment of animals, threats to ecosystems, global climate change, wasteful use of water, land, fuel, widespread hunger and increasing violence.

*Through the efforts of environmentalists, vegetarians and animal rights activists,
the earth will become a healthier, happier place for all species to live."*[52]

Looks to me like somebody's trying to get us to *restrict ourselves of
certain food products* in the Last Days so we can save our planet from certain
destruction. Where have I heard that before? You got it! The Bible says it's a
demonic teaching that would appear on the scene in the Last Days!

1 Timothy 4:1,3 "The Spirit clearly says that in later times some will abandon
the faith and follow deceiving spirits and things taught by demons. They forbid
people to marry and order them to abstain from certain foods."

This demonic behavior and demonic teaching is being promoted *right
now* before our very eyes! In fact, it's even going global! The U.N. recently came
out with a statement demanding us to, "Eat Less Meat to Save the Planet." They
even went on to say, "The world needs to change to a more vegetarian diet to
stand a chance of tackling climate change,"[53] Or in other words, save the planet.
I'll say it again. There's nothing wrong with being a Vegetarian or even being
concerned about animals. I'm not against that. If you want to eat veggies for the
rest of your life go for it. That's between you and God. In fact, if you want to
help save mistreated animals, more power to you. However, the problem is when
you place animals above man, and begin to worship them above God. That's not
only a sin, but it's clearly New Age in teaching and is exactly what the Bible said
would happen in the Last Days! That's just *stage one* of a plan to get people used
to the idea of having a "controlled diet" being a good thing. The Bible also says
we are actually headed for a time when the whole planet is going to be told what
they can and cannot eat and you don't want to be there!

Revelation 6:5-6 "When the Lamb opened the third seal, I heard the third living
creature say, 'Come!' I looked, and there before me was a black horse! Its rider
was holding a pair of scales in his hand. Then I heard what sounded like a voice
among the four living creatures, saying, 'A quart of wheat for a day's wages, and
three quarts of barley for a day's wages, and do not damage the oil and the
wine!'"

As we've already seen, this text deals with the famine conditions during
the first half of the 7-year Tribulation and it says that it's going to be so bad at
that time that the whole world is going to be on some sort of *global food
distribution program* just to stay alive. One day's work and you receive a quart

of *wheat* for yourself, or you could opt out of that for three quarts of *barley*, a less nutritional meal, literally animal feed, to feed you and your family of two. Now, here's the point. This is also what the New Age Movement has been proposing to do for a long time now. That is, get total control of the food supply:

- *In order for the world to be at peace and harmony there must be a New World Order, universal monetary system, world authority on food, health, and water, universal tax, and military draft, one world leader, and the abolishment of Christianity.*[54]

So in light of this, do we see any signs of the world's food supply, health and water, being corralled into the hands of just a few people? Who, ultimately, is going to tell us what we can and cannot eat in the Last Days? It's happening as we speak. *Right now*, all the world's food supply is currently in the hands of just three entities. Cargill/Monsanto, ConAgra, and Novartis/ADM. Believe it or not, they even freely admit that if you want to control the world, forget fuel, forget gas and oil, you need to control the food supply! The following is a quote from Dwayne Andreas, former chairman of ADM:

"The food business is far and away the most important business in the world. Everything else is a luxury. Food is what you need to sustain life every day. Food is fuel. You can't run a tractor without fuel and you can't run a human being without it either. Food is the absolute beginning." [55]

Beginning of what?

"Those who control the global food system, have the ultimate in economic power."[55]

In other words, if you want to control the whole world then you do it by controlling *their food supply*, exactly like the Bible said would happen in the Last Days! Now, if you really think this isn't going on, then you need to explain to me why Bill Gates, along with other elites from around the world, are building a mysterious *"seed vault"* in the middle of the Arctic as this video transcript reveals:

"NBC NEWS Reporter: We have a fascinating story to show you tonight. You are about to see what it means to go to extremes to save the world. Dug deep into a mountain in a remote island near the North Pole-there is a project that is often

called the Doomsday Vault. It's really a giant freezer and inside is something very tiny that could come to the rescue in the case of a global catastrophe.

NBC's Dawna Friesen is 500 miles off the northern coast of Norway tonight on an Arctic Archepelego with this remarkable effort to safeguard the world's food supply.

Dawna Friesen: If the cold doesn't kill you on Svalbard, the polar bears might. Yet 600 miles from the North Pole, high above a fjord deep inside a mountain is a vault, built to one day save mankind. Today the Svalbard vault received its first deposit. Seeds. More than a 100 million of them. Stored to preserve the world's food supply.

Jens Stoltenberg (Norwegian Prime Minister): It is the New World's Ark of today.

Dawna Friesen: 400 feet underground, the bunker is a last ditch reserve, ready to resupply the worlds farmers if all else fails. Seeds are coming in from all over the globe representing every known variety of crop.

Ken Street (Agricultural ecologist) Without this genetic diversity to draw from, um our food security is down the...it's just gone.

Dawna Friesen: We're not only deep inside a mountain here, this place is protected by heavy steel doors, three airlocks and a sophisticated video surveillance system and in case that isn't enough-outside...polar bears. A place so cold and remote-it offers unparalleled security because one day our future might lie in the seeds of the past.

NBC NEWS Reporter: Svalbald's Seed Vault may play a vital role in guarding earth's food supply in the decades to come."[56]

Is it going to guard our food supply, or is it going to *control it*? It's almost like they're preparing for something that they're not telling us about. I wonder what that could be? Maybe total control of the food supply? What they're not telling you, is that one of the three food suppliers on the planet, Monsanto, is not only genetically modifying our food, and that's a whole other issue, but they've also come out with what's called the *terminator gene*. What that is, is a new seed they've developed that *commits suicide* or become *sterile* in the second generation, which means you always have to go back to *them* to get your next batch of seeds. The plants will no longer *self-replicate* which means you always have to go back to them for food![57] That is total control of our global food supply! He who controls the seed vault controls all the master seeds! It's exactly like the Bible said would happen in the Last Days!

4. The Fourth Way the New Age Movement is Seducing People - Promotion of a Heavenly Utopia

Revelation 6:1-2 "I watched as the Lamb opened the first of the seven seals. Then I heard one of the four living creatures say in a voice like thunder, "Come!" I looked, and there before me was a white horse! Its rider held a bow, and he was given a crown, and he rode out as a conqueror bent on conquest."

Now what we have here in a nutshell is the classic passage in the Book of Revelation concerning the Antichrist and his rise to power at the beginning of the 7-year Tribulation. As we already saw, the beginning point of the 7-year Tribulation begins with the fulfillment of Daniel 9:27 where the Antichrist makes a *peace treaty* with the people of Israel. It's this era of *false peace* that the Antichrist starts with Israel yet affects the whole world. He comes riding in on a white horse with only a bow and a crown but no arrows. Most Bible commentators would say this represents how the Antichrist is able to rise to power with a *peaceful coup*. In other words, he overtakes the world by means of diplomacy, not war, with the promises of a *false utopia*, an era of peace. Now here's the point. The New Age Movement and the movers and shakers behind our wicked world system are working on this *false peace utopia as we speak*!

Believe it or not, they are actually building a false global utopia where they get to live in luxury and paradise and the rest of us, at least those they decide who get to live, will serve them forever on planet earth. Isn't that great! I don't think so either! But here's the point. As wild as that is, as crazy as this is, this is exactly what they're doing. They are *reducing the population of the planet* to create this false utopia they plan on having and ruling over and they are using terms to describe it like, "sustainable development," which means *population control*. This is precisely why they are behind such heavy global promotion of feminism, birth control, homosexuality, abortion and even forced sterilization. If you think about it, they all have one thing in common. They all effectively reduce the population of the planet! In fact, abortion alone has now murdered about *1.5 billion babies*.

Now granted, you might be tempted to think, "This is just too far out. This is crazy! It's just a bunch of wacky conspiracy theories. There's no way the leaders in the world are really serious about *reducing the population of the earth to create a False Utopia*. Are they?" Well, don't take my word for it. Let's listen to theirs, including a wicked world leader name Hitler. Here's his so-called "Hit list" which reveals the real reason why he was killing the Jewish people. Not only was Hitler heavily involved in the occult, but he was also an evolutionist and the Jewish people just happened to be at the bottom of his evolutionary list:

HITLER'S HIT LIST
(Species Blood Mixture)

Nordic (blonde, blue eyed)	**Close to pure Aryan**
Germanic (brown hair, blue-eyed or less desirable, brown-eyed)	**Predominately Aryan**
Mediterranean (white but swarthy)	**Slight Aryan preponderance**
Slavic (white but degenerate bone structure)	**Close to Aryan, half-Ape**
Oriental	**Slight Ape preponderance**
Black African	**Predominately Ape**
Jewish (fiendish skull)	**Close to pure Ape**[58]

By the way, Hitler was not planning on stopping with the Jews. He was working his way up backwards from his evolutionary scale. If he could've finished annihilating the Jews, he was going to move on, next with the Black African people, then the Oriental and so on and so forth until he was left with his master race. Now, as shocking as that is, people *today* are still promoting this wicked idea of "cleansing" the planet of so-called "inferiors":

- *Margaret Sanger, Founder of Planned Parenthood called for,* "The elimination of 'human weeds,' for the 'cessation of charity' because it prolonged the lives of the unfit, for the segregation of 'morons, misfits, and the maladjusted,' and for the sterilization of genetically inferior races."

- **David Graber**, *a research biologist with the National Park Service said,* "We have become a plague upon ourselves and upon the Earth. *Human happiness [is] not as important as a wild and healthy planet.* Until such time as homo sapiens should decide to rejoin nature, some of us can only hope for the right virus to come along."

- **David Pimentel**, *a Cornell University Professor said,* "The total world population should be no more than 2 billion rather than the current 5.6 billion."

- **Jacques Cousteau** *wrote,* "The damage people cause to the planet is a function of demographics – it is equal to the degree of development. One American burdens the earth much more than twenty Bangladeshes...This is a terrible thing to say. In order to stabilize world population, we must eliminate 350,000 people per day. It is a horrible thing to say, but it's just as bad not to say it."

- **Bertrand Russell** *wrote,* "At present, the population of the world is increasing...War so far has had no great effect on this increase...I do not pretend that birth control is the only way in which the population can be kept from increasing. There are others...If a Black Death could be spread throughout the world once in every generation, survivors could procreate freely without making the world too full...the state of affairs might be somewhat unpleasant, but what of it? Really high-minded people are indifferent to suffering, especially that of others."

- **Ted Turner** *said, "People who abhor the China one-child policy are dumb-dumbs, because if China hadn't had that policy, there would be 300 million more people in China right now." And then he later advocated that we reduce the world's population from 6 billion to 2 billion.*

- **John Holdren**, *Obama's Science Czar wrote, "Forced Abortions and Mass Sterilizations are Needed to Save the Planet." "Women could be forced to abort their pregnancies, whether they wanted to or not; the population at large could be sterilized by infertility drugs intentionally put into the nation's drinking water or in food; people who "contribute to social deterioration" (i.e. undesirables) "can be required by law to exercise reproductive responsibility" in other words, be compelled to have abortions or be sterilized; a transnational "Planetary Regime" should assume control of the* *global economy and also dictate the most intimate details of Americans' lives using an armed international police force."*

- **Dr. Eric Pianka**, *a scientist, gave a speech at the Texas Academy of Science where he advocated, "The need to exterminate 90% of the population through the airborne Ebola virus. "We're no better than bacteria!" Standing in front of a slide of human skulls, Pianka gleefully advocated airborne Ebola as his preferred method of exterminating the necessary 90% of humans, choosing it over AIDS because of its faster kill period." At the end of Pianka's speech the audience erupted, not to a chorus of boos and hisses, but to a wild reception of applause and cheers.*

- **Dr. Sam Keen**, *a New Age writer and philosopher stated,* "We must speak far more clearly about sexuality, contraception, about abortion, about values that control the population, because the ecological crisis, in short, is the population crisis. Cut the population by 90% and there aren't enough people left to do a great deal of ecological damage."

- *This is why **Dr. Michael Berliner** wrote of the Environmentalist's utter contempt for mankind, "Such is the naked essence of Environmentalism: It mourns the death of one whale or tree but actually welcomes the death of billions of people. Is there a more malevolent, man-hating philosophy than this?"*[58]

Sure looks to me like someone is very serious about controlling, or dare I say, reducing the population of our planet. Is that sick or what? I wish I was making this up, but we have to deal with these horrid facts! This is why the Bible warns us about what is coming to this planet! The world we are headed for in the 7-year Tribulation is so murderously evil that we can't even begin to imagine how horrific of a time it will be! In fact, this desire to see billions of people literally die across the planet may be *yet another reason why* people refuse to repent and get right with God during the 7-year Tribulation. Here's what the Bible says they will be doing!

Revelation 6:7-8 "When the Lamb opened the fourth seal, I heard the voice of the fourth living creature say, 'Come!' I looked, and there before me was a pale horse! Its rider was named Death, and Hades was following close behind him. They were given power over *a fourth of the earth* to kill by sword, famine and plague, and by the wild beasts of the earth."

Revelation 9:15,18,20 "And the four angels who had been prepared for this hour and day and month and year were turned loose to kill *one-third of all the people on earth*. One-third of all the people on earth were killed by these three plagues – by the fire and the smoke and burning sulfur. But the people who did not die in these plagues still refused to turn from their evil deeds."

So could this very well be one of the reasons why the population control elites will refuse to repent and get right with God during the 7-year tribulation? Based on their stated desires they will look upon these two annihilating judgments as a good thing! You can almost hear them stating, "Who cares if one-fourth of the planet gets annihilated and then later another one-third. Keep it coming! We want the population of the planet to be reduced to 500 million people anyway to create our false global utopia!" In fact, as wild as that sounds, this is exactly what the leaders of the New Age Movement are saying is coming:

"A New Age group calling itself the Solar Questers writes, 'Those who hinder will be removed...liquidated...(they) must be wiped clean off the face of the earth.'

The authors of a New Age pamphlet entitled Cosmic Countdown claimed to have received messages from a higher intelligence. The pamphlet says, 'The world should be forewarned to be on the lookout for (the decimation) of populations... these peoples will eventually be replaced by the new root race about to make its appearance in a newly cleansed world.'

But perhaps the most disturbing comments comes from New Age author, Barbara Marx Hubbard. Researchers John Ankerberg and John Weldon report that, 'Due to her vast financial wealth and influence among leading world politicians, and industrialists...[she] is having a major impact behind the scenes. She has been influenced by spirits for almost two decades.'

In her book, Happy Birthday Planet Earth, Hubbard wrote, 'The choice is: do you wish to become a natural christ, a universal human, or do you wish to die? People will either change or die. That is the choice.'

Hubbard says, 'There have always been defective seeds. In the past, they were permitted to die a 'natural death'. We, the elders have been patiently waiting...to take action to cut out this corrupted and corrupting element in the body of humanity.'

Hubbard's spirit guides gave her a vision of things to come. They told her that, 'Out of the full spectrum of human personality, one fourth is electing to transcend...one fourth is destructive and they are defective seeds. Now as we approach the quantum shift from the creature-human to the co-creative human – the human who is the inheritor of god-like power...the destructive one fourth must be eliminated from the social body. Fortunately, you are not responsible for this act. We are. We are in charge of God's selection process for planet Earth. He selects, we destroy. We are the riders of the pale horse, Death."[59]

Wow! No wonder these people don't repent in the 7-year Tribulation! They actually think they're fulfilling Revelation Chapter six, the Pale Horse Rider, death! In fact, they're so brazen about it, they've even set up an *actual monument* celebrating it *right now* here in the United States! It's called the **Georgia Guidestones**. It's a New Age stone monolith similar to Stonehenge and in eight different languages. It is the New Ten Commandments of the New World Order. Listen to what they are:

1. Maintain humanity under 500,000,000 in perpetual balance with nature.
2. Guide reproduction wisely – improving fitness and diversity.
3. Unite humanity with a living new language.
4. Rule passion – faith – tradition – and all things with tempered reason.
5. Protect people and nations with fair laws and just courts.
6. Let all nations rule internally resolving external disputes in a world court.
7. Avoid petty laws and useless officials.
8. Balance personal rights with social duties.
9. Prize truth – beauty – love – seeking harmony with the infinite.
10. Be not a cancer on the earth – Leave room for nature – Leave room for nature.[60]

Now, for those of you who are having a hard time believing this monument is real, the following is a video transcript of just one researcher who went there himself:

"If you go outside the city of Atlanta - go east 60 or 70 miles to the town of Elberton and go north on Hwy 77 about 10 miles. You'll find off to the right what's called the Georgia Guidestones. Looks kind of like Stonehenge – its big, huge granite rocks set up there.

This was done by a guy who gave a pseudo name and came in and paid cash, had this company come in and set these things up in 1980. Called himself R.C. Christian, but that's not his real name-it says there right on the stone – a pseudo name, false name.

On these Georgia Guidestones, it gives the Ten commandments for the New World Order. Ten commandments for the New World Order. The first commandment was to "Maintain humanity under a half billion".

I went there and looked at those things and went-hold on a minute! Today's population is 7.4 billion. They want to maintain humanity under one half billion. Looks like a lot of people have to die for their plan to work, which is by the way the plan.

Jacques Cousteau said we have to eliminate 350,000 people a day- a third of a million people a day would have to be eliminated to save mother earth. Bill Clinton said we have to reduce the population of the earth to 1 billion. There are a lot of folks who want to reduce the population of the earth.

The Bible command is quite the opposite, 'Be fruitful and multiply, replenish the earth,' you know, God said go fill it, have a bunch of kids. The Bible said He designed it to be inhabited so it's definitely the opposite of what God wants.

How does Margaret Sanger tie into overpopulation in this whole propaganda? Well Margaret Sanger was a tragic individual. She believed in reducing the population of the earth using birth control, using homosexuality, using just about anything other than doing what God commanded; to be fruitful and multiply and replenish the earth.

So Margaret Sanger started a group called Planned Parenthood, which many people have heard of. They are one of the key people today in the abortion industry, I mean absolutely murdering. Nearly 5,000 people a day are murdered by abortion. So Margaret Sanger we have largely to thank for that. Other factors are, of course, involved too but it's really sad and I'm sure she is going to have to answer to God for what she's done with her teaching.

She taught that inferior races like Blacks, Jews and Hispanics really need to be eliminated. She wanted to set up her birth control clinics in these lower class neighborhoods. People she didn't think deserved to live and slowly get them sterilized.

She was really involved in the eugenics movement, which became very popular during World War II because Hitler took the obvious conclusion. Hitler was the ultimate evolutionist and if evolution is true, then you find the superior race - Hitler of course thought it was the blonde haired blue-eyed Germans or Norwegians. So they are the superior race and everybody else should be slowly executed - starting with the Jews, then you have the blacks and on and on it goes.

Yeah Margaret Sanger is a tragic person in history and what she did is much worse than Adolf Hitler. Hitler only killed like 6 million. Margaret Sanger and her type with the abortion industry are responsible for killing 150 thousand million – that's 1.5 billion people."[61]

Talk about evil! In fact, speaking of which, the sad thing is that even if the elite who are planning to build this false utopia by the reduction of 90% of the population could pull their dastardly evil off, they have no clue who they're dealing with. This desire to murder is coming from the evil one himself.

John 8:44 "You belong to your father, the devil, and you want to carry out your father's desire. He was a murderer from the beginning, not holding to the truth, for there is no truth in him. When he lies, he speaks his native language, for he is a liar and the father of lies."

This means that even if the elite could pull off this mass murder program to build their *false utopia*, satan, the evil one, would turn right around and murder them too! They're being duped by a false teaching that has come from actual demons in the Last Days, just like the Bible said would happen!

5. The Fifth Way the New Age Movement is Seducing People - Promotion of a Heavenly Host

I'm talking about **UFO's and Aliens**. Believe it or not, this is one of the biggest lies ever to hit planet earth! Again, we just saw in the above passage that satan is the one who is responsible for a *murderous spirit*, but that same passage states he is also the one responsible for *lying spirits*.

John 8:44 "You belong to your father, the devil, and you want to carry out your father's desire. He was a murderer from the beginning, not holding to the truth, for there is no truth in him. When he lies, he speaks his native language, for he is a liar and the father of lies."

Jesus declares that the devil is not only a murderer, but he is also a *liar* and *the father of all lies*. This means that whatever undermines the truth about Jesus and what He came to do and how we can be saved is what satan's all about. He's behind it all. And this is precisely what he's doing with the UFO Alien Movement! It's not only demonic, but it's yet another satanic lie in the Last Days just to draw people away from Christ!

The First Way We Know UFO's are Demonic in Nature - They Lie Like Demons

We know that the whole belief of UFO's and aliens is *a lie from satan* because it's all based on a *lie called evolution*. The whole premise of aliens is that they're a higher evolved race. But wait a second, if evolution is not true and it's not, then how can these things have ever evolved into a higher race in the first place? This means their whole basis for existence and the identity of who they are telling us they are is based on a lie! If evolution can't take place on this planet, then it can't take place on any planet! If evolution can't happen here in the best of conditions, then logically, it can't happen anywhere! This is your first clue that something's wrong here! The whole premise of higher evolved aliens and UFO's is based on a lie and Jesus said lies come from satan. In fact, it's such an obvious lie that even the secular UFOlogists admit something doesn't stack up here with their identity:

"When I got out in 1989 we had cataloged 57 different species. Oh, you have individuals that look very much like you and myself that could walk among us and you wouldn't even notice the difference-except for some of the things that-oh-they might be able to go ahead and even in a dark room and touch an object and go ahead and identify what color that object might be.

They would have a heightened sense of smell, sight-uh- hearing. The situation is that you have various types of what we normally call "greys". We didn't call them greys in the military but you have at least 3 types of the greys. You had some that were much taller than we were. The unique thing that I would like to point out for the most part that the entities that we did catalog, were in fact humanoid.

Now this created a situation where the scientific community was trying to figure out why that would be the case, because you would expect that if life evolved on other planets that they would take on some type of other-uh being so to speak, not necessarily look humanoid or be bi-pedals such as we are but apparently we got quite a few of the species out there that are humanoid in appearance and that creates a question that yet has to be answered by science. "[62]

I'll answer it for you. *It's a lie!* You're right. There is a problem here. If evolution is true, then why are all these supposed alien creatures humanoid, just like us? You'd think you'd get a blob or some random shape once in a while if evolution were true, that is if all of life supposedly came from some random chance event in the universe. But no! These supposed aliens are all humanoid like us. This is simply your first clue that we're being lied to. It doesn't add up because it's a lie that's based on another lie called evolution! When you realize this fact, it makes you think just how dark and cunning and deceptive the enemy really is. In order to pull off this Last Days lie of UFO's and aliens today, you have to *first* get the lie of evolution ingrained into the minds of the people around the world. This means the evil one has been working on this lie for the last 150 years or so, starting with Charles Darwin and then slowly but surely advancing it each succeeding generation until it's now finally coming into fruition in our day! Wow! Is he evil or what? This is exactly what demons do!

The Second Way We Know UFO's are Demonic in Nature - They Teach Like Demons

Demons not only *lie* but they *propagate those lies* with *teachings*, i.e. false teachings! Now, what's interesting is that little do people know, the teachings which are supposedly coming from these Aliens and UFO's have their roots in the occult beliefs of the New Age Movement. What a surprise! Do you see a pattern here? The average person today thinks that they are making contact and receiving new teachings from these heavenly hosts orbiting the planet when in reality they are helping to spread the beliefs of the New Age Movement. To show you what I mean, let's take a look at these teachings that are supposed to be coming from these aliens and UFO's and you tell me if it's not the same lie of the New Age Movement!

• All of us are little gods.

- The earth is a living entity and we need to worship her and change our ways or we will be destroyed.

- Jesus, Muhammad, and Buddha all came from the E.T.'s to assist mankind in our next step of evolution.

- There is no such thing as sin, we do not need to be saved.

- Orthodox Christianity has it all wrong. Jesus' real message was to teach us that each one of us can become "christs."

- To aid in contacting these "heavenly beings" one should refrain from certain foods and practice meditation.

- Mankind needs to unite into a one world government and religion or we will be destroyed.

- The devil or Lucifer is actually a good guy who has come to free us.[63]

Now, let me get this straight. You supposedly come all the way across the universe just to tell me that satan, of all entities, is a good guy? Excuse me? That's sounds demonic! You would think you'd have something better to tell us than that, which is precisely why these researchers state the following:

Dr. Walter Martin: "The big problem is not what they are but who they are. The key to it is their theology. They're all saying the same thing, and all of it is bad-mouthing the Bible. This tells me that what the Bible says was going to take place is taking place. What you're dealing with is another dimension of reality which the Bible frequently mentions. It's called 'the realm of the prince of the powers of the air.' In other words, this is a supernatural manifestation which Christianity calls demonic."

John Ankerberg: "In light of the messages given by the UFO entities, how credible is it to think that literally thousands of genuine extra-terrestrials would fly millions or billions of light years simply to teach New Age philosophy, deny Christianity, and support the occult? Why would they do this with the preponderance of such activity already occurring on this planet? And why would these entities actually possess and inhabit people just like demons do if they were really advanced extra-terrestrials? Why would they consistently lie about things which we know are true, and why would they purposely deceive their contacts?"[64]

Yes, that is a very good question. Why would you supposedly come all the way across the galaxy just to promote the rise of the Antichrist, support Occult New Age teachings and debunk *only* Christianity? You would think, if you were a *real alien,* that you'd share with us some secret technology that's beneficial to us. Perhaps, help us find a cure for cancer or some other disease since you're supposed to be so much more highly evolved and intellectually superior to us. But no! You come all the way across the galaxy just to slam Jesus, Christianity, and the Bible, and promote the Antichrist kingdom saying satan's a good guy! That's totally demonic, just like satan!

The Third Way We Know UFO's are Demonic in Nature - They Communicate Like Demons

Now, if you were paying attention to that list of teachings earlier from supposed UFO's and aliens, you observed how they stated that in order for us to contact and/or communicate with them, we need to abstain from certain food and meditate so we can get ourselves into an altered state of consciousness and only *then* will they speak to us. Now, in the New Age Movement this is called *channeling*! Yet, the Bible declares it *demonic*!

Deuteronomy 18:9-14 "When you enter the land the LORD your God is giving you, do not learn to imitate the detestable ways of the nations there. Let no one be found among you who sacrifices his son or daughter in the fire, who practices divination or sorcery, interprets omens, engages in witchcraft, or casts spells, or who is a medium or spiritist or who consults the dead. Anyone who does these things is detestable to the LORD, and because of these detestable practices the LORD your God will drive out those nations before you. You must be blameless before the LORD your God. The nations you will dispossess listen to those who practice sorcery or divination. But as for you, the LORD your God has not permitted you to do so."

Why? Because God wants us to know the truth and He doesn't want us deceived by demons! Yet, that's precisely what these supposed higher evolved beings say we need to do! In order to contact them, of all methods, we have to use *occult techniques* that God forbids! In fact, here's some people in action talking to so-called aliens using this occult technique. You tell me if demons aren't speaking through them:

"JZ KNIGHT: 'God does not live outside of you. God is you.'

While JZ Knight is one of the more successful mediums, she is certainly not alone. A nearly identical doctrine is preached from a series of channelers who believe they are in communication with extraterrestrial spirits from other planets and galaxies. In a documentary, 'UFO's and Channeling' the late actor Telley Savalas reveals that the purpose of channeling these alien entities is entirely consistent with the purpose of the New Thought/New Age Movement to change the thinking of mankind.

Telly Savalas: 'Tonight we're going to show you some film that might change the way you think about life.'

Next, we are introduced to a woman who channels a spirit calling itself Leah.

"Leah" speaking: 'Hello Phillip, how are you today.'

Phillip: 'Very good Leah, how are you'

"Leah": 'Very good, thank you. So, what is it that you wanted to know?'

Phillip: 'Where are you from?'

"Leah": 'I am from Venus'

Phillip: I don't think anybody is going to believe that you or anybody else could be from Venus. Could you explain to us how you could be when everybody knows it's uninhabitable.

"Leah": 'They think it's uninhabitable because it is not habitable by physical life forms. We have bodies of light.'

While "Leah" rambles on with fantastical ideas, she soon compels the audience toward global unity. A message found throughout the new age movement.

"Leah": 'And what occurs here on this planet will affect the rest of the universe.

Can you, with all of your different ideas, all of your different races-come together as one planet and one people. We have dedicated millennia upon millennia to this idea.'"[65]

Now, let me get this straight again. You not only supposedly come all the way across the galaxy just to slam Jesus, Christianity and the Bible, and to promote New Age teachings including the lie that satan's a good guy. But the *only way* I can receive this "new enlightenment" is by using a demonic practice that the Bible forbids for our own protection so as to not be deceived. You'd think if you're really this higher-evolved, highly advanced civilization, that I could use a walkie talkie, or a new-fangled cell phone or even one of those fancy "Kirk to Enterprise" devices. But no! I have to use, and can only use, a demonic means to communicate with you in order to receive this new information. Give me a break! This is demonic! Again it's exactly what the Bible said would happen in the Last Days.

1 Timothy 4:1 "The Spirit clearly says that in later times some will abandon the faith and follow deceiving spirits and things taught by demons."

The Fourth Way We Know UFO's are Demonic in Nature - They Travel Like Demons

Let's take a look at how demons/angels travel according to the Bible.

2 Kings 6:15-17 "When the servant of the man of God got up and went out early the next morning, an army with horses and chariots had surrounded the city. 'Oh, my lord, what shall we do?' the servant asked. 'Don't be afraid,' the prophet answered. 'Those who are with us are more than those who are with them.' And Elisha prayed, 'O LORD, open his eyes so he may see.' Then the LORD opened the servant's eyes, and he looked and saw the hills full of horses and chariots of fire all around Elisha."

In other words, the hills were full of the angels of the Lord. But what we see here is the classic passage where the prophet of God, Elisha was being hunted down by a foreign King. He asked God to open the eyes of his servant who was freaking out so he could see just how well protected they really were by God's angels. Therefore, it's in this passage, among many others like it that tell us how angels travel, which would include demons who are of the fallen category of angels. They have the ability to appear and disappear, materialize and dematerialize, and pop onto the scene and pop back out. Now, here's the point. This is precisely the same manner in which UFO's and aliens travel:

UFO experts are saying that these beings are not so much physical in nature as they are spiritual.

- *This is because they clock them at speeds up to 15,000 mph making right turns which would instantly destroy anything physical.*

This is also why researchers say they are massless by our physics, i.e. spiritual in nature. (Demons are spiritual, aren't they?)

- *UFO's are not only able to go faster than the speed of sound, but they make no sonic boom like a normal physical object does. Another clue they're spiritual.*

- *Radar has never recorded the actual entering of UFO's into our atmosphere.*

- *Even with supposed millions of advanced civilizations in outer space, it would be almost impossible, if just once a year, for an extra-terrestrial craft to find us out here on the limb of our galaxy. Yet we are seeing literally tens of thousands of these so-called craft yearly.*

- *The so-called "aliens" seem to be able to live in our atmosphere without the help of respiratory devices.*

- *UFO's have been fired upon scores of times by American, Russian, and Canadian pilots, but these pilots have never been able to physically bring down a craft or capture it.*

- *UFO entities seem to have the ability to materialize and dematerialize at will as if coming from another doorway or portal, which is what the Bible says angels and demons can do.* [66]

This is why many UFO experts are now saying that based on decades of research, these beings aren't coming from outer space but inner space. In other words, they're coming from another dimension:

Dr. Jacques Vallee *said, "They're more like windows into another dimension."*

*In fact, in an official statement from Flying Saucer Review by editor **Gordon Creighton** he says, "There seems to be no evidence yet that any of these craft or beings originate from outer space."*

Brad Steiger *said he thinks the chances are very good that, "We are dealing with a multi-dimensional para-physical phenomenon which is largely indigenous to planet earth."*

Arthur Clark, *the famous science fiction writer observes, "One theory that can no longer be taken very seriously is that UFO's are interstellar spaceships."*[66]

In other words, these things are *not* coming from outer-space, they're coming from inner-space. They're coming from another dimension which the Bible calls the *spirit realm*, which fits the profile of *demons*.

The Fifth Way We Know UFO's are Demonic in Nature – They Possess Like Demons

Matthew 8:16,28 "When evening came, many who were demon-possessed were brought to him, and He drove out the spirits with a word and healed all the sick. When He arrived at the other side in the region of the Gadarenes, two demon-possessed men coming from the tombs met Him. They were so violent that no one could pass that way."

The Bible not only clearly says here and elsewhere that demons really are walking around on the planet, but one of the things they like to do is *inhabit people*. This is called *demonic possession*. Now, as creepy as that is, guess what these supposed aliens like to do with people when they come in contact with them? They like to *possess them*, like what this man experienced:

"On the evening of October 25th 1973, a young Pennsylvania farmer, Stephen Fuleski and at least fifteen other witnesses saw a bright object hovering over a field near them. Stephen grabbed his rifle and went to investigate.

It was then that he noticed something walking along by the fence. They were hairy and long armed with greenish-yellow eyes and a smell like burning rubber was present. Stephen sensed that these creatures were not friendly and fired a tracer bullet over their heads. When they kept on coming, he fired directly at one of them.

The creatures then all disappeared into the woods and the glowing object disappeared from the field instantaneously. UFO researchers as well as a State Trooper were called in to investigate.

When they arrived the people there told them that Stephen had been growling like an animal and flailing his arms. His own dog ran toward him and Stephen attacked the dog. Stephen then collapsed and after a time began to come to his senses.

The entire group commented on the nauseating sulfur like odor that was present."[67]

A sulphur-like odor was present? That just so happens to be the same odor the Bible uses to describe the Lake of Fire!

Revelation 19:20 "But the beast was captured, and with him the false prophet who had performed the miraculous signs on his behalf. With these signs he had deluded those who had received the mark of the beast and worshiped his image. The two of them were thrown alive into the fiery lake of burning *sulfur.*"

It's not copper, not cheeseburgers, not even stale milk, but of all things for aliens to smell like when they appear on the scene is *sulphur*, the very stench of the lake of fire, *and* they want to possess the individual! That's by chance? We're dealing with demons here. In fact, UFO researchers also admit that when a person does have an encounter with supposed aliens and UFO's, they habitually do one of three things:

1. They go deeper into the Occult/NewAge.
2. They kill themselves.
3. They go insane and become demonically possessed like that man.

This behavioral trend is why even secular researchers in the UFO field are saying they're demonic. They too see the obvious connection:

Dr. Jacques Vallee: *"We are dealing with a yet unrecognized level of consciousness, independent of man but closely linked to the earth. I do not believe anymore that UFO's are simply the spacecraft of some race of extraterrestrial visitors. This notion is too simplistic to explain their appearance,* *the frequency of their manifestations through recorded history and the structure of the information exchanged with them during contact.*

An impressive parallel can be made between UFO occupants and the popular conceptions of demons. UFO's can project images or fabricated scenes designed to change our belief systems. Human belief is being controlled and conditioned, man's concepts are being rearranged and we may be headed toward a massive change of human attitudes toward paranormal abilities and extraterrestrial life." (i.e. they're deceiving us)

The 'medical examination' to which abductees are said to be subjected, often accompanied by sadistic manipulation, is reminiscent of the medieval tales of encounters with demons. The symbolic display seen by the abductees is identical to the type of initiations, ritual or astral voyage, that is imbedded in the occult traditions of every culture. Thus, the structure of abduction stories is identical to that of occult initiation rituals."

UFO researcher **Lynn Catoe** stated, *"A large part of the available UFO literature is closely linked with mysticism and the metaphysical. It deals with subjects like mental telepathy, automatic writing and invisible entities as well as phenomena like poltergeist or ghost manifestations and 'possession.' Many of the UFO reports now being published in the popular press recount alleged incidents that are strikingly similar to demonic possession and psychic phenomena."*

Dr. Pierre Guerin an eminent scientist associated with the French National Council for Scientific Research says, *"UFO behavior is more akin to magic than to physics as we know it. The modern UFOnauts and the demons of past days are probably identical. What is quite certain is that the phenomenon is active here on our planet, and active here as master."* (i.e they're controlling things)

John Keel one of the most informed persons in the world on UFO's, author of the now-classic *UFO's: Operation Trojan Horse* states: *"The manifestations and occurrences described in this imposing literature on demonology are similar if not entirely identical to the UFO phenomenon itself. The UFO manifestations seem to be, by and large, merely minor variations of the age-old demonological phenomenon."*

John Ankerberg: *"Among UFO contactees or others who communicate personally with the alleged extra-terrestrials, there are also literally 1,000's of* *cases of what can only be termed spirit possession. The fact that these supposedly advanced beings from outer space prefer to possess their contacts after the manner of demons is further evidence that we are dealing with an occult phenomenon."*[68]

If even the secular researchers on UFO's, the so-called experts, are saying these entities are demonic in nature, then I'm kind of thinking they're probably demonic in nature. How much more proof do we need as to their real identity?

The Sixth Way We Know UFO's are Demonic in Nature – They're Rebuked Like Demons

Mark 1:21,23-27 "Jesus went into the synagogue and began to teach. Just then a man in their synagogue who was possessed by an evil spirit cried out, 'What do you want with us, Jesus of Nazareth? Have you come to destroy us? I know who you are – the Holy One of God!' 'Be quiet!' said Jesus sternly. 'Come out of him!' The evil spirit shook the man violently and came out of him with a shriek. The people were all so amazed that they asked each other, 'What is this? A new teaching – and with authority! He even gives orders to evil spirits and they obey Him.'"

Here we see another passage from the Bible dealing with demonic possession, but this time what I want you to observe is just Who it was that has the power and authority over them to cast them out? It was none other than our Lord Jesus Christ. Now what's wild is that there just so happens to be *one surefire way* to get rid of these so-called aliens when they do come your way. Of all things it's when you *command them in the Name of Jesus Christ to leave,* and they do! Now, if that's not a demon I don't know what is, as this researcher also agrees:

"Far from the abductee population including all those with religious beliefs, there is one group of people that, by and large, is notably absent. They are Christians, those who are often (these days unflatteringly) described as 'Christian Fundamentalists.'

Many people in the world claim to be a Christian; that is, they have Christian ideals or morality, and may even regard themselves as good people. But I am talking about what are known as 'born-again,' Bible believing Christians. It is as if ET's tend to avoid this select group of people. This reality has been largely ignored by many UFO researchers.

Muslims, Buddhists, Jews, agnostics, all seemed to claim abduction experiences. As more case studies were examined, a puzzling trend emerged. The so-called Christians reporting the abduction experience tended to be people who intellectually espoused the existence of God, but didn't apply it personally (i.e. not true Christians). But there seemed to be an obvious absence of devout, Bible believing, 'walk the walk' Christians. Where were they in this equation?

One experience by a Mr. Bill D. took place at Christmas in Florida. His abduction started out typically, i.e., late at night, in bed. Earlier in the evening he saw some anomalous lights through his living room window over a forest north of his home. He assumed it was a police helicopter searching for drug runners or something.

Whatever it was, it agitated his dogs for several hours thereafter. He eventually went to bed. He was lying in bed kept wide awake by the barking dogs when paralysis set in. He was unable to cry out. He could see nothing but a whitish grey, like a mist or fog, although he sensed someone or something was in his room. His wife didn't waken.

The next thing he knew; he was being levitated above his bed. By this time, he was alive with terror, but he couldn't scream. Here is where the story becomes very interesting. He states, 'So helpless, I couldn't do anything. I said, 'Jesus, Jesus, help me!'

When I did, there was a feeling or sound or something that either my words that I thought or the words that I had tried to say or whatever, had hurt whatever was holding me up.

I fell, I hit the bed, because it was like I was thrown back in bed. I really can't tell, but when I did, my wife woke up and asked why I was jumping on the bed.'

This was the first time that experienced field investigators had ever heard of an abduction being stopped, and this man did it by just calling on the Name of Jesus.

Another experience of stopping an abduction with the Name of Jesus Christ was a man who states, 'My wife had a strange experience in the middle of the night. At the time we knew nothing about UFO abductions, so we had no category in which to place it other than extremely 'lucid nightmare.' It has many of the abduction 'components.'

The point is that she stopped the entities and the whole experience with the Name of Jesus.' It's vital to get this information out.' I suggest that the answers they have been looking for but do not want to hear may be – 'God is real, and the Bible is true.'

This interpretation is further supported by the 'space brothers' single-minded obsession with undermining the Bible's account of the nature and mission of the only 'One' who appears to be able to stop them – Jesus."

'My name is Joe George and I'm the State Section Director for the Mutual UFO Network from Broward County, Florida. I'm also Lead Field Investigator. When we get a call for an investigation, we take all the information we can over the phone and then we send investigators out sometimes myself-sometimes other investigators working with me. And we follow up to do an investigation report. To these people they were sincere. They have sincere experiences and a lot of them are looking for help and they feel that being as we were involved as researchers and investigators that we can be of some help to them.'

Joyce Erins: My name is Joyce Erins…(pause)…um…I'm a floral designer and I was lying in bed, my husband and I. I was laying on my right side and all I could see when I opened my eyes-all I could see was this red light above the window and I could see my husband's shoulder but I was like paralyzed. Their skin, looked a lot like elephant skin. They had the big bulbous head with the big red-brown eyes.

Joe George: As an honest researcher, I realized that I couldn't just count these people out because the stuff that they had was so bizarre. Most of the researches in the realm said it wasn't possible to stop an experience. Knowing that, I called some of the leading researchers in the country. So I said, 'Guys. I have a very unusual case here.' This man-we'll use the name Bill-and during his experience in fear he calls out 'JESUS! JESUS! JESUS!' or 'Jesus, please HELP ME.' By calling out, he abruptly stops his abduction experience. These entities can be stopped in the name and authority of Jesus Christ.

Joyce Erins: Once down in Coco, this was after I had accepted Jesus Christ, they tried to come and I kept saying No. Jesus please help me. And I took on the empowerment of Jesus Christ and I stopped that. [69]

So my conclusion, based on the evidence, is "If it walks like a demon, talks like a demon, travels like a demon, acts like a demon, and is rebuked in the Name of Jesus Christ like a demon; I think we're dealing with demons here!" Of all things to stop an actual alien encounter is to rebuke it *in the Name of Jesus Christ* alone, and it flees? Every time? It's a demon!

The Seventh Reason We Know UFO's are Demonic in Nature - They Deceive Like Demons

Now, as if what we've seen so far wasn't enough proof that we're dealing with actual demons here, and a crazy Last Days deception. Little do people know that UFO's and aliens are also being used to *explain away the Rapture of the Church*. Here's what the Bible says about that imminent event.

1 Thessalonians 4:15-17 "According to the Lord's own word, we tell you that we who are still alive, who are left till the coming of the Lord, will certainly not precede those who have fallen asleep. For the Lord himself will come down from heaven, with a loud command, with the voice of the archangel and with the trumpet call of God, and the dead in Christ will rise first. After that, we who are still alive and are left will be caught up together with them in the clouds to meet the Lord in the air. And so we will be with the Lord forever."

This is just one of the classic passages in the Bible concerning the evacuation of the Christians, i.e. Rapture of the Church, just prior to God's wrath being poured out upon the planet during the 7-year Tribulation. However, little do people realize that UFO's and aliens are actually being used *right now* to explain away this amazing prophetic event. These demonic entities are actually preparing the planet to think that this mass disappearance of people from the planet in a mere flash, the "twinkling of an eye", is not an event from God coming to get His Church. Rather, it's the UFO's who have come to beam these people up into their spaceships for various reasons.

This mass deception makes sense if you put yourself in satan's shoes in the days we live in. Here you have a Last Days event that you cannot deny, you can't spin it away, the Rapture. It really happened, millions of people all over the planet have suddenly disappeared, and it's specifically and *only* Christians. So the logical normal response of those left behind after this shocking event would be something like, "Oh no! Why didn't I listen to my Christian wife or brother, Christian co-worker, Christian friend etc.? They were right, the Bible's true! I better get right with God now!" In short, you would think that people in mass would get saved all over the world due to the shock of the Rapture. Maybe not. Think of what the devil has been up to. This is what his deceitful lies have been leading to. This is what he put into motion 150 years ago with Charles Darwin! When the population of the planet witnesses other people disappear all across the planet in the blink of an eye, they may very well not even connect it with God or the Rapture or even Christianity. Rather they have been conditioned by Hollywood, the New Age, and the lie of evolution to think it was the UFO's and aliens that came and got them. Therefore, those that remain will be just fine. They don't need to repent. That's not just a convenient theory, that's exactly what your average UFO enthusiast is being taught *right now*:

Barbara Marciniak is a very famous New Age author and channeler. In her book *Bringers of the Dawn* she documents what she claims extra-terrestrials from the star system of the Pleiades have told her. *"There will be great shiftings within humanity on this planet. It will seem that great chaos and turmoil are forming, that nations are rising against each other in war, and that earthquakes are happening more frequently. Earth is shaking itself free, and a certain realignment or adjustment period is to be expected. The people who leave the planet during the time of earth changes do not fit here any longer, and they are stopping the harmony of earth. When the time comes that perhaps twenty million people leave the planet at one time, there will be a tremendous shift in consciousness for those who are remaining."*

Channeler Thelma Terrell, who goes by her spiritual name, "Tuella," wrote a book called Project World Evacuation, these are some quotes from that book: *"Our rescue ships will be able to come in close enough in the twinkling of an eye to set the lifting beams in operation in a moment, and all over the globe where events warrant it, this will be the method of evacuation. Mankind will be lifted, levitated shall we say, by the beams from our smaller ships. These smaller craft will in turn taxi the persons to the larger ships overhead, higher in the atmosphere, where there is ample space and quarters and supplies for millions of people. The Great Evacuation will come upon the world very suddenly. The flash of emergency events will be as a lightning that flashes in the sky."*

Various UFO Channelers say, *"The cataclysms are all part of purifying this Earth back to a millennium. What is going to happen when you reach a certain point is that you will have the first wave of ascension. Those whose bodies cannot take this change will go in the first wave of ascension. They will be taken up and their bodies will be changed in the twinkling of an eye. In the twinkling of an eye they will be removed from the physical completely into the new spiritual body. There will be many visits from the galaxies by inter-dimensional beings, as from the Pleidades, to assist and in some cases to rescue people and take them into higher places. Those are the flying machines that you are seeing coming into your galaxies that have been preparing themselves for up to the last forty years. Some never die on this earth, these missing persons have already been taken, as their time was not up and they were not meant to go through a demise. They went through a lift-off in UFO's."*

Just to make sure the planet falls for this *Last Days lie*, Hollywood is right there helping satan out. Here's a transcript of just one of their movie trailers promoting it:

"On August 28th, 2009 NASA sent a message into space farther than we ever thought possible...

...In an effort to Reach Extraterrestrial Life.

(Scene flying over a nighttime city skyline)

NBC Reporter: Stephen Hawking, astrophysicist and inarguably the smartest man on the planet warned us about the possibility of aliens from outer space.

(Flashes back to the city: A blue beam of light shoots down towards the ground)

Another Reporter: Hawking says that if extraterrestrials visit us-the outcome might be similar to when Columbus landed in America. In other words, it didn't turn out to well for Native Americans.

(Back to the city-many blue beams of light hitting the city streets)

MAYBE WE SHOULD HAVE LISTENED

(Scene of beams causing damage as large clouds of smoke emanate from the

ground)

(Scene changes to untold numbers of people screaming as they are being beamed into the sky towards the inside of a large UFO)

DON'T LOOK UP"[70]

That's just one of their movies promoting this Last Days lie to explain away the Rapture of the Church. If you've been paying attention, they continue to pump out tons of them all brainwashing people to come to the same faulty conclusion. Sometimes they just beam them up. Sometimes they suck them up. Sometimes Hollywood has the aliens landing and flat out grabbing people. But as you can see, *right now* Hollywood is being used to help plant into people's minds many different scenarios to "visualize" away the Rapture of the Church and instead believe the *lie* that it was aliens and UFO's. In fact, in this example, they even specifically said *don't look up* when that's exactly what Jesus says we *need to do*.

Luke 21:28 "When these things begin to take place, stand up and *lift up your heads*, because your redemption is drawing near."

No need for that apparently. The enemy of our souls has been working on this lie for 150 years. To train us into not looking up, not turning to Jesus, not getting right with God, so as to avoid the worst time in the history of mankind. In fact, they even go so far as to get people to think that being left behind is a good thing and they have chosen to enter the Age of Utopia, rather than the 7-year Tribulation! This is not only a *Last Days lie*, it's a lie from the pit of hell! What more does God have to do? Jesus warned us ahead of time. We are headed for the *greatest time of deceit* our world has ever seen or will ever see again and you don't want to be there! Yet, even with all this amazing evidence pointing us to the signs of Christ's soon return, some people still refuse to listen to any kind of request, like this lady:

"In the 18th-century in England, a vagabond was exhausted and famished, when he came to a roadside inn with a sign reading, 'George and the Dragon.' So the hungry man knocked on the door of the inn.

At this, the innkeeper's wife stuck her head out a window, so the vagabond asked, 'Could ye spare some porridge?'

The woman took one look at his shabby, dirty clothes and shouted, 'No!'

Then the man asked, 'Well then, could I have a pint of broth?'

And without missing a beat the woman yelled back, 'No!'

Undaunted, the vagabond now requested, 'Could I at least use your washroom?'

But the woman just shouted back again, 'No!'

Well at this the vagabond said, 'Might I please...?'

'What now?' the woman screeched, not allowing him to finish.

'D'ye suppose,' he asked, 'that I might have a word with George?'"[71]

Now, that lady didn't want to listen to any requests. Unfortunately, she's not alone. The Bible says that in the Last Days many people would also refuse to listen to God's request to repent and be saved before it's too late.

Revelation 3:3 "Remember, therefore, what you have received and heard; obey it, and repent. But if you do not wake up, I will come like a thief, and you will not know at what time I will come to you."

I hope you're not one of those who are refusing to listen to God's loving request to be saved, because if you are, you might wake up one day and discover that *you've been left behind*. And you know what? God doesn't want you left behind. Because He loves us, He has given us the warning sign of **The Rise of Falsehood** to show us that the 7-year Tribulation is near and that Christ's Coming is rapidly approaching. Again, Jesus stated this:

Luke 21:28 "When these things begin to take place, stand up and lift up your heads, because your redemption is drawing near."

Like it or not, we are headed for *The Final Countdown*. We don't know the day or the hour. Only God knows. The point is, if you're a Christian, you need to know that all we are given in this life is a little bitty dash between two dates. I am of course speaking in regards to the dash on our tombstones. Therefore, life is short, pray hard and take somebody to heaven with you. It's high time we Christians speak up and declare the good news of salvation to those who are lost and dying all around us. But please, if you're not a Christian, give your life to Jesus today, because tomorrow may be too late! Just like the Bible said!

Chapter Five

The Rise of Wickedness

"It was a sunny morning in the Big Forest and the Bear family is just waking up. So Baby Bear goes downstairs and sits in his small chair at the table. But he looks into his bowl and notices that it's empty.

So he squeaks, 'Who's been eating my porridge?'

Well, next Poppa Bear arrives at the table and sits in his big chair. He too looks into his big bowl and sees that it's empty as well!

So he roars, 'Who's been eating my porridge?

At this, the Momma Bear puts her head out from the kitchen and yells, 'For Pete's sake, how many times do we have to go through this?

It was Momma Bear who got up first.

It was Momma Bear who unloaded the dishwasher from last night and put everything away.

It was Momma Bear who set the table.

It was Momma Bear who put the cat out, cleaned the litter box and filled the cat's water & food dish.
And now that you've decided to come down stairs and grace me with your presence....

Listen good because I'm only going to say this one more time.......I haven't made the porridge yet!!!"'[1]

How many of you would say that Momma Bear was just a little bit on the edge there? She was having a seriously *rough day*! Did you know there's an even *rougher day* for others coming down the pike after the Rapture of the Church? For those who refuse to accept Jesus Christ as their Personal Lord and Savior, the Bible is clear, they will be catapulted into the 7-year Tribulation and it's not a joke! It's an outpouring of God's wrath on a wicked and rebellious planet. In fact, Jesus said in Matthew 24 it's going to be a "time of greater horror than anything the world has ever seen or will ever see again. And that "unless that time of calamity is shortened, the entire human race will be destroyed." But praise God, God's not only a God of wrath, He's a God of love as well. Because He loves us, He's given us many warning signs to show us when the Tribulation is near and Jesus Christ's Second Coming is rapidly approaching.

Therefore, in order to keep others from experiencing the ultimate rough day of being left behind, we're going to continue in our study, *The Final Countdown*. So far we've already seen how the **tenth sign** on The Final Countdown was **The Jewish People**. The **ninth sign** was **Modern Technology**. The **eighth sign** was **Worldwide Upheaval**. In the last chapter we saw how the **seventh sign** was **The Rise of Falsehood**. What we saw there was that God lovingly foretold us that when we see an **increase of False Christs**, **False Myths**, **False Teachings** and tons of **False Prophets** spreading New Age lies in the Church like, Hollywood, Environmentalism, Food & Population Control and even the Last Days lie of UFO's and aliens to explain away the Rapture of the Church, it's an indicator from Him *we're living in the Last Days*!

The **sixth sign** on *The Final Countdown* is none other than **The Rise of Wickedness**. In other words, in the Last Days, people would get really, really wicked right before Jesus comes back. Here's what God says about that end time prophetic behavior:

2 Timothy 3:1-5 "But mark this: There will be terrible times in the Last Days. People will be lovers of themselves, lovers of money, boastful, proud, abusive, disobedient to their parents, ungrateful, unholy, without love, unforgiving, slanderous, without self-control, brutal, not lovers of the good, treacherous, rash, conceited, lovers of pleasure rather than lovers of God – having a form of godliness but denying its power. Have nothing to do with them."

The Bible simply informs us that one of the major behavioral characteristics of the Last Days society is that it would be one filled with absolute unadulterated wickedness. During that time the people of the planet would become selfish, greedy, boastful, prideful, abusive, disobedient, ungrateful, unholy, unloving, unforgiving, slanderous, out-of-control, brutal, evil, treacherous, rash and conceited! The point is, if you're paying attention to the news, *every single one* of those wicked behaviors is *commonplace* in our society *right now*! This means we are living in that Last Days society the Bible talks about! Now, once again, the skeptic will say something like, "Come on! We've always had wicked behavior. This is no big deal." Granted, yes, throughout history, since the fall of man, we've always had some form of wicked behavior going on. But what's *not common* is how *in the last century alone*, there has been a literal explosion of every single one of these wicked behaviors that the Apostle Paul listed here. In fact, it's getting exponentially worse. Let's take a look at the change of behavior in America in just the last few decades and you tell me if there isn't a clear Rise of Wickedness like the Bible talks about:

LEADING PUBLIC SCHOOL DISCIPLINARY PROBLEMS

Mid-1940's
1) Talking
2) Chewing Gum
3) Making Noise
4) Running in the Hallways
5) Getting Out of Place in Line
6) Wearing Improper Clothing
7) Not Putting Paper in Wastebaskets

Mid-1980's
1) Drug Abuse
2) Alcohol Abuse
3) Pregnancy
4) Suicide
5) Rape
6) Robbery
7) Assault [2]

It sure appears to me that *in the last few decades* there's been a *massive rise of wickedness* in America, just like the Bible said would happen when you're living in the Last Days! In fact, if we're honest with ourselves, it's getting so bad and so commonplace that we're no longer even shocked at this kind of wickedness because it's considered the norm. We expect it, as the news informs us daily that it continues to get worse. You can't go to the movies without getting shot! You can't walk down the street without getting assaulted. People kill each other over a pair of shoes and we act like it's no big deal, "What else is on? Hey honey! What channel is the weather channel on?" Every single news station, twenty-four hours a day reminds us daily just how rotten things have really become, yet the irony is, hardly anyone recognizes the prophetic significance of their broadcasts! How do I know that I'm living in the Last Days? Just turn on your TV! This absolute unadulterated wickedness being reported every single day around the world is one of the clearest signs we're in that generation.

How could there be such an explosion of wickedness in such a short amount of time, especially in America with such a godly heritage? How could a Christian nation turn from loving God to *this*? First of all, let's back the train up a little bit and demonstrate that we really did have a godly heritage as our foundation here in America. I say that because the skeptics are going to say that America was *never* a Christian nation in the first place. However, that is not true. In fact, the skeptics repeatedly shout, "Oh no! Our Founding Fathers demanded a *separation of Church and state* which has basically come to mean, "Keep Christianity out at all costs!" Yet, this is a historical lie! The next time someone cries out to you, "Separation of Church and State" and says that's what our founding fathers wanted, *challenge them*! Ask them. "Where does that appear in the *Bill of Rights*? Where does that phrase, separation of church and state, appear in our *Constitution*?" Why? Because it isn't there! It came from a letter from Thomas Jefferson in 1802 to the Danbury Baptists of Connecticut who were concerned that another *Christian denomination* called the Congregationalists, were going to become the official Christian denomination of the United States. Notice the whole time the context is *Christian and Christianity*. Not Buddhism, not Islam, not Eastern Mysticism, and everything else under the sun! No! When our Founding Fathers talked about religion, they were referring to Christianity.

Jefferson simply referred them to the first amendment, that reads, "Congress shall make no law respecting an establishment of religion, (Christianity) or prohibiting the free exercise thereof..." In other words, Jefferson had full confidence the "original intent" of the first amendment would ensure *no Christian denomination* would be chosen to be the *official* Christian denomination of the United States. That's it! That's what he meant there by the phrase, separation of Church and state.[3] It has nothing to do with keeping Christianity out of every facet of our society. In fact, if you look at the words of the Founding Fathers themselves, you'll clearly see they *wanted to keep Christianity in* at all costs:

John Adams: "The general principles on which the fathers achieved independence were the general principles of Christianity. Without religion, this world would be something not fit to be mentioned in polite company: I mean hell. The Christian religion is, above all the religions that ever prevailed or existed in ancient or modern times, the religion of wisdom, virtue, equity and humanity."

John Quincy Adams: "My hopes of a future life are all founded upon the Gospel of Christ. In the chain of human events, the birthday of the nation is indissolubly linked with the birthday of the Savior. The Declaration of Independence laid the cornerstone of human government upon the first precepts of Christianity.

Patrick Henry: "Being a Christian is a character which I prize far above all this world has or can boast. Righteousness alone can exalt America as a nation. The great pillars of all government and of social life are virtue, morality, and religion. This is the armor, my friend, and this alone, that renders us invincible."

John Jay: (Original Chief Justice of the U.S. Supreme Court) "Mercy and grace and favor did come by Jesus Christ. By conveying the Bible to people we certainly do them a most interesting act of kindness. The most effectual means of securing the continuance of our civil and religious liberties is always to remember with reverence and gratitude the source from which they flow. The Bible is the best of all books, for it is the word of God and teaches us the way to be happy in this world and in the next. Continue therefore to read it and to regulate your life by its precepts. Providence has given to our people the choice of their rulers, and it is the duty as well as the privilege and interest of our Christian nation, to select and prefer Christians for their rulers."

Benjamin Rush: (Father of Public Schools under the Constitution) "The Gospel of Jesus Christ prescribes the wisest rules for just conduct in every situation of life. Happy they who are enabled to obey them in all situations! The great enemy of the salvation of man, (satan) in my opinion, never invented a more effective means of limiting Christianity from the world than by persuading mankind that it was improper to read the Bible at schools. Christianity is the only true and perfect religion; and in proportion as mankind adopt its principles and obey its precepts, they will be wise and happy. The Bible should be read in our schools in preference to all other books."

Noah Webster: (Schoolmaster to America) "The religion which has introduced civil liberty is the religion of Christ and His apostles. This is genuine Christianity and to this we owe our free constitutions of government. The moral principles and precepts found in the Scriptures ought to form the basis of all our civil constitutions and laws. I am persuaded that no civil government of a republican form can exist and be durable in which the principles of Christianity have not a controlling influence."

George Washington: "You do well to wish to learn our arts and ways of life, and above all, the religion of Jesus Christ. These will make you a greater and happier people than you are. While we are zealously performing the duties of good citizens and soldiers, we certainly ought not to be inattentive to the higher duties of religion. To the distinguished character of Patriot, it should be our highest glory to add the more distinguished character of Christian."

Congress U.S. House Judiciary Committee 1854: "Had the people, during the Revolution, had a suspicion of any attempt to war against Christianity, that Revolution would have been strangled in its cradle. In this age, there can be no substitute for Christianity. That was the religion of the founders of the republic and they expected it to remain the religion of their descendants." [4]

- The first colleges formed in America (123 out of 126) were formed on Christian principles.

- Up until 1900 it was very rare to find a university president who was not an ordained clergyman.

- The New England Primer, America's first textbook and used for 210 years taught the alphabet like this: A – In Adam's fall we sinned all. C – Christ crucified for sinners died. Z – Zaccheus he did climb the tree our Lord to see.

- The 107 questions at the end of the New England Primer included questions like, "What offices does Christ execute as our Redeemer?" "How does Christ execute the office of a priest?" "What is required in the fifth commandment?" "What are the benefits which in this life do accompany or flow from justification, adoption, and sanctification?"

- George Washington made it crystal clear that American schools would teach Indian youths the "religion" of Jesus Christ and Congress assisted in doing so.

- In 1782, Congress had 10,000 bibles printed for use in schools.

- Dr. Benjamin Rush said, "The only means of establishing and perpetuating our republican forms of government is the universal education of our youth in the principles of Christianity by means of the Bible."

- Thomas Jefferson wrote the first plan of education for the city of Washington D.C. and adopted two textbooks, the Bible and Watts Hymnal, and hired clergymen to be the teachers.

- The 1854 edition of Webster's Dictionary had Biblical definitions, Bible verses, and Webster's own testimony of personally receiving Christ."

- America's first school was Harvard, founded in 1636 by Reverend John Harvard whose official motto was "For Christ and the Church." Harvard had several requirements which students had to observe, one of which was, "Let every scholar be plainly instructed and earnestly pressed to consider well, the main end of his life and studies is to know God and Jesus Christ, which is eternal life." [4]

In fact, this next transcript reveals some very historically informative artifacts. Wait until you here where the largest Church in America used to be held for many years...

"This is a copy of what the first Bible printed in English in America looked like. This Bible was printed by the U.S. Congress in 1782 and in the records, it says, that this bible is 'a neat edition of the Holy Scriptures for the use of our schools'. So the first Bible printed in America in English. Well that was printed by Congress for the use of our schools? - it's worse than that - on the front of the cover it says 'resolved The United States and Congress assembled recommend this edition of the Bible to the inhabitants of the United States'. So the first Bible printed in English by America was done by the guys who signed the documents, endorsed by Congress and done for the use of schools and we're going to be told that they don't want any kind of religion in education, they don't want voluntary prayer? No, it doesn't make sense.

This document by itself is fairly significant, but in 1830, Congress commissioned these four paintings over here to recapture what the original records said was the Christian history of the United States. In these four paintings, means you have really a span of a few hundred years. If I take you through them chronologically, the first is back there, Columbus landing in the Western world in 1492. They got out, they knelt down and had a prayer service. You see the cross they have. They named the land where they have landed San Salvador, meaning Holy Savior which tells you some of the thinking that was going on then. If you come back over my shoulder here, this is the baptism of Pocahontas in Jamestown and this was in 1613. Over here-the fourth painting is 1620. This is the embarkation of the Pilgrims coming to America. You can see them gathered around the Bible there. You see the prayer meeting they're having.

Now if you take just those four paintings right there in this great secular hall of government. Those four paintings represent two prayer meetings, a bible study and a baptism, which is not bad for a secular building. As a matter of fact, you're standing in what was, in 1857, the largest Church in the United States, the U.S Capitol. Back on December the 4th of 1800, members of Congress, members of the Senate-Thomas Jefferson over the Senate, you had John Trombell over the House. They decided that on Sundays we would turn the Capitol Building into a Church building, and starting on Sunday we started having services in the Capitol.

Now six weeks after that, Thomas Jefferson became President of the United States, but for 8 years as President, he went to Church here at the U.S Capitol. He listened to the sermons here at the Capitol and being Commander-In-Chief, he decided he could help the worship here at the capitol. He ordered the Marine Corp band to play the worship services at the Capitol. Now that would be kind of cool having the Marine Corp as your worship band at Church. That Church went for a better part of a century and by 1857 there were 2,000 people a week who went to Church in the Hall of the House of Representatives and in addition to that, there were four other Churches that met at the Capitol. First Congregational, this was their first home as was First Presbyterian as was Capitol Hill Presbyterian. Churches met here, there was nothing secular or seen to be secular about this building until the last 30-40-50 years."[4]

As these facts reveal, we have been horribly lied to. It is very clear that our Founding Fathers not only believed in Jesus Christ as their personal Lord and Savior, but they also clearly built our Great Nation upon Him and His teachings.

However, it gets even worse. We have not only been lied to, but the same people are desperately trying to *cover up this truth*! If you can believe this, recently a publishing company put an actual "warning label" on the Constitution! As this article reveals:

"Wilder Publications warns readers of its reprints of the Constitution, the Declaration of Independence, Common Sense, the Articles of Confederation, and the Federalist Papers, among others, that, 'This book is a product of its time and does not reflect the same values as it would if it were written today.'

The disclaimer goes on to tell parents that they 'might wish to discuss with their children how views on race, gender, sexuality, ethnicity, and interpersonal relations have changed since this book was written.'"[5]

A *warning label* on the Constitution? It's not only ludicrous, it's blasphemous to the original intent of the Founding Fathers! Therefore, the common sense question is, "How in the world did this happen? How did the U.S.A fall like this, as a Nation giving rise to such rebellion and wickedness in such a short amount of time, especially with such a godly heritage?"

I. Wicked Worldview - Humanism

The First Reason the United States turned from a nation that once loved God to this Rise of Wickedness we see today is by the promotion of a Wicked Worldview. Of course, I'm talking about Humanism. Little do people know that the teachings of humanism and its atheistic ideals have actually aided in this massive rise of wicked behavior that the Bible mentioned as a sign we're living in the Last Days. Now, for those of you who may not know, humanism is the worldview where *man is the center of all things*, not God. So as you can see, at its very ore, it is diametrically opposed to Christianity. In fact, the following is a short summary of their beliefs from the documents called the Humanist Manifesto I and II:

- Faith in the prayer-hearing God, assumed to live and care for persons, to hear and understand their prayers, and to be able to do something about them, is an unproved and outmoded faith.

- We find insufficient evidence for the belief in the existence of a supernatural. We begin with humans not God.

- We do not accept as true the literal interpretation of the Old and New Testaments.

- We include a recognition of an individual's right to die with dignity, euthanasia, suicide, birth control and abortion.

- We believe that intolerant attitudes, often cultivated by orthodox religions and puritanical cultures, unduly repress sexual conduct. Divorce should be recognized. The many varieties of sexual exploration should not themselves be considered evil.

- We oppose any tyranny over the mind of man to shackle free thought. In the past such tyrannies have been directed by churches and states attempting to enforce the edicts of religious bigots.

- Promises of immortal salvation or fear of eternal damnation are both illusory and harmful.

- Salvationism, based on mere affirmation, still appears as harmful, diverting people with false hopes of heaven hereafter. No deity will save us; we must save ourselves.[6]

Sounds like the same familiar attitudes we have to deal with today, doesn't it? Of course it does. That's because it was humanists that forced the Bible, prayer, and the Ten Commandments out of our schools, courtrooms and government under the guise that religion and education do not mix. Again, the lie of separation of Church and state. However, what most people don't realize is that humanism was considered a religion itself by the Supreme Court back in the early 60's. Yet, can you guess just whose "religious" teachings are allowed in the schools today? Humanism it is! They don't even follow their own twisted lie of separation of Church and state! Instead today, faithful and godly teachers have to contend with the wicked behavior in the classroom as well as the wicked goals of humanists who have a *different agenda* for teaching our children. Where is this wicked behavior coming from we ask? The following is the stated wicked agenda that the humanists have for our school system. You tell me if it's not having a horrible effect on our nation's children:

- "(Our) great object was to get rid of Christianity, and to convert our churches into halls of science. The plan was not to make open attacks on religion...but to establish a system of state schools, from which all religion was to be excluded...and to which all parents were to be compelled by law to send their children. For this purpose, a secret society was formed and the whole country was to be organized." **Orestes Brownson (1803-1876)**

- "What the church has been for medieval man, the public school must become for democratic and rational man. God would be replaced by the concept of the public good." **Horace Mann (1796-1858)**

- "There is no God and there is no soul. Hence, there is no need for the props of traditional religion. With dogma and creed excluded, then immutable truth is also dead and buried. There is no room for fixed, natural law or moral absolutes." **John Dewey (1859-1952), the "Father of Progressive Education;" co-author of the first Humanist Manifesto and honorary NEA president**

- "Education is thus a most powerful ally of humanism, and every American school is a school of humanism. What can a theistic Sunday School's meeting for an hour once a week, and teaching only a fraction of the children, do to stem the tide of the five-day program of humanistic teaching?" **Charles F. Potter, Humanism: A New Religion (1930)**

- "I think that the most important factor moving us toward a secular society has been the educational factor. Our schools may not teach Johnny to read properly, but the fact that Johnny is in school until he is sixteen tends to lead toward the elimination of religious superstition." **Paul Blanshard, "Three Cheers for Our Secular State," The Humanist, March/April 1976**

- "We must ask how we can kill the God of Christianity. We need only to ensure that our schools teach only secular knowledge. If we could achieve this, God would indeed be shortly due for a funeral service." **G. Richard Bozarth, "On Keeping God Alive," American Atheist, November 1977**

- "I am convinced that the battle for humankind's future must be waged and won in the public school classroom by teachers who correctly perceive their role as proselytizers of a new faith: a religion of humanity. These teachers must embody the same selfless dedication as the most rabid fundamentalist preachers, for they will be ministers of another sort, utilizing a classroom instead of a pulpit to convey humanist values in whatever subject they teach, regardless of educational level – preschool, day care or a large state university. The classroom must and will become an arena of conflict between the old and the new – the rotting corpse of Christianity...and the new faith of humanism." **John J. Dunphy, "A New Religion for a New Age," The Humanist, January/February 1983**

- "Every child in America entering school at the age of five is mentally ill, because he comes to school with certain allegiances toward our founding fathers, toward our elected officials, toward his parents, toward a belief in a supernatural Being, toward the sovereignty of this nation as a separate entity. It is up to you teachers to make all these sick children well by creating the international children of the future." **Harvard Professor of Education and Psychiatry, 1984**[7]

I'd say that's quite a different agenda for teaching children then what the average American expects is going on when they drop little Johnnie and Susie off at school. So much for reading, writing, and arithmetic! They want to turn all the children of our country away from God! For further proof of this wicked agenda from the humanists, let's listen to one of the ladies who used to work for them but today is blowing the whistle. She freely admits they don't want to educate your child, but indoctrinate them against God:

"My name is Charlotte Thomson-Iserbyt and I served as Senior Policy Adviser in the United States Department of Education under the Reagan administration during which I had access to almost all of the most important documents for the restructuring of not only American education but global education. I am also the author of: 'The Deliberate Dumbing Down of America' which gets into all of this – gives the background of what I saw not only in the Department of Education but as a local school board member.

Just to give you an idea of how blatant they are. Benjamin Bloom said, 'The purpose of education' – and I often say this to parents really listen to this – You really think the purpose of education is reading, writing and arithmetic – 'The purpose of education is to change the thoughts, actions and feelings of students'. He continues explaining how he defines good teaching – and it's even worse from the parental standpoint, as "challenging the student's fixed beliefs."

Interviewer: "When he says challenge. Does he mean 'challenge' or does he mean 'change'...change their fixed beliefs..."

Charlotte: "Yeah, through challenging – It's through challenging. You go up against them and you change them. You asked a good question because then he goes on in one part of the taxonomy that is in my book. He says he can take a student from here (points) to there (points again), from a belief in God or his country or whatever to being an atheist and not believing in his country in one hour."

Interviewer: "Did he do that?"

Charlotte: "Oh yeah, he does it and I've seen it with students. I've seen it with young people."[8]

How could America fall from being a great, mighty Christian nation into this absolute unadulterated wickedness we see today? Because some wicked entity wormed its way in and changed us from the inside out. It's called humanism and they're using our schools to get the job done. In fact, it's worked so well that the average person today thinks the teachings of humanism, not the teachings of Christianity, with the triumph of the human spirit is the antidote needed to cure the wickedness of our world. Yet, in reality they are actually following the teachings of satan, the king of wickedness.

Genesis 3:4-5 "You will not surely die," the serpent said to the woman. "For God knows that when you eat of it your eyes will be opened, and you will be like God, knowing good and evil."

As you can see, the teaching of man being the center of all things, determining his own destiny, in fact being his own god, started with satan. Therefore, is it any wonder that there's been a massive Rise of Wickedness just like the Bible said would happen in the Last Days? In fact, Paul Harvey warned about this subversion *over 50 years ago*. I think we should've listened to him too:

IF I WERE THE DEVIL BY PAUL HARVEY

"If I were the Devil...if I were the Prince of Darkness, I'd want to engulf the whole world in darkness and I would have a third of its real estate and four-fifths of its population, but I wouldn't be happy until I had seized the ripest apple on the tree, thee.

So I'd set about however necessary to take over the United States. I'd subvert the Churches first. I'd begin with a campaign of whispers. With the wisdom of the serpent, I would whisper to you as I whispered to Eve: 'Do as you please.'

To the young, I would whisper that the Bible is a myth. I would convince them that man created God instead of the other way around. I would confide that what is bad is good, and what is good is 'square'.

And the old, I would teach to pray after me: 'Our Father, which art in Washington.'

And then, I'd get organized. I'd educate authors in how to make lurid literature exciting so that anything else would appear dull and uninteresting. I'd threaten TV with dirtier movies and vice versa.

I'd peddle narcotics to whom I could. I'd sell alcohol to ladies and gentlemen of distinction. I'd tranquilize the rest with pills.

If I were the devil, I'd soon have families at war with themselves, churches at war with themselves, and nations at war with themselves until each in its turn was consumed.

And with promises of higher ratings, I'd have mesmerizing media fanning the flames. If I were the devil, I would encourage schools to refine young intellects but neglect to discipline emotions – just let those run wild until before you knew it, you'd have to have drug-sniffing dogs and metal detectors at every schoolhouse door.

Within a decade, I'd have prisons overflowing. I'd have judges promoting pornography. Soon I could evict God from the courthouse, and then from the schoolhouse, and then from the houses of Congress.

And in His own churches I would substitute psychology for religion and deify science. I would lure priests and pastors into misusing boys and girls and church money. If I were the devil, I'd make the symbol of Easter an egg and the symbol of Christmas a bottle.

If I were the devil, I would take from those who have and I would give to those who wanted, until I had killed the incentive of the ambitious. And what will you bet I couldn't get whole states to promote gambling as the way to get rich.

I would caution against extremes in hard work, in patriotism, in moral conduct. I would convince the young that marriage is old-fashioned, that swinging is more fun, that what you see on TV is the way to be and thus I could undress you in public, and I could lure you into bed with diseases for which there is no cure.

In other words, if I were the devil, I'd just keep right on doing what he's doing."[9]

Unfortunately, it looks to me like the devil has been pretty successful in his agenda, and he's been using *humanism* to get the job done!

II. Wicked Teaching - Atheism

The second reason the U.S.A has turned from a nation that once loved God to this Rise of Wickedness we see today is by the promotion of a Wicked Teaching. Of course, I'm talking about Atheism. As a nation, we need to desperately wake up and realize that this atheism has been spawned by *another lie* in our schools other than just humanism, and that is the lie of *evolution*. As we saw earlier, the premise of evolution is that there is no God, we have no hope, we have no future, and we came from nowhere! It's precisely this lie that has spawned these atheistic ideals, these God-hating ideals which have also aided in this *massive rise of wicked behavior* we see today. In fact, God told us this is exactly what would happen to a society if they have the audacity to say He didn't exist.

Romans 1:18-32 "The wrath of God is being revealed from heaven against all the godlessness and wickedness of men who suppress the truth by their wickedness, since what may be known about God is plain to them, because God has made it plain to them. For since the creation of the world God's invisible qualities – His eternal power and divine nature – have been clearly seen, being understood from what has been made, so that men are without excuse. For although they knew God, they neither glorified Him as God nor gave thanks to Him, but their thinking became futile and their foolish hearts were darkened. Although they claimed to be wise, they became fools and exchanged the glory of the immortal God for images made to look like mortal man and birds and animals and reptiles. Therefore, God gave them over in the sinful desires of their hearts to sexual impurity for the degrading of their bodies with one another. They exchanged the truth of God for a lie, and worshiped and served created things rather than the Creator – Who is forever praised. Amen. Because of this, God gave them over to shameful lusts. Even their women exchanged natural relations for unnatural ones. In the same way the men also abandoned natural relations with women and were inflamed with lust for one another. Men committed indecent acts with other men, and received in themselves the due penalty for their perversion. Furthermore, since they did not think it worthwhile to retain the knowledge of God, He gave them over to a depraved mind, to do what ought not to be done. They have become filled with every kind of wickedness, evil, greed and depravity. They are full of envy, murder, strife, deceit and malice. They are gossips, slanderers, God-haters, insolent, arrogant and boastful; they invent ways of doing evil; they disobey their parents; they are senseless, faithless, heartless, ruthless. Although they know God's righteous decree that those who do such things deserve death, they not only continue to do these very things but also approve of those who practice them."

Sure sounds like American society today! The point is, where did God say all this wicked behavior got spawned from? From suppressing the truth about God's existence, in other words, the lie of evolution. Do they not claim there is no God? Do they not suppress the truth about His existence in our schools? In the media and Hollywood? Of course, which I always found interesting. Why do they fight against something so hard that they say they don't believe in? Why don't they just leave the rest of us alone to enjoy our illusion if that's what they really believe in? Unless of course, deep down inside, they know there is a God like the Bible says. They have no excuse, and thus the real reason is they don't want there to be a God so they can become their own god and do whatever wicked thing they come up with.

That's not just a personal convenient theory of mine, it's exactly what the Bible says. What did God do when the Roman society went down this route? *God gave them over* to their wicked desires! In essence, "You don't want there to be a God? Fine! Have it your way! You'll learn the hard way what happens to a society that no longer wants Me! You will immediately go after sexual impurity, shameful lusts and homosexuality. Then you will become filled with every kind of wickedness, evil, greed and depravity, murder, envy, strife, deceit, and malice. You will become gossips, slanderers, *God-haters*, insolent, arrogant, boastful, disobedient to your parents, senseless, faithless, heartless, ruthless, and it will get so bad that you will even invent new ways of doing evil." All because you had the audacity to say there is no God and no proof of His existence, just like the lie of evolution teaches. Therefore, as an act of Judgment from God, He gives you over to your atheistic wicked desires and your society starts to fall apart!

Now, here's the point. Tell me that's not exactly what's happened to society today. Every single one of those wicked behaviors is not only commonplace in our society *right now* but it stems from an atheist mindset created by the lie of evolution. "Why did the U.S.A. fall? How did this Great and Mighty Christian Nation turn into a society of such great wickedness and rebellion?" I'll tell you why! Because they allowed the infiltration of a *wicked teaching* into the school system *on top of* humanism called evolution. It too, like humanism, was a deliberate attack to subvert our nation. For proof that these atheistic teachings of evolution really have also helped to spawn this wicked behavior in this society, just like the atheistic teachings of humanism, let's take a look at the change of behavior in America since the lie of evolution began to take over. The following statistics are from the U.S. Census Bureau from about 1963 onward, which is, again, when evolution became prominent in our school system. Here's the results:

Back in the 1950's, the average textbook only had two to three thousand words about evolution. However, in 1963 it jumped up to 33,000 words. It also just so happened that 1963 is when prayer and Bible reading were taken out of the American school system. Here's the apparent affect it had on our country.

- Since 1963, sexually transmitted diseases among teenagers and young adults have increased nearly 400%.
- Instances of pre-marital sex among teenagers have skyrocketed.
- Unwed pregnancies among young girls are up 553%.
- Unmarried couples living together are up 725%.
- Divorce rates are up to 111%. In some parts of California the divorce rate is one for every marriage.
- Single parent households are quickly becoming the norm.
- SAT scores have plummeted.
- Alcohol and drug consumption have gone ballistic.
- Violent crimes are up 995%.

Is this really a surprise? If you tell kids they came from an ape, then why are we surprised when they act like apes?[10]

I'd say the effects of evolutionary teaching hasn't had a very good impact on our country. Again is it really a surprise? No wonder our world is so hopeless. What is the lie of evolution saying to people? "You are nothing, you came from nothing, and you have no future," That's hopeless! The reason why it creates this hopelessness is because *what you believe determines how you behave*. Again, if we teach kids they came from an ape, then why are we shocked when they act like apes? If you say there is no meaning or purpose to life, why are we so shocked when they so flippantly take a life? If you drill into their heads, from wee high, the lie that there is no God, why are we shocked when they act ungodly? It's a direct correlation. What you believe determines how you behave! This is the rotten fruit of this atheistic lie called evolution. Yet the twisted irony is, even though God clearly warned us that our society and any society would *totally fall apart* when they give into this lie about His existence and *reject Him*, people take one look at our wicked society and actually point a finger back at God and *blame Him*! They say, "Why, God, why? Why are You doing this! Why are You allowing this to happen? Why? Why? Why?" when in reality here's the real culprit to blame:

"Dear God,
Why didn't you save the school children at...

Moses Lake, WA
Bethel, AK
Pearl, MS
West Paducah, KY
Stamp, AR
Jonesboro, AR
Edinborough, PA
Fayetteville, TN
Springfield, OR
Richmond, VA
Littleton, CO
Tabor, Alberta Canada
Conyers, GA
Denning, NM
Ft. Gibson, OK
Santee, CA
El Cahon, CA
Blacksburg, VA?

Sincerely,
Concerned Student

REPLY:

Dear Concerned Student,
I AM not allowed in schools.

Sincerely,
God"

"How did this get started? I think it started when Madelyne Murray-O'Hare complained that she didn't want any prayer in our schools and we said 'Okay.'

Then someone said you'd better not read the Bible in school. The Bible says, 'Thou shalt not kill, thou shalt not steal and love your neighbor as yourself' and we said, 'Okay.'

Dr. Benjamin Spock said we shouldn't spank our children when they misbehave because their personalities would be warped and we might damage their self-esteem. And we said, 'An expert should know what he's talking about, so we won't spank them anymore.'

Then someone said teachers and principals better not discipline our children when they misbehave and the school administrators said, 'No faculty member in this school better touch a student when they misbehave because we don't want any bad publicity and we surely don't want to be sued.' And we accepted their reasoning.

Then someone said let's let our daughters have abortions if they want and they won't even have to tell their parents. And we said, 'That's a grand idea.'

Then some wise school board member said, 'Since boys will be boys and they're going to do it anyway, let's give our sons all the condoms they want so they can have all the fun they desire and we won't have to tell their parents they got them at school.' And we said, 'That's another great idea.'

Then some of our top elected officials said, 'It doesn't matter what we do in private as long we do our jobs.' And we said, 'It doesn't matter what anybody, including the president, does in private as long as we have jobs and the economy is good.'

And someone else took that appreciation a step further and published pictures of nude children and then stepped further by making them available on the internet. And we said, 'Everyone is entitled to free speech.'

And the entertainment industry said, 'Let's make TV shows and movies that promote profanity, violence and illicit sex, and let's record music that encourages rape, drugs, murder, suicide and satanic themes.' And we said, 'It's just entertainment and it has no adverse effect and nobody takes it seriously anyway, so go right ahead.'

Now we are asking ourselves why are our children have no conscience. Why they don't know right from wrong and why it doesn't bother them to kill strangers, classmates, or even themselves. Undoubtedly if we thought about it long and hard enough. We could figure it out. Surely it has a great deal to do with, 'We reap what we sow.'"[11]

"Why God? Why are You doing this! Why are you allowing this to happen? Why? Why? Why?" *It's not Him!* It's *our own doing*! We kicked Him out of our schools, we kicked Him out of our courtrooms, and we kicked Him out of our government! We allowed a wicked teaching into our school system called evolution and it's producing this atheistic mindset that's giving birth to all this wickedness. It's that simple! Therefore, if there's any hope for our nation, we have got to get busy *kicking God back into* our *school system*, back into our *court rooms*, back into our *government* and seek His blessing again!

III. Wicked Attack - Militant Atheism

The third reason we've turned from a nation that once loved God to this Rise of Wickedness we see today is the promotion of a Wicked Attack. Now I'm talking about militant atheism. Apparently it's not enough to just promote these atheistic ideas that spawn from the lie of evolution into our schools and media. These same people, these atheists, will not rest until this *God-hating lie* is permeated in all levels of society and *utterly destroy us* just like Romans Chapter one said would happen. They are *militant* about it and all it does is keep inviting more of the wrath of God upon us. They will not rest until every single memory, every last aspect, every last trace of historical proof of our great Christian heritage is totally wiped out, including the knowledge of the existence of God.

1. The First Attack by Militant Atheists is Upon the Character of God

Revelation 4:8-11 "Each of the four living creatures had six wings and was covered with eyes all around, even under his wings. Day and night they never stop saying: 'Holy, holy, holy is the Lord God Almighty, Who was, and is, and is to come.' Whenever the living creatures give glory, honor and thanks to Him Who sits on the throne and Who lives for ever and ever, the twenty-four elders fall down before Him who sits on the throne, and worship Him who lives for ever and ever. They lay their crowns before the throne and say; 'You are worthy, our Lord and God, to receive glory and honor and power, for You created all things, and by Your will they were created and have their being.'"

When it comes to His character, the Bible not only clearly says that God is Holy, Holy, Holy, but He's also clearly the One Who created us. In fact, He created *all things*! Therefore, it's obvious that God, being the Creator of all things and Infinitely Holy without sin, demands our utmost. But not anymore! Thanks to these militant atheists, we are now being told not only the lie that there is no God, but they've even gone so far as to say that following God's Righteous Holy Character is something that's bad for us, including our kids. They've actually replaced godly events for kids like Vacation Bible School with atheist's camps for kids. Then they've even gone so far as to create opportunities for adults to *de-baptize* themselves with a hair dryer. Here's one report of that blasphemous behavior:

"(Trumpet blowing) WAKE UP!

Reporter: It may be the summer holiday but there's no time to lie in bed at Camp Quest. Twenty-four children aged 7-17 attacking critical thinking, rational query, and a scientific approach to the world in a range of summer camp activities. They will also learn cooperation, tolerance and empathy. All in an atmosphere guaranteed free of religious propaganda. Most of the parents are atheists who want their children to learn ethical behavior but separate from religion.

Samantha Stein: I think that people are possibly getting tired of the influence that religion has in society, possibly an unearned influence um and trying to come up with alternatives.

Reporter: With the sun setting, it was time for a little open air education. It's aimed mainly at encouraging children to think skeptically or not to simply be told what to think. They're likely to talk about religion and be told that religious beliefs can hinder moral behavior."[12]

We wonder why things are getting worse? This kind of atrocious behavior is putting us under the judgment of God. But that's still the tip of the iceberg. The following are even more examples of how these other militant atheists are attacking the character of God:

- Atheism ads are now appearing all across America. Hundreds of thousands of dollars are being spent on Billboards declaring "We Are Good without God," or "Don't Believe in God? Join the Club!" or "Praise Darwin! Evolve Beyond Belief" and "Christianity: Sadistic God; Useless Savior, 30,000+ Versions of "Truth" Promotes Hate, Calls it "Love" just to name a few.

- Atheists in Florida are scrubbing away a blessing with unholy water that Christians prayed for on a highway. They say it made them uncomfortable and that they were not going to tolerate bigotry.

- Various atheists across the country are hosting "Rapture Parties" because "If the Rapture indeed occurs, and Christians worldwide are transported to heaven, we know as atheists, we're not going. If it occurs, it's a good thing for us. We get the real estate and cheap cars, and we won't have to worry about separation of Church and state."

- There's a new website out there called (www.if-jesus-returns-kill-him-again.com) where atheist Darwin Bedford, the self-proclaimed "atheist messiah" states among other blasphemous things, "If that self-made "blank" Jesus returns again, I think we should hire some Jews to throw Him off the rooftop once again. Or maybe we could hire some of Mel Gibson's extras from "The Passion of the Christ" to punish Him first."

- And if that doesn't work, believe it or not there is now a new web filter out there for the Internet called, "God Block" that blocks all religious content to protect kids from, "The often violent, sexual, and psychologically harmful material in many holy texts, and from being indoctrinated into any religion."

And the reason why they say they developed this device for parents and schools was because there's been a resurgence of fundamentalist religion.[13]

Yet, people still have the audacity to ask, "Why God? Why are You doing this?! Why are You allowing this to happen? Why is this going on! Why is our society going down the tubes?" I'll tell you why! Because we've allowed militant atheists *to attack the character of God* and therefore we're under His judgment! It is high time that we the Church stand up and speak up against this atheistic nonsense if there's any hope for our nation!

2. The Second Attack by Militant Atheists is Upon the Name of God

Exodus 20:7 "You shall not misuse the Name of the LORD your God, for the LORD will not hold anyone guiltless who misuses His name."

Here we see that the Bible now informs us that God is not only Holy, but that even His Name is Holy. Therefore, the last thing anyone would ever want to do is *misuse* His Holy Name. This is why He said He will not hold *anyone guiltless*, or in other words, He will punish those who treat His Name as a common word let alone a cuss word. In fact, breaking this command has always amazed me. For instance, why is it when people smash their hand with a hammer they don't cry out, "Buddha, Buddha, Buddha!" Or when somebody driving gets cut off the road by another driver they don't yell out the window, "Ah Muhammad!" Why is it always *Jesus Christ*? I personally don't think this behavior is by chance. If you combine it with Philippians Chapter 2 that states, "Every knee shall bow and every tongue confess that Jesus Christ is Lord over all," including satan and the demons, as well as the fact that it's only through the Name of Jesus Christ that anyone could be saved from hell, then this is precisely what the enemy would do! Turn the blessed Holy Name of Jesus Christ into a common cuss word when it's worthy of our utter respect. Yet, believe it or not, this is precisely what these militant atheists are doing! They're not only encouraging adults and children alike to speak the Name of God *in vain* as a *common cuss word*, but to also use the Name of Jesus Christ in a *blasphemous manner*. One researcher exposes this horrible behavior:

"The Ten Commandments given to us by God warns that we should treat even the mention of His name with great awe and respect, never using it in a casual or disrespectful way. The Old Testament saints took this command very seriously. Insisting that Scribes wash their hands and use a new pen when even writing the

name of God. Many of the Jews were even afraid to say it out loud in any circumstance. Choosing, instead to refer to it indirectly as 'The Name.'

Contrast that to our day. To a time when God as an act of incomprehensible grace and mercy chose to fully reveal Himself in Christ as Immanuel-'God With Us' and has given us the true Name of the LORD our God. The only 'Name under heaven given to men by which we may be saved' Acts 4:12. The Name of the Lord Jesus Christ."

God's Name is degraded, blasphemed and reduced to a cheap expletive by so many in today's entertainment industry.

Ken Kesey, the author of Sometimes A Great Notion and the Academy Award winning One Flew Over The Cuckoo's Nest provided perhaps the best summation of the pride and irreverence that characterizes so much of today's art and entertainment.

'The job of the artist is to say, 'F*** you, god! F*** you and the Old Testament you rode in on!''---Esquire, Sept. 1992, p210

Larry King: "We're gonna run the unedited version"

Kathy Griffin: "What!?"

Larry King: "Be forewarned people, you may be offended. Watch."

Larry King Live showing video clip of Kathy Griffin's Emmy acceptance speech:

Kathy Griffin: "Now look, a lot of people come up here and they thank Jesus for this award. I want you to know that no one had less to do with this award than Jesus. He didn't help me a bit. If it were up to him Caesar Milano would be up here with that d-mn dog."

(Laughter erupts from the audience)

Griffin: "So all I can say is 'S-ck it Jesus, this award is my god now!"[14]

We wonder why our society is going down the tubes? "Why God? Why are You doing this?! Why are You allowing this to happen? Why is this going on! Why is our society going down the tubes?" I'll tell you why! It's because we've allowed militant atheists *to attack the Name of God* and He will not hold anyone guiltless who misuses His Name! We're being *punished*! It's high time we the Church stand up and speak out against this atheistic nonsense if there's any hope for our nation!

3. The Third Attack by Militant Atheists is Upon the Word of God

Psalm 119:73,97,101,105 "Your hands made me and formed me; give me understanding to learn your commands. Oh, how I love your law! I meditate on it all day long. I have kept my feet from every evil path so that I might obey your word. Your word is a lamp to my feet and a light for my path."

It is very clear that God is now informing us that the Word of God, that is the Bible, is something that is good for us, not bad for us. God says it keeps us from evil, it lights our path, it illuminates the darkness and it can even show us the way out of the current mess we're in. This is good news! Here's the answer! We just need to get busy utilizing the Word of God and we can get out of this spiritual black hole we're in. But not anymore! Thanks to the rise of militant atheism, we are now being encouraged to turn in and hand over our Bibles for copies of pornography! Here's the proof:

"Reporter: *A program that has been turning heads and dropping jaws on the UTSA campus since Friday is in the Home Stretch. Through tomorrow an atheist group is offering free pornography to people willing to give up their Bibles. It's made more than a few people angry, but the University says the group hasn't broken any rules and should be allowed to exercise their right.*"[15]

So let me get this straight. We're allowing people to exchange Bibles for pornography right here in America? Yet, we wonder why our country is going down the tubes? Our Founding Fathers must be rolling over in their graves! Speaking of Founding Fathers, I wonder what they would say today of people in office who would treat the Bible with utter contempt and mockery, like this man did. See if you can guess who it is:

"*Moreover, given the increase in diversity of America's population, the dangers of sectarianism are greater than ever. Whatever we once were, we are no longer a Christian nation, at least not just. We are also a Jewish nation, a Muslim nation, and a Buddhist nation, and a Hindu nation and a nation of unbelievers.*

And even if we have only Christians in our midst, if we expelled every non-Christian from the United States of America, whose Christianity would we teach in the schools? Would it be James Dobson's or Al Sharpton's?

Which passages of scripture should guide our public policy? Should we go with Leviticus? Which suggests slavery is okay and that eating shellfish is an abomination. Or we could go with Deuteronomy, which suggests stoning your child if he strays from the faith.

Or should we just stick to the Sermon on the Mount. A passage that is so radical that it is doubtful that our own Defense Department would survive its application."[16]

For those of you who don't know, that was former President Barack Obama. I not only find his words blasphemous as a Christian, but it offends me as a Christian. He told us in the past that we shouldn't say anything bad about the Koran, but it's okay to mock the Bible? Again, why is our society going down the tubes? This blasphemous behavior towards the Holy Word of God is putting us under the wrath of God! We've got to get back to respecting the Word of God, not mocking it, not exchanging it for pornography, and allow it to illuminate our path once again! If you don't think that'll really work, then you better ask this American President. He knew better:

"You see the statue to the left of the door over there? That wide marble statue? That is President James A Garfield. President Garfield was one of the young Major Generals in the Civil War. He was a war hero. He became Speaker of the House. He became the 20th President of the United States and, by the way, that man founded Howard University. General O.O. Howard took it over after he founded it.

Just a really cool guy but what we never really hear about that President of the United States, was that he was a minister during the Second Great Awakening. This is actually one of his letters, signed James A Garfield, 1858. In this letter, President Garfield recounts that he just finished preaching a revival service where he preached the Gospel nineteen times in the revival. He says as a result of his preaching that 34 folks came to Christ and he baptized 31.

Now that doesn't sound like a typical presidential activity today. That's what we used to do as Presidents in the past. Again, you walk through, you see that statue and you think oh there's a President. You'd never think there's a minister.

We've so compartmentalized Christianity in such a small box that we don't realize our Military Leaders are ministers, are educators. Our Presidents used to be ministers. That's why I say about one fourth of these statues are ministers of the Gospel."[17]

Now, wait a second. You mean to tell me that our Presidents used to be Ministers, and that they preached the Word of God to help bring revival to our Great and Mighty Nation in times of trouble? Yes! And dare I say that if revival is ever going to come our way again, then we need leaders, we need people, we need Churches who will do it again! As far as these militant atheists *who do not make up the majority of America*, they're an extreme minority who just have a loud voice. The rest of us just need to do what our Founding Fathers did and speak up and speak out against this blasphemy like this man did:

"Life, liberty or the pursuit of happiness will not be endangered because someone says a 30-second prayer before a football game. What's the big deal?

It's not like somebody is up there reading the entire Book of Acts. They're just talking to God, in whom they believe in, and asking Him to grant safety to the players on the field and the fans going home from the game.

But what about the atheists? What about them? Nobody is asking them to be baptized. We're not going to pass the collection plate. Just humor us for thirty seconds. If that's asking too much, bring a Walkman or a pair of ear plugs.

Go to the bathroom. Visit the concession stand. Call your lawyer!

Unfortunately, one or two will make that call. One or two will tell tens of thousands of Americans what they can and cannot do.

But it's a Christian prayer, some will argue. Yes, and this is the United States of America, a country founded on Christian principles. According to every phone book, Christian churches outnumber all others 200-to-1.

So what would you expect -- somebody chanting Hare Krishna?

If I went to a football game in Jerusalem, I'd expect to hear a Jewish prayer.
If I went to a soccer game in Baghdad, I'd expect to hear a Muslim prayer.
If I went to a ping pong match in China, I'd expect to hear a Buddhist prayer.

But this is America and so why are we shocked when we hear a Christian prayer!

Our parents and grandparents taught us to pray and our Bible tells us to pray without ceasing. Now a handful of people and their lawyers are telling us to cease from PRAYING and whatever you do, STOP mentioning the NAME of JESUS.

God, help us. And if that last sentence offends you, sue me!

The silent majority has been silent too long. And it's high time we tell that one or two who scream loud enough that the vast majority doesn't care what they want. It is time that the majority Rules!

It's time we tell them, 'You don't have to pray; you don't have to say the Pledge of Allegiance; you don't have to believe in God or attend services that honor Him. That is your right, and we will honor your right; but by golly, you are no longer going to take our rights away. We are fighting back, and we WILL WIN!'"[18]

This kind of godly boldness is exactly what our nation was founded upon. A people who were not afraid to declare that we belong to God and He's the One we need. That's what our Founding Fathers believed and that's what made our country so great. Therefore, if we're ever going to get back to being that great Christian nation again then it's high time we the Church get motivated with the same boldness again! We've got to get busy putting Jesus Christ back in our government, back in our schools, back in our court rooms, and yes, back in our pulpits and turn this country around!

IV. Wicked Worship - Self-Love, Self-Esteem, Secular Psychology

The fourth reason we've turned from a nation that once loved God to this Rise of Wickedness we see today is the promotion of a Wicked Worship. Now I'm talking about the self-love, self-esteem movement. Little do people know that the teachings of secular psychology have actually aided in this massive rise of wicked behavior. In fact, God warned us that this one *selfish* behavior would spawn all kinds of wicked behavior.

2 Timothy 3:1-5 "But mark this: There will be terrible times in the Last Days. People will be *lovers of themselves*, lovers of money, boastful, proud, abusive, disobedient to their parents, ungrateful, unholy, without love, unforgiving, slanderous, without self-control, brutal, not lovers of the good, treacherous, rash, conceited, lovers of pleasure rather than lovers of God – having a form of godliness but denying its power. Have nothing to do with them."

Now, we have already seen this text earlier and how it revealed that one of the major characteristics of the Last Days society is that it would be one filled with absolute unadulterated wickedness. People at that time would be, selfish, greedy, boastful, prideful, abusive, disobedient, ungrateful, unholy, unloving, unforgiving, slanderous, out-of-control, brutal, evil, treacherous, rash and conceited. We also saw that every single one of those wicked behaviors is commonplace in our society right now. But here's the point of bringing it up again. What was the apparent *root* of this wicked behavior? What was the *very first thing* mentioned there? Apparently this list of wickedness stems from *a love of self instead of a love for God*. It says there that people in the Last Days would be lovers of themselves. It just so happens that this is the number one virtue being celebrated in our society *today*! Our world not only says you have to be a lover of yourself, but that you have to love yourself *first* if you're going to be able to love God and other people. This is supposed to be the psychological panacea of all our ills and problems. Yet, the Bible says it's this very preoccupation with self and the promotion of it, which is causing all the wicked behavior we have to deal with today! So, once again, that's the question. "How in the world did this happen? How did our once great mighty Christian nation go from being lovers of God to lovers of self?"

1. The First Reason We Became Lovers of Selves Instead of Lovers of God – We Listened to Teachings of Satan instead of the Word of God

The average person today thinks that the teachings of the self-love, self-esteem movement from secular psychology are the antidote needed to cure the wickedness of our world today. Yet, in reality, they've been duped into following the teachings of the king of wickedness, that is, satan. Here's where this self-love, self-worship started.

Isaiah 14:12-14 "How you have fallen from heaven, O morning star, son of the dawn! You have been cast down to the earth, you who once laid low the nations! You said in your heart, I will ascend to heaven; I will raise my throne above the stars of God; I will sit enthroned on the mount of assembly, on the utmost heights of the sacred mountain. I will ascend above the tops of the clouds; I will make myself like the Most High."

As you can see, the Bible shares how satan has a very serious "I" problem. He wanted to be God. He wanted to call the shots. He wanted to be first and top priority in life. So much so that he wanted people to worship him. This is the epitome of *self-love*. It declares like satan that *self comes first*. It takes priority over everything. It's all about what the individual wants, what they like, what they want to do, how they want life to be, and so on and so forth. The Bible says this is the *birthplace of sin* and it started with a self-love desire from satan. In fact, it makes total sense because if you think about it, every time we sin against God, what are we doing? We're doing the same thing! In essence we're saying *I love myself first* more than God to the point where I choose *my will* above His. So is it any wonder why things have gotten so *devilish* lately? We're following in the footsteps of satan! Lest you doubt, here's the top two laws of Satanism and you tell me if loving yourself first isn't a prerequisite for being a good Satanist:

- **First Law of Satanism:** *Do what thou wilt shall be the whole of the law.*

- **Second most important Law of Satanism** *is the law of self-awareness: Man is a divine being within. Life's purpose is to realize the divine within. When this is achieved, you now recognize you are God!* [19]

Self-love is simply the same old satanic lie mentioned in Genesis Chapter three that is being promoted today. This is why things have gotten so rotten and satanic. Yet, if that's still not enough proof for you that self-love and self-esteem teachings originated from satan, then maybe you should listen to actual Satanists themselves. Even they admit it:

"So many people reject the charge of 'satan worship' because they have a caricature of the devil and his religion in their minds.

He's the horn headed demon in red pajamas and serving him shouldn't even exist but involves sacrificing babies, drinking blood or something else equally horrible or bizarre. In reality though, following satan is far more mundane and universal than most people realize or would care to admit.

"Crowd at Woodstock 99 concert: 'Do what we want! We do what we want!'

Anton LaVey of the Church of satan: 'But I can do anything that I want to. I can pursue any kind of lustful desires that I might feel. I can engage in any activities that are so-called sinful activities and not really worry about any ecumenical councils making it right for me to do these things.'

Zeena LaVey (Daughter of Anton): 'Living for, as I said, all the earthly and carnal pleasures.'

Interviewer to Lilith Sinclair: 'If a Christian were to say you were just worshiping yourself what would you say.'

Priestess Lilith Sinclair of the Temple of Set: 'In a sense they would be right. It is a form of self-worship.'

Anton LaVey: 'We feel that there's no reason why these people shouldn't just flip the coin completely over and simply call themselves what religionists have been calling them for many many years. Call them devil worshippers or disciples of evil or satanists. Of course it's very hard for a person to hang a complimentary label on themselves, and for this reason for many years there will be people practicing satanism and as good Christians or other religions and they will instinctively pursue the very same things we are as they always have.'" [20]

INTERVIEW WITH A FORMER SATANIST

"Phil: 'You were a Satanist for how long?'

Mike Leehan: 'Twelve years.'

Phil: 'Twelves years? How on earth did you get involved with something like Satanism. First of all, what is Satanism? Let me get a definition-what does it mean to be a Satanist.'

Mike Leehan: 'To adore...to serve one god. You're serving satan. You're serving self, more than anything else; it's ego-centric, self-centered, serve me, all is me, immediate gratification. That's what it's all about.'

As the occult magazine Gnosis acknowledged: 'If there's anything horrifying in its (Satanism's) teachings, it's that these are the principles by which most people live most of the time usually without admitting it even to themselves.'"[20]

"Why God? Why? How did we fall? How did this happen? How did our once great and mighty Christian nation turn into a society of such satanic wickedness and rebellion?" I'll tell you why? Because we allowed the infiltration of a *wicked worship* into our schools, into our media, into our hearts, and even into our Churches, that promotes self-love and self-worship above God, just like satan! Therefore, if there's any hope for our nation then it's high time we the Church get back on track and start promoting Savior-Love, Savior-Esteem, and Savior-Respect *first*!

2. The Second Reason We Became Lovers of Selves Instead of Lovers of God – We Listened to the Teachings of Man Instead of the Word of God

To me, that's the question. "How did he do it? How in the world did satan get us, even born again Christians, to act just like him, being lovers of self rather than lovers of God, fulfilling this Last Days prophecy?" The answer is he did it by getting us to buy into a false teaching from man called **Secular Psychology**. Even though, as we just saw, this self-love self-esteem teaching was started by satan in Isaiah Chapter 14, it was slowly but surely introduced into our society by secular, God-hating, non-Christians and it's now being elevated above God. In fact, if you'll recall, not that long ago when a crisis hit our country, or when some horrible tragedy occurred, the standard procedure was to call in a Pastor to offer the victims godly counsel. But not anymore! Have you been paying attention? When a crisis hits, who do they call? Not a Pastor, but a secular psychologist who's been trained in the teachings of man. I'm not saying all teachings from man are bad. That's not my point. Yet what you need to realize is that no matter how good man's wisdom might seem to be at the time, to give so-called helpful counsel, in comparison to God's wisdom, its total nonsense.

1 Corinthians 1:19-20 "As the Scriptures say, 'I will destroy the wisdom of the wise and discard the intelligence of the intelligent.' So where does this leave the philosophers, the scholars, and the world's brilliant debaters? God has made the wisdom of this world look foolish."

Or as some translations say, *nonsense*! According to the Bible, no matter how good it might look, no matter how much society tries to tell us to the contrary, even the world's most brilliant minds are *nothing* compared to God's wisdom. Therefore, who in their right mind would seek counsel from the mind of man over the Word of God? This is what secular psychology is. It is a teaching based on the so-called wisdom of man. Yet, herein lies our problem. We're tempted, even in the Church, to no longer go to *Father God* for wisdom, but to seek out a *Freudian psychologist* for wisdom. Are we not told by our society to seek "professional help" instead of the power of God? But again, I don't care how professional something sounds, that still doesn't make it right nor does it make it wise. As long as we'd rather listen to a psychologist instead of our Savior, we're headed for trouble because everything they teach is opposite of what the Bible teaches:

- *The Bible says man is the creation of God. But psychology says that man is a creature of evolution.*

- *The Bible says man's purpose is to glorify God. But psychology says man's purpose is to fit in with their fellow man.*

- *The Bible says God is the Ultimate Supreme Authority. But psychology says man is the supreme authority.*

- *The Bible says the Word of God is the standard of our behavior. But psychology says the norm of society is the standard of our behavior.*

- *The Bible says the biggest obstacle in life is sin. But psychology says life's biggest obstacle is mental illness.*

- *The Bible says bad behavior comes from our internal sin nature. But psychology says it comes from sexual repression and our external environment.*

- *The Bible says repentance and faith in Christ can effectively change sinful behavior. But psychology says the way to change sinful behavior is to place the guilt on others, free your repressed desires, take drugs, or submit to psychoanalysis, sensitivity training, group therapy, etc.*

- *So the choice is yours. The Holy Bible inspired by Almighty God or modern psychology invented by wicked sinful man.[21]*

   Personally, I think I'll stick to the Word of God. But it gets even worse. As you just saw, not only do the teachings of secular psychology totally contradict Scripture, but the lives of these secular psychologists *are totally wacked out*! Yet, we're supposed to listen to them for advice? Here's a small life sampling of the founders of secular psychology and you tell me if they don't need some psychological help:

- *SIGMUND FREUD was an evolutionist who believed that man had evolved from lower animals and that the idea of an Almighty God was just a myth made up by our forefathers to cope with life. Freud was also a believer in the positive health benefits of cocaine and was a user himself for many years and had a severe addiction to nicotine to the tune of smoking an average twenty cigars a day, which eventually led to his death. Oh, by the way, Freud refused to be psychoanalyzed himself even by his own teachings.*

- *ABRAHAM MASLOW said that the motivation for his life's work was his absolute hatred of his mother.*

- *KAREN HORNEY decided she wasn't happy with her marriage after two years so she began a life of constant sexual affairs to which her husband did not object. She also was said to have a serious sexual addiction for young men, which included her students and fellow colleagues, and even had sexual relations with other women as well.*

- *CARL JUNG made a wooden man out of a ruler that he called Manikin and kept it in a wooden case and frequently talked to it in times of trouble and even had a mystical experience while sitting on a rock where he couldn't tell if he was the rock or the rock was him. Then he later had what he considered a major breakthrough in life when he had a vision of God supposedly going to the bathroom on a Church sanctuary from the sky.*

   However, what most people don't realize is that Carl Jung was also completely absorbed in the occult and studied their teachings, attending séances, listened to mediums, practiced necromancy, and had daily contact with disembodied spirits, which he called archetypes. In fact, much of what he wrote was inspired by such entities, one of which he called Philemon.

Listen to his own words, "Philemon and other figures of my fantasies brought home to me the crucial insight that there are things in the psyche which I do not produce, but which produce themselves and have their own life. Philemon represented a force, which was not myself. In my fantasies I held conversations with him, and he said things, which I had not consciously thought. For I observed clearly that it was he who spoke, not I. Philemon was a mysterious figure to me. I went walking up and down the garden with him, and to me he was what the Indians call a guru." [22]

I'd say those psychologists had a few *psychological problems*! These are the "founding fathers" of modern secular psychology where this self-love self-esteem teaching came from? I'm supposed to listen to them for godly counsel above God? These people were totally unbiblical, God-haters, drug-addicts, sexually immoral, people involved in the occult, *yet* we still listen to them over the Word of God. Can you believe that? In fact, they have so convinced us and repeatedly brainwashed us to be lovers of self rather that lovers of God, that we are now being told that we must do so *at all costs*, even if it means ignoring sinful behavior, refraining from discipline, blaming others and avoiding personal responsibility. They say if we force people to deal with their own wicked behavior then that will damage their self-esteem which will then supposedly ruin all hope of having a fulfilling life.

Now, lest you think no one in their right mind would ever fall for this nonsense, let me give you some proof. It's precisely because of this self-worship that parents in Connecticut have taken their son's school to court. Why? Because he was caught destroying school property and was expelled by the school. But the parents say their son now has "feelings of unworthiness" and his "self-worth" has been damaged, so they're suing. In Maine, signs saying "Happy Holidays" and the singing of Christmas carols are now being banned for fear of making somebody feel excluded. In fact, in Manhattan, Mother's Day is now being eliminated because some kids may not have a mother and this could damage their self-esteem. But apparently so do kickball and dodgeball and similar games. Why? Because they promote competitiveness and make some kids feel excluded and that's no longer tolerated.[23] This is not only ludicrous, it's absolutely ridiculous, especially when you look at the track record of this false teaching. Self-love self-esteem teachings are being sold as the panacea for the ills of society, but does it even work? No! Researchers decided to test the effectiveness of self-esteem teaching in schools by measuring how high the students thought of themselves academically. As it turned out, the more highly they thought of themselves and their supposed abilities, the less ability they had. A case in point was how kids in Washington D.C. ranked number one in the country for self-esteem. Yet they came in second to last in academic performance. One researcher simply stated, "Years of self-love propaganda succeeded only in producing self-deluded kids."[24] In other words, it's doesn't work, like this man shares:

"Society is at an all-time moral low. But statistics show Americans are feeling better about themselves than ever. In a survey conducted in 1940, 11 percent of women and 20 percent of men agreed with the statement. 'I am an important person.'

In the 1990s, those figures jumped to 66 percent of women and 62 percent of men. Ninety percent of people surveyed in a recent Gallup Poll say their own sense of self-esteem is robust and healthy.

Incredibly, while the moral fabric of society continues to unravel, self-esteem is thriving. All the positive thinking about ourselves seems not to be doing anything to elevate the culture or motivate people to live better lives.

Can it really be that low self-esteem is what is wrong with people today? Does anyone seriously believe that making people feel better about themselves has helped the problems of crime, moral decay, divorce, child abuse, juvenile delinquency, drug addiction, and all other evils that have dragged society down?

Could so much still be wrong in our culture if the assumptions of self-esteem will finally solve society's problems? Is there any shred of evidence that would support such a belief? Absolutely none. The notion that self-esteem makes people better is simply a matter of blind religious faith.

Not only that, it is a religion that is antithetical to Christianity, because it is predicated on the unbiblical presupposition that people are basically good and need to recognize their own goodness."[25]

You know, just like satan. Yet we still have the audacity to ask, "Why God? Why? How did we fall? How did this happen? How did this once great and mighty Christian nation turn into this society of such wickedness and rebellion?" I'll tell you why? Because we allowed the infiltration of a *wicked worship* in our schools, in our media, and in our Churches that promotes self-love self-esteem and self-worship above God! The Bible says once you become a society of people who are *lovers of themselves* instead of lovers of God you better watch out! It's not only a sign you're living in the Last Days, but it's going to open the floodgates to all kinds of wicked behavior and everything will start falling apart! Therefore, if there's any hope for our nation, then it's high time we the Church get back on track and lead the way back with what needs to come *first*, that of Savior-Love, Savior-Esteem, and Savior-Respect.

3. The Third Reason We Became Lovers of Selves Instead of Lovers of God– We Listened to the Twistings of Scripture Instead of the Word of God

Now, as if what we've already seen wasn't bad enough, what's even crazier is that some people *in the Church* have actually twisted the Scripture to try to make the Bible say that we *should* love ourselves. Even self-love and self-esteem teachings are clearly satanic in origin and being promoted by secular men who were atheists involved in the occult, not to mention the fact that they don't even produce the benefits they promise. The following is one of the favorite passages these deluded people try to twist:

Matthew 22:37-39 "Jesus replied: Love the Lord your God with all your heart and with all your soul and with all your mind. This is the first and greatest commandment. And the second is like it: Love your neighbor as yourself."

Well, there you have it. We need to love ourselves more than God, and certainly much more than other people. It said so right there; we need to love our neighbor as we love ourselves. Wrong! That's what deluded people twist it to mean, but that's not at all what the context means. First of all, if you read the context, you'll see it's the by-product of loving God first that gives us the ability to love our neighbors. Two, if we're honest, it's not that we have a difficulty in loving ourselves. Ask anybody who's married. What causes half of all marital problems? It's because somebody's being *self-centered*! In fact, for those of you who might say, "Well, I know somebody who doesn't love themselves. They actually hate themselves," if you think about it, this is still a preoccupation with self as this man points out:

"In Dr. Martin Bobgan's book Prophets of PsychoHeresy II regarding self-hatred he states: 'Now we are not saying that there are no individuals who genuinely think that they hate themselves.

However, what they generally hate is something about themselves or their circumstances. They exhibit actual love for themselves in that they continue to spend most of their time concerned about themselves, even if it is with unhappy thoughts.

They generally get to the point where they are unhappy about themselves because a discrepancy exists between their aspirations or desires and their performance or condition. This intensive hate is evidence of high self-interest.'"[26]

Therefore, the challenge as the Bible states, is to take this natural ongoing inclination to love ourselves first, no matter how you want to mask it, and now extend it to others. That's the pathway to happiness. It's *outside* of you. Furthermore, notice there are only *two* commandments in the above passage, not three. One: Love God. Two: Love your neighbor. That's it! Jesus *did not* say there were three and He certainly did not say that third one was to love yourself first. Yet, the self-love self-esteem proponents not only create this third supposed commandment out of the two, they even go so far as to say unless you do this third commandment, i.e. love yourself first, then you won't have the ability to do the other two, i.e. love God and your neighbor. Wow! Talk about twisting the Scripture! No wonder there's so much rebellion and unhappiness in people's lives today.

The second verse these deluded people twist is in Matthew 10. Let's take a look at that one:

Matthew 10:29-31 "Are not two sparrows sold for a penny? Yet not one of them will fall to the ground apart from the will of your Father. And even the very hairs of your head are all numbered. So don't be afraid; you are worth more than many sparrows."

Well, there you have it. We need to acknowledge our self-worth. It says we are worth more than many sparrows, therefore we need to acknowledge how incredibly worthy we really are. Wrong! That's what they try to twist it to mean, but that's not at all what the context means. First of all, if you read the context, you'll see clearly that Jesus is saying two sparrows are sold for a penny. Now anybody with an accounting degree can tell you that this is not going to add up to a great worth. If your "many sparrows" meant let's say 500 sparrows, how much are you worth? At one penny per two sparrows you'd be worth about $2.50! Or maybe you've been really good lately so your "many sparrows" adds up to be 1,000 sparrows. That's still only $5 bucks! Read the context. This passage is not dealing with the so-called great worth of us, but rather the greatness of God's great providential care for us! To make matters worse, they even turn a blind eye to obvious passages in the Bible that teach us just the exact opposite of self-love self-esteem teachings. The Bible commands us to *not* love ourselves and instead deal honestly with our sin.

Ezekiel 20:43 "There you will remember your conduct and all the actions by which you have defiled yourselves, and you will *loathe yourselves* for all the evil you have done."

Romans 7:18, 24 "I know that *nothing good lives in me*, that is, in my sinful nature. *What a wretched man I am*! Who will rescue me from this body of death?"

Ezekiel 36:31-32 "Then you will remember your evil ways and wicked deeds, and you will *loathe yourselves* for your sins and detestable practices. Be ashamed and disgraced for your conduct, O House of Israel!"

Job 42:6 "Therefore I *despise myself* and repent in dust and ashes."

2 Corinthians 5:15 "And he died for all, that those who live should *no longer live for themselves* but for Him Who died for them and was raised again."

1 Corinthians 13:4 "Love is neither anxious to impress *nor does it cherish inflated ideas of its own importance*."

Philippians 2:3 "Let nothing be done through strife or vainglory; but in lowliness of mind let each *esteem others better than themselves*."

Matthew 16:24 "Then Jesus said to His disciples, If anyone would come after Me, he must *deny himself* and take up his cross and follow Me."

As you can see, the Bible plainly tells us to be honest with and deal appropriately with our sinful behavior. We are not to excuse it away or blame others for it and we are certainly not supposed to sue others who rightfully discipline us for it. In fact, this false teaching of self-love self-esteem is actually ripping us off of the greater news of where our real identity lies. It's not in our own self-inflated self-important statements of self-love. Rather, it's in being forgiven, accepted and loved by God through Jesus Christ; and that's what gives us eternal value! Because of that, as a Christian, I am now the following:

"I am His beloved, I am His child, I'm an ambassador for the King of Kings and the Lord of Lord, I am blameless, spotless, without blemish and considered a beautiful Bride.

I am blessed in the heavenly realms, I am born again and I belong to God. I cannot be separated. He calls me a saint and I'm now a citizen of heaven. I cannot lose my salvation. I'm complete in Christ and I cannot be condemned.

I am dearly loved, I'm delivered and I have direct access to the throne of grace. I am dead to sin. I am healed from sin and I can do all things through Him Who strengthens me.

I'm a friend of Jesus. I've been forgiven by Jesus. I am established, anointed and sealed by God.

I'm free from the past. I'm kept by God's power. I'm prayed for by Christ and I'm not going to hell! Why? Because God had mercy upon me and made me a new creation in Christ! That's where our value lies!" [27]

It's in *Jesus* and what He has done for me and made me into, not in my own self-inflated self-important statements of self-love that makes this life valuable. The first one gives glory to God, the other one gives glory to self, just like satan. Yet, even as a born again Christian, if you want to listen to this false teaching from satan called self-love self-esteem and still be a lover of self rather than a lover of God, then be prepared to reap what you sow:

"D. Martin Lloyd-Jones says, 'The real cause of failure, ultimately, in marriage is always self, and the various manifestations of self. Of course that is the cause of trouble everywhere and in every realm.

Self and selfishness are the greatest disrupting forces in the world. All the major problems confronting the world, whether you look at the matter from the standpoint of nations and statesmen, or from the standpoint of industry and social conditions, or from any other standpoint - all these troubles ultimately come back to self, to 'my rights,' to 'what I want,' and to 'who is he?' or 'who is she?'

Self, with its horrid manifestations, always leads to trouble, because if two 'selfs' come into opposition there is bound to be a clash. Self always wants everything for it-self. That is true of my self, but it is equally true of your self. You at once have two autonomous powers, each deriving from self, and a clash is inevitable.

Such clashes occur at every level, from two people right up to great communities, empires and nations."

Self-esteem teachings distort the Bible, reflect the world, and appeal to the natural man. The Bible teaches believers to esteem others better than self, to love one another as we already love ourselves, and to deny our self daily."[28]

This is why great nations, great countries, great families, great marriages, great businesses, and even great Churches fall apart, fail, crumble and go out of existence. It's the fruit of this satanic lie called self-love self-esteem. Where did all this wickedness come from? Why is it getting so bad! Why are people being so evil! I'll tell you why! Because we allowed the infiltration of a *satanic self-worship* into every aspect of our society, even in the Church, and the Bible says once you become a society of *lovers of self* instead of lovers of God you are doomed to destruction! Therefore, if there's any hope for our nation, then we the Church need to get back on track and show our country the way back out of this mess we're in. We need to start promoting Savior Love *first*, Savior Esteem *first*, Savior Respect *first*, and putting Jesus Christ *first*, not ourselves! We need to lead the way back by example. Even satan admits that a life of total self-centeredness leads to a life of total slavery and depravity. But don't take my word for it. Let's listen to his:

AND NOW A WORD FROM THE FATHER OF LIES...

I've been here since the beginning
Know exactly how you work
I know all of your cravings
Know what makes you go berserk
Been lying from the start just to make you play a part in my infinite rebellion
against the Father God

Hate
Everything He is

And I make you hate Him too
Make you hate Him with your actions it's so easy for me to do
'Cause you like it...
Sin feels good for the ego...
You love it...
Oh, come on baby let your hair go

And all the time, I'm winding you up
Like my perfect little puppet, you're my favorite robot, welcome to the show but
I'm watching you and all of hell is with me too, helping me make my lies look
true

Oh and there is a lie that works for everyone, everyone
A lie that opens your hearts so I can get me some more of your free will
I'm winding you
Winding you
Give me the control that's why I'm telling you
Selling you
Anything
Everything
Appealing to your human way of being and I use it all against you to just keep
your eyes from seeing past the life you're living
Past the moment you're in
Past the pleasure of your sin

Or the cigarette you're smoking
Choking on your lust
I'll make you drunk with pride
So deeply spun into my system that you won't see the light
Never mind that I'm drowning you
I keep deceiving you...

But I'll say that millions of years ago an accident exploded
And you're the result of this cosmic unknown with no real purpose
Created for no real intent
The reason for your living is just coincidence
So all the remains is what you can gain
Whatever meaning you attach to your days you decide
Mmm, but I help you recognize the important things in life

Introducing money, it's the root of all, evil they say so
I attach your self-worth to the salary you're paid, be a slave to your property
Your jewelry
Your cars and things
Advertise that lie up on the TV so you want that bling
Selling bit by bit the little pieces of your soul
Climbing up the ladder of economic control
Oh, the greed of man makes it so easy to pervert the Father's plan

Or I'll tell you...
There is a heaven but there's many ways to get in
Keep you so confused that you stay bound to your sin
Tell you there are many ways to the same God
Keep you distracted with your methods so your heart stays hard,
I'll make you think you've got spirituality, but it's really just emotional alchemy
Oh, the vanity of self-idolatry I never let you see that it breeds
Hedonism! Whoo!
And it's the anthem of this generation
Come on, drink it, snort it, smoke it, swallow it
Chew on my illusion of freedom 'til you vomit it

And still I don't tell you
Bout the God in heaven
Who loves you
Who yearns for you
No I don't tell you
Bout the freedom of forgiveness and truth
Why would I tell you?
Why would I tell you the truth? [29]

It's high time we stop listening to the father of lies and get back to listening to the Father of Truth, God. We need to deny ourselves, not love ourselves. His way is the only way that leads to an abundant life and puts a stop to all this wicked behavior we have to deal with today.

V. Wicked Lifestyle - Hedonism

The fifth reason we've turned from a nation that once loved God to this Rise of Wickedness we see today is by the promotion of a Wicked Lifestyle. Of course, I'm talking about hedonism. Little do people know that all these teachings we've seen so far, humanism, atheism, and selfism have not only created this massive rise of wicked behavior that we see today, but they've also led to a whole new wicked *lifestyle* called hedonism. Or in other words, *the pleasure principle*. God warned that this too would occur in the Last Days.

2 Timothy 3:1-5 "But mark this: There will be terrible times in the Last Days. People will be lovers of themselves, lovers of money, boastful, proud, abusive, disobedient to their parents, ungrateful, unholy, without love, unforgiving, slanderous, without self-control, brutal, not lovers of the good, treacherous, rash, conceited, lovers of pleasure rather than lovers of God – having a form of godliness but denying its power. Have nothing to do with them."

Again, this passage tells us how one of the major characteristics in the Last Days society is that it's going to be one filled with absolute unadulterated wickedness. Then we just saw how the apparent *root* of this wicked behavior stemmed from a love of self rather than a love of God. Now, here's the point of bringing up this passage again. Notice the *last behavior* mentioned there. It states that people would be *lovers of pleasure rather than lovers of God*! If you think about it, this is the perfect capstone of the wicked behavior mentioned in this list. You start off loving yourself first, then you end up pleasing yourself first. It makes total sense if you put it all together. Hedonism, or "seeking to please yourself more than God" is simply the party attitude we see today of, "Hey, if it feels right or if it feels good do it." It's the logical outcome to this promotion of humanism, atheism, and selfism. If man is the center of all things, *humanism*, and there is no God, *atheism*, and you're supposed to love yourself first, *selfism*, then what's left to do? Hey, it's *party time*! You have to live it up! You have to do whatever you want and please yourself as many ways as you possibly can because tomorrow you could die and go back to the ground to become worm bait. Or to put it another way, "Eat, drink, and be merry for tomorrow we die!" You've heard that saying because it's the average person's attitude *today*! This is their marching orders when they get out of bed. Party it up, please yourself as many ways as you can before you die. *This is hedonism* and it is simply *wickedness unrestrained* and the Bible says once it hits your society *as a way of life*, judgment is coming! In fact, the Bible mentions two other societies that God wiped out for their hedonistic wicked ways.

Genesis 19:4-7,24-25 "Before they had gone to bed, all the men from every part of the city of Sodom – both young and old – surrounded the house. They called to

Lot, 'Where are the men who came to you tonight? Bring them out to us so that we can have sex with them.' Lot went outside to meet them and shut the door behind him and said, 'No, my friends. Don't do this wicked thing.' Then the LORD rained down burning sulfur on Sodom and Gomorrah – from the LORD out of the heavens. Thus He overthrew those cities and the entire plain, including all those living in the cities – and also the vegetation in the land.'"

Genesis 6:5-7 "The LORD saw how great man's wickedness on the earth had become, and that every inclination of the thoughts of his heart was only evil all the time. The LORD was grieved that He had made man on the earth, and His heart was filled with pain. So the LORD said, 'I will wipe mankind, whom I have created, from the face of the earth – men and animals, and creatures that move along the ground, and birds of the air – for I am grieved that I have made them.'"

The Bible not only declares that God is *grieved* by our wicked behavior, but unless we turn around, He is also going to *judge* our wicked behavior. So that's the question, "Do we see any signs of our society today engaging in that level of wicked behavior like Sodom and Gomorrah and even being continually wicked all the time like in Noah's day?" Yes! We're already there, which means whether or not we want to admit it, we too are headed for judgment, folks. Here's just a small sampling of the proof:

- Schools are also teaching kids that religion is a "disease" and entertainers are saying that, "the Bible is a work of fiction."

- New York City principal nixes the song "God Bless the USA" at kindergarten graduation, but when the kids went ahead and tried to sing it anyway, adults chanted back "Burn in hell."

- Divorce cakes have now become a new trend.

- Epidemic growth of Internet porn cited.

- Sexually transmitted disease rates have hit record highs in U.S.

- Girl scouts are now supporting abortion and sexual promiscuity.

- MTV wants you to lose your virginity in a new reality show.

- The U.N. is calling for the legalization of prostitution worldwide.

- A PC game has been released called Rapelay that allows players to gang rape virtual women and then force them to have an abortion.

- A chastity ring has become the source of a new problem in school. A Christian teenager will go to the high court this summer to challenge the decision of her school to ban her from wearing a celibacy ring on school grounds.

- Live baby treated as "medical waste." Crematorium workers found an infant crying in a "medical waste" receptacle on its way to being cremated.

- Planned Parenthood kills 329,445 babies in one year using $487.4 million in taxpayer funds. In fact, since 1973, we have now murdered 54,559,615 babies in America alone. This is almost 10 times the amount of people killed in Hitler's Holocaust of the Jews. We've also murdered just under 1.3 billion babies worldwide just since 1980.

- According to the new healthcare law, even pro-life Americans will be forced to pay for other people's abortions, and British teens are having as many as seven abortions.

- A senior girl believes that abortion is a medium for art. A female senior student will be displaying her senior art project, a documentation of a nine-month process during which she artificially inseminated herself "as often as possible" while periodically taking abortion drugs to induce miscarriages. Her exhibition will feature video recordings of these forced miscarriages as well as preserved collections of the blood from the process.

- Undertakers are now washing the dead down the drain by dissolving them in a caustic solution and flushing them into the sewer.

- A publicly funded exhibition encouraged people to deface the Bible in the name of art. Visitors have responded using abuse and obscenity with comments such as "This is all sexist "blank" so disregard it all," and another wrote on the first page of Genesis, "I am Bi, Female & Proud. I want no god who is disappointed in this."

- The U.S. is using foreign aid to promote gay rights.

- Pentagon to hold its first gay pride event.

- Politicians say they're okay with a second grade teacher reading gay prince fairy tale called, "King and King."

- Schools are now observing a homosexual sponsored "Day of Silence." Several thousand schools across the nation will be observing "Day of Silence" in a nationwide push to promote the homosexual lifestyle in public schools. Students are taught that homosexuality is a worthy lifestyle, homosexuality has few or no risks, and individuals are born homosexual and cannot change. Those who oppose such teaching are characterized as ignorant hateful bigots.

- Recent California laws will eventually require all public school instruction and activities to positively portray transsexuals, bisexuals, and homosexuals to children as young as kindergarten. And another California law barring people from "curing" gay children was recently signed into law.

- Proposed law would force Churches to host gay weddings.

- Play depicting Jesus as gay packs Church.

- A lesbian nativity is being promoted by another Church. "And when the Holy Family arrived, it was two women with their baby."

- A new version of "The Last Supper" has come out in San Francisco. Amidst black leather, tattoos, and feather boas, homosexuals pose as the apostles who in the original painting are depicted gathered at a table with Jesus to partake of the last meal together. In the "new version" the table no longer has the traditional bread and wine symbolizing Christ's body and blood being given for us, but rather sex toys symbolizing the god of sex and unlicensed physical pleasure. And Nancy Pelosi stated, "Christianity has not been harmed by this!"

- A publication is now promoting incestuous pedophilia as healthy sex ed. Booklets for Family Affairs encourage parents to sexually massage their children as young as one to three years of age and psychologists are pushing to decriminalize pedophilia.

As one man stated, "It seems that America has become the land of the special interest and the home of the double standard. If we lie to Congress it's a felony, but if Congress lies to us it's just politics. The government spends millions to rehabilitate criminals, but they do almost nothing for the victims. In public schools you can teach that homosexuality is okay, but you better not use the word God in the process.

You can kill an unborn child, but it's wrong to execute a mass murderer. We don't burn books in America, we simply rewrite them. We got rid of the communist and socialist threat by renaming them progressives. If you protest the President you're a terrorist, but if you burned an American flag it's your 1st Amendment right. You can have pornography on TV or the internet, but you better not put a nativity scene in a public park during Christmas. We can use an aborted murdered baby for medical research, but it's wrong to use an animal.

We take money from those who work hard for it and give it to those who don't want to work. We still have freedom of speech, but only if we are being politically correct. Parenting has been replaced with Ritalin and video games and the land of opportunity is now the land of handouts. What has happened to the land of the free and the home of the brave?"[30]

I'll tell you. We've turned into Sodom and Gomorrah! You still don't think judgment is coming? I like what one guy said, "If God doesn't judge us, He needs to apologize to Sodom & Gomorrah." But God is not in the apology making business so therefore, unless we turn around *now* and *repent* as a nation, including the Church, He is going to judge us too! Why? Because we've become just as wicked as Sodom and Gomorrah and our hearts are just as evil *all the time* just like in Noah's Day. Now, if that doesn't wake you up, you need to listen to what Jesus said concerning this wicked behavior. He stated that once this happens to the planet again, once we become a wicked hedonistic society like in Noah's day, He's getting ready to come back!

Matthew 24:37-39 "As it was in the days of Noah, so it will be at the coming of the Son of Man. For in the days before the flood, people were eating and drinking, marrying and giving in marriage, up to the day Noah entered the ark; and they knew nothing about what would happen until the flood came and took them all away. That is how it will be at the coming of the Son of Man."

We are not only seeing a repeat of the same wicked behavior in Noah's day, but we are also seeing a repeat of the same lackadaisical nonchalant "whoop-de-do-dah" attitude concerning the Second Coming of Jesus Christ today. Correct me if I'm wrong, but what do most people say today when we tell them about Christ's return and God's impending judgment? "Yeah, right! So what! Who cares! You guys are wackos anyway...Noah." They go right on eating and drinking, marrying and giving in marriage, partying, acting like it's no big deal. Just like Jesus said was going to happen, in the Last Days, right before He came back. It looks to me like we're on a spiritual precipice and we better wake up before it's too late, like this man shares:

" 'But as the days of Noah were, so shall also the coming of the Son of man be...'

When God said "come into the Ark, you and all your household". Noah saw God closed the Ark. And the people on the outside did not wonder if he slept those seven days before the rains came.

'...For as in the days that were before the flood they were eating and drinking, marrying and given in marriage, until the day that Noah entered into the Ark...'

I know if it was me, I couldn't have slept. I know there are sleepless nights that I have. And I'm pondering the faith of God that He has showed me what is coming to this country.

'...And knew not until the flood came, and took them all away; so shall also the coming of the Son of man be.' Matthew 24:37-39

Can you sleep? I don't see how you can sleep at night. The bingo halls are full but the Churches are empty. And you may be saying – 'stay up the night the Church is full'. Full of what? Dead men's bones? The casinos are full but no one will give to God? Concerts are packed, but no one will praise the Almighty. We will scream and shout for a rock star but sit quietly bored when hearing about God Almighty. We will sit through a movie for two hours but we can't even pray for two hours. We will drive out of state for a game or a race and we can't even get up on Sunday mornings or Sunday nights or Wednesdays to hear the Word of God and these are so-called Christians that do this.

Not only is the world asleep and the fire getting ready to come upon this earth, but the Christians are asleep. This is Christians that do this. They give God crumbs while they dine on the fruits of the world. They demand unconditional love and they give God lip service. They demand blessings though they curse His name. They demand the flesh but they crucify the Spirit.

They say they can't go to Church services every time the doors are opened but they can take their kids to football, baseball, basketball, wrestling, dance, circus, the fair or just sit in front of a TV all night long. But to go and be in the presence of the Heavenly Father is just too much to ask from them. We will work eight, ten, twelve hours a day to pay the bills and buy the bass boat but we will tell the one who breathed life into us, 'One hour should do God.'

We sit in Church services but we are godless. We have a form of godliness but we deny the power thereof. I don't see how the lukewarm Christians can sleep at night. Before the rains came, I believe Noah couldn't sleep. But the world outside was sleeping just fine. They fell asleep. If it were today, they would have fallen asleep watching TV. They would have just gotten home from their favorite game or their movies. They would have been doing everything under the sun. Eating and drinking and being merry not knowing that tomorrow they shall die. You cannot say you were not warned.

In Luke 21:11 it says that 'great earthquakes shall be in diverse places and famines and pestilences and fearful sights and great signs shall there be from heaven'. In verse 25 it says 'in perplexity the sea and the waves roaring'. You cannot say you were not warned. You cannot say that you had not a Noah that did not preach to you for a hundred and twenty years because you ignored him and said, 'Who is that man? Oh just Noah. He's going to the Church house. That's just Noah. He's always talking negative. That's just Noah, let's go back to sleep.'

At least when Jesus was praying in the garden, while the disciples slept, at least they woke up. When the servant slept and the enemy came and sowed the tares, at least the servants woke up. But when Jesus Christ comes back, His kingdom will be likened to the ten virgins – the five wise and the five foolish – and they will be sleeping. All of them. Oh that we may open our eyes and see. And see what is coming and yet, we sleep on. God have mercy."[31]

Yes, may God have mercy on us. "Why God? Why? How did we fall? How did this happen? How did our great and mighty Christian nation turn into a society of such wickedness and rebellion just like Sodom and Gomorrah and as in the Days of Noah?" Because we allowed the infiltration of a *wicked lifestyle,* called *hedonism* into our schools, our hearts, our media, and even into our Churches! It's the logical response of an unrestrained diet of humanism, atheism, and selfism. Therefore, if there's any hope for our nation then it's high time we the Church *wake up* and *repent ourselves* if there's any hope to turn things around. We simply need to get back to that Biblical attitude of *seeking to please God* not ourselves.

VI. Wicked Belief - Relativism

The sixth reason we've turned from a nation that once loved God to this Rise of Wickedness we see today is by the promotion of a Wicked Belief. This is the question, "How did he do it? How in the world did satan get us, even here in America with our godly heritage, to justify this hedonism even to the point where we act like it's no big deal. Pass the chips! What else is on?" Simple. Our archenemy did it by getting us to buy into a wicked belief system called Relativism. For those of you who don't know, relativism is the belief that says there is no right or wrong. In other words, you make up the rules as you go. You do whatever feels right. It's encapsulated in the popular saying, "Whatever you believe is true for you, is true for you, and whatever I believe is true for me, is true for me." If you've been paying attention, this *relativistic mantra* is commonplace. It states that *truth is not absolute* and that *it is relegated to the person*. It might sound good and pleasing to the flesh, yet the Bible warns us to never go down this relativistic route.

Judges 17:6 "In those days there was no king in Israel; *everyone did what was right in his own eyes.*"

Deuteronomy 12:8 "You shall not at all do as we are doing here today – *every man doing whatever is right in his own eyes.*"

This is *relativism*, everyone doing what is right in their own eyes, and as you can see, God warns against it. Why? Because if you read the context of those passages, this popular mindset *always leads to trouble*! God is the One Who makes the rules and all His rules are good for us. That's why when we stray from His commands, we end up in trouble. Therefore, if we want to prosper personally, let alone as a society, we need to follow God's *absolute standard of right and wrong*. We *do not* do whatever is right in our own eyes. That always leads to trouble! This is precisely why our Founding Fathers built this great nation on the *absolute principles of God's Word*. This is why Andrew Jackson stated, "That book, sir, is the rock on which our republic rests." Why? Because he and the Founding Fathers knew that the last thing you would ever want to do as a nation is to repeat the same mistake that Israel made. Getting to the point where, "We do as we're doing here today, every man doing whatever is right in his own eyes." It will destroy us as a people and a nation and lead to serious trouble every single time. This is because once there is no longer any standard or "rock" for your society to stand firmly upon, your society will start falling apart. It leads to *chaos* and this is exactly what's happening *today*!

In fact, relativism is not only dangerous, it's also *ludicrous*. Truth by its very nature is absolute. Otherwise it wouldn't be truth! Think about it. 2+2 will *always* be 4 whether you like it, lump it, leave it or not. Try saying 2+2=5 on your math test and you'll get an "F" every single time. But you can hear them say, "Well, in my world I thought it was 5?" So what. Math principles don't care how you *feel*. Neither does science or history. You can think all you want that you can jump out of an airplane without a parachute on and think you'll fly upwards but the absolute truth of gravity will turn you into road pizza. You can feel in your heart, very sincerely by the way, that Abraham Lincoln was not a President of the United States, but he was a Wild West Cowboy and you'll still flunk your history exam every single time. Why? Because truth by its very nature is absolute! That's what makes something true!

Furthermore, when a person states, "There are no absolutes," *they just made an absolute statement*! You can't escape it. So the next time they make that statement, "There are no absolutes," just ask them, "Are you absolutely sure about that?" The fact is, sincerity of opinion is no measuring rod for something to be "true" or "right." All it means is that you can be "sincerely wrong." Even the real Abraham Lincoln knew about the absurdity of this relativistic mindset:

"Abraham Lincoln was trying to make a point in a debate but his opponent was unconvinced and stubborn. So Lincoln tried another tactic. He said to the man, 'Well, let's see now. How many legs does a cow have?'

The disgusted reply came back, 'Well, four, of course.'
And Lincoln agreed and said, 'That's right. Now, suppose you call the cow's tail a leg; how many legs would the cow have?'

And the opponent replied confidently, 'Why, five, of course.'

And Lincoln came back, 'Now that's where you're wrong. Calling a cow's tail a leg doesn't make it a leg!'"[32]

Now, me personally, if calling a cow's tail a leg could *make it* a leg, I would be seriously excited. That's just that much more meat to eat off that baby. But seriously, the point is this. Even if I did make that statement, as Lincoln pointed out, it wouldn't change a thing. Yet, it still doesn't keep people today from trying. One researcher shares how people today are actually trying to call a cow's tail a leg, in essence, by *redefining* our morality based on relativism. Here's why we have gone full-blown hedonistic and our society is falling apart:

"What our Founding Fathers referred to as drunkenness because of their Christian heritage, we now call it alcoholism and deem it a social disease, rather than a sin.

What the Law-Word called sodomy, we now call an alternative life style. Pornography is a perversion that brings death to a nation, and yet we call it adult entertainment.

What our Founding Fathers called immorality, we now call the new morality; what the law called adultery or fornication, we now call stepping out or fooling around; and what the Law called abhorrent social behavior (like stealing or filthy language), we now call abnormal social development or anti-social behavior."[33]

Here's a news flash that people desperately need to hear today. *God is not going to change His mind on sin just because we've changed the name of sin!* Unfortunately, it gets even worse. This relativistic mindset has gotten so deep and so popular today that people are not only redefining sin, but they are now *demanding* our praise and acceptance of sin. Another researcher unveils our society's *new definition of tolerance* and how they are using it to brainwash our kids into a sinful relativistic mindset:

"Some of you are saying, 'Wait a minute, I thought tolerance was good?' That's the problem. That's the problem! Little Johnny comes home from school and that very sincere Christian mother from the most fundamental evangelical church meets little Johnny and says, 'How was school today?'

'Oh Mommy.'

'What you talk about?'

'We talked about tolerance'

And that Christian mother goes, 'Oh that's wonderful. You know Jesus told us to be tolerant.'

ABSOLUTELY NOT!! That mother is undermining everything she believes and it won't take years. It will only take months to come back and haunt her.

You're saying hold on a minute, I don't get this. The reason is this. Right now there are two distinct definitions of tolerance. One, I call a historical traditional tolerance. It's the one almost everyone who is here has been conditioned to think by and how you're listening to me through traditional tolerance. I am speaking from a whole new definition of tolerance.

Traditional tolerance would be defined by Webster: To bear or put up with someone or something that is not especially liked. Or you know in our circles we say, 'God has called me as a Christian to love the sinner but to hate the sin.' That's one of the most bigoted statements you could make today. You make that statement in the average classroom today and that entire class would turn on you. The bigotry and the intolerance to say, 'Love the sinner hate the sin.'

The reason is, there is a second definition of tolerance and I would say that 80% of the time, outside the walls of the church, when you hear the word tolerance whether the media, the magazines, the school or what - it's not the tolerance you were conditioned to think by. It's a whole new definition of tolerance, 80% of the time-it's a new definition.

The tolerance you were brought up with is now referred to as negative tolerance. The new tolerance is called positive tolerance. It's defined this way. Every single individual's values, beliefs, lifestyles and claims to truth are equal. Let me repeat that - ALL values, ALL beliefs, ALL truth, ALL lifestyles are equal and if you dare to say there is a value, belief, a lifestyle or claim to truth greater than another that is called hierarchy and that's the new definition of bigotry. A bigot today has nothing to do with racism or anything. A bigot today is someone who's committed to moral hierarchy that there are differences in values and beliefs, lifestyles or claims to truth.

Positive tolerance adds the word 'praise'. What it means is this; 'we not only want your permission, we demand your praise and if you do not praise my value, my lifestyle, my claim to truth as equal to your own'--now listen to this--'as equal to yours, from the heart, you are a bigot and you are intolerant.' From the heart. It's called positive tolerance.

Let me show you just how it's hit the Church. Just in a little brief one. Can you tell me historically what has been the number one verse quoted from the scriptures by Christians and non-Christians, Christian young people, non-Christian young people, the media, everyone? What's the number one verse quoted historically by the Scriptures? John 3:16. Do you know what it is now? Have you all been listening? Have you even been listening to your own young people? Can anyone tell me now, by far, way out far from everything what's the number one verse quoted even from Christian young people from the Bible? Number one now, what is it? 'Judge not, that you not be judged'. Listen! Why? The moment you make a judgment you're saying there's a hierarchy and that makes you a bigot and intolerant and it makes you stand against the number one virtue in culture. Tolerance. All is equal.

Christian love and the number one virtue of culture today cannot coexist. In fact, I'll go as far as to say that Christian love is the number one enemy of the number one virtue in the culture: Tolerance. In fact, men and women, I'll say this. I believe now, it's a point as a Pastor, as an evangelist, someone like that. It is very difficult to be popular and faithful.

Jesus loved that woman at the well. In love and compassion, He said to her, 'Go call your husband.' she said, 'sir, I don't have a husband.' And in loving compassion Jesus said, 'That's right. You've had five husbands and the one you're living with right now is not your husband.' Jesus exposed her lifestyle. He was witnessing to her. He exposed her lifestyle. Now speak to me. Did Jesus expose her lifestyle as an alternate lifestyle or a sinful lifestyle?

Audience: 'Sinful lifestyle.'

'You're a BIGOT! What right do you have to say that?! You're INTOLERANT! Who do you think you are to think you have the corner on truth? What right do you have to make any moral judgment on someone?'

He did it in love. If you don't believe me that that's not true - you try it anywhere in culture right today. You just travel with me into the high schools and universities. And Jesus did it in love. Christian love and tolerance cannot coexist. We had better wake up. "[34]

Yes, we better wake up as Christians and we better wake up soon! Everything we believe in is at risk! If this relativistic mindset and this new definition of tolerance isn't put into check, *we Christians* will become the new enemies of the state! This is because all that we believe in, all of Christianity, and all of Scripture is based on God's absolute standard of right and wrong which does not, cannot, and never will tolerate sin! Jesus said He is the *only* way to heaven, not one of many ways. The Bible declares that there is *only* one God; not many or that we ourselves can become gods. The Bible says that man lives *once* then faces judgment, not many lives coming back again as a second chance. In fact, the very Ten Commandments are all *absolute statements* from God! You *shall not* murder, you *shall not* commit adultery, you *shall not* steal, etc. These are not moral suggestions from God to ponder over a cup of coffee, they're *commands*. Even to this day, we have based our legal system on these basic commands from God and we *do not tolerate* a relativistic approach towards them. For instance, if a person is caught stealing at work, is it acceptable for the person to simply respond relativistically, "In my world I sincerely believe it's okay to steal.' You and I both know that person's next stop will be in the unemployment line or even jail! In fact, if there is no right or wrong, why do we have a Judicial System in the first place? Why do we have a Court of Law? Why would we dare prosecute someone, punish them, and send them to jail against their own wishes? I'm sure they were just following their *claim to truth*.

In addition, how can all values be equal? What if it was someone's "value" to molest his or her children? Is that right? If you bought into the new definition of tolerance, you would have to say yes, even though every fiber of your being says *no!* Or what if it was another person's "value" to teach their children to steal for a living? Or what if it was a mother's "value" to introduce her daughter to prostitution as a fulfilling lifestyle? Or how about a father who's "value" is to teach his son to be an abuser of woman? If everyone's values, beliefs, lifestyles and claims to truth are equal then does that mean that Hitler's slaughter of millions of Jews was okay? No? Why not? Are you being a *bigot*? I'm sure he was just following his *claim to truth*. The facts are, if there are no absolutes then there is no difference between an Adolph Hitler and a Franklin Graham!

"Why God? Why? How did we fall? How did this happen? How did our once great and mighty Christian nation turn into this society of such hedonistic wickedness and rebellion?" I'll tell you why? Because we allowed the infiltration of a *wicked belief* into our schools, our hearts, our media and even into our Churches that promote full-blown hedonism unrestrained and thus we're headed for judgment! I didn't say that; God did.

Isaiah 5:20 "Woe to those who call evil good, and good evil; Who substitute darkness for light and light for darkness; Who substitute bitter for sweet and sweet for bitter!"

If we're honest with ourselves, our society is unfortunately doing this today as well. We are calling evil good and good evil, while at the same time substituting darkness for light and light for darkness. God says, when you have the audacity to do that as a nation, you are clearly headed not for a wild time, but woeful times! Therefore, if there's any hope for our nation then it's high time we the Church *wake up* and *repent ourselves* and lead the way back, *now!* We've got to get busy working together and stop fighting against each other, and start standing on God's truth! Jesus Christ is the *only way* to escape God's wrath that is coming to our planet. Like it, lump it, or leave it, this is an *absolute truth!* No matter how you *feel about it*, Jesus is the only way out of the mess we're in. The fact that God has even provided a way out for us from our dilemma is great news, because the last place you ever want to be is under the wrath of God. He knows who's a real Christian and He knows who's a fake one. The point is, *make sure* before it's too late, as this man shares:

"GOD'S WRATH is coming. Are you ready?

Saving faith is the desperate thrust of a helpless soul upon the arms of an Almighty Savior. Are you doing what Jesus, who speaks the Words of the Father, are you doing what He says? Seek first the Kingdom of God. Are you taking every step necessary to stop feeding your lust?

In God's name, WHY? WHY? WHY? WHY? Will you sit through another service and stand by a sign post that points you away from Hell and the wrath of God and points to Heaven and life and forgiveness and hug death to your breast. Oh the madness. You are a vile, filthy, helpless, hell deserving son or daughter of Adam. You know nothing of true repentance and therefore, a true and saving Faith.

Or do you just occasionally have a little whimper in the closet when your conscience gets so active that you can't live with it and you whimper and cry and ask God for a little help and then you go right back with your hand and your eyeball firmly attached. Oh yes, once in a while you will take a dull paring knife and scratch your hand and occasionally you scratch around your eyeballs. But you haven't begun to CUT OFF AND PLUCK OUT.

You better listen to the words of Jesus, 'Not everyone who says 'LORD, LORD' shall enter but he who does the will of My Father in Heaven. If ye by the Spirit do mortify the deeds of the flesh Ye Shall Live. If ye live after the flesh you'll DIE.' The Cross does not give us a minor shift or two with regard to a few of our ethical and moral and religious values. The Cross RADICALLY disrupts the very center and citadel of your life from self, to Christ. And if the Cross has not done that, YOU'RE NOT A CHRISTIAN!!

My friend, face it. Young rogue, you're not a Christian until the Cross has radically disrupted the very center and citadel of your life and brought you away from a life of commitment to serve self. Whether it's religious self, moral self, proud self, covetous self, lustful self, prideful self, unforgiving self, lazy self. It doesn't matter! What are the focal points of the reign of your SELF? If you've gone to the Cross in union with Christ it's been SHATTERED!

I want you in that Day, when you stand with me before the Judge of the World, to have Him say, 'Come ye blessed.' I don't want to look at you standing there saying, 'LORD, LORD! LORD, LORD! I named you in earth. I named you before the elders. I named you before the Church! I named you in prayer meeting. I named you in witness and now LORD, LORD, LORD LORD! Did I not do this. Did I not do that?'

I do not want to hear Him say, 'DEPART FROM ME. I NEVER KNEW YOU. YOU WORKER OF INIQUITY. You never were made a doer of the will of God.'

You learned enough, and you learned what to say properly enough to be accepted for what you professed yourself to be on earth, but now the Day of Judgment has come and the Truth is now to be known."[35]

Make sure you're a true born again Christian who not only takes sin and wickedness very seriously, but who also refuses to go along with a *Wicked Belief* system called *relativism* that condones sin and wickedness. The price for getting God's *absolute truth* wrong is horrible beyond belief, and that's no lie!

VII. Wicked Chemical- Drug Usage

The seventh reason we've turned from a nation that once loved God to this Rise of Wickedness we see today is by the promotion of a Wicked Chemical. Of course, I'm talking about drug usage. Little do people know that all these *just say no to drug campaigns*, all these *drug wars*, all these *drug lords* and all these *drug problems* that we see around the world, are actually a major mega sign that we're living in the Last Days.

Revelation 9:12-21 "The first woe is past; two other woes are yet to come. The sixth angel sounded his trumpet, and I heard a voice coming from the horns of the golden altar that is before God. It said to the sixth angel who had the trumpet, 'Release the four angels who are bound at the great river Euphrates.' And the four angels who had been kept ready for this very hour and day and month and year were released to kill a third of mankind. The number of the mounted troops was two hundred million. I heard their number. The horses and riders I saw in my vision looked like this: Their breastplates were fiery red, dark blue, and yellow as sulfur. The heads of the horses resembled the heads of lions, and out of their mouths came fire, smoke and sulfur. A third of mankind was killed by the three plagues of fire, smoke and sulfur that came out of their mouths. The power of the horses was in their mouths and in their tails; for their tails were like snakes, having heads with which they inflict injury. The rest of mankind that were not killed by these plagues still did not repent of the work of their hands; they did not stop worshiping demons, and idols of gold, silver, bronze, stone and wood – idols that cannot see or hear or walk. Nor did they repent of their murders, their magic arts, their sexual immorality or their thefts."

So much for the human potential movement that states how mankind is supposed to be full of great and wonderful people who do all kinds of wonderful great things! This simply informs us to the contrary, that mankind is going to be so wicked in the Last Days that even though they're clearly being judged by God, it still doesn't wake them up. They are so full of evil that they refuse to repent and get right with God. Nothing seems to get their attention. Not even the judgment of God. They just continue on in their absolute unadulterated wickedness like it's no big deal, thumbing their noses against God. The question is, "Why?" Well notice the word there in the text, "magic arts." They did not repent of their "magic arts." It's actually the Greek word "pharmakeia" which means "drugs or druggings." It's where we get the English word *pharmacy* from. I believe this one word gives us an important clue as to why the people in the Last Days become too evil and even refuse to repent and get right with God even though they're in the midst of being judged by God. Apparently their minds are going to be elsewhere. There's going to be *a massive amount of drug usage* across the planet *clouding their minds* in the Last Days. Now, lest you think we are not even coming close to approaching this level of evil, I simply invite you to *turn on your TV!* What do we see and hear every single night? Drug this, drug that, drug problem here, drug raid there, drugs in schools, drugs in homes, drugs in streets, drugs in the government, drugs around the world! Drug usage has gone ballistic everywhere all at the same time spawning all kinds of *wicked behavior!*

In fact, they're even creating new drugs called "designer drugs." One of the latest ones is called, "Krokodil." It's called "krokodil" because of what it does to people. It turns their skin greenish and scaly in appearance and eventually causes their blood vessels to rupture and kills the surrounding skin tissue. This in turn creates huge chunks of dead flesh on their bodies, kind of like a zombie type of creature, and I quote, "Once you're an addict at this level, (using this stuff), any rational thinking doesn't apply."[36] Which of course would include getting right with God in the midst of being judged by God. Now, speaking of zombies and horror flicks, another new designer drug outbreak is given the name "bath salts." It's actually causing people to eat other people's faces off! Talk about wicked behavior! Furthermore, experts are now saying it is going to get even worse. This is because there's another drug out there that states are starting to legalize, that drug experts are saying is a *gateway drug* to using all different kinds of drugs, and that is the drug *Marijuana.* Experts are saying if that drug continues to get legalized, we haven't seen nothing yet! Drug usage is going to go nuts! It's a gateway drug that will spawn all kinds of wicked behavior, even worse than what we see today.[37] Speaking of wicked behavior, wait until you hear who in the Church is saying legalizing marijuana is a good thing:

"Martin Bashir: Legalization of marijuana has been sung about by Peter Tosh but who would have thought that television evangelist Pat Robertson would now support the idea.

Pat Robertson: I became sort of a hero of the hippie culture, I guess, when I said I think we ought to decriminalize the possession of marijuana. I just think it's shocking how many of these young people wind up in prison and they get turned into hard-core criminals because they have possession of a very small amount of a controlled substance. I mean the whole thing is crazy."[38]

Yes, I agree it's crazy! Who would've thought that a so-called Christian leader would be promoting the legalization of marijuana! Again, the problem is, the experts are saying, once this happens, once marijuana gets legalized, it's a gateway drug to using all other kinds of drugs and this will create such a full-blown massive drug problem all over the world that you can't even dream how wicked it's going to get! This is because most people don't realize that once you start using drugs, you don't just open *physical* doors with your mind, you open up *spiritual* doors. You're not just taking a physical trip. You're taking a spiritual trip. The usage of drugs put you into an "altered state of consciousness" that opens a spiritual contact. In fact, drugs are not the only way you can accomplish this. Other ways would include *hypnotism* by a psychotherapist, *repetitive movement* like the Hindu Yogis encourage, and even the *repetitive speech* like the Hare Krishnas practice by repeating their mantras over and over again, certain *body postures* and *stretches* in *Yoga*, which mean to "yoke" yourself with the Hindu gods, i.e. demons, and even various forms of *breathing exercises* and *meditation*. All of these practices, along with drugs, get you into an altered state of consciousness. Once you do this, you open yourself to *demonic spiritual forces* to come in and take control of your body and mind, as this researcher shares:

"No one knows what hypnosis is. No one knows what goes on in the mind. It's an altered state of consciousness like yogis and witchdoctors have been practicing. It loosens the normal connection between your spirit and your brain and of course if the hypnotists can control you – and they can make all kinds of suggestions, make you think things are happening that are not happening, make you think you have powers that you don't, experiences that you haven't, and they can even implant memories. Other beings – if there are other minds out there – could also do the same thing.

Sir John Eckels, Nobel Prize Winner for his research on the brain, describes the brain as quote, 'A machine that a ghost could operate,' unquote. What he means by that is your spirit operates your brain in a normal state of consciousness. In an altered state reached under Yoga, TM (transcendental meditation), Hypnosis - you have loosened the normal connection between your spirit and your brain and that allows another spirit – other entities, other minds to interpose themselves and begin to tick off the neurons in your brain to create a universe of illusion. I believe that it's demonic. I think that all the evidence indicates this."[39]

So let's put all this together. Drug usage in general causes people to do some pretty horrific things, like eating other people's faces off. New drugs are being designed to create even more horrible behaviors. Drugs are currently being used all over the world with talks of legalizing even more of them. Finally, using drugs spiritually opens a person up to be *controlled by a demon.* If this keeps up, I'm thinking this would create a level of wickedness that we can't even dream of, including people refusing to repent and get right with God even though they are being judged by God. It's all happening *right now* before our very eyes exactly like the Bible said would happen when you are living in the Last Days!

VIII. Wicked Connection - Demon Worship

The eighth reason we've turned from a nation that once loved God to this Rise of Wickedness we see today is by the promotion of a Wicked Connection. Now I'm talking about demon worship. Little do people know that drugs are not the only interaction people are going to be having with actual demons in the Last Days. Believe it or not, they will become so wicked that they will also be *worshiping those demons.* Again, God said this would happen too.

Revelation 9:20 "The rest of mankind that were not killed by these plagues still did not repent of the work of their hands; they did not stop *worshiping demons,* and idols of gold, silver, bronze, stone and wood – idols that cannot see or hear or walk."

As wild as it sounds, the Bible clearly says that in the Last Days, during the 7-year Tribulation, people will become so evil, that they will even get to the point where they will be worshiping demons, actual agents of evil! So that's the obvious, question, "Do we see people today actually worshiping demons?" Yes! In fact, demon worship, including the worship of the biggest evil entity of all, *satan,* is on the rise. We've already seen that he's done a masterful job of getting people to *act like him* by getting us to live for nothing but ourselves and to love ourselves more than God, which is the number one law of satanism. However, it's gotten so bad and so dark that we now have full-blown *worshipers of satan* entering all levels of society *openly* and it's on the rise! I think part of the reason why is due to our disbelief. We have been conditioned to think, even in the

Church, that satan doesn't exist, and so satanists get to sneak in under the radar with virtually no opposition.

Furthermore, this rise of satanism is also due to its ease of access. No longer do you have to go to some dark alley in some creepy bookstore in the backwoods of town to find out about satanism. Today, it's all over the place, including the Internet! I quote, "A surge in satanism is now being fueled by the internet and has led to a sharp rise in the demand for exorcisms."[40] Even some schools in California are saying, "Lucifer is a model and a guardian. Most of what contributes to our work as teachers – preparation work, artistic work, even meditative work, is under the guardianship of Lucifer. We can become great teachers under his supervision."[41] There was even a prayer offered up by Jack Black to satan at an MTV video awards ceremony where he urged the audience to join hands and pray, "Dear dark lord satan," and asked him, that is satan, to "give the musicians and nominees continued success in the music industry."[42] Yet we wonder why satanism is on the rise? It's now permeated all over the place, as these people share:

"Anton Lavey: We believe in greed. We believe in selfishness. We believe in all the lustful thoughts that motivate man because this is man's natural feelings.

1st Woman: This lady in a black robe came forward with this little baby...

2nd woman: I had my incredibly sharp knife...

1st Man: I would strap the animal into the middle of the pentagram

2nd Man: There were things here that weren't quite as they should be.

1st Woman: ...and she just laid it on the altar

2nd Woman: ...and then I just cut its head off like that, suddenly.

1st Woman: ...then the high priest just cut the baby's head off.

3rd man: They taught me how to kill someone.

2nd woman: Through the powers that was raised through this ritual was used for killing off Christians.

Reporter: Where is the dividing line between something which is a bit of a giggle, and full blown satanism?

Anton LaVey: "Hail satan!" His followers: "Hail satan!"

2nd woman: There's something about sacrifice, if you do it once, you want to do it all the time.

Anton LaVey: All religions are coming around to satanism. We're in the very throes of a new satanic age. The evidence is all around us. All you have to do is look at it."[43]

But that's just it, we don't want to look at it do we? We don't want to deal with the facts that satanism. Yes, demon or devil worship is on the rise, just like the Bible said would happen in the Last Days! In fact, another thing we don't want to deal with is how satanism is not only clearly on the rise, but that satanists themselves are getting so bold they're even going into Churches to take them out! They aren't hiding in the shadows anymore. With all this help in Hollywood and the media, they're getting extremely bold! Just ask these former satanists:

"Doreen (Former satanist/black witch): Christians are the satanists' worst enemy. They are out to torment you. They are out to blackmail you. They will even kill you. They even tried to kill me when I came out of black witchcraft.

Bill: If you're in a church where the Spirit of God is really moving and where the Word of God is really being preached and where prayer is really going up to heaven for the salvation of souls, then they are going to regard you as their mortal enemies and they are going to be out there trying everything they can to destroy, to kill, and to maim because that is, of course, the nature of satan and it is also the nature of his followers. They will try to infiltrate your church. They will try to set up whispering campaigns against the pastor and the elders. They may even try to seduce the pastor.

Glen (former satanist): For two years I was involved in the Baptist Church. I was constantly complaining about the pastor's sermons being too long, being too dry, sowing discord between the people, gossiping about others.

Doreen: As each member is initiated into the coven, they are commissioned to do a job. One individual's job may be to desecrate a Church.

Jack Roper (Occult Researcher): They'll destroy or desecrate churches where they'll spray paint 'satan' right on the altar, just to put fear into that Christian Church.

Doreen: Some satanists who were handpicked, the most powerful ones, were sent into Churches to disrupt the meeting and we stopped people from going forward-when they asked the people to go forward and accept Christ as their Savior.

Bill: I was, in fact, trained to learn all the Christian jargon, you know, to say, 'Haleluejah!' and 'Praise the Lord' and do all the right things and I had no more an idea of Jesus being my Savior than a man in the moon.

Glen: If you can tear down the prayer foundation of a Church, then you've destroyed that Church and that's what every witch or satanist plans to do when they go into a Church-is to tear down that prayer foundation and then the rest of the Church goes down quickly after that."[44]

That's eye-opening, isn't it? The weapons satanists use to destroy Churches is to get Christians to just simply start complaining, gossiping and fighting with each other? That appears to be commonplace in Churches throughout America today! Yet we still wonder why Churches are falling apart? Not all our battles are against flesh and blood, sometimes they're *spiritual*. It's high time we wake up to that Biblical truth! But the point is, it's clear that demon or devil worship is on the rise all over the place. Therefore, I'm thinking if this unfortunate trend continues, then it will create a level of wickedness we can't even dream of. Even to the point where people will actually refuse to repent and get right with God though they are being judged by God. It's happening *right now* before our very eyes and that's exactly what the Bible said would happen when we are living in the Last Days!

IX. Wicked Coven - The Rise of Wicca

The ninth reason we've turned from a nation that once loved God to this Rise of Wickedness we see today is by the promotion of a Wicked Coven. Now I'm talking about the rise of Wicca. For those of you who may not now know, "Wicca" is simply the modern term for old-fashioned "witchcraft." Not so surprisingly, the Bible says that this wicked behavior would also be on the rise as well in the Last Days.

Revelation 9:20-21 "The rest of mankind that were not killed by these plagues still did not repent of the work of their hands; they did not stop worshiping demons, and idols of gold, silver, bronze, stone and wood – idols that cannot see or hear or walk. Nor did they repent of their murders, their *magic arts*, their sexual immorality or their thefts."

Now as we saw earlier, the words there in the above text "magic arts" is actually the Greek word "pharmakeia" which means "drugs or druggings." However, it also carries with it the connotation of, "drug usage that's fostered by the dark arts." This is precisely why some translators have simply translated that word "pharmakeia" to just that, "magic arts, sorcery, or literally witchcraft." Now, if you've been paying attention, this too is also on the rise! People all over the world, including children, are practicing witchcraft and the dark arts. As shocking as that is, one of the seductive ways they're getting people to join in this wicked behavior is through the promotion of *Wicca*. Again, all that is, is the new term for old-fashioned *witchcraft*. Re-label it, call it what you will, but Wicca's teachings and practices are not only demonic, but they've *already infiltrated our thinking*. For instance, witchcraft believes that the entire earth is a living, breathing organism and is the manifestation of the mother goddess. Sounds like *environmentalism*, doesn't it? Witchcraft also says that the mother or female goddess is to be worshiped above all, not a male god. Sounds like *feminism*, doesn't it? Furthermore, witchcraft also states that truth is what is true for you. There are no absolutes. Sounds like *relativism*, doesn't it? Witchcraft even says that in order to contact these gods and goddesses for personal power you need to practice astrology, divination, incantations, psychic power and speaking with the dead.[45] Sounds like *New Age* doesn't it?

In addition, they also promote their wicked teachings through the promotion of all these TV programs *today* where people are supposedly talking with the dead like "Psychic Hotline" or "Crossing Over" with John Edwards, or one of the latest ones with that lady named Theresa Caputo called, "Long Island Medium." In fact, thanks to movies and shows like "Charmed" and books and movie series like "Twilight" and "Harry Potter," witchcraft has a whole new appeal *even for kids*. Yet, amazingly, some adults, even Christian adults, will still state something like this, "These movies and books don't affect my child. They know it's just entertainment." Really? You the adult may be able to differentiate between reality and entertainment, but the facts show that the kids can't and aren't! In fact, after exposure to witchcraft teachings via these various forms of media, children are actually saying that they want to *become full-blown witches*.

Listen to their own words. Apparently, they're more honest than the adults about this media saturation of witchcraft:

"J.K. Rowling, the author of the Harry Potter series admitted that she got many, many requests from children that wanted to attend Hogwart's School of Witchcraft and Wizardry and we know this from books that are out there and interviews with children.

They really wonder at night, while they're lying awake, if there is a Hogwarts that they can go to. If you go to the Warner-Brothers site, they ask you to enlist into Hogwarts. Well there are sites out there that are pulling in your children who are interested in learning more in various different schools of witchcraft and wizardry." [46]

'Occult sites 'lure' teenagers.' - BBC News
'This goes far beyond a case of reading a Harry Potter story. This represents an extremely worrying trend among young people.' - Association of Teachers and Lecturers [46]

QUOTES FROM CHILDREN:

"'I want to go to wizard school and learn magic. I'd like to learn to use a wand to cast spells.' - Dylan, age 10

'If I could go to wizard school, I might be able to do spells and potions and fly a broomstick.' - Mara, age 12

'It would be great to be a wizard because you could control situations and things like teachers.' - Jefferey, age 11

'I'd like to go to wizard school, learn magic and put spells on people. I'd make up an ugly spell, and then it's payback time!' - Catherine, age 9

'I feel like I'm inside Harry's world. If I went to wizard school, I'd study everything: Spells, counterspells, and defense against the Dark Arts.' - Carolyn, age 10

'I liked it when the bad guys killed the Unicorn, and Voldemort drank it's blood."' - Julie, age 13

'The books are very clever. I couldn't put them down. When I was scared I made myself believe it was supposed to be funny so I wasn't too scared.' - Nurya, age 11" [46]

Yes, they are *very clever.* They're indoctrinating kids into witchcraft via various forms of media, and to top it off, their parents are even condoning and encouraging it! In fact, witchcraft is not only appealing to kids, environmentalists, and feminists, but now even to *psychologists,* who are starting to use witchcraft's occult techniques to treat their patients. [47] In addition, Wicca has now been recognized as an "official" religion and the United States Army has allowed approximately one hundred witches to have their own covens at Fort Hood in Texas. [48] Then, as if that wasn't bad enough, one of the male deities that is worshiped by those in Wicca is the "horned god" called Pan. In the ancient cult of Pan, the rites of passage included the use of *drugs* to entice the "spirits" to come. If someone was possessed by Pan, from which we get the English word "panic", it often resulted in an obsession with sex and the need for immediate gratification. Furthermore, it just so happens that Pan is the universal symbol for satan and the Antichrist! [49] Because of this slick new campaign presented by witchcraft in its various forms, Wicca is now considered by some to be the *fastest growing religion in the U.S.* and the second most popular religion among teens. [50] I wonder why?

So if you put this together, it would appear that witchcraft and paganism are exploding all across the planet, *right before our very eyes* just like the Bible said would happen in the Last Days. This means we are headed for one of the most dark, evil and deceptive times this planet has ever seen, as these people admit:

"Female pagan: The fear has gone out of the general public. The craft is more and more acceptable

Paganism has infiltrated the mainstream thought pattern of most Americans today. There is a pagan revival. There are more people practicing true paganism than there are practicing true Christianity.

Female Pagan: Many people were seeking something apart from Christianity. The thing that attracts young people is the power. It's immediate power. Whenever you drink blood, you gain incredible power.

You choose only to let the general public see what you want them to see. Magic is about getting what you want. Magicians are people who are getting what they want. Slowly but surely, the beauty of the craft is becoming widespread.

"Bella" from Twilight: I'm not scared of you.

"Edward" from Twilight: You really shouldn't have said that.

'Psychic vampirism and physical vampirism were very viable ways of achieving power in black magic.'

'Why hide in this day and age. I've hidden in the shadows for centuries. Time to share myself with the world.'

'I'm very proud to be a witch.'
We live in a kind of post-Christian era. People are moving towards a kind of neo-paganism. The neo-pagan revival has proceeded so rapidly. They have had the co-operation of the media in getting their message spread. (Harry Potter, Twilight, True Blood etc.)

A lot of what we do has been taken over by the Church. "Christians" really have married into occult practices. They really no longer know the difference because they've become desensitized to the things of evil.

From Twilight:
Edward: 'Are you afraid?'
Bella: 'No!'"[51]

We should be afraid. We too, even as Christians, have allowed ourselves to become desensitized to evil, sin, including the sin of witchcraft in the Last Days, just like the Bible said would happen. In fact, not only satanists, but witches are getting so bold that *they too* are infiltrating Churches to take them out. Observe the following report:

"Several high-profile pastors have urged me to put into print what we now know, in order to alert the Church to some of the dangers we are now facing.

We now know of a large number of Churches that have been successfully infiltrated by witches. In fact, in one town, witches boast that they have infiltrated every Church in the town and judging by the devastation caused in some of the Churches in this town, their claim is probably correct.

Their plan is meeting with amazing success. One Church that we have been told of, originally had a membership of well over 100. The membership is now down to 30 and the remaining members are almost totally demoralized.

This is now happening to an increasing number of Churches and many promising young Pastors are now leaving the ministry because of it.

These witches are working a carefully laid out plan which has been operating for many years, right under our noses without our even suspecting it. Some profess to be fine Christians. They dress well, speak well, are usually well educated and in some cases are knowledgeable in spiritual matters.

Some witches appear content to just sit in congregations and mumble their incantations while others go out of their way to gain acceptance in a Church and then carefully work their way into positions of influence.

They become members and begin to take an active part, singing in the choir or joining the diaconate etc. Then they work a highly effective plan which is aimed at destroying the Pastor's reputation (seducing him or spreading rumors about him).

They also create factions within the Church and pit one group against another and thus create division. They may lay charges against the pastor and put these charges in writing and send them to the diaconate. This ploy often divides members of the diaconate against each other or sometimes turns the diaconate against the pastor.

The results stemming from these methods are obvious and manifold - confusion, suspicion, loss of confidence in the pastor, emotional problems, tension, disunity - the list is almost endless, and we are certain that this is only the tip of the iceberg.

Unfortunately, the Church in these Last Days has become so worldly and materialistic, that it is no longer any real threat to its enemies.

I constantly hear Christians talk about 'spiritual warfare' and 'putting on the armor of God' etc., but it would appear that with most, their knowledge of these things is theoretical rather than experiential. They are familiar with the 'jargon' but that is as far as it goes."[52]

In other words, this is serious, we really are in a *spiritual battle* and it's high time we wake up! We need to get busy working together as Christians and stop fighting against each other and stop falling for these wicked traps laid out by satanists and witches! We've got to get busy sharing the Gospel while there's still time, even to these same satanists and witches! Do we really want to get a *letter from hell?* As this man shares:

"What if? What if you had a friend who died without knowing Jesus as their personal Savior? What if he or she went to Hell? What if one day you received a letter in the mail from beyond? A LETTER FROM HELL. A letter from your friend in the flames of eternal torment.
"I've been thinking about YOU. You're a Christian. You told me so, yourself. I mean we talked about it three different times today. Kelly brought it up and you laughed it off. Coach Adams brought it up and you changed the subject. I mean it came up right before the wreck. Well the question I can't get out of my mind is this. Why haven't you ever told me about how to become a Christian? I mean you say you're my friend-but if you really were-you would have told me about this Jesus. Told me how to escape this terrible place that I'm headed for.

I can feel my heart pounding in my chest. The angels that have been chosen to cast me into hell are coming down the hallway. I can hear their footsteps. I've heard about this Hell. They call it the Lake of Fire. I can't stand it. I am terrified.

Oh no the angels are at the door! Oh no! NO! They're coming in and they're pointing at me. They are grabbing me and carrying me out of the room. I can already smell the burning sulfur and brimstone. I can see the edge of the cliff where hell burns. This is it. I am without hope.

We're coming closer. Closer. CLOSER. My heart is bursting with FEAR. They are holding me over the flames. I'm damned FOREVER. This is it. They are throwing me in! FIRE! PAIN! HELL!

Why? WHY?! Why didn't you ever tell me about...JESUS.

Signed,

Your friend

P.S. Wish you were here." [53]

This is not a game. Lives are really on the line here for all eternity. Let's not allow ourselves to ingest wickedness to the point where we become desensitized to sin. Rather, let us spend our time wisely telling others about Jesus, showing them how to be spared from hell, the horrible place for sin. We are living in the Last Days and we need to start taking this mission from God seriously. Yet, believe it or not, even with all this amazing evidence pointing to the signs of Christ's soon return, some people still refuse to listen to any kind of godly message, like this lady:

"Two Church members were going door to door sharing God's message of love to be saved and knocked on the door of a woman who was not happy to see them. She told them in no uncertain terms that she did not want to hear their message, and slammed the door in their faces.

To her surprise, however, the door did not close and, in fact, bounced back open. So she tried again, really put her back into it, and slammed the door again with the same result, the door bounced back open.

Convinced that these rude young people were sticking their foot in the door, she reared back to give it a slam that would teach them a lesson, when one of them said, 'Ma'am, before you do that again, you might want to move your cat.'" [54]

Now that lady caused a lot of unnecessary pain by refusing to listen to God's message, didn't she? Unfortunately, she's not alone. The Bible says that in the Last Days, many people will also refuse to listen to God's message to be saved before it's too late.

2 Corinthians 6:2 "For God says, 'At just the right time, I heard you. On the day of salvation, I helped you.' Indeed, God is ready to help you right now. Today is the day of salvation."

I hope you're not one of those who are refusing to listen to God's message to be saved. Now is the time. Today is the day of salvation. Don't delay because you might wake up one day and discover that *you've been left behind.* And do you know what? God doesn't want you left behind. Because He loves us, He has given us the warning sign of **The Rise of Wickedness** to show us that the 7-year Tribulation is near and that Christ's Coming is rapidly approaching. Jesus Himself said this:

Luke 21:28 "When these things begin to take place, stand up and lift up your heads, because your redemption is drawing near."

Like it or not, we are headed for *The Final Countdown.* We don't know the day or the hour. Only God knows. The point is, if you're a Christian and you're not going to shoot at the enemy, satan, then will you at least carry bullets for those who will? Let's roll! It's high time we the Church speak up and declare the good news of salvation to those who are dying all around us. But please, if you're not a Christian, give your life to Jesus *now,* because tomorrow may be too late! Just like the Bible said!

How to Receive Jesus Christ:

1. Admit your need (I am a sinner).

2. Be willing to turn from your sins (repent).

3. Believe that Jesus Christ died for you on the Cross and rose from the grave.

4. Through prayer, invite Jesus Christ to come in and control your life through the Holy Spirit. (Receive Him as Lord and Savior.)

What to pray:

Dear Lord Jesus,

I know that I am a sinner and need Your forgiveness. I believe that You died for my sins. I want to turn from my sins. I now invite You to come into my heart and life. I want to trust and follow You as Lord and Savior.

In Jesus' name. Amen.

Notes

Chapter One
The Jewish People

1. *Joke About Man Having a Bad Day*
   (Email story) – Source Unknown
2. *Quote About Jerusalem Being the Center of the Earth*
   (Internet video) – Source Unknown
   (http://www.johnsnotes.com/Thedesertblossominglikearose.htm)
3. *The Sign of Israel Returning to the Land*
   (http://www.100prophecies.org/page2.htm)
4. *The Sign of Israel Being Brought Forth in One Day*
   (http://www.bibledesk.com)
5. *How Israel Was Brought Forth in One Day*
   (http://www.youtube.com/watch?v=nNWgfei6wO8)
   (http://www.youtube.com/watch?v=ra9so-TLP28&feature=related)
6. *The Sign of Israel Being a United Nation Again*
   (http://www.100prophecies.org/page3.htm)
7. *The Sign of Israel's Currency Being the Shekel*
   (http://www.bibledesk.com)
8. *Quote How Special the Land of Israel Is*
   (http://www.johnsnotes.com/Thedesertblossominglikearose.htm)
9. *Quote Josephus Says Israel's Land is Good*
   (http://www.johnsnotes.com/Thedesertblossominglikearose.htm)
10. *Quotes on Israel's Land Being a Wasteland*
    (http://www.johnsnotes.com/Thedesertblossominglikearose.htm)
    (http://www.mastnet.net/~shucka/Israel.htm)
    (http://www.100prophecies.org/page2.htm)
    (http://rr-bb.com/showthread.php?t=27867&highlight=100+reasons)
11. *Tree & Fruit Statistics of the Israel's Land*
    (http://www.johnsnotes.com/Thedesertblossominglikearose.htm)
12. *Quote Water Under Israel Causes Desert to Bloom*
    (http://www.youtube.com/watch?v=AlUfCpuGl8k)
13. *The Sign of Israel Blossoming as a Rose in the Desert*

(http://www.johnsnotes.com/Thedesertblossominglikearose.htm)
(http://www.mastnet.net/~shucka/Israel.htm)
(http://www.100prophecies.org/page2.htm)
(http://rr-bb.com/showthread.php?t=27867&highlight=100+reasons)

14. *The Sign of Israel Having a Powerful Military*
    (http://www.mastnet.net/~shucka/Israel.htm)
    (http://www.100prophecies.org/page3.htm)

15. *Odds of Eight Prophecies Being Fulfilled in One Entity*
    (http://www.carm.org/bible/prophecy.htm)

16. *Track Record of Psychic Predictions*
    Norman L. Geisler, *Baker Encyclopedia of Christian Apologetics*
    (Grand Rapids: Baker Books, 1999, Pg. 615)

17. *World Leaders Saying "Peace & Security"*
    (http://johnclaeys.com/the-coming-of-peace-and-security/)
    (http://www.youtube.com/watch?v=w9xivoAv8-U)
    (http://www.squidoo.com/prophesiesunfolding)

18. *Announcement of Having the Plans Made for the Temple*
    (http://www.templeinstitute.org/blueprints-for-the-holy-temple.htm)

19. *The Sign of Israel's Temple Having a New Location*
    (http://www.templemount.org/theories.html)

20. *The Discovery of the Priestly Line Through Genetics*
    (http://www.cohen-levi.org/jewish_genes_and_genealogy/the_dna_
    chain_of_tradition.htm)

21. *Priests Being Trained for the Temple*
    (Online Video Report in Jerusalem: Source Unknown)

22. *Stone Altar Rebuilt for the Temple*
    (http://www.templeinstitute.org/building-an-altar-9th-av-5769.htm)

23. *Sacrifices Started Again for the Temple*
    (http://prophecybeyond.ning.com/forum/topics/jews-practice-pesach-
    sacrifice-declare-we-are-ready?xg_source=activity)

24. *Golden Menorah Reconstructed for the Temple*
    (http://www.templeinstitute.org/moving-menorah.htm)

25. *The Sign of Israel Rebuilding Articles for the Temple*
    (http://www.templeinstitute.org/gallery.htm)

26. *High Priests Crown Made for the Temple*
    (http://www.prophecynews.co.uk/content/view/537/2/)
    (http://www.israelnationalnews.com/News/News.aspx/124443)

27. *The Sign of the Return of the Red Heifer*
    (http://www.templeinstitute.org/current-events/RedHeifer/index.html)

28. *Announcement that a Kosher Red Heifer is Now Here*
    (Online Video: Source Unknown)
29. *Jewish Rabbi Says the Messiah Will Come in Our Lifetime*
    (http://www.cbn.com/cbnnews/348570.aspx)
30. *The Sign of the Rebirth of the Sanhedrin*
    (http://www.israelnn.com/news.php3?id=70349)
    (http://www.traditioninaction.org/bev/060bev12-20-2004.htm)
    (http://www.israelnationalnews.com/news.php3?id=76624)
31. *History of Failed Peace Treaties with Israel*
    (http://news.bbc.co.uk/2/hi/middle_east/6666393.stm)
    (http://en.wikipedia.org/wiki/Peace_process_in_the_Israeli%E2%80%93Pale
    stinian_conflict)
    (http://en.wikipedia.org/wiki/List_of_Middle_East_peace_proposals#Peace_
    process_in_the_Israeli-Palestinian_conflict)
32. *Quote from Newspapers About Jewish Expectation of the Messiah*
    (http://www.thejewishpress.com/news_article.asp?article=5370)
    (http://worldnetdaily.com/news/article.asp?ARTICLE_ID=45743)
    (http://www.israelnationalnews.com/News/News.aspx/89850)
33. *Signs America is Worshipping a Political Figure*
    (http://www.wnd.com/2009/06/101217/)
    (http://www.wnd.com/2009/01/87040/)
    (http://www.wnd.com/2009/04/96417/)
    (http://www.wnd.com/2009/09/111399/)
    (http://www.wnd.com/2009/01/86695/)
34. *Various False Teachings Saying You Are God*
    (http://www.carm.org/lds/lds_doctrines.htm)
    (http://www.carm.org/wicca.htm)
    (http://www.religioustolerance.org/hinduism2.htm)
    (http://www.khouse.org/articles/2001/345/)
    (http://www.canadafreepress.com/2002/main90902.htm)
    (http://members.fortunecity.com/alahoy33/msg04.htm)
    (http://www.spiritfind.net/jump.pl?ID=1818&Cat=Channeling/Channeled_M
    aterial&Dir=SpiritFind)
    (http://www.spiritfind.net/jump.pl?ID=2257&Cat=Channeling/Channeled_M
    aterial&Dir=SpiritFind)
    Caryl Matrisciana, *Invasion of the Godmen,*
    (Hemet California: Jeremiah Films Inc., 1991, Video)
    Shirley MacLaine, *Out On a Limb,*
    (Los Angeles: ABC Video Enterprises Inc., 1986, Video)

35. *False Teachers in the Church Saying You Are a God*
(http://www.bereanfaith.com/heresy.php?action=tquote&id=6)
(http://www.bereanfaith.com/heresy.php?action=tquote&id=7)
(http://www.bereanfaith.com/heresy.php?action=tquote&id=8)
(http://www.bereanfaith.com/heresy.php?action=tquote&id=45)
(http://www.bereanfaith.com/heresy.php?action=tquote&id=47)
(http://www.bereanfaith.com/heresy.php?action=tquote&id=32)
Hank Hanegraaff, *Christianity In Crisis*
(Eugene: Harvest House Publishers, 1993, Pgs. 11, 21, 24-25, 26-27)
36. *Current Statistics of Israel's Population*
(http://www.jewishvirtuallibrary.org/jsource/Society_&_Culture/newpop.html)
37. *People Not Knowing Who Hitler Was & Would Help Bury Jews Alive*
(http://www.christianpost.com/news/ray-comfort-180-filmmaker-felt-sickened-by-response-to-holocaust-question-56989/)
(http://180movie.com/)
38. *Quote About Anti-Semitism Being as Bad as It was in the 30's*
(http://www.haaretz.com/news/u-s-envoy-anti-semitism-in-europe-nearly-as-bad-as-in-1930s-1.113884)
39. *Story The Bridge is Out*
(Email story) – Source Unknown

Chapter Two *Modern Technology*

1. *Story of Scared Taxicab Driver*
(Email story) – Source Unknown
2. *History of Horseback Travel*
(http://www.mastnet.net/~shucka/time.htm)
3. *Horse Traffic Problems in New York*
(http://www.lunarpages.com/stargazers/endworld/signs/toandfro.htm)
4. *Statistics on Cars and Their Usage*
(http://www.lunarpages.com/stargazers/endworld/signs/toandfro.htm)
5. *Statistics on Boeing 747*
(http://www.lunarpages.com/stargazers/endworld/signs/toandfro.htm)
6. *Tracking Plane Travel on Internet*
(http://www.lunarpages.com/stargazers/endworld/signs/toandfro.htm)
7. *Article on Flying Car*
(http://www.terrafugia.com/)

(http://www.speakup.com.br/index.php/extras/2011/291/156-291-the-flying-car.html)
(http://www.youtube.com/watch?v=iE2Ij7Rfw1Q)
8. *Statistics on Worldwide Shipping*
(http://www.lunarpages.com/stargazers/endworld/signs/toandfro.htm)
9. *Statistics on Space Travel*
(http://www.lunarpages.com/stargazers/endworld/signs/toandfro.htm)
10. *Article on Virgin Galactic Spaceport*
(http://www.virgingalactic.com/news/item/sir-richard-branson-and-new-mexico-governor-susana-martinez-dedicate-the-virgin-galactic-gateway-/)
11. *Article on Space Elevator*
(http://www.youtube.com/watch?v=kik_3ZPsj1c)
(http://www.squidoo.com/elevator-to-space-just-science-fiction)
12. *Teleporting Light Particles*
(http://www.news.ft.com/ft/gx.cgi/ftc?pagename=View&cid=FT3HW4CJGIC&live=true&tagid=IXLMS1QTICC&subheading=global%20economy)
13. *Information on Information*
(http://www.countdown.org/armageddon/knowledge.htm)
(http://www.lunarpages.com/stargazers/endworld/signs/knowledge.htm)
(http://en.wikipedia.org/wiki/Nanotechnology#Applications)
(http://articles.cnn.com/2007-02-08/tech/ft.nanobots_1_motor-bacteria-rotor?_s=PM:TECH)
(http://www.youtube.com/watch?v=Z4gt62uAasE)
(http://www.youtube.com/watch?v=lUMf7FWGdCw)
(http://www.youtube.com/watch?v=7XyWTGepCHo)
(http://www.youtube.com/watch?v=NB_P-_NUdLw)
14. *Quote on Singularity*
(http://en.wikipedia.org/wiki/Technological_singularity)
(http://mindstalk.net/vinge/vinge-sing.html)
15. *Statistics on Educational System*
(http://www.countdown.org/armageddon/knowledge.htm)
16. *Statistics on Societal Behavior*
(http://www.lunarpages.com/stargazers/endworld/signs/knowledge.htm)
17. *Quote on Being in a Rush*
(http://www.lunarpages.com/stargazers/endworld/signs/toandfro.htm)
18. *Quote on Mad Dash Society*
(http://www.lunarpages.com/stargazers/endworld/signs/toandfro.htm)
19. *Quote on Definition of Insanity*

(http://www.lunarpages.com/stargazers/endworld/signs/knowledge.htm)
20. *Story of The Stanger*
    (Email story) – Source Unknown
21. *Quote on TV Versus the Bible*
    (Web Comment) – Source Unknown
22. *Story of satan's Meeting*
    (Email story) – Source Unknown
23. *Quote Global Television Channel*
    (http://www.aim.org/aim-column/global-television-for-our-future-global-leader/)
    (http://www.onenewsnow.com/Printer.aspx?id=409270)
24. *Google Launches Street View of Israel*
    (http://www.google.com/hostednews/ap/article/ALeqM5gmsSqtg7 Rz4eL0-VaEPIq5EsHokA?docId=310c5370d5644b2780014d8135 9b5df9)
25. *HAARP Technology Controls Weather & Earthquakes*
    (http://www.youtube.com/watch?v=jcmMtUb0mh8&feature=related
    (http://www.youtube.com/watch?v=Wi8F77sEvUg&lr=1&feature=mhum)
26. *HAARP Technology Created Death Ray*
    (http://www.newsofinterest.tv/video_pages_flash/environment/haarp/holes_in_heaven/weather_modification.php)
27. *HAARP Technology Controls Mind*
    (http://www.youtube.com/watch?v=QkLTzesBxGE)
    (http://www.youtube.com/watch?v=Zi1nLmlicxU&feature=relmfu)
    (http://educate-yourself.org/mc/mctotalcontrol12jul02.shtml)
28. *Quote Voice of God Weaponry*
    (http://www.wired.com/dangerroom/2007/06/darpas_sonic_pr/
    (http://www.washingtonpost.com/wp-dyn/content/article/2005/08/23/AR2005082301227_pf.html)
    (http://www.nytimes.com/2003/03/23/magazine/the-sound-of-things-to-come.html?pagewanted=all&src=pm)
29. *Quote Strange Noises in the Sky*
    (http://www.ufodigest.com/article/strange-sounds-heard-around-world)
30. *Quote How the Occult Sees the Last Days*
    (http://www.cuttingedge.org/n1052.html)
31. *Quote Mass Mirage Seen in China*
    (http://www.huffingtonpost.com/2011/06/20/china-mirage-video_n_880591.html)
32. *Examples of Hologram Technology*

(http://news.cnet.com/cnns-human-hologram-on-election-night/)
(http://news.sky.com/home/article/1301500)
(http://www.washingtonpost.com/business/technology/how-the-tupac-hologram-works/2012/04/18/gIQA1ZVyQT_story.html)
33. *Quote Japanese Anime Hologram*
(http://singularityhub.com/2010/11/09/cant-miss-videos-of-japans-3d-hologram-rock-star-hatsune-miku-in-hd/)
34. *Quote Boy Called Milo & Touchable Holograms*
(http://www.shacknews.com/article/58907/lionhead-details-xbox-360s-virtual)
(http://xbox360.ign.com/articles/991/991348p1.html)
(http://english.ntdtv.com/ntdtv_en/ns_asia/2009-09-16/163021253061.html)
35. *Quote Download Brain into Computer*
(http://www.youtube.com/watch?v=oCHuWQrThYo&feature=relmfu)
(http://www.youtube.com/watch?v=6jBVhICzi5U&feature=relmfu)
36. *Story of Senior Citizens*
(Email story) – Source unknown

Chapter Three   *Worldwide Upheaval*

1. *Story of Man Playing Bagpipes for Septic Tank*
(Email story) – Source Unknown
2. *Statistics on Famines*
(http://www.countdown.org/armageddon/famine.htm)
3. *Statistics on Desertification*
(http://www.lunarpages.com/stargazers/endworld/signs/famines.htm)
4. *Statistics on China's Desertification*
(http://thefamily.org/endtime/article.php3?id=4)
5. *Statistic on One of China's Famines*
(http://en.wikipedia.org/wiki/The_Great_Chinese_Famine)
6. *Statistics on World Desertification*
(http://www.cnn.com/TECH/science/9806/21/growing.desert/)
7. *Statistics on Global Famine*
(http://library.thinkquest.org/C002291/high/present/stats.htm)
8. *Quotes on Famine*
(http://www.ft.com/cms/s/0/5f6f94ac-b6bc-11df-b3dd-00144feabdc0.html#axzz1vieoZUbN)

(http://the-end-time.blogspot.com/2010/08/wheat-prices-going-through-roof.html)

(http://www.cbsnews.com/2100-202_162-20083500.html)

9. *Quote on U.S. Drought*
    (http://www.nytimes.com/2011/07/12/us/12drought.html?pagewanted=all)
    (http://photoblog.statesman.com/dry-season-the-texas-drought-of-2011)

10. *Photo of U.S. Drought*
    (http://www.nytimes.com/interactive/2011/07/11/us/DROUGHT.html?ref=us)

11. *Quotes on World Global Food Crisis*
    (http://news.bbc.co.uk/2/hi/uk_news/7951838.stm)

12. *Quote on Family Eating Dirt to Stay Alive*
    (http://www.youtube.com/watch?v=q6gYK7474sE)

13. *Examples of Earth Cracking Up*
    (http://thewatchers.adorraeli.com/2011/03/07/scientists-are-sounding-the-alarm-the-mysterious-cracks-appear-across-the-planet/)
    (http://thewatchers.adorraeli.com/2011/03/07/scientists-are-sounding-the-alarm-the-mysterious-cracks-appear-across-the-planet/)
    (http://www.newscientist.com/article/dn18114-giant-crack-in-africa-formed-in-just-days.html)
    (http://www.esa.int/esaEO/SEM14GBUQPE_index_0.html)
    (http://news.nationalgeographic.com/news/2001/10/1001_lostlake.html)
    (http://news.nationalgeographic.com/news/pf/43658447.html)
    (http://ehextra.com/main.asp?SectionID=12&SubSectionID=35&ArticleID=8713)

14. *Statistics on the Increase of Earthquakes*
    (http://www.countdown.org/armageddon/earthquakes.htm)
    (http://www.mastnet.net/~shucka/6_signs.htm)
    (http://earthquake.usgs.gov/eqcenter/recenteqsus/)
    (http://earthquake.usgs.gov/earthquakes/world/historical.php)

15. *Statistics on the Death Toll of Earthquakes*
    (http://en.wikipedia.org/wiki/1976_Tangshan_earthquake)

16. *Quote Scientists on the Increase of Earthquakes*
    (http://www.countdown.org/armageddon/earthquakes.htm)

17. *Quote Scientists Say Earth is Cracking Up*
    (http://www.croatiantimes.com/?id=26423&print=1)

18. *Quote Future Fatalities from Earthquakes*
    (http://www.lunarpages.com/stargazers/endworld/signs/earthquakes.htm)

19. *Statistics on Pestilence*
    (http://www.lunarpages.com/stargazers/endworld/signs/pestilenc.htm)
20. *Statistics on Influenza Outbreak of 1918*
    (http://en.wikipedia.org/wiki/1918_flu_pandemic)
21. *Statistics on AIDS in Africa*
    (http://bible-prophecy.com/plagues.htm)
22. *Statistics on AIDS Contact*
    (http://www.lunarpages.com/stargazers/endworld/signs/pestilenc.htm)
23. *Statistics on Tuberculosis*
    (http://www.voanews.com/content/report-red-cross-says-10-million-
    might-die-of-tuberculosis-by-2015-118643934/160297.html)
24. *Statistics on the Return of Infectious Diseases*
    (http://www.countdown.org/armageddon/plagues.htm)
25. *Statistics on Bird Flu Mortality Rate in Cambodia*
    (http://english.pravda.ru/science/mysteries/27-02-2011/117027-
    cambodia_virus-0/)
26. *Quote on the Overuse of Antibiotics*
    (http://www.lunarpages.com/stargazers/endworld/signs/pestilenc.htm)
27. *Quote from the American Association of Advancement of Science*
    (http://www.lunarpages.com/stargazers/endworld/signs/pestilenc.htm)
28. *Quote How Europe is Losing Superbugs Battle*
    (http://www.bbc.co.uk/news/health-12975693)
29. *Quote Experts on the Rise of Pandemic Possibilities*
    (http://abcnews.go.com/GMA/video/change-preparing-viral-storm-
    14711126)
    (http://abcnews.go.com/Health/Wellness/deadly-antibiotic-resistant-
    superbug-spreads-southern-california/story?id=13218978)
    (http://news.discovery.com/human/bird-flu-studies-120503.html)
30. *Statistics on Wars*
    (http://www.flashnet/~venzor/chapter2signs.htm)
31. *Statistics on Wars After WWII*
    (http://www.lunarpages.com/stargazers/endworld/signs/wars.htm)
32. *Statistics on Wars in 1993*
    (http://www.countdown.org/armageddon/war.htm)
33. *Statistics on Wars in 1995*
    (http://www.lunarpages.com/stargazers/endworld/signs/wars.htm)
34. *Description of Gog & Magog Prophecy*
    (http://www.lightsource.com/ministry/ankerberg-show/the-background-of-
    the-ezekiel-38-nations-281765.html)

(http://www.youtube.com/watch?v=eR1kj0PdXHk)
35. *Statistics on Nuclear Bombs*
    (http://www.bibledesk.com)
36. *Russia Using Lignostone in Weaponry*
    (http://www.spreadinglight.com/prophecy/gog.html)
    (http://www.lignostone.com/)
37. *Statistics on China's Army*
    (http://www.flashnet/~venzor/chapter2signs.htm)
38. *Quote China's Military Buildup Funded by U.S. Debt*
    (http://www.Raptureready.com/nm/399.html)
39. *Quote China Building Railway to the Middle East*
    (http://edition.presstv.ir/detail/164339.html)
    (http://www.telegraph.co.uk/finance/china-business/7985812/China-to-build-2bn-railway-for-Iran.html)
40. *Description of D.U.M.B.'s*
    (http://projectcamelot.org/underground_bases.html)
41. *Quotes on Solar Activity*
    (http://www.foxnews.com/scitech/2012/05/08/monster-sunspot-threatens-to-unleash-powerful-solar-flares/)
    (http://articles.latimes.com/2012/may/04/science/la-sci-solar-storms-20120505)
    (http://www.guardian.co.uk/news/2011/jan/24/weatherwatch-sunspots-solar-flares)
    (http://www.prisonplanet.com/massive-solar-storm-to-hit-earth-in-2012-with-force-of-100m-bombs.html)
    (http://www.foxnews.com/scitech/2010/06/10/electronic-armageddon-solar-flares-disaster/)
    (http://www.wired.com/wiredscience/2012/03/gigantic-solar-tornado/)
42. *Scientist Warns About Sun Activity*
    (http://www.youtube.com/watch?v=WPdqr2v1rTQ)
43. *Quotes on Asteroid Impact*
    (http://www.universetoday.com/12733/another-asteroid-passes-close-to-earth/)
    (http://www.sliceofscifi.com/2008/01/29/first-images-of-near-miss-asteroid/)
    (http://afp.google.com/article/ALeqM5g6fIS_34_CxE8-vcC5Gvbj D4MIOQ)
    (http://news.bbc.co.uk/2/hi/science/nature/2147879.stm)
    (http://en.wikipedia.org/wiki/Impact_event)

44. *Quote on Japanese Tsunami*
    (http://newsfeed.time.com/2012/05/30/what-the-waves-brought-japanese-tsunami-debris-in-north-america/#radioactive-tuna-fish)
    (http://simple.wikipedia.org/wiki/2011_T%C5%8Dhoku_earthquake_and_tsunami)
    (Various Online Video News Reports) – Source unknown
45. *Explanation of Sun Turning Black Like Sackcloth*
    (http://www.gty.org/resources/print/sermons/66-26)
46. *Quote Current Global Volcanic Eruptions*
    (http://www.telegraph.co.uk/science/9195178/Iceland-volcano-and-you-thought-the-last-eruption-was-bad....html)
    (http://www.arenal.net/costa-rica-volcanoes.htm)
    (http://www.huffingtonpost.com/2011/11/28/ecuador-tungurahua-volcano_n_1117598.html)
    (http://www.volcano.si.edu/reports/usgs/)
47. *Quote on Yellowstone Caldera Devastation*
    (http://www.dailymail.co.uk/sciencetech/article-1350123/Worlds-largest-volcano-Yellowstone-National-Park-wipe-thirds-US.html)
48. *Quote Yellowstone Super Volcano*
    (http://ngm.nationalgeographic.com/print/2009/08/yellowstone/achenbach-text)
49. *Map of Current Active Volcanoes Around the World*
    (http://en.wikipedia.org/wiki/File:Map_plate_tectonics_world.gif)
50. *Examples of How God Controls the Weather*
    (Study Derived from Online Bible Study Tools
    (http://bible.crosswalk.com)
51. *Quotes on the Rise of Global Catastrophes*
    (http://www.cbn.com/cbnnews/healthscience/2010/December/2010s-World-Gone-Wild-Quakes-Floods-Blizzards-/)
    (http://www.msnbc.msn.com/id/45353104/ns/us_news-environment/t/heat-waves-floods-storms-scientists-warn-world-prepare-extreme-weather/)
    (http://www.msnbc.msn.com/id/40739667/ns/us_news-2010_year_in_review/t/s-world-gone-wild-quakes-floods-blizzards/)
52. *Quotes, Statistics, & Map of Global Catastrophes*
    (http://www.cbc.ca/news/world/story/2011/05/10/disaster-report.html)
    (http://theeconomiccollapseblog.com/archives/why-is-the-heartland-of-america-being-ripped-to-shreds-by-gigantic-tornadoes-that-are-becoming-more-frequent-and-more-powerful)

(http://www.cbn.com/cbnnews/healthscience/2011/August/Sign-of-the-Times-Natural-Disasters-Prevalent-in-2011-/)
(http://standeyo.com/NEWS/10_Earth_Changes/100305.nat.diz. increasing. warning.html)

53. *Quotes on the Rise of Global Animal Deaths*
(http://www.treehugger.com/natural-sciences/mass-animal-deaths-around-the-world-dead-birds-fall-from-sky-millions-of-fish-crabs-wash-ashore.html)
(http://www.youtube.com/watch?v=9SSsL2K4H54)
(http://www.thebereancall.org/print/book/export/html/9058)

54. *Quotes on the Rise of Global Insect Invasions*
(http://www.washingtonpost.com/wp-dyn/content/article/2010/09/24/AR2010092403357.html)
(http://deltafarmpress.com/freakish-insect-invasions-plague-mid-south-farmers)
(http://www.semissourian.com/story/1738391.html)
(http://crisisboom.com/2011/06/13/locusts-invade-russia-and-china-threatening-food-supply/)
(http://www.youtube.com/watch?v=swHhWG-qioE)
(http://www.chinadaily.com.cn/china/2011-05-24/content_12572049.htm)
(http://phys.org/print190448921.html)
(http://www.dailymail.co.uk/sciencetech/article-1386233/US-states-braced-cicadas-invasion-hatch-13-years-underground.html?printingPage=true)
(http://www.youtube.com/watch?v=1YNy2R3hg2Q)
(http://www.youtube.com/watch?v=tI6WMV6E_4o)

55. *Quotes on the Rise of Global Hail Storms*
(http://www.telegraph.co.uk/news/worldnews/asia/china/9263425/40-killed-during-hour-long-hailstorm-in-China.html)
(http://www.youtube.com/watch?v=DuMX9AM9BrE)
(http://www.wfaa.com/news/texas-news/Spring-hailstorm-pelts-Texas-Panhandle-147083055.html)
(http://www.keloland.com/News/NewsDetail6371.cfm?Id=102949)
(http://www.youtube.com/watch?v=w47HxYgG7bg)

56. *Story of Bill Clinton*
(Email story) – Source Unknown

Chapter Four   *The Rise of Falsehood*

1. *Story of Men Trapped at Lake Mead*
   (Email story) – Source Unknown
2. *Quote Sun Myung Moon*
   (http://www.gospelcom.net/apologeticsindex/u05.html)
   (http://www.salon.com/2004/06/21/moon_7/)
   (http://www.andrewcusack.com/2004/06/14/sun-myung-moon-crowned-
   messiah-in-washington-dc/)
3. *Quote Jesus of Siberia*
   (http://www.guardian.co.uk/g2/story/0,3604,721088,00.html)
   (http://www.youtube.com/watch?v=yZodGXxi7KI)
4. *Quote What's Your Name?*
   (http://news.bbc.co.uk/hi/english/world/americas/newsid_645000/645182
   .stm)
   (http://www.thejesusguy.com/)
5. *Quote MI5 Messiah David Shayle*
   (http://www.dailymail.co.uk/news/article-475616/The-MI5-Messiah-
   Why-David-Shayler-believes-hes-son-God.html#)
6. *Quote Jesus of Australia*
   (http://www.youtube.com/watch?v=IEs7SORT9P4)
7. *Quote Supposed Signs & Commercial from Maitreya*
   (http://www.shareintl.org/)
   (http://www.youtube.com/watch?v=2FvA6BbMeb0)
   (http://www.youtube.com/watch?v=rjwdFkapK1w)
8. *Statistics on People in U.S. Claiming to be Jesus Christ*
   (http://members.christhost.com/ResourceCentre/Jesus_lastday_prophecies.ht
   m)
9. *Beliefs of Jose Luis de Jesus Miranda*
   (http://www.allaboutcults.org/jose-luis-de-jesus-miranda.htm)
   (http://www.cnn.com/2007/US/02/16/miami.preacher/)
10. *Statistics on Jerusalem Syndrome*
    (http://news.bbc.co.uk/hi/english/world/middle_east/newsid_577000/577180.s
    tm)
11. *Quote Supposed I-35 Prophecy*
    (http://www.cbn.com/media/browse_videos_info.aspx?s=/vod/PST58v4)
12. *Quote Jesus on Different Thing*
    (http://stuffthatlookslikejesus.com/?p=18)
    (http://abcnews.go.com/US/video?id=8248774)

13. *Quote 50 People Lose Eyesight After Looking for Vision of Virgin Mary*
    (http://www.dnaindia.com/india/report_50-people-looking-for-solar-image-
    of-mary-lose-sight_1152984)
14. *Proof of Intelligent Design of Creation*
    (http://www.evolution-facts.org/3evlch36.htm)
    (http://www.answersingenesis.org/docs/3521.asp)
    (http://www.answersingenesis.org/creation/v16/i4/eye.asp0
    (http://www.straight-talk.net/evolution/eye.htm)
    (http://www.straight-talk.net/evolution/ear.htm)
    (http://www.algonet.se/~tourtel/hovind_seminar/seminar_part4b.html)
    (http://www.straight-talk.net/evolution/brain.htm)
    (http://www.icr.org/newsletters/btg/btgdec01.html
    Radio Broadcast of *Focus on the Family* featuring Dr. Richard Swenson
    from a physicians conference entitled "The Heart of a Physician."
    (http://www.evolution-facts.org/3evlch32.htm)
    (http://www.evolution-facts.org/nature1.htm)
    (http://www.evolution-facts.org/nature2.htm)
    (http://www.answersingenesis.org/home/area/faq/design.asp)
    (http://cryingvoice.com/Evolution/Design1.html)
    (http://www.defendyourfaith.com/proving-creation-main.htm#animals)
    (http://www.evolution-facts.org/1evlch08.htm)
    (http://www.evolution-facts.org/3evlch28.htm)
    (http://www.answersingenesis.org/home/area/faq/design.asp)
    (http://www.defendyourfaith.com/proving-creation-main.htm#animals)
    (http://www.evolution-facts.org/Ev-V2/2evlch16.htm)
    (http://www.evolution-facts.org/Ev-V2/2evlch12.htm)
    (http://www.straight-talk.net/evolution/cells-dna.htm)
    (http://www.answersingenesis.org/creation/v20/i1/design.asp)
    (http://www.pathlights.com/ce_encyclopedia/08dna02.htm)
    (http://www.allaboutcreation.org/proof-of-god.htm)
    (http://www.icr.org/pubs/imp/imp-313.htm)
    (http://www.answersingenesis.org/docs/4192msc1-10-2000.asp)
    (http://www.algonet.se/~tourtel/hovind_seminar/seminar_part4b.html)
    (http://www.umich.edu/news/MT/04/Fall04/story.html?molecular)
15. *Quotes on the Odds of Evolution*
    Mark Eastman, M.D., *The Origin of the Universe*,
    (http://www.marshill.org)
    (http://www.algonet.se/~tourtel/hovind_seminar/seminar_part4b.html)
    (http://www.returntogod.com/Science/lifebegn.htm)

(http://soamc.dynu.com/tfh/FILES/Creation,%20Origin/EVIDENC_/index1. htm)
(http://www.pathlights.com/ce_encyclopedia/Encyclopedia/08dna04. htm)
(http://www.pathlights.com/ce_encyclopedia/Encyclopedia/08dna05. htm)
(http://www.pathlights.com/ce_encyclopedia/Encyclopedia/08dna02. htm)
(http://www.allaboutthejourney.org/common/printable-creation-of-life.htm)

16. *Quote Scientists Admit Intelligent Design*
(http://www.wasdarwinright.com/Scientificquotes.html#God)
(http://www.godandscience.org/apologetics/quotes.html#05)
(http://www.godandscience.org/apologetics/quotes.html)

17. *Quote Evolutionists Admit Circular Reasoning*
(http://www.pathlights.com/ce_encyclopedia/12fos11.htm)
Andrew Snelling, *The Revised Quote Book*,
(Acacia Ridge: Answers in Genesis, 1990, Pgs. 24-25)
Kent Hovind, *Seminar Notebook*,
(Pensacola: Creation Science Evangelism, 2001, Pgs. 32,34,70,71)

18. *Faulty Dates from Evolutionary Dating Methods*
Kent Hovind, *Seminar Notebook*,
(Pensacola: Creation Science Evangelism, 2001, Pg. 56)
(http://genesis.amen.net/carbon14.html)
(http://www.pathlights.com/ce_encyclopedia/06dat5.htm)
(http://www.bible.ca/tracks/dating-radiometric.htm)
(http://www.pathlights.com/ce_encyclopedia/06dat4.htm#Problems%20 with%20Radiodating)
(http://www.drdino.com/QandA/index.jsp?varFolder=CreationEvolution &varPage=CarbonPotassiumargondating.jsp)

19. *Quotes on Contamination Problems with Evolutionary Dating Methods*
(http://www.pathlights.com/ce_encyclopedia/06dat4.htm)
(http://www.pathlights.com/ce_encyclopedia/06dat2.htm)
(http://www.pathlights.com/ce_encyclopedia/06dat4.htm#Problems%20 with%20Radiodating)
(http://www.pathlights.com/ce_encyclopedia/06dat5.htm)
Andrew Snelling, *The Revised Quote Book*,
(Acacia Ridge: Answers in Genesis, 1990, Pg. 21-23)

20. *Quote Insane Dating Quote*

Kent Hovind, *Seminar Notebook,*
(Pensacola: Creation Science Evangelism, 2001, Pg. 56)
(http://genesis.amen.net/carbon14.html)
(http://www.pathlights.com/ce_encyclopedia/06dat5.htm)
(http://www.bible.ca/tracks/dating-radiometric.htm)
(http://www.pathlights.com/ce_encyclopedia/06dat4.htm#Problems%20
with%20Radiodating)
(http://www.drdino.com/QandA/index.jsp?varFolder=CreationEvolution
&varPage=CarbonPotassiumargondating.jsp)

21. *Quotes on Evolutionists Real Reasons for Believing Evolution*
(http://www.wposfm.com/HTML%20files/Darwin%20Sunday.htm)
(http://www.allaboutscience.org/intelligent-design.htm)
(http://evolutionexamined.homestead.com/)
(http://www.coralridge.org/impact/2004_May_Pg8.htm)
(http://www.present-truth.org/Creation/Creation-not-EvolutionTOC.htm)
(http://nwcreation.net/evolutionquotes.html)
Radio Broadcast of *Truths That Transform* featuring Dr. D. James
Kennedy entitled "Eden Revisited."
(http://personal.georgiasouthern.edu/~etmcmull/Noev.htm)
(http://uplink.space.com/showflat.php?Cat=&Board=humanbio&Number
=393624&page=11&view=collapsed&sb=5&o=0&fpart=2)

22. *Quote God Reversed My Thinking*
(http://www.youtube.com/watch?v=jgFU5Ak88-k)

23. *Quote Lies of Evolution*
(http://www.straight-talk.net/evolution/misslinks.htm)
(http://www.christiananswers.net/q-eden/edn-c008.html)
(http://www.algonet.se/~tourtel/hovind_seminar/seminar_part2.html)
(http://www.christianity.gr/ef_ag/2001/july_august/sci.htm)
(http://www.geocities.com/johnh_vanbc/bible/mythed.html)
(http://www.nwcreation.net/evolutionfraud.html)
(http://emporium.turnpike.net/C/cs/evid4.htm)
(http://www.fillthevoid.org/Creation/Hovind/Brainwashed.html)
(http://www.alexfound.org/creation/dewitt/hoaxes.htm)
(http://www.wasdarwinright.com/Earlyman.asp)
(http://emporium.turnpike.net/C/cs/evid5.htm)
(http://emporium.turnpike.net/C/cs/evid6.htm)
(http://www.darwinismrefuted.com/origin_of_man.html)
(http://www.trueauthority.com/cvse/moth.htm)
(http://www.trueorigin.org/pepmoth1.asp)

(http://www.apologeticspress.org/inthenews/2003/itn-03-36.htm)
(http://www.exchangedlife.com/Creation/pepper.shtml)
(http://www.cryingvoice.com/Evolution/NaturalSelection.html)
(http://www.fillthevoid.org/Creation/Hovind/Brainwashed.html)
(http://www.alexfound.org/creation/dewitt/hoaxes.htm)
(http://www.darwinismrefuted.com/mechanisms04.html)
(http://www.pathlights.com/ce_encyclopedia/09nsel03.htm)
(http://www.pathlights.com/ce_encyclopedia/09nsel05.htm)
(http://www.fillthevoid.org/Creation/Hovind/Brainwashed.html)
(http://www.christiananswers.net/q-eden/edn-c024.html)
(http://www.nwcreation.net/evolutionfraud.html)
(http://www.sermonaudio.com/new_details.asp?8360)
(http://strengthsandweaknesses.org/news.10.01.2003.htm)
(http://www.apologeticspress.org/rr/rr1994/r&r9409a.htm)
(http://www.apologeticspress.org/docsdis/2001/dc-01-06.htm)
(http://www.apologeticspress.org/docsdis/2001/dc-01-06.htm)
(http://www.darwinismrefuted.com/embryology_04.html)
(http://www.answersingenesis.org/creation/v18/i2/haeckel.asp)
24. *Quote Evolution of Forks*
    (http://www.wiseoldgoat.com/papers-creation/old/hovind-seminar_
    part4b_1999.html)
25. *Evidence of Animals Fitting on Noah's Ark*
    (http://www.christiananswers.net/dictionary/ark.html)
    (http://www.christiananswers.net/q-abr/abr-a001.html)
    (http://www.christiananswers.net/q-eden/edn-c013.html)
    (http://www.nwcreation.net/noahsark.html)
    (http://www.drdino.com/read-article.php?id=76)
    (http://www.drdino.com/read-article.php?id=27)
    (http://www.evolution-facts.org/Ev-V2/2evlch19b.htm)
    (http://www.exchangedlife.com/Sermons/gen/the_flood.shtml)
    (http://www.worldwideflood.com/ark/hull_form/hull_optimization
    .htm#ref02)
    (http://www.answersingenesis.org/articles/am/v2/n2/caring-for-the-
    animals)
    (http://www.solarnavigator.net/noahs_ark.htm)
26. *Quote Evolution Says We Came from a Rock*
    Kent Hovind, *Why Evolution is Stupid*, Video
    (Pensacola: Creation Science Evangelism, 1996)
27. *Evidence of Noah's Flood Destroying the Dinosaurs*

(http://thetruth.uv.ro/_books/_answ_book/Cap_04.html)
(http://cs.joensuu.fi/~vtenhu/hovind/CHP-5.htm)
(http://siriusknotts.wordpress.com/2008/09/08/darwins-dyke-what-the-fossil-record-actually-shows/)
(http://www.answersingenesis.org/home/area/cfol/ch3-how-fast.asp)
(http://www.s8int.com/boneyard1.html)
(http://www.s8int.com/boneyard2.html)
(http://www.s8int.com/boneyard3.html)
(http://www.s8int.com/boneyard5.html)
(http://www.bearfabrique.org/Catastrophism/floods/mfloods.html)
(http://evolution-facts.org/Appendix/a19a.htm)
(http://christiananswers.net/dinosaurs/j-extinct3.html)
(http://christiananswers.net/dinosaurs/j-extinct4.html)
(http://christiananswers.net/dinosaurs/j-age1.html)
(http://christiananswers.net/q-aig/aig-c026.html)
(http://www.bible.ca/tracks/rapid-fossils-rapidly-perishing-detail-preserved.htm)
(http://www.usatoday.com/tech/science/discoveries/2007-12-03-dinosaur-mummy_N.htm)
(http://creation.com/dinosaur-bonesjust-how-old-are-they-really)
(http://creation.com/sensational-dinosaur-blood-report)
(http://www.answersingenesis.org/creation/v14/i3/dinosaurbones.asp)
(http://creation.com/the-creation-music-man-who-makes-dinosaurs)
(http://creation.com/fascinating-four-chambered-fossil-find)
(http://creation.com/dinosaur-heart-update-just-a-lump-of-mud)
(http://creation.com/still-soft-and-stretchy)
(http://creation.com/first-ever-dinosaur-brain-tumour-found)
(http://creation.com/sue-the-t-rex-another-missionary-lizard)
(http://www.genesispark.org/genpark/old/old.htm)
(http://www.answersingenesis.org/creation/v25/i2/footsteps.asp)
(http://www.genesispark.org/genpark/grave/grave.htm)
(http://www.pathlights.com/ce_encyclopedia/Encyclopedia/14flod05.htm)
(http://www.answersingenesis.org/articles/1999/11/05/dinosaurs-and-the-bible)
(http://www.answersingenesis.org/creation/v15/i4/dinosaurs.asp?vPrint=1)

28. *Quote Mormon Beliefs*
(http://carm.org/mormonism)

29. *Quote Jehovah's Witnesses Beliefs*
   (http://carm.org/jehovahs-witnesses)
30. *Quote Christian Science Beliefs*
   (http://carm.org/christian-science)
31. *Quote Seventh Day Adventist Beliefs*
   (http://carm.org/seventh-day-adventism)
32. *Quote New Age Beliefs*
   (http://www.religioustolerance.org/newage.htm)
   (http://www.jeremiahproject.com/prophecy/newage01.html)
   (http://www.victorious.org/newage.htm)
   (http://www.youtube.com/watch?v=Ll3I7ry2fcA)
   (http://video.google.com/videoplay?docid=2705909436303599510)
33. *Quote New Age Plan*
   (http://www.victorious.org/newage.htm)
34. *Quote New Age Statistic*
   (http://www.religioustolerance.org/newage.htm)
35. *Quote New Age Promotion by Oprah Winfrey*
   (http://www.youtube.com/watch?v=JW4LLwkgmqA)
36. *Quote New Age Beliefs*
   (http://www.religioustolerance.org/newage.htm)
   (http://www.jeremiahproject.com/prophecy/newage01.html)
   (http://www.victorious.org/newage.htm)
   (http://www.youtube.com/watch?v=Ll3I7ry2fcA)
   (http://video.google.com/videoplay?docid=2705909436303599510)
37. *Quote People Crying Over Trees*
   (http://www.youtube.com/watch?v=ElJFYwRtrH4)
38. *Quote Earth Worship on the Rise Among Evangelical Youth*
   (http://www.onenewsnow.com/Church/Default.aspx?id=68203)
39. *Quote Pledge Allegiance to the Earth*
   (http://www.youtube.com/watch?v=GDehIG6k7TE)
40. *Quote U.N. Gives Mother Earth Same Rights as Humans*
   (http://www.canada.com/technology/document+would+give+Mother+Earth+
   same+rights+humans/4597840/story.html)
41. *Quote New Age Beliefs*
   (http://www.religioustolerance.org/newage.htm)
   (http://www.jeremiahproject.com/prophecy/newage01.html)
   (http://www.victorious.org/newage.htm)
   (http://www.youtube.com/watch?v=Ll3I7ry2fcA)
   (http://video.google.com/videoplay?docid=2705909436303599510)

42. *Quote Sierra Club*
    (http://www.jeremiahproject.com/prophecy/earth1.html)
43. *Quote James Coburn on Mother Earth*
    (http://www.worldviewweekend.com/worldview-times/article.php?
    articleid=6089)
44. *Quote Environmental Religion*
    (Video Transcript of a CNN Report called "What Would Jesus Drive" –
    Source Unknown)
45. *Quote Green Religion Taking Over Christian Religion*
    (http://www.nationalreview.com/planet-gore/303379/christ-turns-green-un-
    earth-summit-literally-david-rothbard)
46. *Quote Environmentalists Say Tribulation is Good*
    (http://www.insight-books.com/new/0671759000.html)
    (http://www.crystalinks.com/hopi2.html)
47. *Quote Feminism & The Goddess is Alive*
    (http://www.youtube.com/watch?v=nTaTGsh7Cvc)
48. *Quote Christian Feminists in the Church*
    (http://www.thebereancall.org/content/goddess-and-liberal-church)
    (http://wwwcalcatholic.com.newsArticlePrintable.aspx?id=ecf48aa8-
    8c1b-479f-9f08-c14a1a185fdd)
    (http://www.ltwinternational.org/fact_sheet.htm)
    (http://www.crossroad.to/articles2/08/shack.htm)
49. *Quote New Age Beliefs*
    (http://www.religioustolerance.org/newage.htm)
    (http://www.jeremiahproject.com/prophecy/newage01.html)
    (http://www.victorious.org/newage.htm)
    (http://www.youtube.com/watch?v=Ll3I7ry2fcA)
    (http://video.google.com/videoplay?docid=2705909436303599510)
50. *Quote Banned PETA Commercial*
    (http://www.youtube.com/watch?v=HjKRxa7ZyMs)
51. *Beliefs of the Vegetarian Movement*
    (http://www.serv-online.org/)
52. *Quote Interfaith Beliefs of the Vegetarian Movement*
    (http://www.serv-online.org/)
    (http://www.recipenet.org/health/aboutme.htm)
53. *Quote U.N. Says We Need to Eat Less Meat*
    (http://www.telegraph.co.uk/earth/earthnews/7797594/Eat-less-meat-to-save-
    the-planet-UN.html)
54. *Quote New Age Beliefs*

(http://www.religioustolerance.org/newage.htm)
(http://www.jeremiahproject.com/prophecy/newage01.html)
(http://www.victorious.org/newage.htm)
(http://www.youtube.com/watch?v=Ll3l7ry2fcA)
(http://video.google.com/videoplay?docid=2705909436303599510)

55. *Quote Food Suppliers that Control Global Food Supply*
(http://www.greens.org/s-r/gga/heffernan.html)
(http://www.counterpunch.org/1999/11/20/food-central/)

56. *Quote Doomsday Seed Vault*
(http://www.youtube.com/watch?v=U3xE8k9_W1I)
(http://www.youtube.com/watch?v=vUlToC4lxX8)
(http://globalresearch.ca/index.php?context=va&aid=23503)

57. *Quote Terminator Gene for Seed Production*
(http://www.greens.org/s-r/gga/heffernan.html)
(http://www.counterpunch.org/1999/11/20/food-central/)

58. *Quotes on Population Control*
(http://www.acts2.com/thebibletruth/Evolution_Hitlers_Racist_Theories
.htm)
(http://www.radioliberty.com/pca.htm)
(http://www.thegatewaypundit.com/2011/01/dr-gosnell-arrested-for-
murdering-7-babies-who-survived-abortion-something-barack-obama-
supports-has-voted-for-4-times/)
(http://www.aynrand.org/site/PageServer?pagename=objectivism_environme
ntalism)
(http://www.prisonplanet.com/john-holdren-obamas-science-czar-forced-
abortions-and-mass-sterilization-needed-to-save-the-planet.html)
(http://www.prisonplanet.com/articles/april2006/030406massculling.htm)

59. *Quote New Ager's on Population Control*
(http://www.youtube.com/watch?v=UMKW2DVcAqo)

60. *Quote Georgia Guidestones*
(http://www.radioliberty.com/stones.htm)

61. *Quote Researcher Visiting Georgia Guidestones*
(http://www.youtube.com/watch?v=XWJAyviFLsI)

62. *Quote Why Are Aliens Humanoid Just Like Us*
(http://www.youtube.com/watch?v=7vyVe-6YdUk)

63. *Quote Teachings from UFO's*
(http://www.khouse.org/pages/special_events/alien_encounters/)

64. *Quote Why Are UFO's Promoting New Age*

(http://www.scribd.com/doc/46005425/The-Facts-On-UFOs-And-Other-Supernatural-Phenomena-Answers-To-The-Most-Asked-Questions-by-Dr-John-Ankerberg-and-John-Weldon-1992)

65. *Quote People Channeling UFO's*
(http://www.youtube.com/watch?v=UMKW2DVcAqo)

66. *Quote How UFO's Travel*
(http://www.scribd.com/doc/46005425/The-Facts-On-UFOs-And-Other-Supernatural-Phenomena-Answers-To-The-Most-Asked-Questions-by-Dr-John-Ankerberg-and-John-Weldon-1992)
(http://www.khouse.org/pages/special_events/alien_encounters/)

67. *Quote Man Acting Possessed After UFO*
(http://www.youtube.com/watch?v=hpbp-jOMoZo)

68. *Quote Researchers Say UFO's Are Demons*
(http://www.scribd.com/doc/46005425/The-Facts-On-UFOs-And-Other-Supernatural-Phenomena-Answers-To-The-Most-Asked-Questions-by-Dr-John-Ankerberg-and-John-Weldon-1992)
(http://www.khouse.org/pages/special_events/alien_encounters/)

69. *Quote Aliens Rebuked in the Name of Jesus*
Gary Bates, *Alien Intrusion: UFO's and the Evolution Connection*
(Green Forest: Master Books Inc., 2004, Pgs. 255-268)
(http://www.theforbiddenknowledge.com/hardtruth/premise_spiritual_warfare.htm)
(http://www.youtube.com/watch?v=5R4_Vtcpi4A)

70. *Quote UFO's Explaining Away the Rapture*
(Barbara Marciniak, *Bringers of the Dawn*,
(Santa Fe: Bear & Company Publishing, 1992, Pgs. 166, 167)
(http://www.khouse.org/pages/special_events/alien_encounters/)
(http://www.spiritandflesh.com/aliens_Rapture_Aliens_ascension_New_Age.htm)
(http://www.alahoy.com/msg04.htm)

71. *Story of Innkeeper's Wife*
(Email story) – Source Unknown

Chapter Five   *The Rise of Wickedness*

1. *Story of Momma Bear*
(Email story) – Source Unknown
2. *Statistics on School Discipline Problems from the 40's to the 80's*

(http://www.lamblion.us/2012/04/decay-of-society-schools-as-mirror.html)

3. *Origins of the Phrase Separation of Church & State*
   (http://lcweb.loc.gov/loc/lcib/9806/danpre.html)

4. *Quote Founding Fathers on Christianity*
   (http://www.wallbuilders.com/libissuesarticles.asp?id=8755)
   Vaughn Shatzer, *History of American Education*,
   (Hagerstown: Word of Prophecy Ministries, 1999, Pgs. 3-9,12-13)
   (http://www.youtube.com/watch?v=Qrqf2JasMJw)

5. *Quote Warning Label on the Constitution*
   (http://www.foxnews.com/us/2010/06/09/publishing-company-putting-
   warning-label-constitution/)

6. *Quote Beliefs of Humanist Manifest I & II*
   (http://www.SecularHumanism.org)

7. *Quote Humanist Agenda for Schools*
   (http://www.lunarpages.com/stargazers/endworld/signs/occult.htm)

8. *Quote Dumbing Down of America*
   (http://www.youtube.com/watch?v=DDyDtYy2I0M)

9. *Quote Paul Harvey If I Were the Devil*
   (http://www.youtube.com/watch?v=H3Az0okaHig&feature=related)

10. *Behavioral Statistics from 1963*
    (http://www.linda.net/graphs.html)
    (http://www.algonet.se/~tourtel/hovind_seminar/seminar_part1a.html)
    (http://www.geocities.com/Heartland/Village/8759/youth-stats.html)
    (http://www.biblesabbath.org/bacchiocchi/endtimewickedness.html)
    (http://www.seebo.net/crisis.html)

11. *Quote Video God Kicked Out*
    (http://www.youtube.com/watch?v=mNjpddyn0HE)

12. *Quote Video Atheist Camps & De-baptisms*
    (http://www.youtube.com/watch?v=r3cqPA0gJ-o)
    (http://www.youtube.com/watch?v=wAo_rEgR4xU)

13. *Examples of Atheists Attack on God*
    (http://cityroom.blogs.nytimes.com/2009/10/19/good-without-god-atheist-
    subway-ads-proclaim/)
    (http://atheistbillboards.com/)
    (http://www.theblaze.com/stories/florida-atheists-scrub-away-highway-
    blessing-with-unholy-water-because-theyre-not-going-to-tolerate-bigotry/)
    (http://seattletimes.com/html/localnews/2015071658_Rapture17m.html)
    (http://www.if-jesus-returns-kill-him-again.com/index.html)
    (http://www.godblock.com/)

14. *Video Using God's Name in Vain & Kathy Griffin Blasphemy*
    (http://theapologeticsgroup.com/product/pandoras-box-office-hollywoods-war-on-family-values/)
    (http://www.youtube.com/watch?v=RYcOHrxNJjg&feature=related)
15. *Video Atheists Exchanging Pornography for Bibles*
    (http://www.youtube.com/watch?v=KX7rhKfaG-A)
16. *Video President Obama Comments on the Bible*
    (http://www.youtube.com/watch?v=1RWHdQBMgb4)
17. *Video President James Garfield and His Godly Usage of the Bible*
    (http://www.youtube.com/watch?v=Qrqf2JasMJw)
18. *Quote Christian Prayer at a Football Game*
    (http://home.comcast.net/~ray.ammerman/prayer.html)
19. *Quote First Two Laws of satanism*
    (http://www.dowhatthouwilt.com/)
    (http://www.tex-is.net/users/csbrocato/occult.htm)
20. *Quote satanists Admit that Self-love is satanic*
    (http://www.youtube.com/watch?v=VJrcSuO2V9g)
    (http://www.soluschristusministries.com/media)
21. *Quote Psychology Versus the Bible*
    (http://www.fundamentalbiblechurch.org/Tracts/fbcpsyc1.htm)
22. *Quote Lives of Secular Psychologists*
    Matthew Olson, *An Introduction to Theories of Personalities,*
    (Upper Saddle River: Prentice Hall, 1999, Pgs. 20, 23, 47, 48, 65, 66, 67, 70, 129, 502)
    (http://www.wayoflife.org/fbns/jung.htm)
23. *Quote Examples of Self-love Court Cases*
    Tucker Carlson, *Go Ahead, Hurt My Feelings,*
    (Reader's Digest: August 2002, Pgs. 43, 44, 46)
24. *Quote Statistics & Effects of Kids & Self-esteem*
    Tucker Carlson, *Go Ahead, Hurt My Feelings,*
    (Reader's Digest: August 2002, Pg. 46)
25. *Quote John MacArthur on Self-esteem*
    John F. MacArthur, *The Vanishing Conscience*
    (Dallas: Word Publishing, 1995, Pgs. 80-81)
26. *Quote Dr. Martin Bobgan on Self-love*
    (http://www.pamweb.org/selflove32.html)
27. *Quote Who I Am in Christ*
    (http://www.ficm.org/newsite/index.php?command=textwhoamiinchrist)
    (http://64.233.169.104/search?q=cache:loznB9wxiGMJ:www.kenboa.org

/downloads/pdf/IdentityAffirmations2.pdf+i+am+redeemed+forgiven+
beloved+god%27s+child&hl=en&ct=clnk&cd=4&gl=us)
(http://www.solidrockchurch-stillwater.org/whoiaminchrist.html)
(http://www.persevering.org/perceiv.html)
(http://truth4freedom.wordpress.com/the-heart-god-revives/who-i-am-in-christ/)

28. *Quote D. Martin Lloyd Jones on Self*
    (http://www.pamweb.org/selflove32.html)
29. *Quote In the Words of satan*
    (http://www.youtube.com/watch?v=lYDCMg4d7ks)
30. *Examples of Modern Day Wickedness*
    (http://cnsnews.com/news/article/un-commission-calls-legalizing-prostitution-worldwide)
    (http://www.theepochtimes.com/n2/china-news/live-baby-treated-as-medical-waste-37383.html)
    (http://www.lifesitenews.com/news/planned-parenthood-2010-report-4874-million-in-taxpayer-money-329445-unbor/)
    (http://www.christianliferesources.com/article/u-s-abortion-statistics-by-year-1973-current-1042)
    (http://www.numberofabortions.com/)
    (http://www.foxnews.com/politics/2012/03/17/rep-smith-slams-administration-over-abortion-surcharge-rule/)
    (http://www.breitbart.com/Big-Hollywood/2012/05/18/MTV-Lose-Virginity-Reality-Show)
    (http://usnews.nbcnews.com/_news/2012/06/11/12169715-nyc-principal-nixes-god-bless-the-usa-at-kindergarten-graduation?lite)
    (http://www.lifenews.com/2012/05/25/shock-british-teens-have-as-many-as-seven-abortions/)
    (http://www.liveleak.com/view?i=9cf_1248445408)
    (http://www.guardian.co.uk/education/2007/may/14/schools.uk2)
    (http://www.cbn.com/CBNnews/269476.aspx?option=print)
    (http://www.yaledailynews.com/news/2008/apr/17/for-senior-abortion-a-medium-for-art-political/)
    (http://radio.foxnews.com/toddstarnes/top-stories/proposed-law-would-force-churches-to-host-gay-weddings.html)
    (http://action.afa.net/Blogs/BlogPost.aspx?id=2147519995)
    (http://www.ocregister.com/articles/church-219451-play-jesus.html)
    (http://www.lifesitenews.com/news/archive//ldn/2007/jul/07073008)

(http://www.theblaze.com/stories/after-hhs-says-children-are-sexual-beings-psychologists-push-to-decriminalize-pedophilia/)
(http://rescueyourchild.com/The_Problem.html)
(http://www.wnd.com/2011/08/329429/)
(http://www.cbsnews.com/8301-201_162-57337524/u.s-to-use-foreign-aid-to-promote-gay-rights/)
(http://godfatherpolitics.com/2245/girl-scouts-support-abortion-and-say-any-type-of-sexual-activity-is-okay/)
(http://www.foxnews.com/story/0,2933,298307,00.html)
(http://townhall.com/columnists/sandyrios/2007/09/27/da_vinci_code,_move_over!/page/full/)
(http://www.lifesitenews.com/news/archive/ldn/2007/sep/07092803)
(http://www.fmwf.com/media-type/news/2009/11/when-parting-really-is-sweet-divorce-cakes-sparked-by-trend-for-separation-celebrations/)
(http://articles.cnn.com/2012-06-14/us/us_pentagon-gay-pride_1_gay-pride-pentagon-transgender-pride?_s=PM:US)
(http://www.washingtontimes.com/news/2010/jun/15/epidemic-growth-of-net-porn-cited/)
(http://www.telegraph.co.uk/technology/4611161/Rapelay-virtual-rape-game-banned-by-Amazon.html)
(http://www.foxnews.com/politics/2012/08/18/california-law-barring-parents-from-curing-gay-children-moves-through/)
(http://www.theblaze.com/stories/burn-in-hell-adults-heckle-nyc-schoolchildren-while-they-sing-god-bless-the-usa-in-protest-to-principals-ban/)
(http://nation.foxnews.com/culture/2010/06/24/school-teaches-kids-religion-disease)
(http://newsbusters.org/blogs/nathan-burchfiel/2010/06/25/garofalo-bible-work-fiction-child-audience)
(http://www.naturalnews.com/035550_America_special_interests_civil_rights.html)

31. *Quote the Church is Asleep*
    (http://www.youtube.com/watch?v=4IpebXQRxqc)
32. *Quote Abraham Lincoln on Relativism*
    James S. Hewett, *Illustrations Unlimited,*
    (Wheaton: Tyndale House Publishers, 1988, Pg. 483)
33. *Quote Jeffrey Baker on Redefining Sin*
    Jeffrey A. Baker, *Cheque Mate the Game of Princes*
    (St. Petersburg: The Baker Group Inc., 1993, Pgs. 206-207)

34. *Quote Josh McDowell on New Definition of Tolerance*
    Josh McDowell, *The Tangled Web of Christian Tolerance*, Video
    (Coeur d' Alene: Compass International, 1998)
35. *Quote The Wrath of God*
    (http://www.youtube.com/watch?v=9LYgWfLv77Y)
36. *Statistics on Krokodil*
    (http://www.foxnews.com/us/2011/06/28/dea-now-monitoring-krokodil-
    deadly-morphine-derivative/)
37. *Statistics on Marijuana*
    (http://healthland.time.com/2010/09/16/is-drug-use-really-on-the-rise/)
    (http://www.drugabuse.gov/publications/drugfacts/nationwide-trends)
38. *Quote Pat Robertson on Legalizing Marijuana*
    (http://www.bing.com/videos/watch/video/pat-robertson-legalize-
    marijuana/6gcefun)
39. *Quote Dave Hunt on Altered States of Consciousness*
    (http://www.youtube.com/watch?v=h4zn_Z-7Zt4)
40. *Quote on the Surge of satanism and Exorcisms*
    (http://www.telegraph.co.uk/news/religion/8416104/Surge-in-Satanism-
    sparks-rise-in-demand-for-exorcists-says-Catholic-Church.html)
41. *Quote California Schools Saying Lucifer is a Model Guardian*
    (http://www.onenewsnow.com/legal-courts/2010/08/17/schools-claim-
    lucifer-as-model-and-guardian)
42. *Quote Jack Black Prayer to satan*
    (http://archives.onenewsnow.com/Perspectives/Default.aspx?id=724962)
43. *Quote Proof of the Reality & Rise of satanism*
    (http://www.youtube.com/watch?v=W1yK3IsQKwA)
44. *Quote satanists Infiltrating Churches*
    (Patrick Matrisciana, *devil Worship: The Rise of satanism*,
    (Hemet: Jeremiah Films, 1989, Video)
45. *Beliefs of Witchcraft*
    (http://www.gospelcom.net/apologeticsindex/w02.html)
    (http://www.gospelcom.net/apologeticsindex/w04.html)
46. *Quote Kids Comments on the Affects of Harry Potter*
    (http://www.youtube.com/watch?v=745X5b5qniM)
47. *Psychologists Using Witchcraft*
    (http://www.gospelcom.net/apologeticsindex/news/an200215b.html)
48. *Witch Covens Allowed in U.S. Army*
    (http://www.bible-prophecy.com/apostasy3.htm#Current)
49. *The Identity of Pan*

(http://www.forerunner.com/champion/X0044_Witchcraft_and_satan.html)

50. *Statistics on Wicca*
(http://www.gospelcom.net/cgi-apologeticsindex/dbman/db.cgi?db=
default&uid=default&keyword=wicca&mh=10&sb=4&so=descend&view_r
ecords=View+Records&nh=3)

51. *Quote Paganism on the Rise*
(http://www.youtube.com/watch?v=-6UBO7IOStA)

52. *Quote Witches Infiltrating Churches*
(http://www.christianissues.biz/pdf-bin/brycehartin/thelastdays.pdf)

53. *Quote Letter from Hell*
(http://www.youtube.com/watch?v=RbKhMJiQK4g)

54. *Story of Going Door to Door*
(Email story) – Source Unknown

233

No aliens
seem to be
non-human
like = strange
if evolution
were true

77, 78, 79
93
HAARP

Anti-Evol.
192 →

cults
197 →

Code Weather
137

Temple 3D

False Cults
161-164

cults
197 →

Made in the USA
Middletown, DE
17 September 2017